Zealots and Rebels

Zealots and Rebels

A History of the
Communist Party of Czechoslovakia

Zdenek L. Suda

HOOVER INSTITUTION PRESS
Stanford University, Stanford, California

Hoover Institution Publication 234

© 1980 by the Board of Trustees of the
  Leland Stanford Junior University
All rights reserved
International Standard Book Number: 0−8179−7342−7
Library of Congress Catalog Card Number: 80−8332
Printed in the United States of America

Designed by Elizabeth Gehman

Contents

Editor's Foreword

The history of the Communist movement in Czechoslovakia is the eighth volume in a series dealing with the origins and development of ruling Communist parties. The volumes are intended to supplement insufficient existing sources on this subject in the English language. They also provide a corrective to frequently biased material published under the auspices of the parties themselves. In some cases, Communist movements have not produced their own histories. This has not been the case in Czechoslovakia, but official literature on this topic remains both ideologically prejudiced and incomplete.

Dr. Zdenek Suda begins by depicting the difficult process of amalgamation by the various components of the radical left before a unified movement could be established in 1921. The Communist Party of Czechoslovakia (CPCS) always has been an important part of the world Communist movement. Its importance has rested on the geopolitical location of the country as well as on the fact that it is one of only two modern industrial nations to have come under Communist control. What further sets the experience in Czechoslovakia apart from that of other countries is that its Communist movement had operated legally until the Second World War and thus could take advantage of constitutional guarantees.

Prior to 1939, not unlike certain other countries in East-Central Europe, ethnic minorities were strongly represented in the Czechoslovak Communist party. This situation changed radically after the war, owing to large population movements. However, the party continued to have a significant following among the two major nationalities, Czechs and Slovaks. Sympathy for the Communist cause, especially in the formative years of the party, stemmed from a long-established tradition of socialism within the Czechoslovak political culture.

Seizure of power in 1948 was greatly facilitated by the electoral support given the CPCS in the elections held two years earlier. This increased popularity to a large extent had been due to the role played by the USSR in the liberation, adroitly exploited by Communist propaganda. At the same time, the CPCS became a mass movement, totaling more than 10 percent of the population. This characteristic has been maintained and even further accentuated. The size of the Czechoslovak Communist party has been the exception among all political movements, in power or in opposition. This has caused serious problems for party leaders, who have been concerned about preserving a more class-conscious, disciplined, and elite party membership.

The few rare attempts by the CPCS to strike a more independent course, the most spectacular in 1968, were unsuccessful, and the party was reduced to the status of a docile instrument of the Moscow power center. Unqualified subjection to USSR control also precluded any meaningful degree of autonomy in foreign policy. Since the last Soviet intervention in the internal affairs of the CPCS, during which crude force had to be applied, a genuine legitimacy crisis developed, which still persists. The present leaders' mandate has been questioned by a considerable segment of the party rank and file, and it seems to be upheld more by the Soviet military presence in the country than by any CPCS consensus.

RICHARD F. STAAR
Director of International Studies

Hoover Institution
Stanford University

Preface

As this volume reaches the reader, there seems to be little need to insist
on the usefulness of an analytical history of the Communist Party of
Czechoslovakia. About a decade ago, a deep crisis in this party and the
dramatic confrontation of its leadership with the political and military
power of the Soviet Union made headlines in the world press. Nine years
later, the still undefeated opposition to Soviet control voiced a courageous protest and aroused sympathies throughout the West. The
topicality of the subject, therefore, appears to be beyond doubt. Yet the
importance of better knowledge of the Communist movement in general
and of its Czechoslovak branch in particular exceeds the context of the
immediate historical situation. It is from the perspective of this more
lasting impact that the task of writing this book has been undertaken.

The benefits for all open societies of understanding the process of
social change in the systems governed by Communist parties has been
recognized for a long time. Communist-sponsored reforms of economic
and political institutions have been viewed as alternative solutions to the
problems of modern industrial nations. It has been assumed that the
success or the failure of these reforms will testify to the value of the
Communist blueprint. Scientific interest in Communist parties and their
program, however, has aims other than that of approving or discrediting
the Communist model as a response to the challenges of modern
societies. Nations under Communist rule actually are vast sociological
laboratories. In them, not only will the viability of the Communist
program stand trial; for those who are able and willing to observe
carefully, answers will be supplied to much more general questions and
the cogency of a number of important sociological propositions will be
tested.

Among the Communist parties that have had the opportunity to
implement their programs by monopolizing decision making in their

societies, the Communist Party of Czechoslovakia occupies a very important place. The experiences of this party and of the Czechoslovak population over the last thirty years are of special value because of several unique circumstances. The geopolitical location of the country, in the critical zone where all major forces and currents of recent history have encountered one another, has put the Communist experiment in the forefront of attention. The fact that in Czechoslovakia a Communist polity had been grafted onto a nation with a clearly Western political culture has added to the interest in the changes taking place under the leadership of the Communist party. The Czech party itself, on the other hand, has been deeply influenced by its formative years in a pluralist regime; in this respect it has been an exception among the various national components of the world Communist movement and the only exception among today's ruling Communist parties.

An historical analysis of the Communist Party of Czechoslovakia thus should be at the same time an inquiry into the significance of idiosyncratic political cultures in interaction with universalistic—or foreign-grown and imposed—political ideas and programs. The results of this inquiry may not only shed more light on the resilience of national systems of political values under prolonged massive exposure to political resocialization pressures from outside their orbits; it could also permit conclusions of a more general nature about the validity of the convergence proposition in the theory of contemporary social change. Any one of these potential rewards would in itself justify the enterprise attempted here.

It is odd that in the official literature approved and circulated in contemporary Czechoslovakia, only two volumes claim to be more or less comprehensive presentations of the origins and development of the Communist party. Moreover, they are by the same author, and even the more recent version does not cover events beyond the the early sixties.[1] In view of the attention the party generally pays to the study of its own past, and of the considerable research facilities now at the disposal of Communist scholars, this bibliography is hardly impressive. The reasons for this paucity may lie not in a lack of data sources, material means, or talent, but in the peculiar Communist position on history, including the history of the Communist movement, which requires constant reinterpretation in the light of the currently prevailing ideological line and discourages objective historical analysis. Although it is true that accents in historical work have always varied in all cultures according to the given zeitgeist, the Communist historiography has come closest to the Orwellian nightmare where "the past is in the hands of the Party." Under such circumstances, there is little enthusiasm among Communist historians for writing on sensitive subjects, and the party's own past is usually the first casualty.

Non-Communist analyses, on the other hand, mainly by authors living outside Czechoslovakia, are both more abundant and more reliable. These sources are duly credited whenever they have been used in the text, and a complete list of background literature is included in this volume. However, not even among writings of Western origin has there so far been a complete history of the Communist Party of Czechoslovakia. This fact makes of the present volume a pioneer study, with all the risks and shortcomings that such an enterprise entails. The author hopes, nevertheless, that filling an important gap will be one of its redeeming features.

CZECHOSLOVAK COMMUNIST

Name	Born	Year Elected	Party Office	(Government Post)	Other
Presidium Members					
Vasil Bilák	1917	1964	Presidium Member Secretary (international politics & agitprop) Chairman, Ideological Committee		
Peter Colotka	1925	1968	Presidium Member	Prime Minister, Slovakia; Deputy Prime Minister, Czechoslovakia	
Karel Hoffmann	1924	1971	Presidium Member		President, Trade Unions
Václav Hůla	1925	1975	Presidium Member	Chairman, State Planning Commission	Chairman, CMEA Planning Committee
Gustav Husák	1913	1968	General Secretary	President	Chairman, National Front
Alois Indra	1921	1971	Presidium Member	Chairman, Federal Assembly	
Antonin Kapek	1922	1970	Chairman, Prague		Chairman, Czechoslovakia National Front
Josef Kempný	1920	1969	Secretary; Chairman, Economic Committee		Deputy Chairman, National Front
Josef Korčák	1921	1970		Prime Minister, Czechoslovakia	
Jozef Lenárt	1923	1970	First Secretary, Slovakia		Chairman, Slovakia National Front
Lubomir Štrougal	1924	1968	Presidium Member	Prime Minister	

PARTY LEADERSHIP

Name	Born	Year Elected	Party Office	(Government Post)	Other
Candidate Members					
Miloslav Hruškovič	1925	1971	Candidate to Presidium Chairman, Committee for Technical & Scientific Development		
Miloš Jakeš	1922	1977	Candidate to Presidium; Chairman, Agriculture and Food Committee		
Secretariat (not in presidium)					
Mikuláš Beňo	1930	1977	Secretary		
Jan Fojtik	1928	1971	Secretary; Rector, Political Academy		
Josef Haman	1933	1978	Secretary		
Josef Havlín	1924	1975	Secretary		
Jindřich Poledník	1937	1976	Secretary; Chairman, Committee for Work among the Youth		
Secretariat Members					
Marie Kabrhelová	1925	1976			Chairman, Union of Women
Oldřich Švestka	1922	1970			Chief Editor, Rudé Právo

SOURCES: Central Intelligence Agency, *Czechoslovak Communist Party* (Washington, D.C., 1979). CR–79–12585. Borys Lewytzkyj, and Juliusz Stroynowski (eds.), *Who's Who in the Socialist Countries* (New York: K. G. Saur Publishing, 1978), pp. 736. RFE Archives, Munich.

Chapter One

A Difficult Birth

From the Socialist Scission to the Merger Congress of 1921

"In the beginning there was a schism": the story of the birth of the Communist Party of Czechoslovakia does not differ from that of the origin of most other Communist parties, as if it were evidence to support the view of the Chinese leader Mao Tse-tung on the necessity of schisms for the progress of social movements. A very important element in this schism was the psychological effect of the October Revolution in Russia in 1917. To fully appreciate the psychological and moral impact of this event, the student of history has to realize that it occurred after more than half a century of struggles, hopes, theoretical discussions, and ideological disputes within the socialist and workers' movements of Marxist inspiration. In the course of these fifty-odd years, the socialists experienced many disappointments and frustrations. The original goal of building a new social order through proletarian revolution appeared more and more remote. More immediate and pragmatic tasks seemed to call for the attention of the socialist leaders, such as improving the condition of the working class and securing its share of political power within the given constitutional order. Confronted with this new situation, the socialist ranks divided between those who accepted the challenge of immediate opportunities and those who were not willing to give up the revolutionary dream. As the latter position, which we could call radical or dogmatic, could not engender an alternative policy to the pragmatism of the reformist majority, and the disagreement between the two concerned mainly the long-term prognosis of the development of industrial capitalist society, the division did not result in organizational separation. Nevertheless, radicalism constituted a distinct current of socialist thought that was particularly attractive to definite personality types. These were to respond the most enthusiastically to the Russian Bolshevik revolution.

Radical wings had existed, before 1917, in all socialist parties enjoying legal status and operating in pluralist systems. The Czecho-Slav section of the Austrian Social Democracy, the parent of the later Czechoslovak Social Democratic Workers party, has also had its radical chapter. The ideological climate of Austrian socialism before the First World War was to a large extent influenced by the aspirations to self-government of the various non-German ethnic groups. The position of the radicals on the ethnic issue was neither uniform nor simple. Many radicals in the Czech section put the objective of world proletarian victory above the goal of political emancipation of the Czechs, but an equal number saw the desired social revolution and the national revolution merging into one. From this point of view, many adherents to the radical left were heirs to the Czech political tradition. The number of Czech Social Democrats who hailed the October Revolution and felt the Russian example worth emulating, however, included not only the radical left but also many Social Democrats who in matters of domestic socialist policies endorsed a more moderate line. The latter were swung to their position because of their nationalistic pro-Slav leanings; the historical accident that what was referred to as the first state of workers and peasants happened to be Russia thus greatly helped recruitment for the dissident left among the Czech socialists.

In Slovakia in 1917 the situation was comparable, with one important distinction. Since by the end of the First World War the Hungarian socialist movement had only half stepped out of illegality, the differentiation into reformist and revolutionary wings was not as pronounced as in Austria. The Slovak section of the Hungarian Social Democratic party, like all organizations that for a long time had to work underground, showed a greater predilection for radicalism than its counterpart in the Czech provinces. That is why it was predisposed to respond positively to the appeal of the Bolshevik revolution. Nationalist and Pan-Slav motivation, however, may not be overlooked; it was at least as strong among the Slovaks as among the Czechs.

The radicalization of the Hungarian socialist movement brought about by the war and the Russian October Revolution also affected the small Ruthenian contingent, which was later to become the Ruthenian chapter of the Communist Party of Czechoslovakia. As the inclusion of Ruthenia in the new Czechoslovak state was a compromise in the diplo-

matic negotiations about the postwar order in Central and Eastern
Europe, rather than the fulfillment of an articulated political goal of the
Ruthenian ethnic group, the emotional investment of the Ruthenian
elites in the Czechoslovak Republic could not compare with that of the
Czechs and the Slovaks. These elites believed that the status of their
ethnic group was somewhere between that of a nation-building partner
and that of an ethnic minority. Perceptions of this kind influenced the
orientation of Ruthenian Social Democrats in the party crisis. Self-
identification as an ethnic minority promoted the radical cause in almost
all racial groups in Czechoslovakia; in the case of the Ruthenians,
however, additional factors, such as social disruptions of a backward
province in the turmoil of economic and political change, played an
equally important role. On the other hand, Pan-Slav moods and feelings
did not count for much in the radical choices made by Ruthenian Social
Democrats. The geographical proximity of the Soviet Union and the
racial affinity to the Ukrainian nation, which suffered so much at the
hands of the prerevolutionary Russian regimes, made the Ruthenians
more immune to Pan-Slav arguments.

Among the Social Democrats of the largest ethnic minority, the
German-speaking population of Bohemia, Moravia, and Silesia (the
Sudeten Germans, as they came to be called in the 1930s), controversies
concerning the war and the victory of the Bolsheviks in Russia also
produced a schism. Socialist radicals in this section of the Austrian Social
Democratic party had an established history prior to 1917. It was in the
north Bohemian industrial center of Liberec (Reichenberg) that the
most outspoken criticism of the timid position taken by the national
party leadership on the war was voiced in 1914. The spokesmen of
the Liberec organization thus took a stance similar to that of Karl
Liebknecht and Rosa Luxemburg in neighboring Germany. The same
group responded enthusiastically to the October Revolution three years
later, and became the nucleus of the future German chapter of the
Czechoslovak Communist party. The radicalization of the ethnic Germans in Czechoslovakia was naturally not due to any sympathy for the
Russian culture or race. Rather, it was accelerated by their perception of
the outcome of the war, which was the reverse of the Czech socialists'
view. Unlike the Czechs, who at the end of the war saw their national
aspirations either fulfilled or within reach, the German Social Democrats
believed that the position of their ethnic group was threatened because
of defeat in a war of which they had not approved. The new political

order in Central Europe no longer reserved the privileged position for the German language and culture that these had enjoyed in Austria. A keen feeling of humiliation and powerlessness, paired with apprehensions about things to come, led many a German-speaking Social Democrat into the camp of the radical left.

Similar factors helped to establish a radical wing among the Social Democratic following in the regions of Slovakia inhabited by the Hungarian-speaking population. However progressive the Hungarian party had been with regard to equal rights for ethnic groups in Hungary, the shock of the dethronement of the Hungarian language from its status as the exclusive official tongue was too great not to produce a strong psychological reaction among those whom the prewar arrangement had benefited. Before the constitution in 1921 of the Communist Party of Czechoslovakia (CPCS), which was to include the elements of the radical left from the Hungarian minority, polarization within this group was also influenced by other factors. The most important single influence was the radicalization of the mood within the Hungarian Social Democracy proper, culminating in the establishment of the short-lived Hungarian Soviet Republic in 1919. Later this event will be discussed in more detail.

The split in the socialist movement in Czechoslovakia also produced small radical left groups among the numerically weaker ethnic and racial minorities. Of these groups the most active was the Jewish Poale Zion, which later took the name of the Jewish Communist Party in Czechoslovakia and eventually merged with the national party organization. It was supported by a large number of Jewish intellectuals and by the rural proletariat in Eastern Slovakia and Ruthenia, where compact Jewish communities existed until the Second World War.

Beginnings

The split in the Austrian and the Hungarian Social Democratic parties and the emergence of the various left wings and splinter bodies did not in themselves automatically lead to the constitution of a Communist party in Czechoslovakia. Together they may have been a necessary but not sufficient condition for what actually resulted from a long and turbulent process lasting almost four years. A very important element in this process was encouragement and active help from the Soviet Union, channeled after 1918 through the Communist International (Komintern) and given to individuals or groups in socialist parties wishing to follow the Russian example. The support Moscow granted to the Czechoslovak radical left followed a standard pattern since it was part of the universal strategy of world revolution; indeed, this support ultimately evolved into undisguised guidance and control of the national movement by the international center. In the beginning, however, the Bolsheviks contented themselves with assisting the diverse initiatives of Czech and Slovak radicals who sought to organize themselves as counterparts of the Russian party. The latter had established a Czechoslovak section in its Petersburg headquarters, virtually on the morrow of the October Revolution. As early as November 25, 1917, less than three weeks after the storming of the Winter Palace in Petersburg, a conference of the members of the Czecho-Slav Social Democratic party in Russia opened in Kiev. It was attended by Czech socialists of all shades who at that point lived in the Russian prisoner-of-war camps or belonged to the national liberation troops (Czechoslovak Legion) fighting on the side of Russia against the Central Powers. The situation in the Russian empire, especially in the Ukraine, was then rather confused; rival movements and parties were striving to assert their authority and contesting the Soviet claim to control. Nevertheless, the meeting in Kiev showed the direction in which the Czechoslovak radical socialist left would later develop. The resolution adopted at the close of the conference, on November 27, stressed "the bond between the Czechoslovak people and the Russian proletariat, the only worthy and reliable ally of the Czech and Slovak working class." Thus was spelled out the position that in postwar Czechoslovakia would consummate the split in the Social Democratic party organization.[1]

In spite of the sympathies for the Bolshevik revolution expressed at the Kiev conference, the Ukrainian organization of Czech Social Democrats was relatively independent compared with the Petersburg group, which formed but a sector of the Bolshevik party. It was also the more important of the two because of the size of its membership and the reserve of leaders it provided for the future Communist movement in Czechoslovakia, for example, Alois Muna and Josef Hais. The Ukrainian or Kiev group published the periodical *Svoboda* (*Freedom*); the organ of the Petersburg section was *Pochodeň* (*The Torch*). In March 1918, the Petersburg organization moved with the whole Bolshevik party center to Moscow. The subsequent upheaval caused by the civil war in the Ukraine made regular contacts and cooperation between the two groups difficult, even if we disregard the differences in their relationships with and allegiance to the Bolshevik party. The Kiev organization experienced problems and conflicts that the whole Social Democracy in Czechoslovakia had to face later because both groups combined moderate and radical elements. The manner in which the opposition of the two factions was resolved in the Kiev group also indicated what would happen to the socialist movement at home: the left wing seceded and constituted a new radical party, which later merged with the more outspokenly Bolshevik groups. In the beginning, however, the agreement on political goals between the Czech Social Democratic left in Russia and the Czech and Slovak Bolsheviks was only very general. Each of the two partners identified a different task as the most pressing: the Social Democrats were concerned with preparing for the work after the return to Czechoslovakia, and the Bolsheviks, who were participating directly in the October Revolution, viewed the problems of the socialist movement in Czechoslovakia as more remote. Nevertheless, both groups agreed on an issue that was then a crucial one: they rejected the legitimacy of the leadership in the liberation action of the Czechoslovak National Council in Russia.

The council was a branch of a larger organization with headquarters in Paris, directed by Professor Thomas Garrigue Masaryk and representing all shades and currents of Czech and Slovak political life, including Social Democracy. Its office in Russia had been active since the outbreak of the war, successfully coordinating the efforts of the various groups engaged in the campaign for Czechoslovak independence. Soon after the October Revolution, however, the Social Democratic left in Petersburg, Moscow, and the Ukraine began to contest the authority of the National Council on the grounds that it was a bourgeois-capitalist and imperialist instrument. The objection to the council's bourgeois-capitalist character reflected the intolerance exhibited at that time by the left wings and left radical splinters of all socialist parties fascinated by the Bolshevik example. The charge of imperialism, on the other hand, had a special meaning in the context of the history of the Czechoslovak liberation movement. The most significant—and the most visible—aspect of the liberation action was the participation of Czech and Slovak volunteer troops in the military operations of the Allied armies. These units, called Czechoslovak Legions, fought against the Central Powers on all fronts, but the contingent deployed in Russia was by far the strongest; it was estimated at fifty thousand officers and soldiers in 1917.

The presence of a Czechoslovak Legion on Russian territory created serious problems between the National Council and the Bolshevik government, which had made the withdrawal from war one of its primary objectives: since the council remained committed to the pursuit of war on the Allied side, its goals clashed with those of the Soviets; and this situation prompted the Social Democratic left to accuse the council of being an "imperialist tool." Not only did the clash disrupt relations within the Czechoslovak liberation movement at the end of the First World War; as it evolved into an international conflict, it also influenced the attitude of the Soviet Union toward the future Czechoslovak state. Furthermore, it influenced the radical socialist left's perception of the ideology of the First Czechoslovak Republic, a perception that continued to prevail within the later Communist Party of Czechoslovakia. These facts make it desirable for us to deal in more detail with the episode of the Czechoslovak Legion in revolutionary Russia.

The Siberian Intermezzo

As early as 1914, the first battalion of Czech volunteers was established in Kiev. Its members were recruited chiefly from among the Czech and Slovak settlers in the Ukraine. The volunteers called themselves Starodružinníci (The Old Guardians). The importance of the Old Guard would probably have remained symbolic had not spectacular defections of entire units of the Austrian army composed of Czech personnel— such as the Twenty-eighth and the Thirty-sixth Infantry Regiments— supplied considerable reinforcements. The Czechoslovak National Council succeeded, not without difficulties, in obtaining the approval of Russian authorities to set up an army corps from these defectors who, unlike the Old Guardians, were actually prisoners of war and citizens of an enemy nation. The czarist army command looked on the Czech volunteers with some apprehension. It was afraid of a possible contamination of the Russian troops by the liberal ideas, with strong populist and socialist undertones, that had inspired the Czechoslovak movement for independence. And, indeed, it was not until the February Revolution of 1917 that the organization of the Czechoslovak Legion in Russia as an autonomous unit within the Russian army with its own staff of officers could develop on a large scale. As the Russian provisional government, set up after the February Revolution, on several occasions had reiterated its will to continue the war against Germany and Austria-Hungary, it

seemed that nothing stood in the way of full engagement of the Czechoslovak forces on the Eastern front. Complications arose, however, after
the Bolshevik take-over in November. It soon became evident that the
Soviets would conclude a separate peace with the Central Powers, even
under the most unfavorable conditions. The Treaty of Brest-Litowsk,
signed in the spring of 1918, stabilized the German and Austrian front
lines deep in Russian and Ukrainian territory. The Czechoslovak Legion
was in jeopardy. Its political leadership, the National Council, had to
plan how to transfer the Czechoslovak troops safely to the theater of war
in the West.

The task, delicate enough in itself, was further complicated by a host
of partisan interests on the Russian scene that were pushing and pulling
in many directions. The Bolshevik government could see the departure
of the legion as the simplest solution for two reasons. The separate peace
treaty had obliged the Soviet Union not to tolerate the presence of any
army unit of powers hostile to Germany or Austria. In addition, the
Soviets were not sure the legion would not become involved in the civil
war on the side of their opponents. The Central Powers, for their part,
had as many reservations about the transfer of the Czechoslovak army
corps to the Western front as they had about its remaining in Russia. In
1918, with the human potential of Germany and Austria nearing
exhaustion, a reinforcement of the enemy by fifty thousand men was not
a negligible threat. They therefore pressed for the disarming of the
legion and the confinement of its members in prisoner-of-war camps.
Among the Western Allies the desire to use the legion in France
prevailed: such indeed had initially been the official line. Nevertheless,
certain Allied circles kept entertaining the idea of using the Czechoslovak volunteers for the purpose of overthrowing the Bolshevik regime.
These were the interventionists, who hoped that a non-Communist
Russian government would be willing to reopen the front in the East.

The internal Russian interests vying for support from the Czechoslovak army corps were no less complex. There were the opponents of the
October Revolution on the right—the "white" generals Kolchak and
Denikin and other pro-czar groups, next to Ukrainian nationalists—as
well as on the left—the Mensheviks and Social Revolutionaries (the
"Esers"). In the eyes of all these groups the existence of a well-organized,
well-armed, and well-equipped military force of significant size, with
high combat morale, was too much of a temptation. They could hardly
abstain from various attempts to employ it for their own ends. Finally,

there were the Czech and Slovak radical left socialists, organized partly among the Bolsheviks and partly on their own, to whom the enthusiasm and the dedication of the legion posed a challenge; its members represented the strength of national consciousness outweighing class consciousness, and thus gave a foretaste of the psychological obstacles the radical left would have to overcome before it could take root among the working class in its home country. Many members of the Social Democratic left in Russia put forth considerable effort to convert the officers and soldiers of the legion to the Communist cause and eventually make them join the Red Army. Local Russian or Ukrainian Bolshevik agitators also often approached the legionnaires with the same intention.

It can be assumed that Communist proselytizing among the Czechoslovak troops was the result of the initative of lower echelons of the party organization, and that the Soviet government on the whole sincerely wished to remove the discomforting, ideologically alien body represented by the legion from Soviet territory as quickly as possible. Such an operation, however, was not easy in the extremely complicated situation of the Russian civil war, even though both interested parties might have agreed to it. Among the difficult questions to be solved was the itinerary for the evacuated troops. The Soviets and the Allies preferred to use the two north Russian seaports, Archangelsk and Murmansk, as embarkation points. This seemed to be the shortest way via Russia and the fastest route to France, since both the Baltic and the Black Sea routes were under the control of enemy navy. However, some Western advisers feared that the transports might be attacked by German submarines. Also, the advance of the armies of the Central Powers in Russia after the signing of the Brest-Litowsk treaty had obliged the legion's detachments to retreat far to the east, whence the distance to Archangelsk and Murmansk was considerable and the railroad connection uncertain. Another itinerary, although much longer, now appeared to be more practicable: via Siberia to the Russian Pacific port of Vladivostok. This then was the real choice; the bulk of the legion returned home this way, after having made a trip, literally, around the world.[2]

Another question discussed during the negotiations between the Czechoslovak National Council's headquarters in Paris, represented by Professor Masaryk, and the Soviet government, represented by People's Commissar of Defense Leon Trotsky, concerned the kind of arms and equipment the legion would be allowed to retain on its way to the port of embarkation. The talks seemed to take a smooth course. In the agree-

ment signed by both parties in March 1918, the transport of the Czechoslovak troops was referred to not as the movement of an army, but as the
evacuation of a group of free citizens who for their own protection
would carry light arms and ammunition. Heavier equipment was to be
handed over to local Soviet authorities. The transports were routed via
the Trans-Siberian Railroad, but the itinerary via Archangelsk and
Murmansk was preserved as an alternative.[3]

In the beginning, both parties seemed to live up to the terms of the
agreement. The officials and military authorities in the communities
along the railroad helped the transports to move eastward, and everywhere the legion surrendered heavy arms and equipment to the Soviets.
In all, about forty-five thousand troops started out on their world
journey in the hope that they soon would leave behind the chaos of
revolutionary Russia and join their fellow countrymen in Europe. The
circumstances, however, proved stronger than both their hope and the
desire of their representatives to avoid involvement in the Russian civil
war. Various units of the Red Guards and other revolutionary groups
often unconnected with the Soviet power and not subject to its authority
began to harass the legionnaires. Local Bolshevik party organizations,
disregarding or unaware of the agreement concluded in Moscow, tried
to persuade the troops to defect. Anti-Communist groups operating in
Siberia also attempted to win the legion over to their side. Incidents of
seizure of light arms to which the Czechoslovak units were entitled, and
of provisions, as well as cases of imprisonment of the legionnaires,
multiplied. In some places Czech and Slovak soldiers and officers were
attacked and killed by irregular armed bands claiming to represent the
local Soviets or to belong to the Red Army. Thereupon, the legion's
headquarters decided to discontinue the surrender of heavy equipment
and ordered the occupation of the Trans-Siberian Railroad. The Soviet
government responded by instructing the Red Army to take the members of the legion prisoner. The result was an armed confrontation
between the Czechoslovak troops and the Bolshevik power in which the
legion, thanks to exceptional circumstances, not only repelled the attack
but soon extended its control over the entire area of the railroad. It
exercised this control for another two years.[4]

This conflict might not have mortgaged future Czechoslovak-Soviet
relations and increased the prejudice of the Communist party against
the Czechoslovak state so strongly had it remained merely an accidental
collision between an expeditionary army corps and a nation in revolu-

tionary turmoil. However, in the hotbed of the Russian civil war and in the general world situation of 1918 it could not fail to have international consequences. The fact that the legion had to fight the Bolsheviks made unsolicited allies of the various anti-Communist elements of right and left. These elements began to seek shelter in the territories under the legion's control. Soon the Czechoslovak troops found themselves entangled in the intricate web of revolution and counterrevolution, a situation they had always wished to avoid. The most serious complication arose when the Allied command, against the counsel of several experts, decided to include the occupation of the Trans-Siberian Railroad by the Czechoslovak Legion as an important resource in the plans for anti-Soviet intervention. These plans were as ill-conceived as the determination to carry them out was halfhearted. George Kennan pointedly observed that the Allied intervention in Russia had the worst of both worlds: it was too weak to achieve its objectives, but it was strong enough to adversely affect relations between the Soviet Union and the West for two generations.[5] As for Czechoslovakia, it can be claimed that it, too, had to pay the political and diplomatic price of this hapless venture, although its leaders had tried their best to stay out of such involvements.

The Masaryk Trauma

To duly assess the significance of the Siberian episode, we have to keep in mind that the occupation of the railroad by the Czechoslovak Legion continued for more than two years after the end of the war—during a period critical for the Soviet Union and during the formative years of the CPCS. The traumatic experience of the confrontation between the Czechoslovak independence movement and the emerging power of the first Communist nation of the world not only determined the way Soviet and Komintern leaders were to perceive the Czechoslovak Republic, but also influenced the attitude of the Czechoslovak Communists toward the political system of their country. This influence grew stronger as the part the activists coming from the Soviet Union played in the constitution of the Czechoslovak Communist party became increasingly important. Some of the leaders of the Czechoslovak left in Russia had even started their political careers as officials of the National Council and traveled a long way to their ultimate political home, which was to be communism. They were not just adversaries of the liberation action headed by T. G. Masaryk, but disappointed and frustrated believers converted to a hostile cause. They viewed the republic established by the victorious independence movement not as a fortress to be seized and transformed but as an objectionable edifice to be destroyed.

An element that contributed significantly to the negative attitude of the Czechoslovak Communists—and indeed of the entire world Communist movement—toward the First Republic was the vital role played by Thomas G. Masaryk in the action for the liberation of Czechoslovakia, and his leadership of the Czechoslovak Legion. It can be claimed that the dramatic circumstances surrounding the evacuation of the Czechoslovak volunteer army from Russia aroused the Communists' antagonism toward Masaryk in the same manner that Masaryk's undisputed authority over the legions made the latter politically suspicious in the eyes of the Soviets. Masaryk had been known to the Marxist-inspired left everywhere in the world long before the war because of his scholarly work on social problems of modern industrial societies, which included a thorough analysis and critique of Marxism; this volume appeared at the turn of the century under the title *Otázka sociální* (*The Social Question*).[6] Here Masaryk evaluated the merits and the inadequacies of historical materialism from the point of view of liberal humanism. The book received considerable attention from sociologists and political scientists, and stirred a very lively debate in the socialist circles of that time. The value of Masaryk's contribution was then compared with that of the revision of Marxism by the German socialist Eduard Bernstein. Masaryk himself, of course, had never been a socialist, much less a Marxist, but the fact that he approached the problems that had concerned Marx from a progressive liberal position made him appear congenial to theoreticians of socialism. This presumed affinity did not make the Marxists any more lenient discussion partners of Masaryk. The orthodox Marxist left saw in Masaryk's views dangerous ideas capable of subverting, because of their plausibility, the revolutionary spirit of socialism. On these grounds, they had to be rejected even more vehemently than the arguments of the conservative opponents. These critics scornfully labeled Masaryk "a bourgeois eclectic," a type they often lumped together with democratic socialists and other "revisionist and reformist renegades."[7] The more moderate Social Democrats held Masaryk in great esteem even though they, too, disagreed with him on a number of points. The Czech socialists, for example, did not accept his contention that the modernization of Czech political life was possible on the ethical basis provided by the Protestant Reformation; they believed that this goal could be achieved by promoting the universal ideals of the working class as represented in the Socialist International.

The war increased these differences. Although Masaryk's open struggle against the Hapsburg empire for national independence in a more modern political system eventually brought about a rapprochement between him and democratic socialists, it also deepened the mistrust of the radical left. Now more than ever Masaryk appeared to be a dangerous rival. His ability to formulate concrete and realistic political goals that were intelligible to the masses as well as to the elite, his diplomatic skill, and above all, his appeal to the simple working people whom the left considered to be exclusively subject to its influence and leadership challenged the self-assurance of the orthodox Marxists. A sizable segment of the orthodox wing in the Czech section of the Austrian Social Democratic party also questioned the correctness of the national liberation program Masaryk adopted at the outbreak of the war. They did not approve of the idea, which this program implied, of breaking up the Austro-Hungarian empire; instead they proposed a radical constitutional reform that would satisfy the national aspirations of the various ethnic groups and preserve the assets, especially the economic ones, of a large political configuration. This position was associated with the so-called Austromarxist current in Social Democracy, represented by prominent names such as Viktor Adler, Otto Bauer, and Karl Renner, but it also had its advocates among the Czech socialists. Not all Czech Austromarxists were members of the radical left, nor were all Czech radical socialists Austromarxists; however, those who subscribed to both positions had one more reason to oppose Masaryk's national independence campaign.

Soviet Communists, for their part, shared the perception of Masaryk as an ideological opponent who had to be taken seriously. Many knew his writings about Marxism and Russia from before the war.[8] Their rather reserved attitude turned into open hostility after the conflict with the Czechoslovak Legion. In the eyes of the Soviets Masaryk was a protagonist, if not the architect, of the Allied intervention in Siberia. Yet it would seem that by far the most serious offense the Bolsheviks attributed to him was his success in the national liberation and in the creation of a new viable polity in an area that they had long considered to be ripe for a Communist revolution. To a notable extent Masaryk foiled the designs of the Kremlin and the Communist International—a crime that could not be pardoned—and in the later postwar years, the Czechoslovak

Republic continued to be an obstacle to the Komintern's world strategy. The "drunkenness with nationalism" and "national fanaticism," as Moscow referred to the developed Czechoslovak civic culture, occasionally even contaminated the Czechoslovak communist movement itself. Sporadic glimpses of political realism, of tolerance of differing opinions, and of respect for the will of grass-roots organizations manifested by the CPCS could all be traced back to the impact of the democratic traditions and Masaryk's leadership. Soviet critics of these influences usually spoke of "socialdemocratism," and less often of "Masarykism," even where the second label would have been more suitable.

Although the position and the policies of the Kremlin on Czechoslovakia have undergone several changes in the course of time, the Soviet Communists' rejection of Masaryk and his ideas has always been unqualified. Even as late as 1968, the teachings of Czechoslovakia's first president were blamed for having subverted the intellectual elite of the Communist party. And in the numerous postmortems of the Prague Spring, the Soviet-obedient commentators continued to link the idea of Socialism with a Human Face, promoted by the Dubček group, with Masaryk's political philosophy of democratic humanism.[9]

Thus, prior to the establishment of the Czechoslovak Republic and long before the founding of the CPCS, conditions were created in which the latter would take an exceptionally hostile view of the former. The attitudes of the Bolsheviks and the entire European radical left toward the Czechoslovak liberation movement were strongly influenced by the wartime experience and by the perception of Masaryk, the movement's leader, as a political thinker. To these leftists, the movement appeared to be tool of counterrevolutionary intervention, and its foremost sponsor to be a subtle bourgeois ideologist bent upon, and capable of, diverting the popular masses away from the path of socialist revolution. It was in this light that Czechoslovak Communists saw the Czechoslovak state, the product of the liberation movement inspired by Masaryk's ideas. Communist parties in almost all countries of the world, since they are revolutionary parties, have always been radically critical of the prevailing socioeconomic system and political order. In Czechoslovakia, however, the Communists started from a position of total rejection of the raison d'être of the Czechoslovak polity. This rejection, which became almost an article of faith with the party leadership after the Moscow power center assured itself of undisputed control over the Czechoslovak party organization, was to determine Communist policies practically until the end of the First Republic.

Preparing for Action

The two centers of the Czechoslovak radical left in Kiev and Moscow helped the Soviets in their conflict with the Czechoslovak Legion by agitating among the legionnaires to make them defect and join the Bolshevik forces. The Executive Committee of the Czecho-Slav Social Democratic party in Kiev, which had been since November 1917 in the hands of the left wing, decided early in 1918 to set up a Czechoslovak Red Guard. This military formation was to recruit members among the Czech and Slovak settlers in the Ukraine and also to enlist deserters from the Czechoslovak Legion. The Red Guard had not much opportunity to prove its appeal since the advance of the armies of the Central Powers in the spring of 1918 had obliged the Kiev organization of the Czecho-Slav Social Democracy to move to Moscow. Here the organization fused with the Czechoslovak section of the Bolshevik party led by František Beneš and Karel Knoflíček, which as we have seen, had been constituted in Petersburg in November 1917. The fusion was carried out at the merger congress in Moscow held on May 26 and 27, 1918. On this occasion it was reported that in all 1,850 Czechs and Slovaks in Russia had joined the Red Army. It is not known how many of these individuals were former soldiers and officers of the Czechoslovak Legion, but information from other, non-Communist sources suggests that the pro-Bolshevik propaganda campaign conducted among the legionnaires at that point had definite results, although the core of the legion remained intact.[10] The merger congress ended with the constitution of a Czechoslovak Communist party in Russia. The final resolution of the congress declared the new party to be "the only legitimate spokesman of the Czechoslovak proletariat living on the territory of the Russian Federative Soviet Republic," and denounced the National Council, as well as what it termed "the rebellion of the Czechoslovak Legion against the Soviet power." It pointed out, nevertheless, that the newly created party did not claim to be a substitute for a Communist party that still was to be founded in Czechoslovakia, but wished only to be "an avant-garde of the Czechoslovak working class" that might speed up the birth of a genuine Communist party organization from domestic revolutionary elements.[11]

The Czechoslovak radicals in Russia and their Bolshevik sponsors had very definite ideas about how the establishment of a truly proletarian socialist party in Czechoslovakia could be accelerated. Above all, they had a very precise notion of the type of party organization the Czechoslovak proletariat should create: it was a type to suit the needs of the world revolutionary strategy of the Komintern. This strategy would have been best served by parties with national rank-and-file following but with leadership supplied by, and unreservedly obedient to, the international headquarters. Preparing and training such leadership was from the start the primary task of the Czechoslovak Communist party in Russia. Several training centers were set up for this purpose in major Soviet cities and operated until the early 1920s. Civil war in Russia and in the Ukraine disrupted this work several times. The first trainees, mostly officials of the Czechoslovak Communist party in Russia, arrived in Czechoslovakia as early as the end of 1918. Along with Bolshevik-trained cadres equipped with large quantities of propaganda material and supplied with money to finance the political action came a number of former Austrian prisoners of war who had not joined the legion, or enlisted in the Red Army, or participated in any other way in the revolution, but had opted for the relative security of the Russian prisoner-of-war camps. Among these returnees were many supporters of the radical left as well as many demoralized and uprooted individuals who also, once they had regained their native place, espoused the radical cause. This was especially true of the prisoners of war from ethnic groups that were not Czech or Slovak, such as the German and Hungarian groups; these prisoners had undergone political education and conversion to radical socialism in Russian captivity during the revolution and civil war. Their consciousness of belonging to a defeated nation inclined them more than the Czechs to extremist ideologies. Thus the impact of the Bolshevik revolution and the Soviet influence upon the left wing of the Czechoslovak socialist movement was strengthened.

However, as the activists and agitators returning from the Soviet Union gradually discovered, the development toward a separate organization of the socialist left in Czechoslovakia did not depend entirely on the will and plans of the Moscow center. In Czechoslovakia, as in most European countries, the radical wing of the socialist movement had grown out of domestic traditions, even though the example of the October Revolution notably contributed to the polarization within this movement. It was flattering and encouraging for the leaders of the left to see themselves as part of a world community of revolutionaries, but not all of them were prepared to accept the role of insurgent agents under direct orders from the Bolshevik party. Many suspected that the epithet "Section of the Communist International" appended to the name of every Communist party only concealed the hard fact of its subservience to the power center in Moscow. In the long run, this fact was hard for a very large proportion of the Czechoslovak socialist left elite, regardless of background or origin, to accept. Even some of the prominent officials of the Czechoslovak Communist party in Russia, who had received their political education in the Soviet Union and had been specially trained by the Bolsheviks for their tasks in Czechoslovakia, eventually disagreed with the policies of the Komintern and had to be dismissed from their functions or expelled. In short, the development of the Czechoslovak radical left had its own dynamics, a circumstance that the Moscow planners had to take into account and that on several occasions produced serious crises in the formation of the CPCS.

The Socialist Movement at the End of World War I

While the Soviet-sponsored cadres prepared the part they would play after they returned to their home country, the regrouping of the socialist forces in Czechoslovakia continued. The left had enjoyed an initial advantage over the center and the right because the leadership of the Czecho-Slav section of the Austrian Social Democratic party during the last two years of the war had been in the hands of the Austromarxists and the internationalists, who leaned towards radicalism more than did the nationalist wing. One of the most prominent Czech Austromarxists, Dr. Bohumír Šmeral, a popular Prague lawyer, was elected chairman of the Executive Committee of the Czecho-Slav Social Democratic party in 1916. Shortly before his election to this key post, Šmeral had represented Czech socialists at the Zimmerwald/Kienthal peace conference in Switzerland. There he had endorsed the radical line promoted by the Russian delegates, especially Lenin. In November 1916, he and Vladimír Tusar, a centrist, took seats in the coordinative caucus of all Czech political parties in the Vienna Imperial Council (the Austrian parliament).

The center and the right of the Czecho-Slav section of the Austrian Social Democracy were more strongly represented in the Czech National Committee in Prague, a body comprising all political, economic, and cultural interest groups among the Czech population of Bohemia,

Moravia, and Silesia. The National Committee, constituted in the fall of 1916, had played a key role in the campaign for Czechoslovakia's independence. The distribution of the protagonists of the two main tendencies in the Social Democratic party—the internationalist left and the nationalist center and right—among the various Czech political organs and agencies reflected the differing images each wing held of the future of Austria-Hungary. The internationalists and the Austromarxists counted on the continuing existence of the empire, albeit in a changed (possibly federalized and socially more progressive) form. The nationalist group expected the disintegration of Austria into a number of independent states based upon the principle of self-determination. For reasons already given, a correlation existed between Austromarxism and the socialist left and between nationalism and the centrist-rightist current in the Social Democratic party.

The newly constituted leadership of the Czecho-Slav section participated in the peace conference called by the Socialist International in Stockholm in June 1917. The Czech delegation included radical as well as moderate elements. A spokesman for the latter group, Gustav Habrman, submitted a resolution calling for the creation of an independent state of Czechs and Slovaks within a federation of the Danube area nations. This resolution was supported by all delegates, but Dr. Šmeral candidly admitted that he did not see a sovereign national state as the best political solution for the Czechs; since a majority of the Czech people desired complete independence, however, he would respect their wish.[12] The reference to a Danubian federation in the Czech resolution was obviously a compromise between the nationalist and the Austromarxist positions. Nothing else indicated a coming split in the party; the event that was to precipitate the schism, the Bolshevik revolution, occurred later in the same year.

Nevertheless, the polarization within the Czech socialist movement increased sharply prior to the storming of the Winter Palace in Petrograd. Other factors were at work, among them the trauma caused by the failure of European socialism to make a serious attempt at preventing war in 1914, as well as the movement's manifest impotence in stopping or even limiting the bloodshed once it had begun. Growing discontent among the population because of rapidly deteriorating economic conditions favored political radicalism. Communist historiography has interpreted the unrest behind the front lines during the last period of World War I as a sign of a genuine revolutionary situation. According to this interpretation, all that was needed to achieve a successful socialist revolution was competent political leadership. The fact that this supposedly unique historical chance was passed up is blamed by Communist historians on Social Democracy, partly on its "renegade rightist wing" and partly on the radical left. In reality the circumstances in Austria in general and in the Czech provinces in particular at that time were much more complex than Communist analysts depict them, and they were not altogether favorable to a socialist take-over.

The protest against the shortages of food and basic commodities, as well as against the rising cost of living and other hardships caused by the war, became general by the end of 1916. It was not only the objective economic situation, however, that prompted these manifestations of discontent; one could argue, in accordance with widely accepted sociological theory of expectation gap,[13] that the protest movement expressed frustrated hopes that had been raised not long before by a perceptible political relaxation. In the summer of 1916, Emperor Francis Joseph I had died and had been succeeded by Charles I, his grandnephew. The change on the Austrian throne was accompanied by a number of measures restoring constitutional rule and facilitating the activity of political parties. The Viennese court, under the new monarch, acknowledged that the war could not be ended by any decisive victory of the Central Powers and began to seek reconciliation both abroad and at home. Far from improving, however, the material conditions of the Hapsburg empire continued to worsen in a typical case of expectations outstripping actual developments.

Early in 1917 a series of strikes broke out in the major Austrian industrial enterprises, most of them in the economically highly developed Czech provinces. In July of the same year, the workers in the Škoda armament plant in Plzeň (Pilsen) and in the large steel mills of Vítkovice, in Silesia, stopped working for several days. On August 14, 1917, martial law had to be proclaimed in the entire Pilsen area as a consequence of strikes, riots, and plundering of stores. In January 1918, Austrian trade unions declared a general strike that was observed all over the country. Another general strike in the industrial districts of Prague followed on January 22, 1918. Finally, a province-wide strike was called and successfully carried out in Bohemia on October 14, 1918. This strike also had marked political overtones: a change of government and recognition of the Czechs' right to self-determination were some of the demands spelled out on this occasion. Thus, the strike is viewed as one of the most important manifestations of the Czech national liberation movement, which achieved its goal two weeks later, on October 28, 1918, by the proclamation of the Czechoslovak Republic in Prague. Communist historians like to contrast the strike of October 14 with the events of October 28. They claim that whereas the general strike had been a truly popular and proletarian action and an expression of the will to socialist revolution, the establishment of the Czechoslovak Republic by the National Committee in Prague, in agreement with the independence movement leaders abroad, was a "bourgeois-capitalist undertaking that snatched away from the Czech working class the fruits of its long struggle."[14]

Another important element in Austria's internal situation toward the end of the war was the progressive collapse of the discipline and morale of the Austrian and Hungarian troops. Although it was only at the very end of the hostilities, in the late summer of 1918, that the disintegration of the armed forces reached proportions comparable to those observed in the Russian army in 1917, sporadic acts of disobedience and isolated cases of mutiny had multiplied since 1917. The most spectacular of these was the revolt of the garrison at the naval base in the Bay of Kotor, on the Adriatic coast, in the spring of 1918. Since 1917, an ever-increasing number of Austrian soldiers had deserted their units or failed to return to them after a temporary leave. Hiding in the countryside, they began forming irregular bands that often secured the necessary supplies by raiding military depots and civilian homes. After the war, these so-called Green Cadres (an allusion to the forests that were their hideouts) stimulated the imagination of many a Communist writer; the stories they inspired might lead readers to believe that these bands were potential nuclei of partisan troops. In reality, the activities of the Green Cadres, which remained very restricted in scope, were not part of a scenario of social revolution, but rather a sign of general fatigue after more than three years of senseless war.

Moreover, conscious acts of rebellion, whenever and wherever they occurred, had one peculiar characteristic: they were perpetrated almost exclusively by soldiers and civilians belonging to ethnic minorities. Although the discontent caused by the privations and hardships of war was general in Austria and Hungary, open rejection of state authority was an attitude displayed mostly by individuals and groups whose language and origins were neither German nor Hungarian. The denial of the legitimacy of the political order was always paired with the protest of underprivileged ethnicity. The "nation-building" ethnic groups, German and Hungarian, in the Austro-Hungarian empire based their opposition to the government upon concrete issues, particularly those of war and peace. However critical of the government some of the spokesmen of the German and Hungarian populations might have been, even the most radical of them never questioned the existence of the Austro-Hungarian state. The acts of open rebellion in Austria at the end of the war, for example the Kotor mutiny, must therefore be seen primarily as manifestations of ethnic protest. If there was a revolutionary mood in the Danubian monarchy at that time, it was directed toward a national, not a proletarian revolution. Indeed, such a revolution eventually did take place and succeeded, but its outcome, naturally, was not socialism. It led to the break-up of the empire and the birth of a number of smaller national states.

Neither the Austromarxist left nor the Russian Communists themselves expected the war to have these results. They had hoped that Austria-Hungary would remain intact and thus become a rewarding target of the world revolutionary strategy. This belief was reinforced by the experience of the multi-ethnic czarist empire that was being rebuilt into a strongly centralized Union of Socialist Soviet Republics. The Bolsheviks in particular had difficulty in understanding the virulence of the nationalist currents in Austria and Hungary; these reminded them, rather disconcertingly, of the centrifugal forces threatening the territorial integrity of the Soviet Union. Unprepared for the turn of events in Austria, they had to devise new policies concerning the emerging successor nations on a more or less impromptu basis. The thesis of "national revolutions growing into social ones" had not yet been formulated at that time; in fact, it was distinctly spelled out only during the world conference of the Communist parties in Moscow held in 1957. Stalin's work on nationalism,[15] written in 1909, despite its apparent radicalism, was too abstract to be of practical use in the given situation. Besides, whatever concessions Stalin's theory had made to nationalism and to the search of the ethnic groups for national identity were obliterated by later oppressive practices of the Soviet government toward minorities in Russia.

The official position that the Bolshevik party and the Komintern eventually took on the national revolutions in Austria-Hungary combined lip service to the principle of self-determination with a lament over the "poisoning of the proletariat by the drug of nationalism." This was a

sign of badly veiled embarrassment at the fact that the Marxist doctrine
and its Leninist version failed to predict the actual course of events. Only
much later did Soviet and Komintern leaders recognize that the resistance movement among the underprivileged ethnic groups in the
Hapsburg empire had also had a national character. They then blamed
the socialist left in Czechoslovakia and other successor states ex post facto
for not having given the national movements "proper guidance towards
the goal of socialist revolution."

Actually, the Czechoslovak Social Democratic left could not have been
any wiser to the situation than the Bolsheviks; the conclusions it drew
had been based on the same dogmatic premises. The position of the
center-right wing of the party, on the other hand, was more realistic.
The center-right did not underestimate the strength of the nationalist
current and considered the demise of Austria-Hungary to be very likely.
It was also rather skeptical about the prospect that the Russian revolution would become universal. These differences between the two wings
in the interpretation of the situation aggravated the internal tensions in
the Social Democratic party and rendered major policy decisions difficult, but in themselves they would not have made a split inevitable. To
complete the schism, deliberate interference from Moscow was necessary. In 1917 and 1918, however, this interference had not yet reached
significant proportions. At that point, both wings were still anxious to
preserve the unity of the party; each still hoped that its point of view
would ultimately prevail. Thus the Czecho-Slav Social Democracy
entered the new historical era, after the proclamation of Czechoslovak
independence, as an apparently intact body. For a brief while it even
appeared that in the wake of national liberation an earlier split would be
healed: on September 6, 1918, the leaders of the Social Democratic party
and of the Czech National Socialist party (the latter having seceded from
the Social Democracy at the beginning of the century) declared their
intention to work toward the constitution of a single Czechoslovak
socialist party organization.[16] Although this project did not materialize,
the initiative demonstrated that at that time, the Social Democracy, far
from wishing to promote a schism, planned on further growth. At its
first postwar congress, held in December 1918 in Prague, the party,
among other things, officially adopted the name Czechoslovak Social
Democratic Workers party, and in its final resolution voiced the will to
"pursue a revolutionary socialist course" while condemning the violent
methods used by the Bolsheviks in Russia.[17] This wording reflected the

polarization into the left and the center-right camps, as well as a concern with maintaining a common platform on which proponents of both tendencies could meet and coexist.

The first sign that it might be difficult to preserve such a platform appeared early in 1919. On January 15, the Central Committee of the party renewed its condemnation, first voiced at the Twelfth Party Congress, of the ruling practices of the Russian Communists and included in its criticism the German Spartacans, a radical wing of the Social Democratic movement in the neighboring German Republic. The left-oriented members of the Central Committee refused to endorse the statement. Shortly afterwards, on February 28, 1919, the left wing, frustrated by what it believed to be discriminatory coverage by the party's central press organ, *Právo lidu*, announced the publication of its own periodical. Characteristically, the new review was called *Sociální demokrat* (*Social Democrat*). The editorial board identified itself on the front page of the journal as the Social Democratic Workers party, with the word "levice" ("the left") added in brackets. The desire of the editors was clearly not to precipitate a split that the adoption of another label, such as Communist, could have brought about. In spite of these precautions, the party's internal crisis became publicly known.

Ethnic Problems of the Socialist Left:
The Impact of the Hungarian Communist Revolution

At the beginning of 1919, the two wings of the Social Democracy appeared to be comparable in strength. The representatives of the center-right current were in the majority among the members of the Central Committee, but the distribution of the most influential positions seemed to favor the left. As early as in the summer of 1918, Bohumír Šmeral was re-elected to the post of party chairman. Increasing numbers of activists trained in the Soviet Union began to arrive and gradually occupied key posts in the regional and local party organizations. Some were co-opted directly into the various governing bodies at the party headquarters. The trend toward the left in the Czechoslovak socialist movement was further reinforced by developments within the Social Democratic sections set up by ethnic minorities, such as the Germans and Hungarians.

The division among the German-speaking socialists in Czechoslovakia into center-right and left wings dates back to the beginning of the war. In 1914, the industrialized north of Bohemia, which was inhabited by ethnic Germans, became the center of opposition to the ambiguous position of the Austrian party leadership on the expansionist policies of the Vienna court. These radical pacifists were concentrated in the regional organization of Liberec and their mouthpiece was the daily *Vorwärts* (*Ahead*). After the Bolshevik revolution, Liberec became the center of the extreme left. Thus, even before the formal constitution of the German Social Democratic party in Czechoslovakia and the severance of the original tie to the national Austrian body, the socialist movement of the German ethnic minority had to face the split between the left and the center-right. After the party congress held in Teplice-Šanov (Teplitz-Schönau) in October 1919, a showdown became unavoidable. The left adroitly exploited the national resentments among the ethnic Germans, taking an uncompromisingly radical view with regard to the right of self-determination and blaming the centrist leadership for "selling out to Czech bourgeois chauvinists."[18] The militancy of the left had considerable appeal for German nationalists of all shades, especially for the German-speaking prisoners of war who had just returned home.

Nationalistic passions and the antagonism between left and center were dramatically escalated as the political leaders of the German ethnic group failed in their attempt to establish an independent state in the German-speaking regions of Bohemia, Moravia, and Silesia. In March 1919, invoking the fourteenth point of U.S. President Woodrow Wilson's October 1918 peace declaration, in which the right to self-determination had been acknowledged for "all nations of Austria-Hungary," the representatives of the German minority proclaimed a sovereign Deutschböhmen ("German Bohemia"). This proposed entity, however, included sections of the other two Czech provinces and was to become part of Deutschösterreich ("German Austria"), corresponding to today's Austrian Federal Republic. The initiative in this act came from political parties other than the Social Democracy. The socialists were involved insofar as they called a general strike of the German-speaking industrial workers in support of the ethnic Germans' claim to self-determination. The movement was quickly suppressed by the police and the army, but the attendant bloodshed left a lasting scar on German-Czech relations. Politically, and above all geopolitically, German Bohemia could never have been a viable entity. It would have created a thin ring of highly industrialized districts around the Czech provinces. Its economic problems would have been insurmountable. Nevertheless, the fate of this ill-conceived project supplied the left wing of the German Social Democracy with useful propaganda arguments against both its own party leadership and other, nonsocialist German parties. The left now could unmask the capitalist bourgeoisie of the German ethnic group as a traitor to the national cause and the Social Democratic center as bankrupt and inept, completely incapable of defending German ethnic interests. The indictment of treason appeared all the more justified to the radicals since not long afterward the German parties agreed to participate in the Czechoslovak Parliament and in local government. Although the left could not fully capitalize on its propaganda among the Germans since German nationalism soon became the domain of the extreme right, the thrust of its attack indicated what would later be a major source of recruitment for the Communist cause: disaffected minorities with strong ethnic resentments.

Meanwhile developments in the eastern part of the Czechoslovak state promoted the establishment of a radical leftist stronghold among the Hungarian ethnic group and ensured that the future Communist party in Slovakia would wield appreciable influence. These events were part of the immediate postwar history of Hungary, but they were indivisibly connected with the early history of the Czechoslovak Communist movement. After the collapse of the Austrian war fronts in October 1918, the abdication of Emperor Charles I, and the constitution of independent Czechoslovakia, the crisis in the eastern half of the double monarchy began to escalate. Despite growing opposition among all segments of the population, especially among the non-Magyar ethnic groups, the Hungarian government, unlike its Austrian counterpart, had stubbornly maintained its hard conservative line until the end of the war. The collapse of the regime in Vienna, however, rendered this policy untenable. Eventually, a Hungarian National Council composed of liberal and progressive elements and supported by revolutionary units of the Hungarian army took power in Budapest on October 31, 1918. It appointed a coalition government with Count Károlyi as prime minister, and placed Social Democrats from both the center and the left wings of the party in important cabinet posts. Following the pronouncements of the National Council, postwar Hungary was to become a democratic republic with strong socialist tendencies. The new course aimed at a complete break with the conservative past, particularly as far as policies towards various ethnic groups and minorities were concerned. Károlyi's program was to transform Hungary into a federation where all races and languages would enjoy equal status and cultural as well as territorial autonomy. However, the October Revolution, as these events have frequently been named, came too late to save the integrity of Hungary's historic borders. Still, it was an important step on the road to the short-lived Hungarian Soviet Republic, and in turn profoundly influenced the development of the Communist movement in Czechoslovakia in general and in Slovakia in particular.

The concrete accomplishments of the Károlyi ministry could not measure up to expectation. The Hungarian liberal revolution failed precisely because of that issue it seemed initially to have resolved successfully. Károlyi had performed an almost incredible feat of statesmanship when he rallied the support of the Hungarian-speaking population, the most favored ethnic group under the old regime, for policies that signified the surrender of its privileges. Later, however, it became evident that Hungarian nationalism had merely been muted in the euphoria of the revolution; it retained enough force to prevent Hungarian society from adjusting to the realities of postwar Europe, in which Hungary belonged to the losing camp. When the Allies demanded, under the terms of the peace conditions formulated by President Wilson, that Hungary relinquish territories inhabited by Slovaks, Ruthenians, Rumanians, Croatians, and Serbs, the Károlyi government refused to comply. It argued that the Hungarian people—a term that was used somewhat ambiguously in this context—would never agree to the partition of the fatherland. Such, indeed, was the mood of the Hungarian nation-building group, even though at that point Hungary's future borders had not been determined and the outrageous amputations of entire regions where the Hungarian-speaking population clearly constituted the majority had not yet been made. It appeared that the very principle of self-determination for the various non-Magyar ethnic groups was more than the spirit of the Hungarian October Revolution could tolerate. Károlyi resigned and invited the Parliament to set up a new government in which responsibility would be assumed by parties representing the truly popular masses. In the given situation this meant a socialist cabinet, and since the radical left had already gained the upper hand within the Hungarian Social Democracy, the road was open to a leftist experiment.[19]

The radicals did not miss their chance. On March 2, 1919, in Budapest, the Hungarian Soviet Republic was proclaimed. The easy triumph of the socialist revolution, which looked much more like a peaceful, almost constitutional transfer of power, surprised everyone, including Moscow. Despite a certain skepticism, the Bolsheviks hailed the birth of a new Communist state that seemed to end the isolation of the USSR and to confirm the diagnosis that the European situation was ripe for a continent-wide proletarian take-over. The new Hungarian government was not exclusively Communist—it was based on a coalition with the Social Democratic center—but this fact did not seem to disturb the Communist observers, who recalled that in its early beginnings the Bolshevik revolution had taken a similar course. Events in Hungary then mirrored those in Petrograd in November 1917: the initiative and control in Budapest in 1919 were firmly in the hands of the extreme left, headed by Béla Kún. Thus, what actually turned out to be but a short episode, lasting precisely 133 days, appeared initially to be the dawn of a new era. The Kún government made it clear that it regarded the new Hungary as a full fledged Communist society. The Hungarian Soviet constitution and the abundant legislation passed during this brief period testify to the seriousness of this intention. However, the most lasting imprint of the short-lived Hungarian Communist revolution was its effect on the radical socialist movement in the Danube area as a whole. The subsequent development of the radical left in this region and the often extremely intricate relationships among its various ethnic and racial sections can to a large extent be traced back to the 1919 experience. The CPCS, through its Slovak branch, was among the parties most deeply affected by the Kún intermezzo.

The Communist regime fully endorsed the principles of equality for individual ethnic groups in Hungary that had been spelled out by the Károlyi government. Theoretically, it went even farther: it recognized the right of each group to self-determination, including the right of secession, just as the Bolsheviks in the immediate postrevolutionary period had recognized the right of the peoples of the Soviet Union to self-determination. Communist spokesmen in Hungary justified this approach by pointing to what they believed to be the inevitable course of events in the immediate future: a world, or at least European, socialist revolution. After the establishment of the dictatorship of the proletariat, as Béla Kún himself explicitly stated, the national state would become a meaningless entity, and the question of self-determination would retain only minor importance. This reasoning was not devoid of logic; from the point of view of international communism it really mattered little how many new nation-states emerged from the ruins of the two Central European empires, as long as they were all Soviet republics

obedient to the policies of the world Communist headquarters in
Moscow. In reality, however, there was no guarantee that national
aspirations and the socialist revolutionary drive in the Danube basin in
1919 would always converge. The radical internationalism of the Hungarian left was soon put to a test that revealed the left to be as much a
prisoner of the nationalist forces as the previous liberal coalition, born
out of the "Glorious October" of 1918, had been. Perhaps it was even
more so, since the actual course of action adopted by the Kún government toward the new states in Hungary's neighborhood suggested an
even stronger commitment to the principle of territorial integrity than
Károlyi had ever exhibited. Czechoslovakia became the primary object of
this action.

After power in Hungary passed into Communist hands, the Entente
sent South African general Jan C. Smuts to negotiate the conditions of
the armistice between the victors of the war and Hungary, terms that
Károlyi had refused to discuss because of demands by the non-Magyar
minorities for self-determination. Although the Allies were careful to
avoid any appearance that this move was a diplomatic recognition of the
Communist regime in Budapest, Smuts was authorized to offer Kún a
more favorable demarcation line between Hungary and its neighbors
than that actually held by Hungarian troops. The Allies proposed to
defer the question of the final borders to the peace conference and
indicated that at that point some territories could be returned to
Hungary. At the same time, the Entente made it clear that the basic self-
determination rights of the various ethnic groups could not be curtailed.
In other words, the integrity of Hungarian territory as it existed before
the war could not be preserved. Béla Kún in his reply tried to reconcile
the two incompatible concepts of self-determination and territorial
integrity by proposing a popular vote on both issues. Hungarian
Communists hoped that the outcome of the vote would overwhelmingly
favor preserving Hungary's historical borders. They expected that in
Slovakia, for example, no less than 80 percent of the population would
vote this way. Massive support for the territorial status quo would have
been very welcome to Kún since it could have been interpreted as a
demonstration of the legitimacy of the Hungarian Soviet Republic.
Whatever grounds there may have been for optimism over the outcome
of the popular vote, a plebiscite was not a realistic alternative in April
1919, when most of the critical areas were already occupied by troops of
the successor states: Yugoslavia, Rumania, Czechoslovakia, and the

Austrian Federal Republic. Nevertheless, Kún rejected Smuts's offer and decided to use force. His motives probably were, on the one hand, to cement revolutionary solidarity within the country and, on the other, to encourage Communist and radical leftist forces in the neighboring countries to follow the Hungarian example. Of these two expectations, only the first was fulfilled, and only for a short time. The price that had to be paid for this brief success was terrible. Seldom in history has a move been misread so completely, both at home and abroad, as was the offensive of the Hungarian Red Army in the spring of 1919, and seldom had a temporary victory so utterly defeated its own purpose.

The Slovak Soviet Republic Episode

At the time of Kún's talks with Smuts, Hungarian units were confronting two major potential adversaries: the Rumanian army in the east and the Czechoslovak troops in the north. The Rumanians were the stronger of the two because Czechoslovak authorities in Slovakia disposed of only a few police contingents thinly scattered all over the province. Hungarian Communists chose to attack at the point of least resistance. The intervention in Slovakia was preceded, and possibly precipitated, by an unsuccessful attempt to establish a Soviet regime in Ruthenia. Ruthenia, according to a previous regulation decreed by the Károlyi government, was to constitute an autonomous region within Hungary with its own diet (*sejm*) that would be responsible for matters of education, religion, and justice. In view of the fact that the Ruthenians were racially and linguistically close to the Ukrainians, a key ethnic group in the Soviet Union, the Kún regime was prepared to respect all rights granted to them by the October program, and even to further increase Ruthenian autonomy. However, carrying the Communist revolution into Ruthenia was a rather difficult and complicated task since only a small part of the Ruthenian national movement was socialist and the leftist elements among that group were even less numerous. When the Communists took power in Budapest, tension arose between the central government and the Ruthenian regional authorities that in some places turned into open rebellion. Several Ruthenian towns became centers of resistance. To regain control over Ruthenia, Kún sent a Red Army regiment to Berehovo and Mukačevo in western Ruthenia. Mass arrests and deportations of alleged counterrevolutionaries followed. Soon afterward, however, the advance of the Rumanian troops made the Hungarian position in Ruthenia untenable. Rumanian and Czechoslovak detachments occupied both towns at the end of April 1919. On May 8, the Ruthenian Central National Council in Užhorod voted for Ruthenia's incorporation into the Czechoslovak Republic as an autonomous territory. Thus ended the Communist rule in Ruthenia. Despite its short duration, it was long enough to create a lasting polarization in the region. The image of communism as a political program and both sympathies and antipathies toward the Communist party in Ruthenia were to a large extent shaped by this brief experience.

After the failure in Berehovo and Mukačevo, the Hungarian Communist government wished to improve its reputation by asserting control in another part of the former Hungarian kingdom. The provinces annexed by Rumania, especially Transsylvania, were the logical target, but their troops were too well equipped to permit the Hungarian Red Army an easy victory. On the other hand, after the evacuation of Ruthenia, the Rumanian army posed no direct threat to vital centers in Hungary proper. The attack, therefore, was directed against Czechoslovakia. At the end of May 1919, the Hungarian troops broke through the weak Czechoslovak lines and in less than two weeks occupied the territory comprising almost the entire East Slovak Region as it exists today, with two important cities, Košice and Prešov, and part of the present Central Slovak Region—in all about eleven hundred square miles of territory. The Hungarian Communist government took great pains to present this operation as a defense of Hungary's legitimate interests and as the liberation of the Slovak proletariat from an alien, that is, Czech, capitalist yoke. However, all evidence seems to indicate that Kún was not willing to go beyond the formula of a federalized but territorially intact Hungary in his vision of the future political order in the Danube area. It required intervention by the Soviet commissar of foreign affairs, Chicherin, as well as by Lenin himself, to make the Budapest government translate its professed principle of self-determination into concrete action. On June 16, 1919, pursuant to clause 88 of the Hungarian Soviet Constitution, the Slovak Soviet Republic was proclaimed in Prešov.[20]

If the Hungarian Communist regime was short-lived, the Slovak Soviet Republic was even more ephemeral: it lasted exactly three weeks. In Czechoslovak Communist historiography, however, this episode occupies a very important place and has been interpreted in various ways at various times. Between the wars it served as a symbol of the Slovak proletariat's rejection of the idea of a Czechoslovak state; since 1945 it has been invoked as the precursor of the present Czechoslovak Socialist Republic and of Czecho-Slovak solidarity in the framework of the Communist movement. And indeed, the confused circumstances and the many political and constitutional ambiguities surrounding the creation of this peculiar polity made several interpretations possible.

Czechoslovak Communists, hostile to the liberal democratic ideas that had given birth to the First Republic, saw in the brief existence of the Slovak Communist state a welcome symbol of the unity of the national and proletarian revolution untarnished by any bourgeois ingredients. This was a tradition that they believed would be a suitable substitute for the tradition of October 28, 1918, at least in Slovakia. However, the fact that a Slovak Soviet Republic had existed more than two years before the constitution of the CPCS served to strengthen another trend in the Czechoslovak Communist movement, that of Slovak autonomy. This created serious problems for the centralist, overwhelmingly Czech party leadership, especially in the period after Munich. Finally, the Slovak Soviet Republic exhibited certain features that pointed in quite the opposite direction: to the integration of both the Slovaks and the Czechs in a single state, naturally a Communist-inspired and Communist-controlled one. The predilection of the official party exegesis for presenting the abortive Communist rule in Eastern Slovakia in 1919 as the Piedmont of Communist Czechoslovakia is relatively recent, but a few objective facts support this theory. There is the circumstance that Czechs as well as Slovaks played a leading role in the Slovak Soviet Republic. Several commissariats (ministries) of the government of this republic were held by Czechs who came from Budapest and had been members of the International Socialist Federation in Hungary, a body assembling radical left elements of various foreign groups on Hungarian territory. The Czech group in the federation published a weekly in the Czech language called *Armáda proletářů (The Proletarians' Army)*. Special editions of this periodical were distributed among troops of the Czecho-slovak government in Slovakia with the aim of converting them to the Communist cause. The most prominent representative of this group, Antonín O. Janoušek, took the portfolio of foreign affairs in the Council of People's Commissars (the cabinet) of the newly proclaimed Slovak Soviet state. From the available documents and from Janoušek's correspondence it appears that he and his Czech comrades actually did see Soviet Slovakia as the nucleus of the future federal Socialist Czechoslovak Republic. Incidentally, it was on these grounds that Janoušek was later tried by the counterrevolutionary Horthy government; he was accused of "having conspired for the purpose of the separation of the territory of 'Upper Hungary' [i.e. Slovakia] from Hungary and incorporating it in a foreign nation."[21]

The Slovak Soviet Republic, and shortly afterward its Hungarian sponsor, came to an end when the Kún cabinet yielded to an Allied ultimatum requesting the retreat of the Hungarian troops beyond the 1918 demarcation line. The Rumanian army, disregarding the terms of the armistice, scored an easy victory over the demoralized Hungarian Red Army and occupied Budapest on August 1, 1919. The march into Slovakia proved to be a suicidal move on the part of the Hungarian Communists. Without the offensive in the north, it is unlikely that the Entente would have been roused to any energetic action. After the bitter experiences acquired in Russia, the Allies showed little inclination to engage in yet another military intervention for the sole purpose of changing the internal regime of one of the defeated nations, but Kún's invasion changed the mood altogether. Rightly or wrongly, most probably wrongly, this action was perceived in the West as part of a larger aggressive plan that had to be foiled. Given the balance of powers in Central Europe at that time, once the Allies took this view of the situation the outcome of the military adventure of the Hungarian Soviets was easily predictable.

However, the ill-fated march into Slovakia did not merely lead to countermoves by the Entente that the Communist system could ill afford; it also elicited reactions the Hungarian leaders had never anticipated, and even less desired. To begin with, the purpose of the Soviets' action was misunderstood in Hungary itself. Despite the official line concerning aid to the proletarian brethren in territories under capitalist domination, the April 1919 military campaign was seen by the broad masses of the Hungarian-speaking population as an attempt to regain those provinces lost to the successor nations. This may well have been the main reason for its relative success: it provided a strong motivation for the Hungarian troops. By the same token, the retreat in July caused a sharp drop in combat morale, since it made the army despair of the reestablishment of Hungary's old boundaries. It seemed that by having failed to satisfy nationalist aspirations, the Communist regime had lost its raison d'être in the eyes of the entire Hungarian-speaking population, including the working class, so that its demise became inevitable.

Although these facts testifying to the strength of nationalist feelings in the Hungarian Communist movement have been embarrassing to Communist ideologists and historians, they are irrefutable.

The Split Deepens

The occupation of eastern Slovakia, however, was also greatly misunderstood abroad, especially among Hungary's neighbors. It had its most immediate effect upon Czechoslovak public opinion and politics. The invasion and the abortive attempt to set up a Communist regime on Czechoslovak territory could not fail to influence the course and outcome of the crisis in the Czechoslovak socialist movement. An event that seemed tantamount to a conquest by the oppressor of yesterday could not but provoke lively resistance among Czech and Slovak socialists of all shades. This reaction became so salient that the Soviet government showed concern and warned Kún against the risks of the "growth of Czech nationalism as a consequence of the Hungarian Red troop's occupation of non-Hungarian territories." This message cabled to Budapest indicated that the Soviet Union was on the whole unfavorably disposed toward efforts at preserving the territorial integrity of Hungary at all costs. It has to be assumed, too, that the growth of Czech nationalism that so alarmed Moscow referred more specifically to the invasion's psychological impact upon the Czech and Slovak Social Democrats and, above all, upon the left wing of the Social Democratic party. Kún himself substantiated this assumption: in July 1919, in his justification of the retreat from Slovakia, he claimed that the withdrawal would "pull the rug out from under Němec and other chauvinists" (Antonín Němec, a centrist leader of the Czechoslovak Social Democratic party) and would "take the last trump card out of their hands."[22] The Hungarian Communists apparently discovered late in the game that their crusade for the liberation of the proletariat in Czechoslovakia, far from winning the sympathies of the Central European left and igniting another revolution in the heart of the continent, had instead strengthened their enemies and considerably dimmed the prospects for further progress of communism.

These unanticipated effects could be observed in a particularly pronounced form in the subsequent evolution of the dispute between the center and left wings of the Czechoslovak Social Democratic party. The Hungarian Red Army's offensive was immediately answered with a proclamation by the Social Democratic leadership that condemned the move in very strong terms and called upon the Czech and Slovak working class to use every means to defend the republic against the foreign intruder. This proclamation was unanimously endorsed by the party's supreme executive organ, showing that Kún was unable to find advocates of his own "liberation campaign" in Czechoslovakia even among the radical left. The feelings of the Czechoslovak working people concerning the Hungarian invasion seemed to be in agreement with the party leadership's position. In the first nationwide elections for the municipal councils, on June 15 and 16, 1919, the Social Democratic party obtained 30.1 percent of all votes given to Czech and Slovak parties and thus emerged as the strongest political power in the country. The parliamentary elections, held ten months later, merely served to confirm the leading position of the Social Democracy. Loyalty to the young republic, seen by Moscow as an artificial creation of the rapacious Versailles Treaty, was vigorously indicated by the socialist electorate. Nevertheless, while both main currents in the party rejected the Hungarian Communist intervention in Slovakia, the anti-Kún position reinforced the center and the right rather than the left. The public, specifically the Social Democratic voter, associated Russian Bolsheviks and the Komintern with the ill-fated Kún expedition; hence, since the left admired and proposed to emulate the example of the Russian October Revolution, the defeat of the Hungarian Red Army in Slovakia was also viewed as a defeat of the left wing. Electoral success therefore did not cement the ranks of the party. In vindicating the political positions of the center-right, it instead deepened the polarization and accelerated the climax of the crisis.

In the spring of 1919, alienated by the activities of the radicals, a moderate group of Social Democrats, led by František Modráček and Josef Hudec, set up a new organization called the Socialist Party of the Working People. Thus it is a historical fact that the first secession from the socialist movement was centrist, not leftist in character. The left, which was by far the most numerous and influential of the splinter groups, continued to hesitate before the final showdown. However, the proliferation of various socialist reviews and periodicals advocating radical policies was unmistakable evidence of the internal divisions in the party. In October 1919, the first public declaration of the goals of the left, as distinct from the current party program, was made in Prague. On October 5, the radical wing that identified itself as the Marxist left released a "Program Resolution," in which the "historical task of the Social Democracy in Czechoslovakia" was seen to lie in the preparation of a "workers' revolutionary action." Two months later, the split was also consummated from the organizational point of view. At a national conference in Prague on December 7, 1919, the radicals constituted the "Czechoslovak Social Democratic Workers Party of the Left." The secession was probably speeded up by pressure from the Komintern, warning the left wing about the immobilization that might result if the slogan "Party Unity above All!" were too rigidly followed.[23] On the other hand, despite what had occurred at the Prague conference, it seemed that the left had not yet given up hope of preserving party unity—under its leadership, of course. The name given to the new party indicated that the door remained open for an eventual compromise.

In 1919, however, the left was not a homogeneous body. The Marxist left of Social Democracy was by far the most important component of the radical socialist movement, but there were other smaller groups that also promoted radical ideas and programs and often made up in zeal and propagandistic skills for their lack of numbers. Among them should be mentioned the "Party of Czechoslovak Communists," which had strong anarchistic leanings, as well as the "Initiative Group of the Third International," whose goal was obviously to integrate the left into the recently founded world Communist organization. Unanimity on all issues did not even prevail within the Marxist left despite its now formal organizational framework. The Social Democratic Party of the Left had its own extreme left wing composed chiefly of activists trained in the Soviet Union, who tried to make the policies of the new party conform to the general Communist strategy laid down by the Komintern. The extremists often operated completely independently of the elected executive bodies, but in strict obedience to instructions received from Moscow. Thus, for instance, Alois Muna created a separate propaganda center in the industrial region of Kladno, in central Bohemia, and Josef Handlíř set up a Communist underground cell in Prague from which he regularly communicated with the Bolshevik headquarters without any supervision from, and often without the knowledge of, the executives of the Marxist left. The elected officials of the Marxist left found themselves in an increasingly difficult situation. A majority of them were home-grown socialist leaders who had opted for the "revolutionary path to Socialism," but envisaged a revolutionary solution corresponding to the conditions and the needs of the Czechoslovak proletariat. Usually, they set little store by the dream of world revolution that in 1919 was still almost an article of faith of the Bolshevik party and the Third International. The more they saw of the ruling practices of the Communists in Russia, Hungary, Germany, and elsewhere, the less they were inclined to make this dream their own.

The most prominent leader of the left, Dr. Bohumír Šmeral, was a prototype of this home-bred radical socialist. The ultimate failure of his career in what was later to become the Communist Party of Czechoslovakia was chiefly due to the illusions Šmeral had entertained about the freedom of movement a radical left party would enjoy in the domestic and international situation of the early 1920s. He did not correctly assess the significance of the affiliation to the Third International of the party he helped to create. Brought up in the Social Democratic tradition of the early twentieth century, Šmeral imagined that the Komintern would be a new edition—more radical, to be sure—of the Socialist International: he envisioned a coordinative body of national parties each retaining a large measure of autonomy. He seemed to overlook the supranational character of the Komintern, which from the very beginning had claimed the role of the headquarters of the world Communist revolution and the authority of a decision-making center whose policies were to be universally binding. Only gradually, as the Czechoslovak Communist party organization began to take shape, did Šmeral realize that he had joined a club in which the rules of the game were radically different from those he had learned during his political apprenticeship. He shared this disheartening experience with a number of other similarly oriented leaders of the left.

The difficulties of the Social Democratic left did not stem merely from the incompatibility of many of its component elements, which ranged from the left-of-center groups to the extreme left, from radical socialists aware of the specific needs of Czechoslovak society to Communists with exclusive allegiance to Moscow. Many problems were generated by the parallel emergence in Czechoslovakia of radical-left party adherents belonging to other ethnic groups. The cultural differences among these groups were great enough to make the establishment of even a loosely organized national party body a challenging task. However, the Komintern insisted that the party to be set up become a unified centralized organization; hence the title eventually given to it, the Communist Party of Czechoslovakia. This was a goal very hard to accomplish since each ethnic group, in addition to its cultural idiosyncrasies, was marked by its particular experience of the war, which depended upon whether it perceived itself as belonging to the victors or to the vanquished. This perception often determined a group's level of radicalism, which was higher in the minorities formerly privileged as nation-building races— the Germans and the Hungarians—than in the groups to whom the end of the war brought self-determination and sovereign statehood. Thus each ethnic organization of the radical left was in itself a variant of the revolutionary socialist movement, occupying a specific place in the ideological continuum. These differences in background resulted in frequent disagreements among the groups on the order of political priorities. The Czech and the German Social Democratic leftists communicated especially poorly with each other.

The Czechoslovak Socialist Left and the Komintern

Under these circumstances, the establishment of a unified national revolutionary socialist party took much longer than the Komintern leaders had expected and much longer than the development of similar parties in other European countries. Something like a "Czechoslovak problem" began to loom for the Third International as early as at its Second Congress in Moscow, in July and August 1920. The process was further impeded by the necessity, in the absence of a single left party, to select the Czechoslovak delegation from a number of radical socialist organizations of varying size and significance and sometimes with no common ground at all, all of which claimed to represent the Czechoslovak revolutionary proletariat. Some of the groups took advantage of the opportunity to accuse the Social Democratic Party of the Left of lack of "Bolshevik courage," of "centrist illusions," or of various other kinds of ideological failure. Rather than representing a self-conscious national radical movement, the Czechoslovak delegation resembled a cluster of contending factions indifferent to the consequences that their mutual struggle would have for those in whose name they pretended to speak. Lenin and his associates did not overlook the fact that the group that was most criticized by the various splinter organizations and extremist sects, the Czechoslovak Social Democratic Party of the Left, was the only significant political force of the radical wing, and therefore of key importance for the future of the Communist movement in Czechoslovakia. Nevertheless they showed impatience over the slow progress of the integration of the individual leftist groups into one whole and over the delay in the constitution of a new party. That was why, at the close of the Second Congress of the Komintern, a special resolution urged the Czechoslovak Marxist left "to set up a Communist Party of Czechoslovakia in the shortest time possible."[24]

The resolution put pressure of two kinds on the Czechoslovak left, one explicit and one implicit. In addition to the demand to speed up the creation of the national Communist party, there was in the resolution an implied assumption that this party would automatically join the Third International. This premise was by no means self-evident, however, despite the fact that the elected leadership of the Czechoslovak Social Democratic Party of the Left had officially been represented at the Komintern meeting. Šmeral and his comrades had not yet made up their minds on this question, and the issue was to remain open for a long time to come. It looked as if the question of affiliation with the Komintern was to become a new source of internal tensions, especially as some of the ethnic organizations of the left, disregarding the position of the Czech Social Democratic radicals, pre-emptively declared their intention to adhere to the Moscow Communist forum. At the national conference of the Marxist dissidents in Prague on September 5, 1920, membership in the Third International was discussed as a possibility, but no clear decision was reached on this subject. The conference failed to also arbitrate a number of other controversial issues. Thus, for example, although the participants appeared to accept the principle of absolute equality of all ethnic groups and minorities in Czechoslovakia and to recognize their unlimited right of "self-determination to the point of secession," the program declaration of the left, subsequently read in the Prague Parliament by Bohumír Šmeral, did not satisfy the German socialist extremists who had advocated the toughest line on this issue.[25]

The Showdown: The Congress of the Left

If the events of the late summer of 1920 could not solve any of the disputes dividing the core of the Czechoslovak socialist left from other groups with radical leanings, nor speed up the crystallization of a unified Communist party, nevertheless they accelerated the final showdown within the maternal Social Democratic organization. Things now took a swift course. The center-right leadership, which for a long time had watched, more or less passively, the agitation of the left, decided to move. At the meeting of the Social Democratic parliamentary caucus on August 12, members Rudolf Bechyně and Gustav Habrman, speaking for the party Presidium, declared that the left had adopted a line imcompatible with the principles of the Czechoslovak Social Democracy and that a schism was inevitable if the radicals persisted in their course. The left, which was represented at the meeting, took cognizance of the leadership's position but did not submit any counterresolution or explanation of its own. The reply was implicitly but clearly contained in the very fact of the national conference of the leftist groups, held on September 5, which has already been mentioned. The centrist party leadership then called a new meeting of the parliamentary caucus for September 14, at which it was decided to withdraw the Social Democratic ministers from the coalition government on the plausible grounds that burdened with an internal dispute, the party could not fully meet the responsibilities of its participation in the management of state affairs. Only when the membership and the electorate had been consulted, the leadership argued, could a clear picture be obtained of the extent of the support that each of the two major currents enjoyed and that could be cast behind a socialist-led cabinet. In practice, this meant appeal from the center to the rank and file, and, eventually, verdict by general elections. To make consultation with lower-echelon party units possible, the leadership proposed to postpone the Thirteenth Congress, originally scheduled for the end of September, for another three months.

This resolution was adopted against the votes of the left wing, which judged that it had everything to lose whereas the center-right had everything to gain from this postponement. An objective assessment of the support base of the two tendencies was difficult in September 1920 since the party had gone undivided into the April elections. Typically, both wings claimed the spectacular success of the Social Democratic party as a popular endorsement of their respective positions. The left was furthermore convinced that the general mood among the membership favored its line, which could not fail to come to the fore at the party congress, and was not willing to forfeit its chance. It also feared that the leadership, if given more time, could take advantage of its privileged access to the party apparatus and swing some important regional organizations to its side. It therefore refused to submit to the majority decision favoring postponement. The following day (September 15), its representatives met at the Zábranský Café in the industrial Prague suburb of Karlín and announced their intention to hold the congress as originally slated, if necessary without the participation of the center-right. A week later, on September 21, 1920, the left began publishing its own daily called *Rudé právo (Red Right)*, in an obvious attempt to upgrade, in a revolutionary way, the long tradition of the Czech Social Democratic press symbolized by the journal *Právo lidu (The Right of the People)*, founded in 1897, which now became the organ of the center. The break within the Czechoslovak Social Democratic party was thus consummated.

Shortly afterward, the antagonisms between the revolutionary and the reformist forces in other socialist organizations in Czechoslovakia came to a head. On September 19, the Slovak Social Democracy met in a congress at Turčiansky Sväty Martin. The majority of the delegates pronounced themselves in favor of the leftist course.[26] The left wing started a new press organ called *Pravda chudoby (The Truth in Poverty)* that was deliberately similar in name to the Social Democratic daily *Pravda (The Truth)* appearing in Bratislava. Everything seemed to confirm the assertions of the radical leaders that the political winds continued to blow from the left. At the congress of the Ruthenian Social Democratic party in Užhorod, held June 20, 1920, radical tendencies had become manifest, and at the constituting congress of the Union of Young Ruthenian Workers in Bratislava in September the delegates voted for affiliation with the Third International.[27] On the other hand, the congress of the German Social Democratic party in Czechoslovakia, which met in Liberec in October 1920, ended in the victory of the center group led by Josef Seliger over the Communist-oriented wing led by Karl Kreibich; nevertheless, the success of the center could not prevent the ultimate split.[28] It is only possible to speculate about the outcome of the congress of the Czechoslovak Social Democracy had it been held as a meeting of the whole organization, with both tendencies represented. There, too, the left would probably have come out strongly; yet it should be kept in mind that the trauma of the invasion of Slovakia by the Hungarian Communists was still very recent among the Czechoslovak public, including the socialists, and that public opinion did not make much distinction between the radical Marxists and the Communists, seeing all as part of a worldwide conspiracy. The large electoral support for the party in the elections of April 1920, rather than explicitly approving either of the two competing fractions, might simply have indicated that the working masses were not estranged from Social Democracy despite the already manifest internal crisis.

The congress of the left, claimed by the sponsors to be the Thirteenth Ordinary Congress of the Social Democratic party, took place in Prague on September 26–29, 1920. While it demonstrated to the whole world the willingness of the radicals to pursue the revolutionary line even at the cost of a complete break with the rest of the socialist movement, it was far from being the constitutive meeting of a Czechoslovak Communist party that was so impatiently awaited by Moscow. In virtually all essential points of the agenda, the congress reflected the caution and the hesitation of the leaders headed by Šmeral. Before the congress opened, the left once more approached the centrist core and argued that the unity of the party could still be saved if the original schedule of the congress were observed. If the center-right would yield on this point, the left was prepared to make "an acceptable compromise" in the matter of membership in the Komintern (meaning that the issue could, at least temporarily, be shelved). At the congress itself, Šmeral and other top leaders of the Marxist left stressed that they did not consider the Soviet example, either in substance or in form, suitable for emulation under Czechoslovak conditions. Šmeral explicitly stated that an essential difference between the Bolshevik party and the Czechoslovak Social Democratic Party of the Left lay in the concern of the latter for the preservation of the unity of the socialist movement. He and other speakers repeatedly pointed out that the situation in Czechoslovakia was not ripe for a proletarian revolution, and that such a revolution, even if it broke out, could succeed only if it were accompanied by similar revolutions in other countries of Central and Eastern Europe. On the other hand, the political program of the left was truly radical. It called for the expropriation of large landholdings, nationalization of industry and the banks, and workers' control of enterprises. These goals, however, as Šmeral indicated, were to be reached by parliamentary means. The revolutionary program of the left first had to win over to Social Democracy all the voters of worker and peasant origin who still supported other parties, and thus ensure a socialist majority in the government.[29]

Leaving aside the question of the political realism of such expectations, the tenor of the congress quite faithfully reflected the perspective from which Šmeral and his associates viewed the future of radical socialism in Czechoslovakia. It also showed that the left still believed it possible to commit the entire Social Democratic party to the radical course. The relatively broad attendance of the Thirteenth Congress—67 percent of

the various party organizations invited to the congress were represented—reassured the left that this was a real possibility. As the minutes
of the congress testify, the left hoped for a new, reborn and unified
socialist party capable of implementing the classical Marxist program in
Czechoslovakia, with full consideration of the specific national conditions.
International affiliation came second in importance. The Soviet promoters of the world revolutionary movement had little sympathy for this
order of priorities. In its message to the Thirteenth Congress, the
Executive Committee of the Communist International warned the Social
Democratic left of the "danger of sinking into a political morass" that
could result from "excessive stress upon the slogan of party unity."[30] The
disappointing outcome of the congress from the viewpoint of the
Komintern, which had expected more progress toward the creation of a
Communist party obedient to Moscow, further increased apprehensions
in the Kremlin. The Third International now faced what later came to be
called the "Czechoslovak question." On November 11, 1920, the Executive Committee rather peremptorily called upon Šmeral and his group to
"finally resolve the problem of the new organizational form" of the
revolutionary left. In other words, they demanded the convening of
another congress at which a Communist party integrating all ethnic
groups of the radical socialist movement would be established as a
section of the Komintern.[31]

The December 1920 Strike

Yet not even at this point did Šmeral comply with the demands from
Moscow. Soviet impatience, as well as criticism from several radical
groups at home, continued to grow. Ironically, the expectations that had
led the leadership of the Social Democratic left to wait beyond the
Thirteenth Congress, did not materialize. Further inroads into the
positions of the center-right could not be made, nor could the unity of
the Social Democratic party be preserved. On the contrary, immediately
after the Prague congress, the party executive assembled in an emergency
session and expelled Šmeral, along with fifteen other leftist ringleaders.[32]
The schism in the Czechoslovak party organization now became general.
In October, at the second congress of the Social Democratic Youth
Union in Prague, the left got the upper hand and made the union adopt
a resolution proposing membership in the Communist Youth International. The center-right minority thereupon founded its own youth

organization. In November, the left wing of the Slovak organization of the Social Democratic party, which had gained a victory at the party congress in Turčiansky Sväty Martin in September, constituted its own action committee and held consultations in Nitra, in southern Slovakia.[33]

A counterattack of the center-right followed. The postponed congress was called for November 26–28 in Prague. This, as the leadership argued, was the legitimate Thirteenth Party Congress of the Social Democracy: the September meeting of the left had been "a secessionist enterprise." The congress endorsed the centrist positions and decreed global expulsion of all members and officials associated in any formal way with the left.[34] A struggle now broke out over the control of party property. Some of the assets in dispute had considerable symbolic value, for example, the Lidový Dům ("The House of the People"), the original seat of the Social Democratic party Secretariat in Prague. Since the split, the building had been occupied by the partisans of the left who installed there the editorial offices of their new daily, *Rudé právo*. After the party headquarters complained to the Prague district court, the Ministry of the Interior ordered the left to evacuate the House of the People and to return it to its lawful owner, the leadership of the Social Democratic party. The left appealed the decision. The legal issue was a difficult one, since neither in Austria-Hungary nor in the Czechoslovak republic did political parties enjoy the status of legal persons. Moreover, the formal distinction between the two wings was extremely hard to draw. Eventually the issue was handled as a civil suit by the official representative of the Socialist Publishing House and the managing editor of *Právo lidu*, Antonín Němec, who charged unlawful occupancy of premises under his authority; the decision of the lower instance was upheld. As the left refused to comply, the situation developed into a crisis. Two weeks later, however, the radicals themselves supplied a pretext for an immediate court action. The editorial board of *Rudé právo* fired the owner of the printing license of the Socialist Publishing House, whereupon publication activities at the House of the People ceased to be legal. Following the issuing of an injunction, the police forcibly removed the party officials and the journalists of the left from the building.[35]

The evacuation of the party headquarters by the police triggered a sharp response from partisans of the left all over the country. The left-oriented union leaders, who were in a clear minority among the elected union functionaries, called a general strike. Although the strike order was followed in some industrial regions and in some districts of the capital city, the stoppage proved to be neither general (affecting all categories of production) nor nationwide. The strike broke out on December 10, 1920, but after six days during which violent clashes with the police and the army occurred, chiefly in the western provinces, it had to be called off. While it unfolded, the strike movement was justified by the spokesmen of the left as a protest against the ejection of the radicals from the Social Democratic party center; later, however, Communist historiography began to build up this event into an abortive attempt at a political take-over, a kind of Communist revolution. Curiously enough, this interpretation of what is referred to as the December strike of the Czechoslovak proletariat resembles that of the commentators on the conservative right, who also claimed that in December 1920 Czechoslovakia had escaped, by a hair's breadth, a Bolshevik dictatorship.[36]

The myth of the failed revolution at the end of 1920 served a twofold purpose: it provided the CPCS with a prehistory, and it supplied one additional proof for the later critics of the left leadership that the left, because of alleged "ineptitude, opportunism and betrayal," had missed a unique chance to seize power in Czechoslovakia. The truth, however, is that the left had merely called a protest strike; it had not planned anything even remotely resembling a revolution. Nevertheless, the unsatisfactory outcome of the December mass protest marked the end of the wave of postwar social unrest. A period of consolidation set in. It was yet another message to the strategists of world communism that they should give up the dreams of an imminent, universal socialist revolution. Oddly enough, although this failure refuted one of the basic premises of the Komintern's current line, it simultaneously decreased the maneuvering ability of the Czechoslovak left and increased its dependence on the Kremlin: as the advent of a socialist regime became ever more unlikely, the significance and the political weight of the left diminished. The Czechoslovak working class now could expect more from the Social Democratic center and from the reformist unions than from the radical wing. The international position of the left, too, had been weakened considerably. It had to prepare for a possibly extended period of hibernation, until the return of conditions favorable to a revolution. Under these circumstances, it had to rely more and more upon support from Moscow, and Moscow consequently could more easily enforce its will.

Despite this objective change in the scenery, the birth of a new party was not any faster in coming. In the first weeks of 1921, meetings of various leftist groups and declarations of their intentions to join the Third International multiplied, but the decisive move of the largest component of the Czechoslovak left was not yet in sight. The Slovak socialist left held its constitutive congress in the Tatra health resort Lubochňa on January 16 and 17, 1921. The Union of Communist Youth, the Komsomol, was founded in Prague on February 6. In the same month, the left wing of the Jewish Social Democratic party, the Poale Zion, accepted the famous twenty-one conditions of membership stipulated by the Komintern. Meeting March 12–15 in Liberec, the Marxist left of the German Social Democratic party in Czechoslovakia, whose representatives had been expelled by the reformist majority, constituted itself the Communist Party of Czechoslovakia—German section. The organizations of the ethnic groups and minorities thus moved much faster toward the goals defined by the Komintern than did the core of the Czechoslovak left. It required repeated intervention from Moscow, as well as considerable pressure from various Komintern-obedient centers in Czechoslovakia, to make Šmeral and his comrades take the final step. Šmeral tried to gain recognition in Moscow of the special situation of the radical left in Czechoslovakia. He used the recent failure of the general strike as an argument in support of his view that "Soviet yardsticks could not be applied to Czechoslovak conditions." Some of the splinter groups, among them the "Communist Center" led by Josef Handlíř, supported him in his position.[37] It looked as if the Czechoslovak question would become a major concern of the Komintern.

April 1921 Consultations in Dresden and the
Constitutive Congress of the CPCS

Lenin and the Komintern leaders were aware that the Czechoslovak situation was more complex than that of other European countries where Communist parties had long since been successfully constituted. They were not, however, prepared to make any exceptions to the basic principles binding all members of the international Communist movement. Instead, they suggested that the difficulties be removed by comradely discussion between the representatives of the Third International and the Czechoslovak left. These talks were to be held on a neutral soil, in the Saxon capital of Dresden. And, indeed, in April 1921, Komintern officials Béla Kún and Gyula Alpári, both prominent functionaries of the Hungarian Communist party, met in Dresden with four members of the Executive Committee of the Czechoslovak Social Democratic Party of the Left and Karl Kreibich, secretary-general of the Communist Party of Czechoslovakia—German section. In the Czechoslovak delegation, only Kreibich was an official of high rank. He came mainly because he had been the most severe critic of the "opportunism" and the "inconsistency" of Šmeral's leadership. Šmeral, for his part, in sending to Dresden officials of second rank, demonstrated his displeasure with the Komintern for forcing his hand. This gesture must have antagonized Kún, who was at that time the head of the Komintern office for questions of the national parties and already held a grudge against the leadership of the left wing of the Czechoslovak Social Democracy because of its indifferent, if not hostile, stand on the Hungarian Soviet revolution and the Slovak Soviet Republic established by the Hungarian Red Army during its advance to eastern Slovakia in 1919. The talks in Dresden did not lead to any concrete results, beyond a very general clearing of the atmosphere between the Komintern and its prospective Czechoslovak section.[38] It is interesting to note that Communist historians hardly ever mentioned the Dresden consultations, and to wonder whether the choice of Dresden for another meeting of the representatives of the international Communist movement concerning, the problems of the Czechoslovak party, about half a century later, in March 1968, was purely accidental or inspired by the near-forgotten example of the talks of April 1921. At any rate, there is a striking similarity between the two events, in the cool reception the Czechoslovak comrades accorded to the Soviet initiative on both occasions.

Despite its obvious reluctance, the Šmeral leadership was forced to acknowledge that it was fighting a losing battle. The hour of decision finally struck in May 1921; the long-postponed gathering that was to lead to the constitution of a unified Czechoslovak Communist party finally took place in Prague from May 14 to May 16. It was attended by 569 voting delegates, former officials of the Czechoslovak Social Democracy in the Czech provinces who had joined the left wing, and by 56 representatives of the Marxist left of the Slovak and the Ruthenian Social Democratic party organizations. The decision to join the Third International was taken almost unanimously (there were only seven dissenting votes), but this token opposition refused to submit to the majority and quit the new party to join a separate organization called Independent Socialists. The closing resolution of the congress called for the creation of a single Communist party comprising the radical organizations of all ethnic groups, including those who were not represented at the meeting. The road to this desired unitary body was not smooth, however. Another action on the part of the Komintern and personal intervention by Lenin were required before the goal was reached.[39]

Although additional Communist-oriented groups joined the newly constituted party soon after the May congress, certain important factions, such as that of the ethnic Germans, still remained outside the mainstream. The Komintern continued to entertain serious misgivings about the political line of the future Czechoslovak Communist party. All these problems and difficulties were subjected to a thorough discussion in Moscow on the occasion of the Third World Congress of the Third International, from June 22 through July 12, 1921. The Czechoslovak delegation at that time comprised several, often mutually antagonistic, tendencies. Especially strong were the conflicts between the leadership confirmed at the May congress and the spokesmen of the Communist party organization of the ethnic Germans, Bohumír Šmeral and Karl Kreibich. During the talks in the Komintern Secretariat, at which the top officials of the international were present, Kreibich accused Šmeral of "social democratic opportunism." In these invectives he was backed by almost all the staff of the Komintern's department for the questions of the nationalities, especially Béla Kún, Gyula Alpári, and Matyás Rákosi. Cornered by all these opponents, the Šmeral group threatened to leave the congress and to withdraw their affiliation. It pointed out that among the sects and splinter groups of the Czechoslovak left represented at the congress, the Czechoslovak Communist party constituted in May 1921 was by far the most important; the future of the socialist left depended largely on this party. Lenin, who saw the cogency of the argument, mediated in the conflict by restraining Kún and Rákosi and prevailing upon Kreibich "not to move too far to the left."[40] In the series of the crisis of growth of the Czechoslovak Communist movement this was the last dramatic turn before the final resolution of the structural problem. On Lenin's recommendation, the Third Congress admitted the Czechoslovak party to membership on the condition that all ethnic groups, especially the German, be integrated into the national organization. The understanding that Lenin had demonstrated in his conversation with Šmeral of the specific Czechoslovak situation, however, was not mentioned or even indirectly reflected in the text of the ruling.

On its return from Moscow, the Executive Committee, in the session of August 27, 1921, decided to call a new convention of all leftist groups and parties to broaden the basis of the Communist party. This meeting was scheduled for the coming fall, and later entered history as the Merger Congress of 1921, as distinct from the Constitutive Congress held in May of the same year. The organizational problem now appeared to be on its way to a definite solution. With organizational difficulties subsiding, disagreements among the various currents of the radical left on a number of questions of principle and tactics nevertheless continued. On the whole, the minority groups in the Communist movement found the policy line of the Czechoslovak leadership much too centrist—that is, uncommitted on basic issues—if not downright reformist. The position of the Šmeral executive on an international crisis that broke out in the late summer of 1921 in connection with an unsuccessful attempt by the former Austrian-Hungarian emperor Charles I to regain the Hungarian throne confirmed Šmeral's "opportunism" and "lack of principles" in the eyes of his leftist critics. In October 1921, when the successor nations in the Danubian area, among them Czechoslovakia, protested the presence of the Hapsburg ex-monarch in Budapest and mobilized their armed forces to add muscle to their diplomatic steps, the leadership of the CPCS made a statement condemning the efforts at Hapsburg restoration in Hungary, thus implicitly approving the stand of the Czechoslovak government. As a consequence, it came under fire from left extremists, who, in turn, received support from the Executive Committee of the Third International. In reality, Šmeral's declaration did not stem from Social Democratic opportunism so much as it indicated that in the Communist movement, too, national aspirations and social reform sometimes ran parallel. There were to be more manifestations of this interaction before the Czechoslovak party would turn into a totally passive tool of Moscow.

The Merger Congress convened on October 30 and lasted until November 2, 1921. At this date all hitherto independent Communist groups had already decided to join the national party body, so that the congress had only to formally approve their affiliation. The sole new ethnic chapter that applied to the party for admission on that occasion was the Poale Zion; it, too, was accepted. The two main speakers at the congress were Bohumír Šmeral and Karl Kreibich, a fact that underscored the importance of the two components they represented.

The congress also adopted the first version of party organizational rules and a provisional party program.[41] Thus after prolonged birth pangs, the Communist Party of Czechoslovakia—section of the Communist International—was eventually born. It was a latecomer to the world Communist movement, constituted long after most of the European Communist parties (one exception was the Albanian party).

Chapter Two

The Road to Bolshevization

To a contemporary observer, the Merger Congress of 1921 might have appeared a signal accomplishment from several points of view. It seemed to have put an end to a prolonged period of uncertainty and hesitation. It completed the unification of half-a-dozen radical groups of various ethnic origins, no mean feat in the multiracial and multilinguistic environment of the young Czechoslovak Republic; no political party in the area, of whatever color, could claim similar credit, either under the Austro-Hungarian empire or between the two world wars. The organized following the CPCS believed it could rely on at the moment of its constitution was also impressive: it comprised 350,000 members. Last but not least, after many misunderstandings, the question of the integration of the new party into the world system of Communist organizations seemed also to have been successfully resolved. In reality, however, the establishment of the Czechoslovak Communist party merely marked the end of one phase of conflicts and struggles; another was soon to follow.

None of the achievements of the Merger Congress, for example, could contribute to the solution of the core problem that had been built into the Czechoslovak Communist movement: was the CPCS to be a radical left party, integrated into the party system and the whole political culture of the country, or was it to function as a spearhead of a world revolutionary movement, guided from a remote center and obedient to the imperatives of a global strategy? The implications of the answers to these two questions were crucial, both for the policy and for the type of organization the new party was to have, and the alternative solutions were mutually exclusive. Each point of view had its advocates among the top cadres. In the beginning, most of the key party positions were held by those who saw the Communist party as a regenerated socialist avant-garde, free from the mistakes and the blemishes of the Social Democracy, and with a particularly clean record in the matter of co-responsibility for the war. In their eyes, such a party was clearly qualified to claim the leadership of the workers' movement, which they wanted to guide back to its original revolutionary ethos. In other words, they understood their party and the Komintern to be legitimate heirs to the great socialist tradition.

Party chairman Bohumír Šmeral belonged to this school of thought. He and his associates believed that there was no necessary conflict between the principles the Czechoslovak party had subscribed to in its early days and the official line of the international Communist movement. The content and language of the major resolutions of the Komintern seemed to suggest that the idea of the continuity of Western-originated and Western-oriented revolutionary socialism was firmly established in the minds of the leaders of the Third International at that time. This was natural since the brain trust of the Komintern was to a large extent composed of West European radical Marxists. During the first years of the Komintern's existence, references to the Soviet Union and to the Bolshevik party did not predominate in its public statements and literature. There was no call on individual national parties to accept the Soviet example as binding and to exhibit unqualified obedience to the Soviet Union, a scenario that became familiar toward the end of the 1920s. The Bolshevik revolution was seen only as a beginning of a global upheaval—an upheaval necessary for the preservation of the Soviet regime itself—in which Russia, by historical accident, would play the role of the first nation to be liberated from capitalism and would act as a show-window advertising the cause of radical socialism to the toiling masses of other, especially more developed, countries. It is easy to understand why the whole philosophy of Šmeral and other Czechoslovak Communist leaders continued to thrive under these circumstances.

Nevertheless, a conflict was inevitable, and it began taking shape in the first months after the CPCS was created. Despite the apparent plausibility of the Šmeral group's diagnosis of the immediate situation in the international Communist movement and its perception of the place of the Czechoslovak section in the global strategy of the Komintern, future development of the CPCS was determined by a major historical process then in the making: the progressive departure of the Soviet Union and the Komintern from the assumption that a world revolution was imminent. Theoretically, this process contained both a risk and a promise for the policies of the various Communist parties outside the Soviet Union. It could have reinforced the independence of these parties because it implied a shift in the focus of the Bolsheviks' interest toward Russia's internal problems. However, subsequent events proved this shift to be tragic for the smaller Communist organizations, since the passage from the policy for a world revolution to the policy of Socialism in One Country ushered in the era of Stalinism. The history of the CPCS in the early 1920s was profoundly marked by this change.

The intricate relationships between the Soviet Communists and the international staff of the Komintern were replicated on a miniature scale within the Czechoslovak Communist movement. Not unlike the Bolshevik party, the CPCS counted among its elites both partisans of the Western socialist tradition and followers of the Leninist approach. The former, although duly revolutionized, espoused the Marxist philosophy of history in its more or less original form: that is, they stressed the importance for socialism of accomplished capitalist development of industrial societies. The latter endorsed Lenin's revision of historical materialism and looked to Bolshevik Russia as the principal model of new social order. The Western group, to which most of the leading officials belonged, was more internationalist, but by the same token also more Czechoslovak, since Czechoslovakia was part of the family of the advanced industrial nations of the West. The Leninist group, although more Slavic because of its allegiance to Russia, was actually more alien since it was concerned about the fate of the Soviet Union rather than the well-being of the Czechoslovak working class. As was suggested earlier, these two different positions were often rooted in the background of the individual leader or activist: internationalists usually came from the Austromarxist school, while Leninists got their political education in the USSR. There were many influential persons and groups in the party, however, who took far less clearly defined stands or supported each tendency on occasion.

To an observer in the early 1920s who had not been initiated into the maze of ideas, trends, approaches, and tactics represented in the CPCS, the recurrent conflicts during the first decade of its existence might have appeared to be accidental collisions of varying intensity, on the whole unconnected with each other. There were left as well as right deviations from the party line. Protests, resignations, secessions of entire groups, suspensions, and expulsions were almost everyday happenings. It seemed as if the only lasting result of these crises would be the decimation of all groups, resulting in a general weakening of the party organization. Although this actually happened—by 1929 the organized membership of the CPCS was reduced to little more than 5 percent of its original size—there was a certain logic or meaning in all the apparently incoherent and fortuitous conflicts and confrontations, especially if these are viewed in a longer perspective. Through them the party evolved to the stage at which it was ready to fulfill its historical role as a docile instrument of Stalinist strategy. The Czechoslovak Way to Stalinism may have been stormier than the road to the same destination taken by the fraternal parties elsewhere, but the enormous costs of this process have not been judged too great by those who considered such a goal to be the most important.

Dispute with the Left Ultras: The First Purge

The secession of the centrist group of Independent Socialists from the mainstream of the Communist movement at the May 1921 congress was but a prelude to what was to become almost an everyday spectacle in party life. The first major crisis that confronted the party after its admission to the Komintern was provoked by an attack from the left. It originated in a dispute over the tactics used toward workers' mass organizations, particularly the trade unions.

After the split in the Social Democracy and the constitution of a separate Communist party, the struggle for the allegiance of various interest groups sponsored by the Social Democractic party became inevitable. The Communist leadership launched a systematic campaign in the hope of capturing, if not whole organizations, then at least substantial parts of their followings. The campaign unfolded with the slogan "Turn towards the Masses." In a sense it acknowledged that the new party was not strong enough to wage the political battle alone, depending only on its current membership, and that it had to seek support of wider circles of the working class. The slogan could be interpreted as the application of the principle of the united front with other socialist and workers' parties that had been adopted by the Executive Committee of the Komintern in December 1921. Cooperation with workers' mass organizations was indeed less risky for the revolutionary spirit of the Communist parties than direct involvement with the allegedly reformist, centrist, and otherwise opportunist socialist partners in an eventual government coalition. In the trade unions, for example, the Communist-oriented officials encountered many uncommitted members of the rank and file who were receptive to the party propaganda.

The Executive Committee (in the later phases of the party history, the Central Committee) of the CPCS, which was in session in January 1922, in dealing with the Komintern resolution of December 1921, attempted to give the concept of the united front practical meaning within the Czechoslovak context. At the same time, it laid down the rules to be followed by the party members who were delegates to the trade union congress scheduled for January 22. Official party historiography has blamed the CPCS leadership of that time for delaying its recognition of the Komintern resolution, and has seen in the allegedly belated reaction a sign of "indifference to the question of the work in the unions," a charge hard to sustain if we consider the then-prevailing communication difficulties between the Soviet Union and the rest of Europe. In any event, the strategy the Executive Committee of the CPCS selected as the best for the Communist delegates to follow at the unions convention was a cautious one. The delegates were advised to exploit to the maximum the "left mood," real or postulated, among the union membership, to "unmask the betrayal of the working class by the reformist and centrist leaders," but to avoid, if possible, a fragmentation of the unions that the Executive Committee felt could only benefit the socialist parties of the right at that time.[1]

This approach did not contradict the general directives of the Third International, but it was opposed by a number of radical trade union officials. These preferred an open split in the union organizations both to continued neutrality in the conflict between the Marxist left and other socialists and to the uneasy coexistence of the representatives of the two opposite camps in the various unions' governing bodies. Their discontent with the CPCS policy on trade unions was but a form of the global dissatisfaction of the Communist extremists with a course of party politics that they found to be determined by "reformist and social democratic errors and illusions." Prominent among these extremists were Executive Committee members Václav Bolen, Václav Houser, and Bohumil Jílek. The opposition group began to take shape at the beginning of 1921 when these three officials lent support to the periodical *Komunista (The Communist)*, the successor to *Sociální demokrat*, which had spelled out the views of the Marxist left before the constitution of the Communist party. *Komunista*, however, did not enjoy the authority of being the mouthpiece of the CPCS, and it soon began to advocate rather unorthodox opinions. Its editor-in-chief, Emanuel Vajtauer, criticized the Šmeral leadership for "guiding the party back into reformist waters." According to *Komunista*, the CPCS was not a revolutionary party in 1922 because it had no policy for immediate action. Vajtauer proposed that the party change the class war into an economic war with the goal of the destruction of capitalism. This economic war was to be waged as a wholesale boycott of all capitalist products which, remaining unsold, would have to be distributed to the population according to individual needs. While the boycott lasted, the working class was to be supplied by cheap goods from producer and consumer cooperatives.

The substitution of a revolution of consumers for armed revolt was undoubtedly an original idea in a party that claimed its ideological descendance from Karl Marx. Yet, despite its aberrant character, the tactic reflected a very real problem of the time. In 1922, after the monetary reforms of Minister of Finance Alois Rašín averted in Czechoslovakia the disastrous inflation that had ravaged neighboring Austria and Germany, economic policy followed a very sharp deflationary course. High nominal—and in certain sectors even real—wages became the first casualties of the reform. The cost of living increased considerably. The proposal of a consumer boycott and of the replacement of privately owned production and distribution enterprises by cooperatives was a response to this situation. Deflation and the fear of further loss of the purchasing power of wages also dominated the daily concerns of the unions. These were the main themes of the All-Union Congress of January 1922. It was to be expected that the delegates of the various industrial workers' groups would be less interested in propaganda aimed at converting them to the Communist cause than in possible solutions to the more immediate economic problems of their constituencies. The Communists' objective of making further inroads into the trade-union movement could hardly be served by impractical proposals, but revolutionary rhetoric and partisan quarrels were of even less use.

Long before the All-Union Congress, the left-leaning Communist leaders in the unions had created certain procedural and legal conditions that made the implementation of the CPCS line, as formulated by the Executive Committee, extremely difficult. To a large extent they pre-empted the results of the congress itself. Václav Bolen, chairman of the Agricultural Workers' Union, and Josef Hais, chairman of the Union of

Chemistry Workers, could secure Communist majorities in these two unions. Disregarding the instructions of the party executive, they steered toward a head-on collision with the reformist all-union leadership. Bolen decided to suspend the payment of membership dues from his union to the all-union fund on the grounds that it was "not morally defensible to pour workers' hard-earned money down the gullets of revisionist traitors."[2] His action had the predictable consequence of causing his union to be expelled from the national organization. For his part, Josef Hais provoked the expulsion of the Chemical Workers Union, the Woodworkers Union, the Footwear Industry Workers Union, and the Transport Workers Union. All these organizations together, however, represented only a small minority of the membership of the national trade union body, which thus remained firmly in the hands of the Social Democratic party.

The failure of the Communist bid for power in the trade union movement forced the CPCS to make another choice: to set up its own unions. This, however, was a very long and difficult process, and its final result could hardly be called satisfactory. The so-called Red Unions, as these Communist-sponsored industrial interest groups were called at the time (their official summary title was Mezinárodní všeodborový svaz [International All-Union Association]), soon developed into bastions of nonconformism and resistance to domination by Moscow. Although the Red Unions joined the world federation of Communist trade unions, the Profintern, set up by the Third International in July 1921, the relations between the Czechoslovak contingent and the international organization were a source of constant tensions and conflicts. The CPCS was power-less, too, in the face of manifold centrifugal tendencies in the individual regional unions, especially those organized on an ethnic basis. This inability to influence the unions significantly was characteristic of the situation of the Communist party all through the period of the First Republic. All major union actions during these two decades, including bargaining and strikes, were initiated and directed by workers' organiza-tions sponsored by either the Social Democratic party or the National Socialist party. The Turn towards the Masses did not seem to be a spectacular success in the union sector.

The party leadership correctly assessed the severity of its setback in the struggle for control of the trade unions and had little difficulty in identifying the culprits of the Communist defeat at the All-Union Congress. These admitted their responsibility and suffered the consequences. The party secretary-general, Bohumil Jílek, and a member of the Executive Committee, Václav Bolen, resigned their offices. The change in the office of the party secretary brought to the foreground for the first time Antonín Zápotocký, a committed Communist politician who was to play a very important role in party history in the years to come. When the National Party Conference, held in Prague April 16–17, 1922, condemned in its resolution the tactics adopted by Bolen and Hais in union work, the leftist group conformed to the majority and supported the resolution. At the plenary session of the Executive Committee on June 20, 1922, Jílek also resigned as a member of the Executive Committee. The leadership's position appeared vindicated, all the more since the Enlarged Plenum of the Executive Committee of the Komintern, meeting in Moscow from February 21 through March 4, 1922, sharply criticized the failure of the Czechoslovak section to seize power in the Czechoslovak unions.[3]

Šmeral and his associates interpreted the censure by the Komintern as giving them a free hand in their controversy with the left wing. Consequently they opted for a firm stand and for rigorous application of the principle of party discipline. When later it became clear that despite the admission by the ultraleftists of errors committed in connection with the workings of the trade unions, they were not prepared to cease their opposition to the majority's policies, and their mouthpiece *Komunista* continued and further stepped up the attacks on the party line, the leadership described the conduct of the left as factional struggle, which was in Leninist doctrine an unpardonable crime. A new national conference was called by the Executive Committee to deal with the charges against the ultras; it was held in Prague September 22–24, 1922. At this conference, seven prominent representatives of the extreme left, among them Jílek, Bolen, and Houser, were expelled from the party. The first major example in the CPCS of a purge, a phenomenon that was gradually to become typical of Communist organizations in general, had taken place. The national conference nevertheless recognized the expelled members' right to bring their case before the Komintern. This respect for party statutes was not a sign of Bolshevik virtue; it represented a part of the reformist heritage in the Šmeral leadership. Thus the ultras were given another chance, ironically thanks to what they had most vehemently attacked.

The consequences of the energetic action against the left faction were quite unexpected. It became evident that Šmeral had not accurately interpreted the position of the Komintern on this issue. Although critical of the poor performance of Czechoslovak Communists at the All-Union Congress and in the trade union movement, the Third International remained apprehensive about Šmeral and his team since their reluctance to break with the Social Democracy and their procrastination in setting up the new party were still fresh in memory. The Komintern leaders feared that the removal of the left elements from the CPCS would permit the "Social Democratic anachronisms" to become even more deeply entrenched in party life. That was why the Executive Committee of the Komintern, having heard the appeal of the expelled Czechoslovak officials at its session of October 13, 1922, provisionally suspended the decision of the Prague National Conference and referred the case to the Fourth World Congress of the Komintern, to be held in Moscow at the end of the year.

Before the congress convened, a number of significant events occurred in the Czechoslovak Communist movement. On September 27, 1922, the Czechoslovak Ministry of the Interior disbanded the Komsomol, which had been founded in February 1921. This was another blow to the policy of the Turn towards the Masses. The Komsomol had been constituted after the Communist attempts at subverting and dominating the various national youth organizations had failed. It was a compromise formula similar to the one adopted after the unsuccessful Communist campaign that had been devised to bring trade unions under the control of the CPCS. We have seen that the party, acknowledging the unfavorable situation, decided to organize the Communist-obedient union sections into a separate body. The new organization was officially established on October 26, 1922, and given the resounding name of the International All-Union Association (IAUA), most probably in the hope that the Communist-led unions of other European countries might join it. The hope never materialized, and the IAUA membership figure of ninety thousand registered on the day of its constitution, a small fraction of the total Czechoslovak unionized work force, remained virtually unchanged until the end of the First Republic.[4] The autumn of 1922 also saw a regrouping among Slovak Communist intellectuals. In early November, several prominent Slovak writers and poets, following the example of their Czech comrades associated in the writers' collective, called Devětsil, created an artistic collective entitled DAV. The name was a word-play; it was put together from the first letters of the first names of the three most renowned members of the collective, Daniel Okáli, Andrej Sirácky, and Vlado Clementis, but the word "dav" in Slovak is also the equivalent of the English "crowd" or "multitude," which in this context stressed the mass-oriented nature of Communist culture. Like its Czech counterpart, Devětsil, which included stars like Jiří Wolker, Josef Hora, Vítězslav Nezval, and Stanislav Kostka Neumann, DAV proposed to overcome bourgeois individualism in the arts and to coordinate Communist talent in the service of proletarian revolution. It also launched a literary and artistic review of the same name that appeared regularly until 1937. In the early 1950s, DAV was associated with what was then called the Slovak national bourgeois deviation, and many of its members became victims of the purges and the political trials of that period.

CPCS Proposes, Komintern Disposes

The Fourth World Congress of the Komintern met in Moscow from November 5 through December 5, 1922. It was not the first time, nor the last, that the supreme gathering of the world's radical left had to arbitrate internal disputes of the Czechoslovak Communist party. Following the recommendation of the Executive Committee of the Komintern, the congress annulled the expulsions of Jílek and his associates. At the same time, it condemned the ideological position of the Jílek group as "an anarchic-syndicalist aberration from the principles of the Third International." On the other hand, Šmeral and Alois Neurath, an outstanding functionary of the German ethnic component of the CPCS and a collaborator of Karl Kreibich, were elected members of the Executive Committee of the Komintern. Alois Muna became a candidate to membership in this committee. Jílek was advised to work his way back to the leading position by "a sincere recognition of his errors and selfless cooperation with the leadership of the party."[5] Despite all appearances, the outcome of the conflict with the left opposition left Šmeral in no doubt about the narrow range of choices left to him and, for that matter, to any other future chief executive of the party by the fact of the affiliation of the CPCS with the Third International. To make things worse, although the Komintern's ruling in the Šmeral-Jílek dispute served the needs of Moscow's strategy, it neither solved nor alleviated the problems of the CPCS, but rather perpetuated them. From hindsight, an analyst might be inclined to say that the only real beneficiary of the ultraleft crisis of 1922 was Antonín Zápotocký, since Jílek's temporary eclipse gave him the opportunity to lay the foundations of his brilliant party career, which was to extend over more than thirty years.

In the climate of continuing inner conflicts, frustrated expectations, and new hopes, the party held its First Ordinary Congress from February 2 to February 5, 1923. Taking part in the deliberations were 125 delegates with voting rights and 59 delegates with consultative votes. According to the report of the Executive Committee, the total membership was 132,000, less than half the number estimated to have been represented at the constitutive congress in May 1921. The prolonged disagreements about the best form of the organization and about the party's affiliation with the Komintern, as well as the conflict with the left ultras, had obviously taken a heavy toll. Among the domestic issues discussed at the congress, the most important was the question of the various ethnic groups in Czechoslovakia. The congress adopted a resolution that recognized the existence of a Czechoslovak people in the sense of a linguistic and cultural unit. This actually was a concession to the view advocated by the establishment. Initially, the Communists had been very critical of the idea of "one Czechoslovak nation composed of two branches, the Czech and the Slovak," which underlay the current official theory of the Czechoslovak state.[6] The change in position on this issue further complicated the problem both for the Czechoslovak Republic and for the Communist movement. A chronic crisis in the nation, stemming from unresolved ambiguities in the relations between the Czechs and the Slovaks, eventually came to affect the party itself. For the rest, the resolution concerning the various ethnic components followed the principles formulated by the Komintern. It called for complete equality of all ethnic groups before the law and in politics; in 1923, this was a rather courageous stand, considering the strong wave of Czech and Slovak nationalism that had not yet begun to ebb. Another act braving the intensely anti-German and anti-Hungarian mood of the time was the belated adoption by the delegates of the protest declaration of the Executive Committee of the Komintern issued in July 1919 against the Treaty of Versailles. The declaration spoke of the "predatory terms" the treaty imposed upon Germany and Austria, and although Czechoslovakia was not named among the beneficiaries of the "Versailles robbery and loot," it was nevertheless implicitly indicted. The endorsement of this document was not a step calculated to increase the CPCS's popularity.

By far the most important part of the transactions of the First Congress consisted of discussion of the directives and the recommendations of the Fourth World Congress of the Komintern. The delegates commented at length upon the Komintern's resolution on the issue of the united front with other socialist and workers' parties and organizations, especially on the possibility of participation in workers' governments. The speakers on this topic were Karl Kreibich and Edmund Burian. The united-front resolution reflected the Komintern's new, more realistic assessment of the Communists' chances to seize power on a world scale. It found a very attentive audience among the delegates to the congress. The leaders and a large part of the membership of the CPCS saw in a coordinated action with other parties of the left the only real chance of promoting socialist ends and improving the lot of the working class. This perception of the situation came clearly to the fore in a presentation by Edmund Burian. Yet the principles of the united front, as proclaimed by the Komintern, and Czechoslovakia's concrete political needs and opportunities were then worlds apart. Thus, although the First Congress approved the Komintern resolution without change, the CPCS took no positive action to implement it except repeatedly to urge the "reformist and traitorous" socialists in the Social Democratic and National Socialist parties to join a "common engagement" that was not further defined. These invitations were always coupled with so many qualifications and showed so clearly the intention of the Communists to profit from an eventual collaboration by strengthening their own position that the non-Communist parties of the left rarely bothered to reply. On the other hand, these fruitless attempts did not bring the Komintern and the CPCS leaders any closer: Prague's interpretation of the concepts of the united front and the workers' government caused many misunderstandings between the two.

Another important subject of the First Congress deliberations that the previous resolutions of the Third International had made topical was the question of the work among the unions. Like the united front, this issue was a sensitive one in the relations between CPCS and the international Communist body. The Komintern's censure of the Czechoslovak Communists for their mistakes in dealing with the trade unions and the party's failure to secure at least partial control in this sector were still fresh memories. Moreover, even the splinter union center, the IAUA, which had recently been constituted after so many difficulties, was not functioning satisfactorily. Two diametrically opposed policies seemed to compete in this body: one of strict centralism, imitating the pattern prevailing in the Communist party, and another of a looser, more flexible structure, more congenial to the traditions of the trade union movement. Partisans of both views were present at the congress, each arguing that its approach was the most suitable in the given conditions. The congress finally adopted a stand substantially identical with that of the Third International that seemed to favor centralism rather than the autonomy of the individual branch organizations. Here again, as in the case of the united front, the ruling of the party congress, far from resolving the controversy, made it more or less permanent.

The congress also dealt with the question of the workers' consumer cooperatives. It adopted a document entitled "The Point of View of the CPCS Concerning the Cooperative Movement." This position paper showed more independence from Komintern tutelage than other congress transactions, chiefly because the problem was specifically a Czechoslovak one and cooperatives of all kinds had had a long tradition in Czechoslovak history. Finally, the congress attended to the business of renewing the party's governing organs. Changes in important functions were necessary after the conflict with the left. The provisional appointment of Antonín Zápotocký as secretary-general of the party was made a full-term one. Šmeral was re-elected party chairman. The Executive Committee, in its first session on February 6, 1923, elected Alois Muna its chairman and Karl Kreibich its vice-chairman.[7]

Although the First Ordinary Congress left the party with a number of unresolved internal problems, these difficulties did not immediately come to the fore. One reason for the respite granted to the Czechoslovak Communist movement was, ironically, the danger (or its subjective perception by the party leaders) that the party might be outlawed. On March 1, 1923, after hearing Šmeral's report on the general political situation, the plenary session of the new Executive Committee concluded that the government was preparing a legal action against the party. At that point, a bill was passing the last hurdles in the National Assembly that later became known as the "Law for the Protection of the Republic." It was to empower the executive and the administrative organs to take steps against political associations considered dangerous to the constitutional order. The Communist party, which saw itself as the only party questioning the legitimacy of the Czechoslovak state, believed that it was the main target of the bill. This belief promoted a kind of truce in a besieged fortress among the contending groups and factions within the party. This siege psychosis never completely subsided during the time of the First Republic, with the exception of a short period immediately before the Munich crisis and the Second World War. It is difficult to decide with certainty whether the Communists were completely convinced in 1923 that an era of illegality and persecution was imminent. Interestingly, the group of Communist-obedient members of the Parliament elected in 1920 by the Social Democratic ballot submitted in the National Assembly an amendment to the bill for the protection of the republic: in case the amendment was adopted, they were prepared to vote for the bill. The amendment was to be included in the preamble of the law and would have identified the source of the threat to the republican and constitutional order as emanating "from the circles of former aristocracy, high ranks of the military, the bureaucrats and the great capitalists." In itself, this initiative was a subtle but unsuccessful move on the part of the Communist caucus, but it earned the wrath of the Komintern and was severely condemned by later party historians.[8]

While the CPCS prepared to face being outlawed, it also publicly voiced its apprehensions and protested what it called "anti-Communist legislation." On April 1, 1923, only seven weeks after the First Congress, an "extraordinary manifestation congress" was called to Prague at which the law for the protection of the republic, just enacted by the Parliament and the Senate, was denounced as an "instrument of capitalist persecution" aimed at the working class movement. On the same occasion, Secretary-General Antonín Zápotocký submitted a report on the implementation of the resolutions passed by the First Congress in the matter of the united front. The delegates were forced to learn that the initiative had not yielded any appreciable results because of the refusal of other socialist parties and non-Communist workers' organizations to cooperate. The extraordinary congress was concluded by a "Proclamation to All Working People of All Ethnic Groups in the Republic" soliciting the sympathies and the help of the working class in the party's anticipated fight for survival.[9]

This dramatization, whether real or contrived, of the political climate did not bring the desired mass support for the CPCS, but it accelerated the polarization of the Czechoslovak left. The left wing of the parliamentary caucus of the Czechoslovak National Socialist party (CNSP), which openly manifested its solidarity with the Communists, was expelled by the CNSP's Executive Committee. The expulsion was confirmed by a special meeting of the National Socialist party representatives in Prague on March 22, 1923. The left group, consisting of four members of the Parliament, then joined the club of the "independent Social Democratic parliament representatives," the official name for the club of Communist members of the Parliament, since the CPCS had no formal representation in the National Assembly, the last elections having taken place before the party was established as an independent entity. Within this club of independent Social Democrats, the former National Socialist legislators set up a new caucus called the Socialist Union. In August 1923, the Socialist Union called a conference to create a new party of the left. Considerable differences of opinion on this issue—a majority of the delegates favored joining the Communist party—made an immediate decision impossible. On the other hand, František Modráček, chairman of the Party of Progressive Socialists (PPS), another left-wing but anti-Communist and anti-Komintern splinter of the Social Democratic party, was readmitted to the mother party as an observer in April 1923. The rest of the PPS followed Modráček in early June, with the exception of one Parliament member who entered the ranks of the National Democratic party, a political denomination of the conservative center.

First Tests of Popularity

The second half of 1923 brought an internal political event that was very important for the Communist party. In September and October, municipal elections were held in the capital city and in the three Czech provinces of Bohemia, Moravia, and Silesia. In themselves, communal elections could not compare in political significance with parliamentary elections. In 1923, however, they provided the first opportunity for the CPCS to run an independent ballot. Although the Komintern followed the preparations for these elections very closely and sent several written communications to the Czechoslovak party leaders to ensure their obedience to its directives concerning Communist participation in bourgeois-democratic elections, as approved by the Second World Congress in 1920, the Czechoslovak Communists showed their intention to choose the approach that in their judgment was best suited to specifically Czechoslovak conditions. At the Third Enlarged Plenum of the Executive Committee of the Komintern, party Secretary-General Zápotocký pleaded for the support of a united front in Czechoslovakia. In his plea he explicitly stated that "under the given circumstances, the United

Front is not a mere tactical move (as understood by the 1922 Komintern resolution) but a serious action which can lead to positive results." The plenum did not seem to be much impressed by these arguments. It insisted that the Czechoslovak party abide by the principle that only party members could be supported as candidates in the elections, and such candidates could run only on Communist party ballots. The Executive Committee of the CPCS approved this principle in July 1923. Nevertheless, shortly before the municipal elections in Prague, the same Executive Committee appealed to other parties of the left "to support in every precinct always the most promising socialist candidate," that is, the candidate with the greatest chance of being elected. This appeal clearly implied that the Communists were prepared to cast their vote, in certain circumstances, for a non-Communist contestant or incumbent.[10]

The results of the elections in Prague and of the subsequent vote in the three western provinces seemed to uphold the point of view of the Komintern, for they showed the Communist party strong enough to be able to reject cooperation with other socialist parties. The CPCS became the second strongest party in the capital, with 18 percent of all votes, and in Bohemia, Moravia, and Silesia it often polled the largest percentage of all three socialist parties. Zápotocký and Šmeral could, of course, draw completely different conclusions from the same facts. They could have argued that a united-front formula would have given even better results. For example, in Prague the total vote of the three parties of the left, running separately and often in competition with each other, was only 2 percent short of absolute majority. This was very much the way in which the results of the 1923 municipal elections were evaluated at the plenary session of the Executive Committee of the CPCS on October 11, 1923. Notwithstanding the differences in the assessment between the CPCS and the Komintern, the lesson of the first test of popularity was undoubtedly encouraging for the Czechoslovak Communists. Their optimism was reinforced when parliamentary by-elections, held about six months later in Ruthenia, brought 39.4 percent of all votes to the CPCS and made it the strongest party in the easternmost province of Czechoslovakia. It might have seemed that the working class was prepared to invest its trust in the Communist party despite internal dissent and ideological conflicts, interference from abroad, and commitment to patently nonpatriotic causes, and that nothing could shake this support. In reality, the vote of the Communist electorate reflected a far more complex motivation than mere approval of the confused and esoteric party program or agreement with the Komintern's world revolutionary strategy. In fact, its support really had nothing to do with these issues. (This subject will be discussed in more detail later.) Moreover, for the purpose of properly appraising the popular judgment of the party's performance, the development of an organized following, that is, a body of card-carrying party members, is at least as important as the vote cast at an election. Membership figures since the founding of the CPCS, however, spoke a language different from that of the polls. Although in the early 1920s the leadership had not yet subscribed to the principle of an elite revolutionary party modeled on the Bolshevik example, its following was dwindling rapidly.

The electoral success of the CPCS in 1923 could not resolve or mask the serious difficulties of the Czechoslovak Communist movement. The very voting support given to the party became a new source of disagreement between the leadership and the Komintern, each of whom interpreted these results in its own way. The differences of opinion about the meaning of the voting statistics were but a symptom of a deeper division; what was at stake was the implementation of the united-front policies in Czechoslovakia. It became increasingly evident, in 1923 and 1924, that the Šmeral group had its own notion of the most suitable formula of cooperation with other parties of the left, a notion that was at considerable variance with the principles announced in the resolution of the Fourth World Congress of the Komintern. This notion had already been contained in statements and comments of the CPCS leaders before the Komintern resolution was adopted. The offer they had made to other socialist parties at the time of the municipal elections to support, on a reciprocal basis, the socialist candidates with the best chance of winning, was an attempt to translate the principle of the united front into the language of concrete politics.

Another occasion to test in practice the policy line of the united front was a widespread strike of miners in Bohemia, called by the Social Democratic trade unions in the late summer of 1923. During the strike, which continued into the autumn of the same year, the CPCS offered the reformist unions full political support and agreed that for the duration of the strike "all political quarrels should cease and all polemics should be stopped which could divide the working class."[11] In March 1924, party chairman Šmeral, speaking before the Parliament, formulated the conditions under which the caucus of the former Marxist left, now Communist, would be willing to participate in the government. He stated that such a government would have to "stem from the will of the working population," that is, be elected by the votes of the working people, and be prepared to "grab the big capitalists, big landowners, speculators and other big thiefs by their throats."[12] None of these declarations or concrete steps could be reconciled with the spirit and the letter of the Komintern resolution on the united front and workers' government. Moscow had expected the Czechoslovak Communists to seize the opportunity of the miners' strike to unmask "the traitorous role of the reformist unions" and substitute themselves for the Social Democrats as leaders of the strike. Concerning Šmeral's statement on possible participation in governmental responsibilities, his major error, in the eyes of the Komintern, was in "playing the bourgeois liberal parliamentary game," that is, in accepting the political system without previous transformation of its "bourgeois-capitalist features." The initiatives of the CPCS in all these matters only reinforced the suspicion of the world Communist headquarters that the Czechoslovak party "continued to sail in Social Democratic, reformist and petty-bourgeois waters."[13]

The Communist International was also displeased by many public utterances of the CPCS top officials on topics other than the united front, but equally important. The Komintern was particularly perturbed about the not entirely partisan coverage by the Czechoslovak Communist press of various international events and problems. In particular, occasional flashes of objectivity and fine distinction in the evaluation by this press of Czechoslovak non-Communist politicians, such as President Masaryk and Foreign Minister Beneš, caused concern in the Kremlin. It was shocked at the stance the Czechoslovak Communist leaders took on the attempt at a take-over by the Communists in neighboring Germany. When the attempt failed, the CPCS did nothing to help the fraternal party except to reject the economic blockade of Germany that the Allied Powers then contemplated. The Third International displayed indignation over the fact that even in rejecting the blockade, the CPCS used arguments about a possible loss of vital markets for Czechoslovak products and the resulting increase in unemployment. In short, heads of the Komintern found that the Czechoslovak leadership lacked a class approach to major issues of the time. It was occasionally suggested in Moscow that "Brandlerism," a kind of deviation named after the German party boss whom the Komintern blamed for the failure of the 1923 coup, had its counterpart in Czechoslovakia in "Šmeralism." In both cases, however, the objection was less against an alleged ideological shortcoming than it was against the unwillingness of the two Communist leaders to follow without protest the Komintern's instructions.[14]

The Bolshevization Issue

The uneasy relationship between the CPCS and its Moscow sponsor continued and further deteriorated during the first half of the 1920s. Before this series of misunderstandings and disappointments broke out into an open conflict, however, another bone of contention had to be added. A real crisis developed when the Fifth World Congress of the Third International, in June and July 1924, launched the slogan of the bolshevization of all Communist parties. Bolshevization in this context signified the adoption by all sections of the Komintern of the organizational structure and the working methods that the Bolshevik wing of the Russian Social Democratic party had employed during the period of illegality and the struggle for power.[15] It was thus by far the most serious intervention by the Moscow center in the internal affairs of the individual national Communist movements. It showed utter disregard for the specific conditions of the various societies and countries, disregard that later became one of the basic characteristics of Stalinism. The idea of bolshevization encountered great difficulties in all sections of the Komintern, but it met with particularly strong resistance in countries with parliamentary regimes and democratic traditions. Czechoslovakia was one of these.

Although the bolshevization program was formally endorsed only at the Fifth Congress of the Komintern, the first move toward the introduction of Bolshevik organizational forms and rules had occurred at an earlier date. Already on April 21, 1924, the Bureau of the Executive Committee of the Communist International had advised the Communist Party of Czechoslovakia to replace party local and enterprise groups by local and enterprise "cells." It is generally believed that the immediate motive for this step was the lack of success of the revolutionary movement organized and led by the Komintern in neighboring Germany. The Third International wished to prevent the repetition in Czechoslovakia of Brandlerism. On May 4 and 5, 1924, a National Party Conference, called in the Moravian capital Brno, discussed the directives of the Komintern Bureau concerning the creation of cells, as well as instructions relating to party activity in the trade unions and the problems of the united front and workers' government. The National Party

Conference laid bare strong opposition to the new policy line of the Komintern, both to the suggested organizational formula and to the working methods. The delegates of party organizations at intermediate and lower levels testified that the membership often did not understand the purpose of the cells and found the whole project of restructuring the party extremely artificial and unnecessary under Czechoslovak conditions. At the same time, the conference discussions showed that the bolshevization issue was perceived by the left opposition, which had recently been reprimanded and reduced in influence, as a unique opportunity for a comeback. A confrontation between the majority and the left, as well as polemics with Moscow, was avoided through a rather flexible formulation of the conference resolutions.[16] Nevertheless, it was clear that the party would go to the Fifth World Congress divided on precisely the issue that the Komintern then considered to be the most vital.

The unanimous adoption of the resolutions in no way fooled the leadership of the Third International about the attitude of the Czechoslovak party's governing team and apparatus. This attitude became manifest in speeches at many regional and local meetings and in the manner in which the Czechoslovak Communist press covered and commented on the bolshevization theme. The comments showed how little credibility many CPCS spokesmen gave to the Komintern thesis of the imminence of confrontation with capitalism on a world scale, which was to justify the radical change in the organizational structure of the Communist parties. Some writers of editorials openly declared that the diagnosis of the international situation as a revolutionary one was an "anarchistic, not a Communist assessment," and several went so far as to reject the official Komintern interpretation of the causes of the failure of the 1923 revolutionary attempt in Germany.

Inevitably, the Fifth Congress of the Komintern had to become the scene of an open confrontation between the Czechoslovak Communists critical of the bolshevization line and the Komintern leaders. Already in the advanced general reports submitted by Grigori Zinoviev, the secretary-general of the Komintern, the tenor and the decisions of the Brno national conference were singled out as opportunistic, especially in matters concerning the united front, although some ultraleft positions were equally criticized. Zinoviev's report also criticized several statements on the 1923 revolutionary movements in Germany that had been selected from the Czechoslovak party press. The majority of the Czechoslovak delegation at the congress tried to reconcile the disagreements by presenting the criticized articles as individual perceptions of the events by the various writers. However, the left minority, which was strongly represented among the delegates of ethnic-group party organizations other than the Czech, unreservedly endorsed the position of the Komintern. This stand was acknowledged with satisfaction by the Komintern officials who were already beginning to look for reliable allies within the Czechoslovak party: these would be needed in the eventuality of a conflict with the Šmeral leadership. The left opposition did not restrict its criticism to the united-front policies of the CPCS; it also attacked the majority political line on ethnic problems. It charged that instead of respecting the resolutions of the previous Komintern congresses, which had proclaimed "unlimited right of self-determination to the point of secession," the Communist party had identified itself with the positions of "Czech imperialists and chauvinists" and advocated territorial integrity of the Czechoslovak Republic. Furthermore, it accused the Šmeral team of "constitutional fetishism"—that is, of giving too much attention to the rules of democratic procedure in the Parliament, and pointed out that "the notions of the seizure of power and of the dictatorship of the proletariat had entirely disappeared from the vocabulary of the CPCS."[17]

Šmeral's diplomatic talent, however, and the inborn Communist dislike of differences of opinion succeeded in preventing a showdown at the Fifth Congress. There was no majority vote on any of the major issues concerning the Czechoslovak party, only unanimity. The criticism and the recommendations of the congress were accepted without qualification by all delegates; the left opposition had no grounds for dissent. The leadership may have chosen this course because it was confident that the interpretation and the implementation of the congressional resolutions would be in its own hands. The avoidance of an open split in the international arena also preserved for Šmeral and his group the right to represent the Czechoslovak section in the Komintern. And indeed, the congress elected Šmeral, Muna, and Neurath to the Executive Committee and Karl Kreibich to the International Control Commission, although all of these except Neurath had been the main targets of leftist criticism. Neurath took a wait-and-see position that left him somewhere between the right and the left. Despite this tactical victory, a serious crisis lay ahead. It had little to do with the intrigues of the leftist members of the Czechoslovak delegation at the Moscow congress; rather, it was built into the principal policy decisions taken there. By decreeing obligatory bolshevization of all member parties, the Komintern had supplied ammunition for the struggle between the various factions in the CPCS.

Until the Fifth World Congress, Šmeral could have hoped that the practical application of the often vague or contradictory policy decisions of the supreme Communist authority would be left to the discretion of each national party. The demand to bolshevize was a completely new element in the situation. It did not admit of more than one interpretation; it could only be obeyed or disobeyed. Thus it forced the hand of the Šmeral leadership, which on the whole shared the aversion of the grass-roots organizations for the bolshevization experiment. The leadership's room for maneuvering, on the other hand, was narrowed by the left opposition. Its presence in the party was a guarantee that the issue of bolshevization would be neither shelved nor sabotaged. The Komintern officials were aware of this circumstance. Since an indivisible part of the bolshevization campaign was "comradely ideological discussion," which in practice meant a blanket approval of all kinds of invective against the elected party organs, the Third International could be sure that the differences of opinion within the Czechoslovak party would not soon be resolved. The effects of this discussion were confirmed by later party historians who, although uncompromisingly in agreement with the Komintern's position, admitted that "the party discussion in those years [1923 and 1924] had taken such sharp forms that there existed an acute danger of a split."[18] Nevertheless, the left faction was not strong enough to bring about the desired change or provide an alternative leadership team. Therefore, the Komintern espoused a strategy that, in this phase, would lead to the elimination of at least the most outspoken defenders of the more independent course that was tailored to the needs of the Czechoslovak situation.

Regional Opposition and the Second Party Congress

In this major internal confrontation, which was to extend over six years, the party organization of the capital city played a key role. The suspensions and demotions carried out earlier against the Jílek group affected the party apparatus in the Prague region particularly strongly and brought into the leading positions there Communists of a completely different orientation. Moscow later labeled this orientation rightist, but in reality the Prague organization after the purge of Jílek was in the hands of cadres of all shades. The common denominator of their various positions was the conviction that to be successful, a party policy had to take into consideration the specific conditions prevailing in the given social environment. Among the leaders of the Prague party unit the person who reaped most of the Komintern's wrath was Josef Bubník, the party's regional chairman and a member of the parliamentary caucus of independent Social Democrats. As the top executive official of a party section comprising a great number of units located in large industrial enterprises in one of the most economically developed parts of the country, Bubník kept receiving firsthand reports and complaints and often protest delegations from grass-roots organizations that were unwilling to cooperate in the transformation of relatively well-functioning party enterprise locals into cells, as the Third International required. He made himself champion of this rank-and-file movement of dissatisfaction.

The controversy over bolshevization, only papered over at the Komintern congress, flared up with renewed vehemence after the return of the delegation from Moscow. The Fourth Enlarged Plenum of the Executive Committee of the Third International, which met on July 12 and 13, 1924, in a special resolution admonished the Czechoslovak party to proceed without delay to restructure the party body and to establish enterprise cells. This reminder was discussed at the meeting of the Executive Committee of the CPCS held in Prague on July 31 and August 1. The opinions were so far apart that in the end two different draft resolutions were submitted for vote. Of the two, the text prepared by Alois Neurath and seconded by the leftist elements was carried by a very narrow margin. Some officials felt that the discussion at the Executive Committee session had been manipulated and that the final vote did not truly reflect the view of the majority. They particularly disagreed with the unqualified endorsement of the Komintern criticism contained in the version of the resolution that was adopted. The spokesmen for these dissenters was Josef Bubník, who called a regional party conference in Prague for September 28, 1924. This conference rejected by a great majority of votes the findings and the resolution of the Executive Committee. As the resolution was also dealt with in other regional and local party organizations, it became evident that the left, which had scored a narrow victory at the Executive Committee session, was in the minority not only in Prague, but also in all regional party units in Bohemia, Moravia, and Silesia. Two very important regions, Kladno and Brno, followed the Prague example and held conferences, and here, too, the left was defeated and the Executive Committee's resolution was disavowed. Only party organizations in Slovakia and Ruthenia and some organizations of the German ethnic group gave their support to the left. This insubordination of the regional units appeared to indicate that the left was too weak to be feared any more: apparently the leadership now could hope to shape its policies without too much pressure from the left. Such an interpretation, however, would have underestimated the influence and determination of the Komintern.

Šmeral felt sure that the forthcoming Second Ordinary Party Congress would be a suitable occasion to settle in a more permanent way the protracted dispute with the left. To secure the best position in the anticipated confrontation, the leadership decided to postpone the date of the congress, originally scheduled for September 1924, for another two months, and to await feedback from all regional party organizations on the most urgent questions of party policy. As we have seen, the results of the regional party meetings indicated that the left was not popular with the rank-and-file membership. Barring unexpected factors, the congress could be expected to confirm the position of Šmeral and his group. However, external factors could not be barred. The Komintern, pursuing its project of bolshevization, was determined to exploit to the maximum the divisions within the Czechoslovak party. On October 15, 1924, the Presidium of the Third International issued a resolution "on the nationalities (that is, the ethnic) problems and the specific conditions of the proletarian struggle in Czechoslovakia."[19] This was already the third Komintern resolution within ten weeks concerning the CPCS. This document criticizing and "correcting" the party's approach in matters of ethnic minorities was apparently aimed at "deviant" leaders such as Karl Kreibich and Břetislav Hůla, but Kreibich, despite his nonconformist stand on the ethnic issue, was now a close collaborator of Šmeral and part of the CPCS establishment. Thus the censure of his views was also an implicit criticism of the leadership. It provided an additional topic that in itself included a number of vital points, both ideological and tactical, for the controversy between the team in control and the left opposition. The impending deliberations of the party's supreme organ promised to be stormy.

The Second Ordinary Party Congress met in Prague from October 31 through November 4, 1924. In all, 165 fully accredited delegates and 64 delegates with consultative vote took part in the discussions; they represented 99,700 dues-paying members. According to official data, membership had diminished by about 22 percent between the first and second congresses, and the 1924 total was less than a third of the following claimed at the Merger Congress of 1921. Dimitri Manuilski was the most prominent representative of the Komintern present: the fact that the secretary of the Presidium himself was chosen for this assignment testified to the importance the Third International attributed to Czechoslovak matters.[20] The Komintern, as well as many observers outside the Communist movement, expected that the congress would bring a resolution of the controversy between center and left. However, although the various reports clearly showed significant differences of opinion among the delegates and although the discussions occasionally became very heated, the final battle between the two currents did not take place at the Second Party Congress. In view of the support given by the Komintern to the left opposition, the centrists chose to avoid the ultimate showdown. All resolutions submitted by the leadership were in agreement with the principles laid down by the earlier rulings of the Komintern; thus the left was deprived of the chance to denounce the group in control before the international Communist forum. Outspoken opponents of the bolshevization course, such as Regional Chairman Bubník, Secretary J. Rejlek, member of Parliament František Toužil, or functionaries of other regional party organizations, could not influence the contents of the resolutions. Concessions to the left were also made in the composition of the new Executive Committee. The left filled eighteen seats while the right obtained only fourteen. The rest were allocated to the center, which thus retained decisive power.[21] It could hope that even in the changed conditions it could continue to pursue the established line.

Nevertheless, the Komintern was not happy with the results of the Second Congress. Šmeral's retreat might have saved the left from an imminent disaster, but this tactical gain was more than compensated for by the consolidation of the centrist line. Moscow saw in the apparent smoothness with which the resolutions were adopted a kind of "Kutuzovian strategy"—a "reculer pour mieux sauter." This suspicion was manifest, for example, in the message from the secretary-general of the Komintern, Grigori Zinoviev, to the Second Congress. In it Zinoviev refused to accept the explanation that the curious unanimity of vote exhibited by the Czechoslovak Communist party organs was a sign of the "sense for party discipline." This explanation had been offered to him at the Fifth World Congress of the Komintern by Zápotocký, but Zinoviev considered such party discipline to be most pernicious since in his opinion it "masked serious disagreements and dodged open comradely discussion." He recommended that the Second Congress put "false unanimity" aside and face the issues as they really were.[22]

The Bubník Crisis and the Fifth Plenum of the Komintern Executive

The showdown that the Komintern desired—in the hope that it would benefit its own interests—came much later, however, and in a piecemeal manner. The first crisis after the Second Ordinary Congress was again connected with the party organization of the Prague region. On February 10, 1925, the CPCS called a meeting of industrial workers to the Old City Square to protest inflation and the high cost of living. After the meeting was over, an unorganized group of young participants formed a procession and marched toward the business center. The police tried to disperse the crowd, using force rather indiscriminately. The demonstrators then began throwing rocks at the police, who finally opened fire and wounded several of them. The Communist party leadership thereupon called a new demonstration for February 15, which was to be "the day of protest of the working people." Meetings were to be held on that day throughout the whole country "to denounce and condemn the police terror of the bourgeoisie."[23] Prior to the day of protest, a mass gathering was planned in the capital city on February 13, but this decision was made only forty-eight hours before the scheduled time. The Prague regional party headquarters, charged with the preparations, felt that there was not sufficient time to assure the success of the planned action. Chairman Josef Bubník also feared that such an improvised mass meeting could result in a bloody clash similar to that at the march of young people on February 10. Together with other members of the regional party committee, he therefore called off the mass gathering and the strike order for February 13, which had been issued by the party's top executive organ. Instead, Bubník and his staff worked out a new plan for the February 15 demonstration that they thought substantially reduced the risk of a collision with the forces of public order.

Bubník's step raised a greater furor in the party's national headquarters than even police shooting could have caused. The Politbureau met in an emergency session on February 18, 1925, and expelled the Prague regional chairman from the CPCS because of his "opportunistic and harmful behavior." The Komintern, which classified Bubník among the rightist elements, reacted far more quickly than it had in the case of Jílek. Only three days later its Executive Committee telegraphically approved Bubník's expulsion. It was evident, however, that action against Bubník, which had been initiated by the left wing and condoned by the centrists, did not meet with the approval of the entire membership. The Prague organization protested. On February 20, the party's regional organization in Brno rejected the expulsion of Bubník, pointing out that other individuals in the party, "through-and-through corrupt [. . .] should be eliminated" instead of dedicated party workers such as Bubník. On this occasion, the regional organization removed the left-oriented editorial staff from the Moravian Communist daily *Rovnost* (*Equality*) and put a new editor-in-chief in control. The meeting of the regional executive also adopted a document, which later was to enter the annals of the party as the so-called "Brno memorandum," that was to be submitted for discussion to all party units in the country and that was to be tabled at the Fifth Enlarged Plenum of the Komintern Executive Committee slated for March 1925. The memorandum summed up all the grievances against the "schemings of the left opposition" in the Central (formerly the Executive) Committee of the CPCS, requested the annulment of Bubník's expulsion, and called for an immediate convocation of an extraordinary party congress. The party regional organization in the mining district of Kladno, west of Prague, protested in similar terms. (The three regional units of Prague, Brno, and Kladno represented in 1925 the most important strongholds of the Communist party.)

The CPCS Central Committee, in which the left was more strongly represented than the right, convened on February 28. It made some concessions to the dissatisfied regional groups by expelling a few officials singled out by the lower echelons as corrupt, but it confirmed the ruling of the Politbureau in the case of Bubník. This increased the opposition of the intermediate and grass-roots level organizations. Bitterness toward the leadership increased especially after the leftist members of the Central Committee succeeded in placing a number of their partisans in the CPCS delegation to the Komintern's March plenum, although many of these individuals had previously been denied confidence by the local groups from which they came. The lower-level party organizations demanded that the CPCS be represented in Moscow only by Communists approved by them. They hoped that the Enlarged Executive Committee of the Third International would rescind its original endorsement of

Bubník's expulsion when it had heard all the facts, as they were spelled out in the Brno memorandum. The removal from the party of the Prague regional chairman now became a question of principle. Both the CPCS and the Komintern experienced the Bubník crisis.

The Fifth Plenum of the Executive Committee of the Third International, held in Moscow from March 21 through April 6, 1925, dashed the hopes of the Czechoslovak nonconformists. It dissipated the last illusions about the chances of survival within the framework of the Komintern of a Communist party with a reasonable degree of autonomy and a serious concern with the lot of the working class. The Moscow center, far from putting the left back in its place, openly encouraged the leftist bid for power. In so doing, however, it did not identify with any of the contending factions within the CPCS, but used them for its own ends. Czechoslovakia was a very important area in the Komintern's world strategy and the Czechoslovak question ranked high on the agenda of the Fifth Plenum. Its significance was illustrated by the fact that the Komintern reporter in the subcommittee on Czechoslovakia was no less a personage than Joseph Stalin.

As could have been anticipated, the Fifth Plenum confirmed the Executive Committee's approval of Bubník's expulsion. In the same vein, it condemned the spirit and letter of the Brno memorandum. Speaking in the subcommittee on this subject, Stalin found that the memorandum contained "a peculiar theory of revolution which has nothing in common with Leninism" and that it took a "menshevik position on the question of the party activity among the masses." He further declared the suspension of the editorial staff of *Rovnost* by the party regional organization "a form of banditism or hooliganism in the party," and stated that the reluctance of the Brno group to submit to the authority of the party center was "not bolshevism, but anarchomenshevism of the most unadulterated vintage."[24]

The stance of the Central Committee of the Czechoslovak party was thus vindicated by the most authoritative spokesman of the world Communist movement.* Yet the Bubník affair and the Brno memor-

---

*Or was it? If we read attentively the whole of Stalin's report, we see that although it agrees with the assessment of the gravity of the offence committed by the Prague regional chairman and the officials of the Brno organization, it nevertheless criticizes the way in which the Bubník affair was handled by the CPCS leadership. Stalin says explicitly: "Expulsions are not the decisive weapons in the struggle against the right," and argues that the Central Committee and the Politbureau had "acted with undue haste" in expelling Bubník. This statement is of particular interest to a historian. On this point Stalin's opinion

andum were not the only aspects of the CPCS's situation that preoccupied the Fifth Enlarged Plenum of the Komintern. The Komintern
was seriously concerned with the whole development of its Czechoslovak
section. The CPCS had by then become a problem child for Moscow. The
Third International worried less about the insubordination of a middle-
echelon official or a regional party group than about the general mood
prevailing among the leading cadres and the insufficient support these
cadres were giving its policies. In this respect, the Czechoslovak leadership was found wanting, despite the reinforcement of the left wing at the
Second Congress. The Komintern's Executive Committee was aware of
the lack of enthusiasm with which the Czechoslovak party apparatus had
accepted the directives relative to the bolshevization. It knew that the left
saw in this issue a welcome lever to unseat the team in control, but it did
not believe that the left, as it then existed, would be capable of pushing
through all the necessary reforms, programmatic as well as organizational, required by a successful bolshevization. It placed even less trust in
the Šmeral group, which, in spite of increased influence of the left wing
in the Central Committee, still controlled much of the national party
organization. The recent conflict over the unsuccessful Prague manifest-

---

seems to be close to the view that Šmeral and Zápotocký expressed at the critical meeting of
the Central Committee on February 28. Both top officials held that the Politbureau "had
hurried too much" when imposing the ultimate sanction against the dissident regional
functionary. As we know, the Central Committee overruled their objections and gave satisfaction to the left wing, but there is a strange inconsistency in the manner in which
Communist historiography deals with their caution and with Stalin's reservations. It never
fails to blame Šmeral and Zápotocký for their allegedly "opportunistic approach," but it
quotes Stalin with unqualified approval. It would be difficult to explain this discrepancy
merely by the differences in the power hierarchy. Stalin's view that the expulsion of a
"rightist element" from the CPCS was too hasty is reproduced without comment and two
prominent Czechoslovak leaders are severely criticized for holding apparently the same
view because the two positions are only superficially similar. Stalin, like Šmeral and
Zápotocký, believed that there had been "unwarranted haste" in the punitive measure
against the Prague chairman, but for two entirely different reasons. The leaders of the
CPCS meant what they said: that the case should have been duly examined and both parties
heard before a decision was taken. Not so Stalin. In his report he develops his point in
detail: "This all [what has been said so far] does not mean, of course, that we must
necessarily expel all rightist members . . . . An expulsion, when it becomes really inevitable,
should be but the natural consequence of the moral destruction of the opponent." And
Stalin argued further: "In this sense, the left in Czechoslovakia committed a serious error
because it pressed for a quick expulsion of Bubník, instead of exploiting the Bubník case to
the maximum." The difference between Stalin's point of view and Šmeral's is obvious
However, the historical interest of this episode goes even beyond what happened in the
CPCS in 1925. What we have here, particularly in the paragraph quoted last, is what was to
become one of the essential features of Stalinism. In commenting on the Czechoslovak
party crisis of 1925, Stalin drafted with frightening accuracy the strategy of his future
purges.

ation, on the other hand, indicated that what Moscow called the right remained an influential force in the party; it was from there that further resistance to the restructuring of the CPCS along Bolshevik lines was the most likely to come.

The dissatisfaction with the work of the Czechoslovak party found its expression not only in the report by Stalin, where it received treatment comparable to that of the Bubník incident; the Komintern chairman himself, Zinoviev, addressed the issue in his speech following Šmeral's presentation. He charged that a panicky mood prevailed among the CPCS leaders that in no way reflected the real mood of the Czechoslovak working class. Only the Communist intellectuals who had hoped to defeat the bourgeoisie within two months were disillusioned, declared Zinoviev. His point of view was backed by Executive Committee member Dimitri Manuilski, who derided the alleged oversensitivity of the educated party elites. "These people," Manuilski mocked, "are never satisfied with 'decisions taken in Moscow,' they moan and groan and cry out their eyes in the Prague cafés, and suffer diarrhea from sheer apprehension of a mistake which the party could make, but they are prepared, already tomorrow, to ignite a new conflict in the party."[25]

Accusations and ridicule, however, could not solve the Czechoslovak crisis. In view of the actual distribution of forces within the CPCS, the Komintern chose a more pragmatic approach. It promoted a temporary coalition of the center and the left, the purpose of which was to liquidate the right—a relatively undramatic rehearsal on a miniature scale of what later was to become a typical Stalinist purge. Considering that the right was fairly firmly entrenched in the party structure, the Enlarged Plenum did not advise an immediate all-out attack on its positions, but recommended that a few minor concessions first be made to it. The concessions consisted mainly of upholding the expulsions and suspensions from membership of the officials whom the regional organizations had denounced as corrupt. The "ideological and moral destruction" of the right, following the Stalinist recipe, was to be undertaken only gradually.

Aftermath of the Bubník Crisis:
The Third Party Congress

The establishment of the center-left bloc and the rather cautious strategy it adopted in the internal struggle for party control provoked opposition not only from the right, but also among the younger groups of the left.

These radical groups, recruited chiefly from youth and student organizations and supported by party units in the territories inhabited by ethnic minorities, had hoped that the Fifth Plenum would ensure an unequivocal victory for the left. They had especially expected that the criticism voiced at the Moscow gathering would be aimed at the centrist leadership of Šmeral. The Komintern's stance disappointed them. One of these groups became known through a book it published under the title *Leninismus nebo . . .?* (*Leninism or . . .?*), where the question mark stood for "Šmeralismus."[26] The Komintern did not officially back or approve the publication, but it noted the existence of a young left and included it in its long-term plans for the Czechoslovak party.

The CPCS thus returned from Moscow with a compromise solution that satisfied nobody. The crisis was not overcome, but exacerbated. On the right there was bitterness about the decision in the Bubník affair and the rejection of the Brno memorandum. Meanwhile, Bubník himself, together with several other officials and members of the Communist faction in the National Assembly, founded an independent Communist Party of Czechoslovakia. The new party began publishing its own press organ, the biweekly *Hlas pravdy* (*The Voice of Truth*). The independent party had little success in the political arena—in the 1925 parliamentary elections it received only eight thousand votes nationwide—and disintegrated rather rapidly. The principle contained in its program, however—that the trade union movement should retain autonomy from party control—was adopted by the IAUA (The Red Unions), in flagrant contradiction of the twenty-one conditions of membership stipulated by the Komintern in 1920. The agreement reached at the Fifth Enlarged Plenum did not satisfy the center and left either. Although these two groups were working in an alliance set up in Moscow, they soon began to prepare for an eventual confrontation. At the Central Committee session of April 24, 1925, the familiar spectacle of rubber-stamping of the Komintern resolutions was repeated, even though everyone familiar with the ways of the party knew that the resolutions had lost their force.

The year 1925 was an eventful one for the CPCS. Apart from internal crises and frequent interventions by the Komintern, there was an unusually high rate of turnover in the highest offices because of police and court actions against individual incumbents. In May, Secretary-General Antonín Zápotocký was arrested. The left wing of the party succeeded in obtaining the appointment of its most prominent representative, Bohumil Jílek, who had been out of power since the events of 1922, to Zápotocký's office. This appeared to be an unexpectedly favorable turn for Jílek, but exactly two months later he too was arrested, along with another leading personality of the Communist left, Václav Houser. The office of secretary-general was thereupon entrusted to Čeněk Hruška, who was responsible for the party Secretariat until the Third Ordinary Congress, held in Prague September 26–28, 1925.

The Third Ordinary Party Congress assembled 107 delegates with full, and 122 delegates with consultative, vote. The disproportion between the two categories reflected the unstable, if not confused, state of the party organization, caused both by continuing internal strife and by the impact of bolshevization. In all there were 93,000 dues-paying party members; this represented a loss of about 7 percent since the Second Ordinary Congress in 1924, although the rate of membership loss seemed to be decreasing. On the positive side, the congress marked the entry into the party of the group of former deputies of the National Socialist party who had formed an independent Socialist caucus of their own after their expulsion from this party in 1923. The group was presided over by Bohuslav Vrbenský. The two main reporters at the Third Congress were Josef Haken and Bohumír Šmeral. Haken presented the viewpoint of the leadership concerning the domestic and international situation, political as well as economic, and the resulting immediate tasks of the CPCS. Šmeral gave an account of affairs within the Communist party, especially of the recent crisis in relations between the national center and the regional organizations. When the congress proceeded to the election of the top executive officials and of the Central Committee, it became evident that the left had made further inroads into the party's power structure. Šmeral was not re-elected as chairman, but was replaced by Haken.[27] After the Third Congress, Šmeral played only a marginal role in the CPCS until he completely withdrew from Czechoslovak politics. From the end of the 1930s on he lived in Moscow, where he worked in the Secretariat of the Third International and died in 1941. With Šmeral's departure from the party, the most salient link with the great traditions of the Czech socialist and workers' movement was lost. The chances that the party would be able to maintain a modicum of independence from the international power center and a better orientation toward the real problems of the Czechoslovak working class dwindled rapidly. It was significant that while Šmeral was on his way to political retirement, the list of the new members of the Central Committee included, for the first time, the name of Klement Gottwald, an ambitious party activist who, although a Czech, was elected to the top executive organ as a delegate from the Slovak regional organizations. His name would be in the limelight during the climax of the party crisis, in the late 1920s, and for many years afterward, always associated with the hard line of unqualified obedience to Moscow. Eventually he was to eclipse and oust the reputedly leftist Jílek, who at the Third Congress recovered the key post of secretary-general.

The Central Committee, in its first session on September 29, 1925, elected a new political bureau (Politbureau) and an organizational bureau. The latter organ gained greatly in importance during the subsequent struggle over the bolshevization of the party. Officially, its main task was "to assure contact with the party organizations of all levels."[28] The congress obviously had learned a lesson from the revolt of the regional units during the Bubník crisis and was anxious to facilitate feedback from these vital party components. More often than not, however, the activity of the organization bureau resembled a one-way street: it usually served the purpose of manipulating the grass-roots membership rather than taking the pulse of the rank and file.

The 1925 General Elections:
Ethnicity and the Communist Vote

Not long after the Third Ordinary Congress, the CPCS underwent its first test of popularity on a national scale. In the parliamentary elections of 1925, the party for the first time ran as a separate group with its own ballot. Although the results of the previous municipal elections and of the regional parliamentary elections in Ruthenia had indicated that the party enjoyed a strong following among the electorate, the results of the elections to the National Assembly, held on November 15, 1925, came as a surprise. The Communist party polled 13.2 percent of all votes, obtained forty-one seats in the Parliament, and thus became the second strongest political group in the country. The outcome of the elections was a signal success for the party, all the more remarkable as it was achieved in a period of confusion and turmoil. The large number of voters choosing Communist candidates appeared to be in sharp contrast to the rapidly decreasing number of organized party members. This contradiction was a typically Czechoslovak phenomenon that had its specific causes; it will presently be examined in more detail. The fact is that the party leadership in 1925 could not refrain from wishful thinking nor resist the temptation to interpret the electoral success as proof of the correctness of the policy line. But which line? In view of the continuing struggle of various factions for the control of the CPCS, it was certainly difficult to identify a definite policy. If the election figures were to be considered an endorsement by the masses it could only have been an endorsement of internal party strife; and despite its absurdity, this was the explanation the party leadership chose. Had the team in control really wished to understand the appeal of the CPCS to the Czechoslovak population at large, it would have had to take a closer look at the territorial and ethnic distribution of the Communist vote. This distribution followed, already in 1925, a definite pattern that it maintained until the end of the First Republic.

Contrary to what an orthodox Marxist would have expected, the strongest bastions of the party were not found in the most industrialized regions of the country; almost the opposite was the case. With the exception of the mining district of Kladno and the capital city, where the Communists polled a higher percentage of votes than the Socialist party in 1925 (but not in any of the following elections), all areas with strong Communist support were predominantly rural. However, there was an additional, and even more important, element in this voting pattern: the rural districts in which the Communists received a large proportion of vote were nearly all in the south of Slovakia (an area inhabited chiefly by ethnic Hungarians) and in Ruthenia. Although the actual percentage changed at every subsequent election, the picture of the relative strength of the Communist party, as it was divided among the individual regions and ethnic groups, remained the same from 1925 until 1938. (See Table 1 for more detailed data.)

This curious popularity of communism in electoral districts of a peripheral and backward character in Czechoslovakia led an area specialist, Richard V. Burks, to an interesting theory in the early 1960s. Very briefly, Burks maintained that the communism in Czechoslovakia—and by implication in the whole of Central and Eastern Europe—reflects the frustrated expectations of ethnic minorities.[29] Burks's work, of which a substantial part has been devoted to the analysis of Communist voting in prewar Czechoslovakia, is very well researched. The data seem to bear out his thesis best in the case of the Hungarian ethnic minority. Here, the correlation between what Burks calls Magyarism (the consciousness of being a Hungarian-speaking inhabitant of a territory that in the past belonged to Hungary) and the Communist vote is almost perfect. The

TABLE 1

COMMUNIST VOTE IN SELECTED DISTRICTS DURING THE LAST THREE GENERAL
ELECTIONS IN PREWAR CZECHOSLOVAKIA
(Elections in which the CPCS ran a separate ballot)

District	Dominant or Significant Ethnic Element	Communist Vote (% of Total Vote) Election Year		
		1925	1929	1935
Banská Bystrica	Slovak	11.0	7.6	11.7
Brno	Czech/German	13.8	9.8	8.9
České Budějovice	Czech/German	8.6	4.4	3.2
Hradec Králové	Czech	8.4	6.2	6.4
Jihlava	German	9.4	6.9	5.0
Karlovy Vary	German	9.4	12.0	5.9
Košice	Hungarian/Slovak	20.9	15.6	17.8
Liptovský S. Mikuláš	Slovak	1.4	7.9	16.3
Mladá Boleslav	Czech	15.4	12.8	10.2
Moravská Ostrava	Czech	12.4	10.1	11.4
Olomouc	Czech	7.0	6.5	6.3
Pardubice	Czech	8.8	6.0	6.6
Plzeň	Czech	5.2	4.4	3.2
Praha	Czech	15.5	11.4	12.9
Prešov	Slovak	6.2	4.6	7.4
Trnava	Slovak	13.7	11.3	12.2
Turčiansky S. Martin	Slovak	9.5	6.2	7.8
Užhorod	Ruthenian	31.2	15.2	25.6
OVERALL NATIONAL COMMUNIST VOTE		13.2	10.2	10.3

theory does not appear to work so well for other minorities, especially
ethnic Germans. Burks is aware of this difficulty, which he explains by
the existence of alternative channels of discontent that were open to the
German ethnic group, namely the radical nationalist parties and movements. On the other hand, he also attributes minority status to the
Ruthenian population, and claims that the Slovaks perceived their
political role in Czechoslovakia as that of an underprivileged ethnic
group. These assumptions should explain the large Communist following in districts with Slovak or Ruthenian majorities.

The merit of Burks's analysis, among others, is that it destroys the
myth that the Czechoslovak coup d'état and various other forms of
Communist take-over in Central and Eastern Europe were examples of
socialist revolution carried out by a class-conscious industrial proletariat.
Nevertheless, his alternative solution raises two problems. It is difficult to
accept his assertion that the Slovaks and the Ruthenians in the First Republic belonged, or even believed that they belonged, to the same category of population as the other, non-Slav ethnic groups. It is still more
difficult to explain why, if Burks's theory is correct and a Communist

vote expresses the dissatisfaction of minorities in a political order they do not consider legitimate, the German nationalist parties of the right could deflect the Communist vote to their benefit while the Hungarian right, equally articulate, could not. This paradox was particularly striking during the first two general elections, in 1925 and 1929, when there was no influence, let alone interference, from the German Weimar Republic.

As for the self-perception of the Slovak political elites and their relation to the Czechoslovak state, these were rather complex matters. The attitude of the Slovaks to the Czechs included everything from rivalry and the will to assert their own ethnic personality vis-à-vis a numerically much stronger but culturally very closely related partner with whom they had earlier shared a written language and literature, to a complete identification with the theory of Czechoslovakia as one nation with two ethnic branches that had inspired the constitution of 1920. However, in contrast to the position often taken by non-Czech and non-Slovak ethnic leaders, the occasionally critical views of Slovak politicians could under no circumstances be interpreted as the rejection of the national emancipation movement of 1918. Slovaks of all parties and beliefs were virtually unanimous in their resistance to the assimilation pressures that they had experienced especially during the last decades of the Austro-Hungarian regime, and in their concern about possible territorial aspirations of postwar Hungary. They considered the outcome of the First World War fortunate from the viewpoint of their national interests—a radically different stance from that taken by the German or the Hungarian minority. Thus they saw themselves as a nation-building people (or, to use an untranslatable but very precise German term, a "Staatsvolk"), although they maintained some reservations about the institutional forms their nation-building role was to take.

The Ruthenians had a different perspective but they shared Slovak apprehensions about eventual Hungarian claims on former Hungarian territories, which would have affected Ruthenia even more than Slovakia. Their relations with the Czechs were fundamentally positive, and perhaps less complicated than those of the Slovaks. The "big brother" was geographically remote, and there was less danger of being absorbed into his cultural orbit, since the two languages, Czech and Ruthenian, were distinctly different. They also viewed the Czechoslovak Republic as the historical savior of Ruthenia from Magyarization. The Ruthenian leaders might have differed over the best political solution for Ruthenia, but hardly anyone considered the disintegration of Czechoslovakia to be a condition of such a solution. In their own way, the Ruthenians also felt that they belonged to the nation-building "group" of the Czechoslovak Republic.

The application of Burks's theory is even more problematic in the case of the largest and the most important ethnic minority, indeed the critical minority that in the end broke up the Czechoslovak state: the German-speaking group. The electoral records from the districts populated by ethnic Germans show that the Communist party enjoyed only moderate success in 1925, and fared even worse in the later elections. We have seen that Burks attributes communism's lack of appeal to the German ethnic voter to the availability of a substitute platform for the expression of discontent, the nationalist German political parties. The difficulty here is twofold. First, the radical nationalist party, the Sudetendeutsche Partei, which absorbed not only a significant part of the potential Communist vote but also a lion's share of the electoral support previously given to middle class and peasant parties, emerged only toward the end of the First Republic. Yet in the border areas of Bohemia, Moravia, and Silesia, the Communists never achieved anything comparable to their success in Slovakia and Ruthenia, not even in the elections of 1925 and 1929. Second, and in even greater contradiction to Burks's hypothesis, the great defeat that the Communist party suffered in 1929 did not benefit any of the nationalistic parties of the right in the German-speaking regions but the German Social Democratic party in Czechoslovakia, a political denomination that explicitly recognized the legitimacy of the Czechoslovak Republic and proved its commitment to this republic in the most convincing way during the Munich crisis of 1938. In light of these facts, the Communist vote, at least among the German-speaking population in Czechoslovakia, cannot be seen as merely expressing the frustrations of a subject ethnic group.

The Pattern of the Communist Vote and the Theory of Cleavages

Burks's valuable insight—that communism in Czechoslovakia did not draw its strength primarily from the economic contradictions of a mature industrial society, but instead exemplified a phenomenon observable at several places along the "soft periphery" of Central and Eastern Europe—could be usefully developed in combination with other established sociological theories. Perhaps the most appropriate tool of analysis in this context would be the Lipset/Rokkan concept that political parties respond to various social cleavages.[30] A social cleavage in this context is a disagreement between social groups about values, desirable goals, or interests, strong and permanent enough to create conflicting fronts in society; this disagreement may be due to class or ethnic background, religious affiliation, or differences in occupation or in geographical location. The more general question to ask would be to which of the groups separated by the various cleavages in the Czechoslovak society has the Communist party "catered"?

The answer cannot be a simple one. Lipset and Rokkan themselves caution that not only may the same party satisfy more than one group, but that a party need not cater to the same group all the time; significant political, social, or economic changes may produce situations in which a party may no longer respond to the cleavage that originally provided its main base of recruitment, and a shift in alignment may result. In the case of the CPCS, additional complications are present. As I argued earlier, it would be difficult to speak of one homogeneous Czechoslovak society in the first years after World War I, which were precisely the formative years of the Czechoslovak Communist movement. At that time several societies and cultures, divided along ethnic lines, existed side by side. In applying the Lipset/Rokkan theorem, we must therefore be aware not only of the cleavages resulting from the objective level of development of the entire country, but also of the ethnic diversity that adds another dimension to the existing pattern of cleavages.

A historical accident further complicates the task of the analyst seeking to link the appeal of the CPCS to the system of cleavages in Czechoslovak society, especially in the initial phase of the development of the party organization. Although the party did not run as an independent election group until 1925, the years prior to 1925 were nevertheless crucial for the Communist movement. It would be very hard to identify today the social components that could have supported the Communist cause before 1925. Considering the magnitude and frequency of upheavals within the party during the first five years of its existence, we might well suspect that pro-Communist sympathies in the population shifted as these upheavals occurred.

What, then, could the Lipset/Rokkan model contribute to our understanding of the strength of the Czechoslovak Communist party? According to Lipset and Rokkan, the original—and consequently the deepest, almost subconscious—cleavages in most European nations have resulted from two kinds of revolution: national and industrial. These two polarized every society along two axes: geographic (opposing the interests of the periphery to those of the center) and economic (pitting the interests of the rural elites against those of the industrializing and modernizing elites). The geographic cleavage can further be broken down into: (1) the tension between the nation-building segments of the population and the so-called subject populations on the periphery who may, but more often do not, accept the new definition of the political situation by the nation-building group; and (2) the tension between the claim of the newly emerging nation-state to authority over the formulation of the basic principles of social life that will become the basis of the consensus among the citizenry and the traditional monopoly over such "ultimate truths" of the centers and agencies, chiefly the churches, that held such power prior to the national revolution. The cleavage engendered by the industrial revolution, on the other hand, can also be subdivided into: (1) the conflict of interests between the agricultural producers and the industrial entrepreneurs; and (2) the conflict between employers and labor. The employer/labor conflict would seem to be the most important for our analysis. Nevertheless, for a complete understanding of the relevance of the Lipset/Rokkan hypothesis to the CPCS, a brief sketch of the pattern of cleavages prevailing in Czechoslovakia in the early years of the party's existence appears indispensable.

In terms of the Lipset/Rokkan theory, every social and political mobilization attendant upon the process of nation-building—that forceful redefinition of the political situation and of the objects of solidarity and allegiance—is followed by a countermobilization of the peripheral elements, which are often distinguished from the nation-building group by different ethnic origins. The two processes of mobilization and countermobilization, masterfully presented by K. W. Deutsch, determine not only the depth of the cleavage between center and periphery, but also the success or failure of the attempt at nation-building.[31] In the case of Czechoslovakia, the cleavage pattern, as it existed between the two wars, was the result of two waves of mobilization and countermobilization. The first wave came with the early phase of industrialization, beginning at the close of the Napoleonic wars. It affected all the western and northwestern parts of the Hapsburg empire, but it was most keenly felt in Bohemia, Moravia, and Silesia, where most of the industrial assets were invested. The early industrialization effort had gained momentum by the end of the 1840s: by then the industrial proletariat had begun to represent a statistically significant percentage of the population. The political movements of 1848, including the unsuccessful revolution in Vienna and an abortive uprising in Prague, for the first time involved the industrial working class in politics.

The stormy year 1848 was also the watershed between the wave of mobilization and that of periphery-originated countermobilization. The border regions of Bohemia and Moravia, inhabited predominantly by a German-speaking population, were industrialized faster than the interiors of the two provinces, in which the Czech-speaking population prevailed. At the same time, most of the capital that was invested in the Czech-speaking regions was controlled by German-speaking owners; a Czech capitalist class began to emerge only after the collapse in 1860 of the Austrian political absolutism. For a Czech worker employed in the German-speaking regions of Austria, social mobilization represented a challenge to his ethnic identity. Although the class consciousness of industrial workers at first favored the constitution of multi-ethnic labor organizations and socialist parties, ethnic divisions eventually proved stronger than class loyalties. The countermobilization of the non-German majorities in Bohemia, Moravia, and Silesia split the social structure to its core. In Austria, during the last seventy years of its existence, the classical pattern of economic cleavages was crosscut by the ethnic dimension. The owner-worker cleavage, crucial for the development of the socialist movement, was no exception to this rule. Only briefly was Austrian socialism able to present itself to the world as a unified supra-ethnic force. It soon had to compromise with the forces that in the end disrupted the whole Hapsburg empire.

In terms of the Lipset/Rokkan theory, the Austro-Hungarian nation-building attempt failed because the countermobilization could not be contained. The unsuccessful attempt nevertheless left a legacy of cleavages to all the successor nations. Czechoslovakia was particularly deeply marked by this legacy, because among the multi-ethnic polities erected on the ruins of the Hapsburg monarchy it was the most developed country. In 1918, up to 90 percent of the various sectors of industrial production in Austria-Hungary were located on the territory of the future Czechoslovak Republic. With the constitution of Czechoslovakia, a new process of mobilization and countermobilization was started, this time with the roles of the ethnic groups almost completely reversed. Now the Czechs and the Slovaks became the nation-building groups. The success of their enterprise depended on how much consensus they could build among the remaining ethnic elements over the definition of the new political situation. This proved to be an extremely difficult task, that was further complicated by the delicate and at times equivocal relationship between the two nation-building elites. The ethnic components that in the old Austria-Hungary had been the nation builders, the Germans and the Hungarians, found themselves in the situation of the subjected populations; in any case, this was their perception of the situation, despite the radically liberal constitution of the Czechoslovak Republic and a highly progressive system of protection of the minorities in this state. The center-periphery cleavage, too, was now geographically reversed: instead of leading to Vienna and Budapest, the vital links of communication led to Prague. Also, the southeastern regions of the new state, Slovakia and Ruthenia, which in the old Hungarian setting had measured up to the overall level of national development, dropped to the rank of underdeveloped areas compared with the advanced Czech core. This change opened a new cleavage between the interests of the agricultural way of life and mode of production on the one hand and the needs and requirements of the industrial sector on the other.

These were the consequences, in terms of the system of cleavages, of the national emancipation and the attainment of statehood by the Czechs and the Slovaks. The political party system of the First Republic on the whole faithfully reflected this new pattern of cleavages. The two most developed ethnic groups, the Czechs and the Germans, could choose among parties that, taken together, represented all the antagonisms typical of industrial societies and were separately organized for each group. By contrast, the spectrum of political parties organizing the less developed and less differentiated ethnic components was simpler; even there, however, we find a complete set of voting options for each ethnic minority. Thus in Bohemia, Moravia, and Silesia the Czechoslovak Agrarian and Smallholder party and the National Democratic party each represented one pole of the countryside-city continuum. Among the German-speaking electorate their counterparts were the Peasant Union (Bund der Landwirte) and the German National party (Die Deutschnationale Partei). In the eastern part of Czechoslovakia, the Agrarian and Smallholder party also organized the Slovak liberal peasantry, who were mainly of Protestant faith, but the Czech National Democratic party did not run in Slovakia, and the middle and upper-middle Slovak classes voted for the rather conservative National party (Narodniari) instead.

There were also a Hungarian Peasant party and a Hungarian National party. Opposition to the secularizing influence of the state was, in the Czech districts, expressed by a vote for the People's party (Československá strana lidová), which was Catholic in inspiration, and the German Social Christian party (Deutsche Christlich Demokratische und Soziale Partei) benefited from the corresponding cleavage among the German-speaking population. In Slovakia, this secular-religious cleavage was among the most critical divisions. The party based on the clerical protest against modern secularism, the Slovak Popular party of Andrej Hlinka (Hlinkova slovenská strana ľudová), later became the home of the most radical right opponents of the idea of the Czechoslovak Republic. The Hungarian variant of the Catholic parties, the Hungarian Christian Social party, on the other hand, was a moderate and, for Hungarian conditions, a rather progressive political group. The role of the liberal-radical movement in promoting emancipation from church influences was in the Czech provinces played by the National Socialist party, although historically the party did not have its origins in the anticlerical, lay movement, but had come into existence as a nationalistic splinter of the Czecho-Slav Social Democratic party. Among the German-speaking element, the earlier Deutsch-liberal (German Liberal) current survived in the form of the National Liberal party. In Slovakia, there had never been a distinct secular party before the war (this function had sometimes been filled by the National party), but most of the anticlerical voters usually supported the socialist left. A similar situation prevailed among the Hungarian minority. There were a number of smaller parties on the Czech, German, Slovak, and Hungarian sides that need not be listed here since they accommodated only a fraction of the electorate organized and voting with the major parties. In the eastern-most province, Ruthenia, the situation after the First World War was comparable to that found in many developing countries today: there was a highly mobile population in search of its political identity, whose elites had been brought up and formed in completely different cultures. There were no separate Ruthenian or Ukrainian parties in the strict sense of the term, but most Czech, Slovak, and Hungarian parties vied there for the support of both the Ruthenian and the Hungarian-speaking electorates. The only local political organizations were those of the Ukrainian nationalists, whose importance in the early years of the republic was not very great.

The employer-worker cleavage generated the Social Democratic parties that in Czechoslovakia had formed an independent organization for each ethnic group. In the Czech case, we can count two such organizations if we consider socialist the National Socialist party that had seceded from the Social Democracy in 1908; since then it had been many things to many people. As we have seen, the postwar split in the Social Democratic movement led to the constitution of radical wings in all ethnic chapters of this movement, and these groups eventually merged into a unitary Communist Party of Czechoslovakia.

However, the crucial question still remains to be answered: Which groups separated by this new system of cleavages did the CPCS "cater to," in terms of the general election results of 1925? We have already recognized the cogency of Burks's view that the Communist success could not be attributed, even in the main, to the intensity of the classical cleavage generated by the industrial revolution—the employer-worker conflict of interests. We have also seen that neither is it possible to accept without qualification the hypothesis that the strength of the Communist following in Czechoslovakia was due mainly to the frustration of nationalist feelings and aspirations of ethnic minorities. The voting pattern of the largest minority, the German, does not permit such an interpretation. If we again look closely at the vote cast in 1925, broken down by regions (see Table 1), we find that the Communist-voting electorate was situated, above all, in the underdeveloped areas of the country. This may in itself explain why Communist gains among the German-speaking population were rather modest. The German ethnic group did share with the Hungarian minority the feeling that it was a "dispossessed heir to power," but it did not see itself as an underdeveloped society facing the challenges of a more developed center. It appears that only where disaffection arising out of the loss of political privilege was coupled with a perception of the social costs of economic development and of the general ordeal of change—that is, where the conflict between the nation-building and the subjected population overlapped the industrial-agricultural and the owner-employee cleavages—did strong Communist alignment follow. The last two of the three cleavages seem to be even more important for the Communist vote than the first. This could also explain the strong pro-Communist mood of the electorates in predominantly Slovak-speaking and Ruthenian-speaking districts of the two eastern provinces, which were among the least developed districts. In other words, the statistics of the 1925 elections tend to identify Communist suffrage as a protest vote of the disaffected: segments of the population caught in the turmoil of social change, rejecting the claim to legitimacy of the political order or having an unclear perception of their political role. The subsequent general elections, as well as those held at the local municipal levels, during the First Republic appear to confirm this proposition.

The Power Struggle in the Kremlin and Trotskyism in Czechoslovakia

In 1925 the CPCS leadership failed to read the message of the Communist vote correctly because it was either unable or unwilling to do so (which, considering its dogmatic obstinacy, might have been the same thing). As for the implications of the election results for national politics, the party felt the strength now acquired by the three socialist parties called for common action, in agreement with the Komintern principle of the united front. The conditions stipulated by the Third International, however, did not leave much room for such action. The Central Committee, strongly influenced by the left wing and anxious to abide by the Komintern's instructions, therefore responded to the Social Democratic proposal to establish a socialist government with so many qualifications and restrictions that its reply amounted to a refusal. This position was then confirmed by the party chairman, Josef Haken, before the Parliament on December 6, 1925. The guiding hand of Moscow began to show; after the Third Congress the CPCS manifested much less willingness to participate "in the constitutional game."

In the first days and weeks of 1926, two important meetings of Communist-sponsored mass organizations took place in Prague. The IAUA, which had been formed by the left splinters of the national trade unions, held its second congress on January 1 and 2. The delegates had to concede that in spite of its ambitious name, the IAUA remained a very loosely knit organization assembling but a fraction of the mass of Czechoslovak organized labor. The impotence of the party in relation to the unions was an additional cause of dissatisfaction for the Komintern. Simultaneously with the unions congress, the Communist-obedient left wing of the Social Democratic organization Workers Gymnastic Association (Dělnická Tělocvičná jednota or DTJ) held its extraordinary congress in the capital city. At this congress, the left wing merged with the Communist-sponsored Association for the Spartakist Scout Work, a radical splinter of the national Boy Scout organization, and with other two smaller Communist-oriented sports organizations to form a nationwide, supra-ethnic Federation of Proletarian Gymnastics (Federace pro-letářské tělovýchovy or FPT). Nobody could have suspected in January 1926 that the FPT, which appeared to be only a marginal satellite body, would later by a historical accident become involved in the most severe internal party crisis.

At the beginning of 1926, the unresolved conflicts within the CPCS were further aggravated by the repercussions of the power struggle then unfolding in the Kremlin between Joseph Stalin and his rivals on the left. At the National Party Conference in Prague on January 19, 1926, Bohumír Šmeral, in his capacity as member of the Central Committee and delegate to the Fourteenth Congress of the Bolshevik party, reported on the background of the dispute between Stalin and Zinoviev and his associates. The latter were identified as the Leningrad Opposition because of their party background and their most important stronghold, but soon the official party media began to refer to them as Trotskyists, although in 1926 Trotsky had not yet openly formulated his criticism of Stalin's policies and methods. The Leningrad Opposition rejected the line represented by Stalin that was gradually taking shape under the slogan Socialism in One Country. Stalin's line was based on a new analysis of the international situation that was radically different from that hitherto accepted by the Bolshevik party and the Third International; it seemed that the practical implications of this new analysis would also be very radical, both for the Soviet Union and for the international Communist movement. The concept of Socialism in One Country was built on the obviously correct premise that since the middle of the 1920s all chances of a European continental or even world proletarian revo-lution, if they had ever existed, had been reduced to zero. In these circumstances, the primary task of all Communists was seen to lie in preserving and consolidating the only major power base thus far conquered, the Soviet Union. Zinoviev, Leo Kamenev, and a number of other influential leaders objected to this line not so much because of a different assessment of the prospects for a universal revolution—even they saw that the revolutionary wave of the first postwar years was rapidly ebbing—but because they believed that the Soviet Union could not survive isolated, in a capitalist encirclement. Spreading revolution in their eyes meant saving the Bolshevik regime in Russia. Leon Trotsky later became the most prominent spokesman of this group: hence the label Trotskyism. The apprehensions of the Leningrad Opposition might have been exaggerated—history, as we know, confirmed Stalin's view in this matter—but they were probably due to the still-recent experience of the various interventionist attempts of the Western powers in the civil war.

Inevitably, each of the two conflicting theories assigned a different role to the Third International and to its individual national sections. The importance the partisans of Socialism in One Country attributed to the Komintern in terms of future Communist strategy was considerably less than that foreseen by the proponents of the "export of revolution." As for the relations between the Moscow power center and the individual Communist parties, however, the position of the Socialism in One Country group, especially as it was later implemented by Stalin, was not logically consistent with the first stance. An observer in 1926, not knowing the real nature of Stalin's seemingly more pragmatic line, would probably not have hesitated to predict that these policies would result in more respect for the specific needs of the various national movements and thus leave to the individual Communist parties a greater measure of autonomy. Almost the opposite turned out to be the case. Socialism in One Country became part and parcel of the doctrine known as Stalinism, which eventually achieved a degree of power concentration as yet unsurpassed and led to the establishment of a monolithic totalitarian world empire. In this process there was no room for national or local idiosyncrasies. The Komintern, which had originally been conceived, at least theoretically, as the supreme organ of the world Communist movement in which all sections were to be equal, changed in Stalin's hands into a malleable tool of the domestic and international politics of the Soviet Union. The dependence of the individual member parties on Moscow, far from diminishing, became almost total. If, before the victory of the principle of Socialism in One Country, national Communist organizations could be criticized as remotely controlled by the Komintern, after Stalin's triumph it was possible to assert that both the Komintern and its twenty-odd sections were subject to a much more efficient remote control from the central Secretariat of the Communist Party of the Soviet Union (CPSU).

The polarization of views on the most adequate policy line in the changing international situation also produced new realignments in the CPCS. Already at an early stage of the confrontation in the USSR, initiated leaders were aware of the actual choices the two contending approaches offered to the national parties. This awareness elicited sympathies and allegiances that at the time might have been unexpected.

Official Czechoslovak Communist historiography, for example, has claimed that Trotskyism, a term applied to the whole left opposition in the Soviet party since 1925, was but "an ideological outgrowth of Social Democracy."[32] Ironically, although Communist historians have often claimed that Social Democracy was the archvillain of the Socialist world, there was a grain of truth in this otherwise farfetched statement. Many an advocate of more independent policies in the CPCS, faced with the choice between Stalin and the Leningrad Opposition, opted for the weaker and less dangerous—in this case the radical left alternative. Thus, positions associated in the official party jargon with "Social Democratic anachronisms" formed curious alliances with left extremism. Naturally, not all of Zinoviev's and Kamenev's sympathizers, and later Trotsky's, were recruited from the right wing of the Czechoslovak Communist party. Many joined Trotsky because they unreservedly subscribed to his thesis of the priority of world revolution over all considerations of the national interests of the Soviet Union and of the working class in the capitalist countries. Indeed, these elements, however confused, eventually prevailed in the Fourth International founded by Trotsky. Nevertheless, since Trotsky for a very long time remained the only truly outstanding Communist personality defying Stalin, his platform also became the refuge of anti-Stalinist opposition of all possible colors and shades.

Czechoslovakia has known its own version of the world revolutionary, or Trotskyist, ideology. Emerging from the discussions in a circle of Communist intellectuals led by Professor J. Pollak, it was a very radical variant of the early Komintern thesis of the necessity of bringing about a world proletarian uprising to save the achievements of the Bolshevik October Revolution. The new version advocated an aggressive war by the Soviet Union to prevent the international consolidation of social conditions that, according to the authors of the theory, could only benefit the reactionary status-quo forces. A war, on the other hand, even if lost by the Soviet Union, would inevitably revolutionize the masses and accomplish what the First World War only showed to be possible. It took some time, however, before these ideas crystallized and were made public.[33]

Trotskyism also found supporters among a number of key functionaries in the Czechoslovak party apparatus who belonged to the left opposition and on whom the Komintern had pinned its hopes for successful bolshevization and defeat of the Social Democratic resistance. These cadres had always pledged their loyalty to the international headquarters: for this loyalty they had often been criticized by the more independent-minded and domestic-minded activists. The very same concern for independence and the well-being of the working class, however, caused those activists ultimately to prefer the internationalists of the Komintern to the dictator Stalin. In this way, radically different points of view led to very similar concrete options. By an additional whim of history, those who initially had been branded by their comrades as agents of Moscow and promoters of foreign interference in Czechoslovak affairs in the end became victims of the power with which they had been associated.

In the forefront of the struggle triggered in the CPCS by the conflict between Stalin and the Leningrad Opposition stood one of the main leaders of the German ethnic component, Alois Neurath. In 1926, Neurath held important positions in the party Secretariat and in the Politbureau, and was a full member of the Executive Committee of the Komintern. In the last capacity, he participated in the Sixth Enlarged Plenary Session of the Komintern in Moscow from February 17 through March 15, 1926, where he openly supported Zinoviev and Kamenev against Stalin. He continued to side with the Leningrad Opposition after his return to Czechoslovakia, and sought to convert other leading Communists to his views, despite the fact that the party had already made the opposite choice and endorsed Stalin's line. Neurath's stand reopened the issue, dividing the leadership anew. The party now was left with a choice between disavowing Neurath publicly or remaining silent, which would have been tantamount to approving his position. The conflict in the Bolshevik party thus became a prominent point on the agenda of three plenary meetings of the Central Committee on March 22, May 8, and June 7, 1926. In the end, the CPCS reiterated its pro-Stalin stance. This should have been a warning to Neurath, but he did not seem to heed it, and was explicitly reprimanded at the subsequent meeting of the party top organ on August 21. Later, when it became known that Neurath was continuing to propagate his Trotskyist views through the channels of the regional party organization in Liberec, the Politbureau on October 8, 1926, relieved him of all his party functions; the Central Committee concurred in this punitive measure, which then was applied against a number of other prominent left deviationists in the party apparatus all over the country.

With the first round of the struggle against Trotskyism duly completed, the CPCS might have hoped that it had restored the confidence of the power holders in Moscow. Unfortunately for Haken and Jílek, this was not the case. Stalin, who was now emerging in an unchallenged position of control both in the Bolshevik party and in the Komintern, saw the Trotskyist deviation of Neurath and his associates only as an episode, however deplorable, in the Czechoslovak party's development. The problem with which he was concerned in all Communist parties was that of bolshevization. In the case of the CPCS this meant what Moscow in the 1925 resolution had called "overcoming the remnants of Social Democratic opportunism." The left majority that had been seated in the party's governing bodies by the Third Congress in 1925 had supposedly been charged with this task, but the trust invested in the left by the international power center was now on the wane. Not only did the left prove to have Trotskyist sympathies; it was also increasingly evident that the notion of Social Democratic heritage was understood in two different ways in Prague and in Moscow.

Difficulties in achieving bolshevization were experienced by all of the various sections of the Third International. That was why the Extended Plenary Sessions of the Executive Committee of the Komintern in February 1926 (the Sixth Plenum) and in November of the same year (the Seventh Plenum) had to relaunch the original appeal of the World Congress. The Kremlin's insistence, even after the triumph of Stalin's concept of Socialism in One Country, on bolshevization, which had initially been associated with the theory of an imminent world proletarian revolution, added further confusion among the rank-and-file membership. The grass-roots party units everywhere, including Czechoslovakia, found it incomprehensible that cells—organizations suitable to the conditions of czarist Russia—instead of the usual enterprise units should be set up now that the thesis of impending universal revolution had been abandoned. They, of course, misunderstood the real significance of the bolshevization drive. They failed to see that bolshevization was a key element in the master plan for the final subjection of the entire world Communist movement to the will and the interests of the Soviet Union. Socialism in One Country in this context required one type of organization for all national Communist parties so that these could be better controlled from one center: twenty years later, for the same purpose—better control by the Soviet Union—the same doctrine of the same Kremlin leader meant blind imitation of the Soviet socioeconomic institutions by all people's democracies in Central and Eastern Europe. Nevertheless, even though the leading cadres of the CPCS in 1926 did not, and often could not, anticipate these consequences, they showed great reluctance, on the whole, to follow the call for bolshevization. It took one more mighty shake-up before men could be put in control who were willing to transform the Czechoslovak party into a docile tool of Stalin's policies.

The Fourth Party Congress

At the time of the Trotskyist crisis, the final showdown in the CPCS was still three years away. Thus not even the Fourth Ordinary Congress held in Prague March 25–28, 1927, could bring a resolution of the protracted disagreement between Moscow and the Czechoslovak Communists. The issue of bolshevization loomed large at the congress, but three other major problems preoccupied the delegates. These were: the international situation in general and the internal political situation in Czechoslovakia in particular, in the context of the development of world capitalism; the problems of Czechoslovak agriculture and the opportunities available to the CPCS for political work in the rural countryside; and the perennial complex and delicate problem of the relations between the party and the trade unions. The Fourth Congress assembled 130 voting delegates and 143 delegates with consultatory status. Membership statistics were more encouraging than at the previous congress: for the first time the party could report an increase instead of a decrease. There were 138,000 registered dues-paying members, about 40 percent more than in 1925. In addition to the organizational report submitted by Secretary-General Jílek, there were three substantive presentations on the agenda: party chairman Josef Haken spoke about the general political situation and the resulting tasks to be accomplished by the party; the problems of agriculture and party work among the peasantry and the rural proletariat were treated by Václav Bolen; and the thorny issue of the party's relation to the recalcitrant Red Unions was discussed by Antonín Zápotocký.[34] From today's perspective it seems paradoxical that at the Fourth Congress Zápotocký was viewed with criticism, if not with mistrust by the party left because of his alleged Social Democratic opportunism, for Zápotocký was the only major leader to survive politically the bolshevization crisis: many of his leftist critics were among its casualties.

The discussion of the international and the internal situation at the Fourth Congress revealed a shift away from realism, as a result of the increased influence of the left faction. The analyses of the state of the Czechoslovak economy and of the development of world capitalism were in sharp contradiction to objective data. It was argued that Czechoslovak capitalism was in a deep crisis, whereas in reality 1927 and the two subsequent years marked the peak of postwar prosperity. Moreover, the finding, correct in itself, that the influence of finance capital in Czechoslovakia was growing at an exceptionally fast rate was taken as a point of departure for the preposterous conclusion that Czechoslovak capitalists, under the dictate of the big banks, were out for the conquest of Eastern European markets, which were then supplied by the Soviet Union, and were therefore pressing, in collusion with British and French monopoly capitalists, for a new preventive war against the USSR. Speakers at the congress engaged in lengthy speculations about whether in the case of an "imperialist attack upon the first nation of workers and peasants" Czechoslovakia would directly participate in such a venture or whether the specific economic interests of the Czechoslovak bourgeoisie, for example, the prospects of capturing Soviet markets, would instead dictate a position of neutrality.[35] Later, when the party crisis reached its climax, the proponents of some of these views were called opportunistic.

In the assessment of the domestic political situation, a similar avoidance of the facts prevailed. The leadership presented the view that the Czechoslovak Republic was rapidly changing from a formal (constitutional) bourgeois democracy into an undisguised fascist dictatorship that would wipe out every vestige of civil rights and liberties. Opinion was also divided on this issue, however. A nonnegligible proportion of the top cadres refused to recognize any real fascist danger; they pointed to the marginal role played in Czechoslovak political life by the Czech National Fascist Community, a sect rather than a party, and by other organizations of the extreme right. The proponents of the thesis of progressive fascistization, however, argued that current events would not culminate in a right extremist coup d'etat, but that the liberal bourgeoisie itself would resort to authoritarian methods once it came to the conclusion that the revolutionary movement of the proletariat could not be contained by constitutional means. All these farfetched theories echoed ideas prevailing at that point among the leaders of the Third International, regardless of their Trotskyist or Stalinist allegiances. As a matter of fact, there was little difference between the advocates of a world revolution and the partisans of the principle of Socialism in One

Country in their evaluation of the situations of the individual Communist parties.

The problem of the party's work among the rural strata of the Czechoslovak population was approached with no more realism than international or internal political questions. The line adopted here was one of systematic belittling of the importance of the Czechoslovak land reforms concluded in 1924. Extreme dogmatism in assessing the development of Czechoslovak agriculture, which led to the most fantastic propositions, cost the party any chance of taking more solid root among the progressive and reform-oriented peasantry. Like most Communist parties, the CPCS showed a peculiar inability to understand the rural facts of life. This might have had its origin either in a general theoretical weakness of Marxism or in the absence, characteristic of Marxism, of any specific theory concerning the agricultural segment of society. Not unlike their masters, the disciples of Marx and Engels in the Western world in the first half of the twentieth century lacked a concept that could serve as a basis for a workable policy on rural populations. Marxism, in both its classical and Leninist versions, implicitly defined agriculture as a backward sector of industrial societies, that was destined to disappear in the wake of the great blurring of differences in the coming socialist order. It has always seemed to be insensitive to the fact that whereas industrial activity is mainly an occupation, agriculture is also a way of life. Later revisions of Marxism and Leninism filled in this gap, but in the second half of the 1920s these new theories were not yet in sight. The Czechoslovak party, and all other European parties, were then rather embarrassed by the problems posed by a revolutionary movement that would have included the rural proletariat. All this might have appeared absurd in view of the circumstance that the CPCS in the First Republic owed the bulk of its electoral support to the voters in the underdeveloped agricultural areas, especially those inhabited by ethnic minorities.

The third timely issue discussed at the Fourth Congress was the relation between the Communist party and the Communist-sponsored Red Unions. The delegates had to acknowledge that there had not been much improvement since the previous congress. The activities of the party and the work of the Red Unions could not be successfully coordinated as the principles established by the Komintern had required. The failure of the attempts at controlling the unions has been blamed by official Communist historians on the "much more powerful influence of

Social Democratic opportunism in the labor movement than in the communist party proper." In reality, the poor show of the Communists in the trade unions goes back to another Marxist theoretical blind spot: an indifference, if not hostility, to the idea and the goals of workers' interest groups. The CPCS, oriented like most Communist parties towards an ever more remote goal of universal revolution, had little use for the daily efforts of the unions at improving the condition of the proletariat in the here and now. In the eyes of the Communists, the unions, and for that matter all mass organizations, were but tools of the craft they practiced best, the seizure of power. Therefore the coexistence of the party with the union movement could hardly be peaceful. Additional complications arose from the never-ending criticism and pressure by the Komintern, which found the record of the CPCS in union work very unsatisfactory and insisted on the implementation of its own directives concerning unions. This resulted in further deterioration of the party's image among the Red Union leaders; the party was perceived not only as indifferent to the fate of the Czechoslovak working class, but also as an agent of a foreign power willing to sacrifice to that power the interests of the union membership. These basically incompatible viewpoints produced a stalemate in the efforts at cooperation between the two partners, a problem the Fourth Congress could do little to resolve beyond restating the party's and the Komintern's positions on the issue.

Nor were the changes in the leading functions and in the composition of the Central Committee, carried out by the congress, of great significance. Since the Third Ordinary Congress in 1925 had created a left majority in the party's leadership, the relative strengths of the individual factions remained basically unchanged after the Fourth Congress adjourned. Inevitably, uncertainty about the party's future line and Moscow's apprehensions about this situation, also remained unchanged.

Shortly after the Fourth Ordinary Congress, a domestic political episode further strained the relations between the CPCS and the Third International. In May 1927, presidential elections were due in Czechoslovakia. In an earlier decision, taken prior to the Fourth Congress, the party had nominated its own candidate to run against the incumbent, Thomas G. Masaryk. Three weeks before the elections, however, the conservative National Democratic party announced that it would introduce its most prominent leader, Dr. Karel Kramář, into the presidential race. Dr. Kramář had acquired a nationwide reputation during the national struggles in the Austrian Parliament. During the war he had been condemned to death for high treason, but had later been pardoned; this made him into a martyr for the Czech cause. It was generally assumed in May 1927 that Dr. Kramář's candidacy, because of his great popularity, had some real prospects of success, however strong the appeal of the president then in office. Many observers speculated that Kramář might be supported not only by the conservative right, but also by the center, where the Agrarian party held the largest number of seats both in the Parliament and in the Senate. In the constitution of 1920, the power to elect the president of the republic was vested in the two chambers of the National Assembly, which met for that purpose in a joint session. It was also considered to be likely that the Tradesmen and Middle Estate party, a medium-sized parliamentary faction, would vote for Dr. Kramář. The leaders of the Communist party felt that in this situation they had to abandon their principled opposition to the entire establishment and to support the lesser of the two evils. Consistent with its professed concern about an impending fascistization of Czechoslovakia, the party feared that to have a conservative elected as head of state would increase the chances that the Communist movement would be outlawed. At the plenary session of May 5, 1927, the Central Committee rescinded its original decision concerning the presidential elections, annulled the nomination of the CPCS senator Václav Šturc and advised all Communist deputies to vote for T. G. Masaryk.

This move, which indicated that even with a left majority the party was occasionally capable of a more pragmatic approach to politics, provoked great consternation in Moscow. The international Communist headquarters considered it an unpardonable mistake on two counts. First, the party had taken sides in what the official Communist doctrine called "the bourgeois constitutional game"—a move the Komintern viewed as sheer opportunism. Second, and much more serious in the eyes of the Kremlin, the CPCS had given its backing not to just any bourgeois or reformist politician, but to Thomas Masaryk, one of the statesmen most hated by the Bolsheviks because of his eclectic and pseudo-progressive position on Marxism and his role in the Siberian anabasis of the Czechoslovak Legion during the Russian civil war. The Executive Committee of the Komintern dealt with the case almost immediately and instructed the CPCS by cable to revoke its decision of May 5. The Central Committee complied with the order on May 10. In fact, the position of the party proved to be of no consequence for the outcome of the presidential elections; even without Communist support Masaryk won practically unopposed. However, the abortive attempt at a more imaginative policy deepened the mistrust Moscow already felt toward the Czechoslovak leadership. It was probably on this occasion that the Soviet center realized the need to look for a new team to replace the left led by Jílek if unqualified obedience by the CPCS was to be assured. In a way, too, the Komintern's intervention in 1927 against the Czechoslovak party's support of Masaryk was a precursor of other, much cruder and more far-reaching cases of interference in internal Czechoslovak affairs that occurred after the Second World War—for example, in connection with the decision of the Czechoslovak coalition government, presided over by CPCS Chairman Klement Gottwald, to participate in the Marshall Plan. The stakes at that time were much higher, but the nature of the Soviet intrusion was the same.

Moscow's Allies in the Bolshevization Campaign

It was not easy to find a replacement for the Jílek left, which now had lost all credit with its erstwhile Moscow protectors. Nevertheless, soon after the Fourth Party Congress, the attention of the Komintern officials began to turn to a group of young activists in the CPCS apparatus who were rather vocal in their criticism of the indecision and opportunism of the leadership. The majority of these activists came from the local organization in the Prague industrial suburb of Karlín and had little formal education and still less political experience. Party members and functionaries of longer standing referred to them as the "lads from Karlín" (karlínský kluci); the nickname betrayed the low esteem in which their comrades held them. Nevertheless it was this group that was to eventually carry out the overdue bolshevization and that would remain in control until the end of Stalin's rule a quarter of a century later. Some of the names associated with the Karlín group later achieved notoriety—for example, Rudolf Slánský and his brother Richard—because of dramatic events in which they would be the main protagonists. In the second half of the 1920s, however, the lads from Karlín appeared to be little more than a gang of ambitious young men determined to take advantage of the protracted party crisis. They did not find a leading figure in their midst; this role finally fell to Klement Gottwald, an experienced party apparatchik who had been co-opted into the headquarters at the Third Ordinary Congress in 1925.

Moscow soon recognized in Gottwald and in the Karlín group a potential alternative to the Haken-Jílek leadership. The apparent inexperience and poor theoretical background of the prospective governing team did not much disturb anyone in the Kremlin. As of the summer of 1927, Moscow seemed to have made up its mind. It encouraged, implicitly and explicitly, the various factions in the CPCS to continue their collision course, and waited for the most propitious moment to bring about the ultimate showdown. There was abundant opportunity in 1927 to create embarrassing situations for the top party officials. The specter of Trotskyism had not yet been entirely exorcised; the relations between the party and the Red Unions left much to be desired; the problem of the representation of the interests of the various ethnic groups remained unresolved. One aspect of this last issue, the so-called Slovak question, became topical after the regional party conference in Žilina held in July 1926. At this conference, Slovak Communists called for organizational changes in the CPCS to satisfy the political and cultural aspirations of the Slovak ethnic group. In September 1927, another conference convened in Ružomberok in northwestern Slovakia endorsed earlier demands on the national leadership for the decentralization of the party structure. These demands were wrapped in more general revolutionary rhetoric, such as the slogan "Liberate Slovakia from the oppressive apparatus of the bourgeoisie!" but it was clear that the Slovak party elites expected the CPCS to set an example by first recognizing the rights of the Slovak group within the framework of its own organization. Klement Gottwald, familiar with the mood of the Slovak membership from his previous career in the Slovak party units, decided in 1927 to ride the waves of Slovak nationalism and separatism in the hope of promoting the interests of the "new left." Thus he took a stand that was in sharp contrast with the position he would defend as party head in the Czecho-Slovak dispute during and after the Second World War. The party itself got a foretaste of what was to grow into a major problem twenty years later and become one of the main causes of the collapse of the otherwise fairly resilient Czechoslovak brand of Stalinism.

The Haken-Jílek team was aware of the crisis situation. At the plenary session of the Central Committee on October 29 and 30, 1927, ultra-leftism, by which both Trotskyism and the revolt of the Karlín lads were to be understood, was declared a danger of the same magnitude as right opportunism. The new left, as opposed to the established left group of

Jílek, did not approve of this equation and protested loudly.[36] Before the end of the year, Trotskyism again appeared on the party's agenda. The CPCS headquarters received a complaint from the regional organization in Liberec about secessionist activities of Alois Neurath. In response to these charges, the party Secretariat summoned Neurath to a personal interview on November 30. Neurath was interrogated about his alleged contacts with left dissidents as well as right opportunists in the USSR. The outcome of the interview seems to have been inconclusive. On December 17, the Central Committee renewed its condemnation of Neurath's position on the conflict in the Soviet party, but it abstained from more energetic disciplinary measures against the accused.

Dissatisfaction with the work of the CPCS among the trade unions provided grounds, early in 1928, for the Komintern to intervene again in Czechoslovak matters. At the Ninth Plenum of the Executive Committee of the Communist International held in Moscow February 9–25, a special resolution concerning the Czechoslovak party was adopted, in which the party was exhorted to set up without delay a collective leadership in the IAUA that would assure the alignment of this body with the general policies of the Communist movement. This recommendation, when considered today, is not devoid of irony: the international Communist forum recommended collective leadership as a safe remedy for the ills of bad coordination precisely at the moment when the dramatic resolution of the Stalin-Trotsky dispute ended the experiment of collective leadership in the Kremlin and ushered in the era of the cult of personality, the personal dictatorship of Stalin. The criticism of the inadequacy of the Czechoslovak party in matters pertaining to trade unions was reinforced shortly afterwards by a similar evaluation made by the Third Congress of the International Federation of Proletarian Trade Unions (Profintern) in Moscow, held from March 17 through April 3, 1928.

The CPCS Central Committee dealt with the recommendations of the Komintern on March 26, 1928. The topicality of the union theme at that time was underscored by an ongoing strike in the soft-coal belt of northwestern Bohemia, near the town of Most. This strike, like most of the strike movements since the split in the socialist movement, was organized and led by the so-called reformist unions, which were affiliated with the Social Democratic party and controlled an overwhelming majority of industrial workers in Czechoslovakia. The Red Unions, whose autonomy in relation to the CPCS was in fact greater than the Communists were willing to admit, played only a marginal role in the labor disputes of that period. In the spring of 1928, the IAUA's record of activities was particularly discouraging. The Red Unions had lost a strike that they had launched among the textile workers in northern Bohemia in the fall of 1927. The strike had been called under the pressure of the left opposition, which then controlled the regional party organization in Liberec. In the miners' strike in the Most region, the Red Unions had to leave the initiative to their Social Democratic rivals. Individual actions undertaken by the IAUA during this strike, especially the attempts to organize what it called "a united front from below"—that is, to influence the members of the reformist trade unions and to turn them against their leadership, failed and only further impaired the situation of the striking workers. Thus the experience of practical application of the Komintern directives was not exactly vindicating. Nevertheless, the party endorsed the Komintern resolution and proceeded to set up a collective leadership in the IAUA. The most prominent Communist leader who subsequently acquired the key position in the Red Unions was Antonín Zápotocký, the former chief executive official of the party and the current secretary-general of the IAUA. His nomination did not meet with unqualified approval. The new left in particular mistrusted him. Moreover, the left wing of the preponderantly German-speaking regional party organization of Liberec lacked confidence in Zápotocký and subsequently claimed that opportunism flourished under his secretaryship as it had under that of his predecessor, Josef Hais. It was evident that the Red Unions, which the party considered to be its own domain, were in for further shake-ups, as the chronic internal crisis in the Czechoslovak Communist movement developed toward its final resolution.

The Failure of Red Day and the Sixth Komintern Congress

The immediate cause of the ultimate confrontation in the ideological and power conflict that had plagued the CPCS since 1922 was rather trivial. On the face of it, the victory of the bolshevization course and the eventual unlimited subjection of the Czechoslovak Communist movement to the interests of the Soviet Union seem to have been made possible by a one-time organizational blunder of the Jílek leadership. On April 27, 1928, the police president of Prague pronounced a ban on the second national Spartakiad, which the Communist-sponsored Federation of Proletarian Gymnastics (FPT) had scheduled for July that year. This rather ill-advised step of the center-right government of

Antonín Švehla, in which none of the socialist parties were represented, triggered a chain of events leading to a showdown between the contending factions in the Czechoslovak Communist party. The Communist leaders chose to brave the governmental ban and called a mass demonstration referred to as Red Day in Prague for the date on which the Spartakiad had originally been scheduled to open. Thus the authorities, who were concerned over what might have turned out to be a relatively harmless sports event with radical left undertones, by their actions caused the issue to degenerate into a purely political one. Oddly enough, this excess of zeal did not so much backfire on the forces of order themselves as it supplied the lads from Karlín and their Moscow protectors with the long-sought pretext for an all-out attack upon the team in charge.

The decision of the party leadership to substitute a mass rally for the banned Spartakiad was endorsed by the National Party Conference held in Prague on June 16 and 17, 1928. Red Day, of course, was but one of several points on the agenda of this conference. Much more attention was paid to the difficulties the party was then encountering in its efforts to penetrate and direct the trade unions. With the Sixth World Congress of the Communist International only one month away, the conference also spent a great deal of time in discussing the problems to which the world Communist gathering was most likely to turn its attention, and the areas of party activity that could elicit the Komintern's criticism. These were the same issues that divided the official left in the governing positions of the party from the new left. The heated debate at the National Party Conference suggested the intensity of the conflict that was soon to be brought to a head.[37]

As might have been expected, the police also forbade the Red Day planned in lieu of the Second Spartakiad. On the same occasion, the Ministry of the Interior dissolved the local Prague organization of the FPT. The party Secretariat, which had received an endorsement for the mass demonstration not only from the National Conference but also from the subsequent plenary meeting of the Central Committee, was determined to carry out its plans, the police ban notwithstanding. Red Day thus became a test of strength between the establishment and the Communist party, but as it actually turned out, it assumed much more significance as a catalyst in the chronic intraparty crisis. Jílek and his associates contributed not a little to this turn of events, since they declared Red Day to be "a milestone in the history of the revolutionary movement in Czechoslovakia" and a "show of the strength and the influence of the Party, a testimony to the advancing radicalization of the working class."[38] In this way, the leadership put their prestige at stake in connection with an enterprise that need not have been accorded so much importance. The outcome, for a number of reasons, including insufficient preparation, was disastrous. Instead of the expected 120,000 participants who were to march through the main streets of the country's capital city, only about 6,000 persons turned up for the rally. Even this small number was denied the opportunity at least to allow the demonstration's sponsors to save face: since there was no plan for this eventuality, the demonstrators lacked guidance and the police had no trouble dispersing them before the public could take notice.

The failure of Red Day was exploited by the new left with unprecedented skill. Because of the exemplary dexterity of the opposition in spinning intrigue and twisting arguments, this relatively banal episode provided the rebels with means sufficient for a complete take-over. What was even more unusual was the victorious group's success in getting its interpretation of this ill-fated venture accepted not only by all party historians, regardless of ideological stance and shade, but also by a number of otherwise objective analysts outside the Communist movement.[39] In these terms, the fiasco of Red Day was proof that the "opportunist policies of the CPCS leaders influenced by Social Democratic reformism, pursued without interruption since the Merger Congress of 1921, resulted in the estrangement of the working class from the communist cause." A crucial part of this argument, however, was the assertion that in the 1920s the masses were "more revolutionary than the communist party itself"; hence the "estrangement."[40] This second element in the analysis of the situation was an indispensable part of the entire argument, for obvious reasons: it claimed not only that the leadership had pursued false policies and consequently lost the control of the masses, but also that the only correct alternative to these policies was a radical shift to the left, in order to "catch up with the revolutionized masses"—a move that in the given situation could mean only one thing: the bolshevization of the party.

The leaders around Jílek, who considered themselves part of the left and at one point in the past had even been disciplined for left extremism, argued that the July 1928 demonstration had failed because the masses had "exhibited passivity" when faced with the repressive action of the government. They claimed that although mistakes had been made in the organization of Red Day, the general policy line of the party had been correct. Aware of the main thrust of the attack waged by the new left, the leaders knew that they had to keep the issue of the failed demonstration separate from that of the overall political orientation of party activity. At a stormy plenary meeting of the Central Committee held July 9 and 10, 1928, Politbureau member Viktor Štern defended the party's current policies as basically sound. As for the mood of the masses who had not responded to the appeal of the Red Day, Štern declared that it "was not one of hostility towards the CPCS"; on the contrary, the working class was "sympathetic" to the party, "its heart was with the party," only it was a "passive sympathy," according to Štern.[41]

Of the two points of view, that of the team in power, as expressed by Štern, seems to have been closer to the facts. If we discount the apologetic motive in it, Štern may have hit upon the truth, albeit unwittingly. Passive sympathy was probably the attitude of the party following not only in 1928, but most of the time. It was a stance taken not by the working class as a whole—talking about "masses" has always been a slightly megalomaniac habit of Communist leaders—but by that peculiar segment of the population that supported the Communist cause at various elections in the First Republic. This phenomenon of passive sympathy toward the CPCS can also be defined as an unspecified protest against the established political and social order and its values. It can explain the astounding insensivity of the voters to the quasi-permanent crisis in the party organization and the attending factional disputes, purges, denunciations, splits, and policy reversals, which would have discredited any other party in the eyes of its electorate. The CPCS in fact experienced only one major electoral defeat during its prewar existence. The costs of its internal crises were reflected instead in shrinking membership figures. The six-digit election gains, in comparison with the minute membership base, were but another aspect of what the leadership in the last phase of the bolshevization believed to be passive sympathy for the Communist party. Antonín Zápotocký, who had recently been appointed to a top position in the Red Unions, confirmed this attitude from his own specific experience. Even where the Red Unions were relatively strong, as for example in Zápotocký's home region of Kladno, it had been "impossible to move the masses to an action. . . . The workers have always stopped halfway," complained Zápotocký.[42]

Considering these facts, reason would have suggested less rather than more radicalism if the party wished to have greater influence among the workers. However, the new left, bent upon obtaining maximum advantage from the Red Day aftermath, succeeded in making the party accept a completely opposite point of view. In so doing, it profited not a little from the confusion among the members of the leading team. The coalition that had taken control at the Third Ordinary Congress and had been confirmed at the Fourth Ordinary Congress was heterogeneous; the subsequent conflicts, both in the CPCS and in the international Communist movement, only further fragmented and divided this leadership. In the search for scapegoats after the failure of the mass demonstration, some of the top functionaries joined the chorus of the new left calling for a thorough purge of the party apparatus. The new left also adroitly manipulated the mood among selected rank-and-file elements. It employed new techniques of subversion that later became part of the Stalinist arsenal: proselytizing in the key district and regional organizations and stirring the membership against the party headquarters in flagrant violation of the otherwise sacred Leninist principle of democratic centralism. This was factionalism in its pure form; although the Moscow center seemed to have no objection to it, two decades later scores of party cadres, in Czechoslovakia as well as in other countries, were purged or even physically liquidated for the same activities.

In the late summer of 1928, the new left in the CPCS made unscrupulous use of all these techniques. One of its tools was the so-called Prague Memorandum, possibly so named to underline the contrast between its contents and those of the Brno Memorandum of the independent Communist group drafted in 1925. The Prague Memorandum was actually a manifesto of the new left that the lads from Karlín, thanks to their strategic location in the party organization of the capital city, succeeded in having endorsed by a number of handpicked officials of this body. Although the authorized representatives of the Prague regional organization refused to accept this document as an expression of the opinion of the regional unit, the memorandum nevertheless was published under the title "The Point of View of the Active (in Czech *aktiv*, a term in the Communist vocabulary denoting an ad-hoc group of party members and/or officials deliberating at a given time about a given issue) of the Functionaries of Greater Prague Concerning the Party Policy after the Failure of 'Red Day.' " It was then distributed among the membership and introduced into the set of documents to be submitted to the Sixth World Congress of the Communist International scheduled for July 1928.[43]

The appeal to the Komintern without previous authorization or consultation of the elected party organs was another violation of bolshevik discipline. The leadership of the Prague region responded with a countermemorandum that was also included in the Czechoslovak materials for the Komintern congress. In evaluating the current political consciousness of the Czechoslovak working class, the authors of the countermemorandum made references to the advanced report prepared for the congress by Nikolai Ivanovich Bukharin, head of the Presidium of the Third International and Zinoviev's successor. Bukharin also had concluded that the stabilization of capitalism had had as a consequence "the passivity of the masses" and "lack of understanding for international actions."[44] The sponsors of the countermemorandum believed that invoking the authority of the Komintern's foremost leader would lend more credence to their arguments and improve their position in the dispute with the new left. In reality, the opposite was true. The Jílek group did not know that as the Sixth World Congress convened in Moscow, Stalin was making preparations for another mass party purge, this time affecting the right deviationists, among whom Bukharin was the most prominent target. The countermemorandum of the Prague regional party organization, in citing Bukharin, thus antagonized the real power holders in the Kremlin and ruined its own chances before it came on the congress agenda.

It is doubtful, however, that the prospects of the CPCS leadership would have been much better even without this untimely quote. In the supreme world Communist forum, all signs seemed to point towards the new left. The lads from Karlín had long since been marked by the Komintern as a shadow government of the Czechoslovak party. The real issue in the eyes of the Moscow power center was not so much the shortcomings of organizational work, or as Jílek put it, "the weak party engine," but the degree to which either of the rival groups was prepared to abandon the aspirations of independence and to become an obedient servant of the Third International—which, in the given situation, meant a servant of Stalin. The future absolute ruler of the Soviet Union was not prepared to miss the chance to settle the Czechoslovak question once and for all.

Czechoslovak matters again ranked high on the agenda when the Sixth World Congress of the Communist International convened in Moscow on July 17, 1928. A special commission was set up by the Secretariat of the Nations and charged with fact-finding and making recommendations in the matter. The commission's report was presented in the congress plenum by the Soviet delegate G. K. Gusev. In principle, the report adopted all the views of the Czechoslovak new left, whose spokesman at the congress was Klement Gottwald, and only gently criticized the Prague Memorandum for not being more consistently critical of the CPCS leadership. The lads from Karlín won the day; it was evident that in future confrontations with Jílek and his associates they would be able to count on support from Moscow. The position of the Third International on the crisis in the Czechoslovak section was then formally stated in an "Open Letter to the Membership of the CPCS" that was endorsed by the Sixth Congress and distributed directly to the rank and file, over the heads of the executive officials. The open letter put special stress on the need for the Czechoslovak comrades to comply, without further delay, with the requirements of the fifth plenum of the Komintern's Executive Committee and to reorganize the party following Bolshevik principles. Of particular significance was the recommendation to reinforce the Leninist base of the party by including in the leadership "young communists of working class origin." It was not difficult to guess whom the Komintern had in mind when making this recommendation.[45]

Thus the Komintern did more than just take sides in the Czechoslovak party dispute: it called upon the membership to join the new left in its revolt. By this action it considerably speeded up the final showdown. Even before it left for Moscow, the Czechoslovak delegation had hardly been a unified and loyal group representing a party in which a minimum of consensus prevailed; it returned home divided into two irreconcilable camps, bent upon settling accounts. The fact that the congress still re-elected Jílek to the Presidium could not deceive anyone or conceal the gravity of the crisis.

Final Round in the Power Struggle:
The Fifth Party Congress

Meanwhile, the signs of the approaching storm multiplied. On June 25, 1928, before the abortive mass demonstration, seventy representatives of various dissident Communist groups that had seceded or been expelled from the CPCS had held a conference in Brno. At this meeting they had decided to constitute a provisional coordinating body named "The Communist Party *in* Czechoslovakia." They had declared their willingness to return to the CPCS as soon as fundamental changes occurred at the leadership level.[46] On the other hand, the reaction to the publication of the Komintern's open letter was one of bewilderment and often of refusal. The Red Union officials, for example, voiced the opinion that organized labor should not be involved in the dispute and called for the independence of the IAUA from the party. It was clear that the cleansing of the party of the opportunistic elements that the new left and its Moscow protectors were so anxious to accomplish would be a costly enterprise in terms of the prestige and the influence of the Communist movement.

The setting of the ultimate battle was the Fifth Ordinary Party Congress. The meeting had originally been scheduled for the last week of December 1928, but the new left succeeded, after many heated discussions in the Central Committee at its two sessions of November 1−2 and December 7−8, in having it postponed for another two months. The Central Committee justified the postponement by the necessity of holding preliminary internal consultations in all party echelons and a number of regional conferences before the congress met; but the purpose of the delay, as explained in an article for *Rudé právo* by Klement Gottwald, was to ensure that "the entire party activity from the grass-roots units up to regional groups be reorganized following the principles spelled out in the 'Open Letter' of the Komintern." This was explicit enough: the congress would take place only when the victory of the new left was more or less certain.

The Fifth Congress, which went into the annals of the party as "the most significant milestone of the interwar period," was held in "conditions of semi-illegality" in Prague February 18−23, 1929.[47] It was not the first party gathering from which the public was excluded; prior to that, regional and national party conferences had occasionally been held in secret, allegedly for fear of police persecution. In the context of the Fifth Congress, however, this clandestine quality might have been an ingredient welcome to the partisans of bolshevization. During the precongress discussions in the lower-level organizations, the Jílek leadership had received strong support in several key regions of the country, such as Brno, Kladno, and Ostrava. In the industrial border regions inhabited by the German-speaking population, on the other hand, the Trotskyite group of Alois Neurath proved to be influential. Although Neurath did oppose Jílek, his group nevertheless rejected the international trend represented by Stalin; in any event he had been a potential rival to the lads from Karlín. It took a good deal of devious manipulation on the part of the new left to neutralize these foci of resistance. A congress held in the limelight of public attention might have given the opponents of the new left an opportunity to present a more accurate picture of the mood of the entire party.

The Fifth Congress can legitimately be called Bolshevik not only because it consummated the long-prepared bolshevization of the Czechoslovak Communist movement, but also because of the truly Bolshevik methods by which it was prepared and run. The scenario that unfolded in Prague in February 1929 paralleled the familiar spectacle of all Soviet party congresses since Stalin had assumed power. All resolutions and decisions had been prepared in advance in secret and the majority needed for their adoption was assured by skillful manipulation of the delegate lists. The tenor of the congress was predetermined by plentiful printed material, published for the most part by the new left. In this literature the pivotal thesis, that "the working masses had developed revolutionary consciousness" while the party with its "opportunistic leadership" had lagged behind and "failed to give the masses appropriate guidance towards a revolutionary action," was incessantly repeated.

The position of the left seemed to be strengthened by a simultaneous strike of textile workers that had broken out in the industrial region of north Bohemia, near the city of Liberec, on February 8, 1929. It actually was a wildcat strike, a strike that the Red Unions had neither organized nor recommended and that they only cautiously supported once it had begun. The new left at the Fifth Party Congress used the strike as proof of its claim about the discrepancy between the "objectively revolutionary mood of the working class" and the "opportunistic," "Social Democratic," and "liquidatorial" (a key term in the vocabulary of the partisans of bolshevization denoting the alleged intention of their adversaries to "liquidate the revolution") tendencies among the CPCS leadership.[48] The strike broke down after four days, but it lasted long enough to supply propaganda ammunition to the opponents of the Jílek group, and its very failure was aptly exploited for further indictment of the leadership in power as traitors of the proletariat. The situation of the top party officials was not hopeful. The delegations to the congress had been manipulated by the anti-Jílek opposition; the German-speaking section was only partially represented since the followers of Alois Neurath had been excluded; and as for the Red Unions, only a few minor officials with known allegiance to the new left turned up. Recognizing the terrific odds against him, Jílek gave up and resigned from the role of main congress reporter that had belonged to him as the secretary-general in office. Among the top leaders, only Zápotocký carried out his functions connected with the congress; however, he had already been won over by the new left.

Because of the clandestine conditions under which the congress was held, no impartial detailed reports are available about its workings. Judging from the account given by Klement Gottwald in *Rudé právo* on February 26, 1929, however, the new left had the situation pretty much under control. Participants in the gathering included 124 delegates with full vote and 52 with consultative status. The membership at that point had reached an all-time low of twenty thousand, barely a fifth of those registered at the Fourth Congress and only a little more thar 5 percent of the total reported at the Merger Congress of 1921. The main speakers were almost all representatives of the new left: Klement Gottwald, Josef Guttman, Rudolf Kohn, Pavel Reimann, and Rudolf Slánský. The newly elected party executive clearly reflected the triumph of this group. The promoters of the bolshevization course acquired a majority in the Central Committee; Klement Gottwald became secretary-general; and the congress also replaced Jílek and Šmeral in their functions as members of the Presidium of the Communist International. The completely new leading team was a guarantee to Moscow that its will at last would be done. A number of congress resolutions denounced "Social Democratic anachronisms" in the Communist party, thereby condemning an occasionally more balanced approach to Czechoslovak politics. It was evident that the CPCS had become what the Komintern and the Soviet party had always wanted it to be: a small conspiratorial group blindly obedient to a foreign power center.

Although all these fateful decisions had been taken at the Fifth Congress, to a large extent even before it, the implications of the new course became visible only afterward. The weeks and months immediately following the publication of Gottwald's article brought a series of dramatic events, as a logical consequence of the now successful bolshevization. It was only then that the dwindling party membership and the broad public became aware of the gravity of the internal party crisis. It was no surprise that the new party leadership that had attained power through shady methods at a semisecret meeting could not be accepted without reservations by the rank-and-file members and the Communist-affiliated mass organizations. Sharp confrontations were inevitable. The upheavals began with a stormy session of the Extended Presidium of the

IAUA that was held in Prague on March 10 and 11, 1929. At this meeting, the so-called collective leadership, which had been imposed by the party upon the union organization pursuant to the directives of the Komintern in April 1928, was recalled, and Josef Hais again became secretary-general. On this occasion the IAUA took formal measures, such as registration with the authorities as a legal person, to ensure the control of union assets and to assert its claim to organizational independence. This signified something like a state of war between the Communist party and the Red Unions, but it was only the beginning of the final and the most dramatic phase of the crisis in the Czechoslovak Communist movement.

The conflict between the IAUA and the CPCS broke out two days before the Presidium of the Executive Committee of the Komintern approved the results of the Fifth Ordinary Congress; henceforth any individual or group who chose to defy the Gottwald leadership had to expect to be banned by the world Communist forum. The endorsement by the Third International of a party government that whole party units perceived as illegitimate further exacerbated the opposition. The shake-ups in the party proper began with the protest of the Communist Senate caucus, approved by majority vote on March 21, 1929, against the "domination of the party by young inexperienced communists"—a more than obvious reference to the lads from Karlín, who at the Fifth Congress had secured many key positions in the governing organs. This protest was followed within a week by an emergency joint session of the Communist caucuses of both legislative chambers, at which Alois Neurath submitted a declaration, signed by twenty-six deputies and senators, criticizing the new party line. Considering that in the 1925 national elections the CPCS had obtained forty-one seats in the Parliament and twenty in the Senate, the opposition of twenty-six legislative representatives was a very serious matter. These dissidents were shortly to be joined by others who either resigned their membership in the party or were expelled but could retain their mandates in accordance with the constitutional rules. However, the second National Assembly remained in office only until November 1929, when because of disagreements in the governmental coalition, it was dissolved and new elections were held.

The take-over of the party by the new left also elicited resistance among Communist intellectuals, who had always formed an important element in the Communist movement not so much on account of their numbers but rather because of the prestige their names and their reputation lent to the Communist cause. On March 28, 1929, a group of seven writers and poets, among them Josef Hora, Ivan Olbracht, and Helena Malířová, condemned the methods by which the Bolshevik line had been forced upon the party and called for an extraordinary congress that would give the CPCS a new leadership. Their declaration was countered by a statement of loyalty to Gottwald and his associates by another group of Communist intellectuals and artists. The new party leaders themselves dealt with these manifestations of dissent at the plenary session of the Central Committee on April 21, 1929. The committee decided to reject all criticism and to stress the correctness of the new line. The dissidents received the epithet "liquidators of communism,"' which was then very much in vogue with the Third International. An extensive memorandum, under the title "The Liquidators— Who They Are and What They Want," was published in the languages of all ethnic groups represented in the CPCS by the party Presidium, and widely distributed; its author was Josef Guttman, editor-in-chief of the party daily, *Rudé právo*. In the booklet, the new leadership made it clear that it was prepared to accept any loss of organized support or electoral popularity rather than to compromise in what it believed to be a matter of Leninist principles.[49] Possibly not all members of the new team realized that these principles, as interpreted in Moscow, amounted to little more than a requirement of blind obedience of the national parties to the Soviet power center. Guttman himself, not long afterward, was disabused of his erroneous ideas when he became a victim of the Komintern's wrath for having dared to criticize the Moscow-approved policy line of the German Communist party on the Weimar Republic and Hitler.

One conflict followed another in quick succession. The crisis of the relations between the party and the Red Unions came to a head when the Soviet-sponsored International Federation of Revolutionary Trade Unions (Profintern), after an unsuccessful effort to arbitrate in the dispute, expelled the secretary-general of the IAUA, Josef Hais, and his group from its ranks. Hais responded by severing all links between the IAUA and the CPCS. What was already a second split in the Czechoslovak trade unions was consummated at the Third IAUA Congress in Prague on May 4 and 5, 1929. The CPCS, which until then had lived in a rather uncomfortable partnership with the Red Unions, already represented but a fraction of the entire trade union movement; after the congress it could ensure the allegiance of only part of this fraction. The influence of the Communists upon organized labor in Czechoslovakia dropped to practically zero.

About a month later, Gottwald and his associates carried out the first "surgical intervention" in the party body. At the plenary session of the Central Committee, on June 1 and 2, 1929, a large number of prominent activists of long standing were expelled from the party, among them Jílek, Muna, and Neurath. Many more expulsions took place before the year was over. In addition to the expulsions, a large number of Communist leaders voluntarily resigned from their offices and even from membership: for example Míla Grimmichová and Karel Goliath-Gorovský. The rank and file were defecting en masse. The prestige and the influence of the party reached its lowest point. No membership statistics are available for the period between the bolshevization congress in 1929 and the Sixth Ordinary Congress in 1931; however, it is indicative of the mood then prevailing on the left that in Slovakia, one of the party's most important strongholds, there were only twenty-seven hundred party cardholders at that time.[50]

The Tenth Plenum of the Executive Committee of the Communist International, which was in session in Moscow from July 3 through July 19, 1929, gave its unqualified endorsement to the new bosses of the CPCS and to the measures they had taken. The fact that the Czechoslovak section had lost practically all organized support, far from causing concern in Moscow, was instead perceived as a relief. In its new form, the CPCS was much closer to the Komintern's ideal of a truly bolshevized national party. As a small sect, which it seemed to have become, it could better fulfill the function of the avant-garde of the revolution.

The parliamentary elections in November 1929 showed the costs, in terms of electoral support, of the bolshevization supercrisis. All things considered, they were not excessive. Although the party lost more than 20 percent of the votes gathered in 1925 and fifteen seats in the two chambers of the National Assembly, the function of the CPCS as a mobilization symbol for discontented populations of backward areas and minorities was preserved. The 10.2 percent of the overall national vote cast for the Communists was a protest loud enough to be heard.[51] The party leaders could be reasonably sure that these disaffected population segments would accept the guidance of the CPCS without influencing or modifying the Bolshevik policy line set by the Third International in the framework of its world revolutionary strategy.

Chapter Three

From Bolshevization to Munich

The CPCS in the 1930s

The bolshevization of the CPCS, which was completed at its Fifth Ordinary Congress, was a signal victory for the Komintern, and particularly for Stalin. For the first time since the party's foundation, its leadership was in the hands of people about whose allegiance to the Moscow center there could be no doubt. These leaders demonstrated their loyalty quite convincingly when they sacrificed all material and human assets, as well as the moral credit of the Czechoslovak Communist movement, to meet the demands of the international headquarters. A better proof of proletarian internationalism in Stalinist interpretation was hardly conceivable.

To an observer at the end of the 1920s, the results of the showdown between the new left and the established party cadres might not have seemed favorable for the future of Czechoslovak communism. Bolshevization had wiped out the last vestiges of the genuinely Czech and Slovak traditions of radical socialism. When the Social Democratic organization split in 1920 and the foundations were laid for an independent radical left party, left radicalism had a considerable appeal among many strata of Czechoslovak society, largely because of the presence of congenial elements in the Czech and Slovak political cultures. Thus, in the years immediately following the First World War, the leftist current in the socialist movement stood an excellent chance to rally strong support among the progressive elite.

That opportunity was gradually lost in the process of the Communist party's submission to unrestricted control from Moscow. The widespread dedication of progressive circles to the cause of the radical left depended on a number of premises of which none, in the long run, was compatible with the eventually dominant Bolshevik course. A radical socialist party corresponding to the Czech and Slovak populist traditions would have had to be a mass party; the conspiratorial avant-garde formula of the Russian prerevolutionary period that the Moscow center imposed upon the CPCS could only estrange many potential followers. Even more difficult to reconcile with the Czechoslovak political culture was the dogmatic class perspective that the Komintern indiscriminately applied to all national environments even though it was actually suited only to ethnically homogeneous Western capitalist societies that had not experienced long periods of domination by ethnically alien economic and political elites. The CPCS, as a section of a revolutionary movement controlled from a foreign center, took an uncompromisingly radical stand on the problem of ethnic groups in Czechoslovakia and called for the right of self-determination to the point of secession. Although this position was more consistent than those of the rival socialist parties, its indifference—if not open hostility—to the Czechoslovak state could not win for the Communist program those Czechs and Slovaks who saw social reform as part of their national aspirations.

True, the party's negative stance on the Czechoslovak nation-building idea assured it of the support of disaffected segments in the underdeveloped areas inhabited by ethnic minorities. It was chiefly from these milieus that the CPCS recruited voters, especially after 1929. Indeed, the history of the first decade of the party is told by a continuous shift in the membership base from the left-oriented Czech and Slovak industrial workers and intellectuals to the urban "lumpenproletariat" (the dregs of the lower class) and marginal protesters in depressed and underdeveloped regions. Only so could the party survive: these voters were on the whole uninterested in the ideology or the tactics of the CPCS, and thus were willing to ignore the quasi-permanent internal party crisis. This new electorate, composed of alienated political outsiders, substituted itself gradually for the lost issue and program voters.

The Aftermath of the Fifth Congress

In the fall of 1929, the further prospects of the Communist party on the Czechoslovak political scene might have been considered bleak. Two courses seemed open to it: the party could persist in the approach adopted at the Fifth Congress and "freeze" as a sect, subject to growing ideological rigor and inevitable factional struggles and regular purges, and occasionally polling protest votes at the elections; or it could eventually succumb to the influence of the pluralist environment— actually, the CPCS was the only Communist party in Central and Eastern Europe that enjoyed almost two decades of legality—and end by joining or reinforcing the left operating within the constitutional framework. The bolshevization course chosen by Gottwald and his group was not, after all, irreversible. The fact that neither of these possibilities materialized has to be ascribed to major factors of European economic and political history of the 1930s, which took an unexpected turn after the Fifth Congress.

The year 1929 saw not only the bolshevization of the Czechoslovak section of the Komintern, but also Black Friday at the New York Stock Exchange, which marked the beginning of the Great Depression. The economic crisis of the 1930s hit Czechoslovakia more severely than many other industrial nations since she had inherited more than two-thirds of the industrial production capacities of the former Austro-Hungarian empire, with a population less than one-third the size and a correspondingly reduced internal market. For economic prosperity the new state depended on exports. One of the secrets of the remarkable recovery of the 1920s, a recovery that the Communists had obstinately refused to acknowledge, had been a relatively smooth passage, as soon as postwar reconstruction was achieved and internal consumption saturated, to significant participation in the system of international trade. In 1929 this expansion had reached its limits and begun to slow down, but the world slump transformed this deceleration into the most serious recession in modern Czechoslovak history. Demand shrank rapidly in both the industrial and the agricultural sectors. The number of unemployed reached the record level of 920,000 in February 1933, when population was a mere 14 million. In addition to the difficulties experienced by all the industrial countries of the world, Czechoslovakia suffered from the refusal of its economic experts and leaders to budge from their commitment to the classical principles of capitalist economics, which had worked miracles in the postwar conditions of scarcity but were unsuitable as remedies to a crisis of overproduction and oversupply. Instead of policies stimulating consumption, investment, and employment, the Czechoslovak government (unlike its British counterpart, for example) responded to the depression by saving and retrenchment measures that only aggravated the snowball effect of receding demand. It was not until the second half of the 1930s that more courageous and imaginative economic policies were adopted.

The agony of the Czechoslovak economy during the Great Depression had a very serious effect on the political climate in the country. The initial economic achievements that had helped Czechoslovakia outstrip other European nations struggling to recover after the war—especially its attainment of monetary stability without the catastrophic inflation experienced by all the other nearby countries—had begun to enhance the legitimacy of the new political order in the eyes of those ethnic groups that could not perceive the Czechoslovak state as a fulfillment of their national aspirations. The economic depression seemed to put this new image in doubt. Not only the minorities, however, but also the two nation-building groups experienced a period of serious disenchantment. This was true especially of the Slovaks, for whose elites, because of the relative underdevelopment of Slovakia, the ideals of national emancipation and of economic and social progress had always blended. As in developing areas today, the Slovak elites of the 1930s judged the political system largely by its performance in the field of economic development and modernization. (The widely accepted contemporary sociological theory of modernization, which links the perceptions of legitimacy by the relevant population segments to the level of satisfaction of material expectations, seems retroactively applicable in this case.)[1] The slowdown in economic growth the Great Depression had brought about challenged the claims of the Czechoslovak state to the loyalty of its Slovak citizens. Extremists of all kinds and colors profited from this situation, the right wing as well as the radical left. The Communist party could reap only a small part of the benefits attendant upon the politics of despair; its following and electoral support remained virtually unchanged during the most critical period of the slump. Nevertheless, the crisis provided an opportunity for the party to unleash manifold activity among the industrial and rural proletariat.

This activity unfolded under two slogans typical of the period of the early 1930s: Facing the Masses and Class against Class. The slogans were based on the assumption that the party was the vanguard of the most developed and class-conscious segments of the working force. Although everyday experiences clearly refuted this thesis, the party continued to live in the world of its own imagination. Perceiving itself as a guiding hand of the revolutionary movement, the CPCS led its followers into a number of strikes and mass demonstrations protesting alleged political persecution and war preparations by the Czechoslovak bourgeoisie. The strikes, which took place in the industrial as well as the agricultural sector, were all unsuccessful. The party leadership blamed the failure on the reformist and yellow unions' betrayal of the working class. In reality, the fault was with the Communists themselves, who after the second split in the trade union organizations controlled only a small percentage of labor and yet irresponsibly launched work stoppages that they were then unable to pursue to the end. The collapse of the strike actions was all the more likely since the party, obedient to directives from the Komintern, was not willing to seek alliances or even ad-hoc agreements with the mass of the trade union body. The Moscow formula of joint action consisted of Communist subversion of the membership of other socialist unions. Under these circumstances, naturally, no united front could ever be formed. The futile strikes served only to damage the bargaining position of the workers in future labor disputes and to impose additional hardships upon the individual employees and their families. Yet even the failures were explained away by the party bosses in the best dialectical tradition. They argued that "the worse—the better!" meaning that any worsening of the condition of the proletariat was a gain for the Communist cause because it promoted "the revolutionary spirit of the masses." The public soon began to associate this catchword with the basic philosophy of the Communist party.

The political mass actions initiated by the Bolshevik leadership in and after the summer of 1929 did not fare any better than the abortive strikes. For example, the order to stop working for a brief period on August 1, 1929, as a symbolic protest against the persecution of Communists, was followed by only seventeen thousand employees in the whole country. Compared with the number of workers who, a year earlier, had turned up for the ill-fated Red Day, the response to the strike order was hardly more impressive. At the same time, the party organized a "Day of Manifestations against the Danger of War," also on a national scale. By their talk of an eventual war, the Communists at that time usually meant the possibility of an aggressive war by Western powers against the Soviet Union, made inevitable by the "contradictions of capitalism in its stabilization period."[2] This analysis of the international situation was far-fetched since there was no evidence to support it; however, it was by no means merely a Czechoslovak idea but rather a reflection of the views that the Komintern propagated among the national sections. The

Antiwar Day failed to arouse any more enthusiasm among the target population, however, than had any previous mass action. Participants nationwide numbered about sixty thousand. There was something patently wrong with the thesis that the masses were moving faster along the revolutionary path than the Communist party, in the name of which Gottwald and the lads from Karlín had toppled the Jílek team at the Fifth Congress. Ignoring these signs, the new Bolshevik leadership stuck fast to the cri de guerre Facing the Masses in the hope that it would eventually be possible for the party to catch up with the hypothesized radicalization of the working class and thus assure for itself the role of vanguard of the proletariat.

New Ultraleft Currents: The Slovak Problem

With the imagination that never seemed to be lacking in the ivory tower of communism, it was possible for some to see the failure of the agitation among the workers as a proof that even after the latest shake-up in the party, its adopted course was not left enough, so that the Communists kept lagging behind the masses. This was the interpretation adopted by a group of activists who had only recently acceded to leading posts but showed little gratitude or loyalty toward the clique that had given them their chance. The party thus had another left or ultraleft opposition. The new faction was associated with the name of Politbureau member Evžen Fried, and later party historians have referred to it as to the "ultra-left deviation of the Fried group." Other names cited in connection with Fried's were those of Pavel Reimann, the CPCS's representative in the Komintern Presidium, and Otto Synek, a well-known journalist and leader of the Komsomol. The Fried group enjoyed considerable sympathy among the regional party organizations and in the Komsomol. Fried first challenged the Gottwald leadership while on a mission as the main party representative in the strike committee during the miners' strike in northwestern Bohemia in October 1929. The strike failed and the miners had to resume work without having achieved any of their goals. Although the party headquarters, as usual, put the blame for the unsuccessful enterprise on the reformist union bosses who had failed to support the Communist initiative, it nevertheless recognized that the strike was hopeless and ordered it terminated. Fried, however, disobeyed the instructions from Prague. He insisted that the strike should be continued "in drops," that is by irregular short work stoppages in the individual mines, a method that he believed was as efficient as a collective strike action of entire unions. He argued, in an already familiar vein, that the masses were "more revolutionary than the party" and that they wished to continue the struggle; in such a situation, he believed, the party should "bow to the will of the working class."[3]

The ultraleftists also opposed the policies of the new party leaders on other occasions. They were the most vociferous critics of the unsuccessful political mass actions of 1929. They also pointed out the CPCS's poor showing at the 1929 parliamentary elections and claimed that it was caused by the "disappointment of the revolutionary proletariat" over the cautious party line. As a remedy they recommended the same means the new left had used at the Fifth Ordinary Congress: a mass purge of so-called opportunistic elements. Their views had less chance of being adopted by the party than those of Gottwald and his followers had had in 1928 since they lacked support from Moscow. The Central European Section of the Communist International, in its session of December 1929, condemned Fried's position. Disavowed by the Komintern and condemned by the party leadership, the only courses open to Fried's group were to repent their sins or face expulsion. At the Extended Plenary Session of the Central Committee, on January 5 and 6, 1930, Fried, Reimann, and Synek submitted a declaration recognizing their mistakes and expressing their will to cooperate in the correction of their errors.[4] Thus the new left deviation was wiped out.*

Opportunities for mass action during the years following the bolshevization congress were abundant. Unemployment grew, but did not remain limited to industrial areas; equally, if not more severely, affected were the underdeveloped regions of the east and southeast of the country. Here small entrepreneurs and craftsmen, as well as small farmers, frequently became insolvent because of a catastrophic drop in demand. Their holdings were mortgaged beyond tolerable limits. Seizures of small businesses and farms and bankruptcies multiplied. The growing discontent of these strata was hardly identical with the radicalization of the proletarian masses in the wake of capitalist stabilization so long heralded by the party theoreticians. Instead of automatically

---

*The manner in which this ideological conflict and its resolution were later recorded in the official annals of the party is a model example of Bolshevik self-criticism. The analysis of the theoretical and political mistakes of the Fried group, their critical evaluation, and the description of how the deviant group "found its way back to the Truth," were penned, in both editions (1931 and 1961) of the authorized manual of CPCS history, by Pavel Reimann, himself a prominent representative of the ultraleft faction.

leading to the reinforcement of the left, it largely benefited the groups and movements of the extreme right, especially in Slovakia. Nevertheless it provided an opportunity for the Communists. The early 1930s thus saw the party exploiting to the maximum the misery of the victims of the depression. It organized protest congresses and hunger marches of the unemployed, riots of agricultural workers, resistance to the seizures of insolvent farms and shops, and so on. This policy solidified the party's support among the disaffected marginal segments in the nonindustrial areas. During the economic crisis the CPCS more than ever became the spokesman for the disadvantaged and the alienated. As we will see, however, the immediate political profit of the economic crisis, in terms of electoral statistics, was in no way notable. In the eyes of the broad public, the Communists were political profiteers of human misery. This impression was often supported by the behavior and statements of party officials or functionaries of Communist-front organizations such as the Communist-obedient splinters of the trade unions. These splinter groups repeatedly claimed, for example, that the system of unemployment benefits paid to the Czechoslovak jobless on the basis of the Ghent System Agreement of 1926 was undesirable from the point of view of the revolutionary proletarian movement, since it tended to reduce revolutionary pressures and to perpetuate the capitalist order. These views might have been consistent with the classical Marxist tradition, in tune with Marx's scornful label for union work as "mending social shoe soles," but they did not make the Communist cause any more popular outside the orbit of its habitual supporters.

More insightful, on the other hand, was the stand the party continued to take on the problem of the various ethnic groups in Czechoslovakia. The Communists recognized where the most difficult aspect of the whole complex ethnic problem lay: in the equivocal concept of one Czechoslovak ethnic group as the nation-building element in the Czechoslovak Republic. According to the 1920 constitution, the "bearer of the statehood" in Czechoslovakia was an entity defined as the "Czechoslovak people composed of two branches, Czech and Slovak." In this context, "Czech" and "Slovak" are cultural terms, differentiated according to the peculiarities of the respective languages, and "Czechoslovak" is a political term. "Czechoslovak" lacked precision, however: on the one hand, it was used to denote citizenship in the Czechoslovak state, or "nationality" in the Western meaning of the word, and thus encompassed all citizens of the Czechoslovak Republic regardless of ethnic background, German- and Hungarian-speaking individuals as well as Czechs and Slovaks. On the other hand, in a narrower sense, it referred to the nation-building partnership of the Czechs and the Slovaks. Thus both ethnic groups were requested to give up their separate identities in favor of a larger unit that was not sufficiently differentiated from its constituent parts. This solution contained a certain threat, especially to the Slovaks who, as the smaller party to this contract—the demographic ratio in the beginning was 1 to 4—felt that they might gradually be absorbed into the Czech cultural orbit and be denied strict equality of opportunity. Slovak was the official language in Slovakia but, owing to a critical shortage of educated personnel after 1918, a large number of Czech teachers, civil servants, and other specialists were transferred to Slovakia. As a new Slovak intelligentsia, educated in Slovak schools and universities, gradually emerged, these Czech cadres became less welcome in Slovakia. They were perceived as competitors and a hindrance to the mobility of the Slovaks. The depression considerably aggravated this situation since the acute unemployment in the areas requiring more highly qualified personnel rendered a smooth withdrawal of the Czech personnel and their replacement by domestic applicants very difficult. Thus, economic competition further added to the already existing cultural tension.

During the period of the First Republic, the CPCS was the only nationwide political force led by Czechs that took a position free of the ambiguities of "Czechoslovakism" in dealing with matters of Czecho-Slovak relations. It rejected the concept of "one nation with two branches" and claimed for the Slovaks the same right of self-determination that all other ethnic groups enjoyed. This position reflected the greater freedom the CPCS enjoyed as an opposition party to indulge in the luxury of moral and political principles. Nevertheless, its view, which the liberal establishment considered too radical and subversive, ultimately proved to be the most pragmatic and prevailed. After the Second World War, the Slovaks were recognized as an individual ethnic unit with the right to aspire to national identity and self-determination. Thus, although they were motivated not by concern over the viability of the Czecho-Slovak partnership in nation-building but by the desire to take the maximum political advantage of this unresolved issue, the Communists, as early as the 1920s, indicated the basis on which it would ultimately be settled.

However, this circumstance did not spare the party the problems and the crises that other political groups and movements experienced; ironically, it was under the rule of the CPCS that the Czecho-Slovak dispute developed to its most dramatic forms. The question to which the Communists initially seemed to have a correct answer later became a source of chronic instability within the party organization. It also played a crucial role in the most significant crisis of the Czechoslovak Communist system to date, which occurred in the late 1960s. The reasons for this apparent paradox may lie partly in the logic of the national political culture, which no regime, however radical, can ever escape. All the same, its causes should also be sought in the nature of the party as it evolved, especially since its bolshevization. Later internal party developments showed that it was one thing to profess self-determination to the point of secession as a political maxim, and a completely different thing to apply this maxim within an organizational structure based on the principle of Leninist democratic centralism.

This dilemma first emerged in the formative years of the Czechoslovak Communist movement, before the Merger Congress of 1921. The unitary CPCS was a kind of solution, however imperfect. Later, at the beginning of the economic depression, an appealing argument by the competitors of the CPCS among the Slovak radical right was that the plight of the working people would not be so great if "Slovak affairs were in the hands of Slovaks themselves." The Communists adopted this argument, too, but could not avoid its implications for their own organization. The pressure for better local representation grew, leading ultimately, after two regional party conferences in Slovakia in the summer of 1930, to a reform of the until-then strictly centralist structure. At the constitutive All-Slovak Conference in Trnava on May 10 and 11, 1930, the project of a regional Slovak organization with its seat in Bratislava was ratified. This signified a change in the original organizational pattern, which had made no distinction between the "historical provinces" (inhabited by Czechs and Germans) and Slovakia but had observed only geographical and administrative divisions. The new regional organization for Slovakia had not yet received the name of a Communist party, but it reflected clearly the individual character of the Slovak party component. It was subdivided into nine districts reporting to the Bratislava regional headquarters. After the most prominent leader of the Slovak group and the architect of the regional structure, Evžen Klinger, was disciplined by a censure motion of the Slovak governing party body for ultraleft factional activity in the spring of 1930, the power passed into the hands of the organizational secretary, Karol Bacílek. The fact that no corresponding regional section for the Czech provinces or for the Czech membership was established as a counterpart to the Slovak section, and that its creation was not even considered, revealed the continuing commitment of the national party leadership to the principle of centralism. The revision of the party structure in Slovakia was to remain an exception for many years to come. Few leaders suspected in 1930 that the Slovak problem would eventually develop into a major intraparty crisis because of this inconsistency. At that time, many circumstances, including the staunch commitment of the organizational secretary himself to the principle of centralism, seemed to guarantee that Slovak national aspirations would not get the upper hand.

The Sixth Party Congress

The importance the party ascribed to the problem of ethnic groups in Czechoslovakia was underscored in the program of the Sixth Ordinary Congress held in Prague March 7–11, 1931. Although the consequences of the Great Depression were predictably the leading theme of the congress, the so-called nationalities question received a high priority. The reporter on this topic was Václav Kopecký, one of the lads from Karlín. The radically internationalist stance he took at the Sixth Congress, when considered from a longer historical distance, constitutes a curious contrast to the almost fanatical Czech chauvinism and anti-German demagoguery in which he later indulged as minister of information, after World War II. In 1931 Kopecký advocated that the most intransigent version of the self-determination principle be applied to all ethnic minorities in Czechoslovakia. The Communist party's concern with these questions and its critique of the existing arrangements of ethnic relationships was unwittingly prophetic: less than two years after the Sixth Congress, the Nazi regime was to come to power in neighboring Germany, and at the end of the 1930s it was to use the nationalities question as the main lever in destroying the Czechoslovak Republic.

Topic number one, however, was the economic crisis and its lessons, which the party leadership believed to have vindicated the revolutionary Marxist line adopted in the process of bolshevization. The crisis was perceived, above all, as a major opportunity to increase Communist influence. Considerable attention was paid at the congress to the party's work in the countryside, although it was evident that the party elites did not realize, even after two general elections, what was the real motivation behind the Communist vote among the peasantry. They continued to speak of "revolutionary masses of the rural proletariat" even though the party following was chiefly based on disaffected marginal elements of cultural and ethnic minorities protesting against the costs of social change connected with economic development and modernization.

Youth organizations and the sorry state of the Communist-sponsored trade unions completed the agenda of the Sixth Congress. It seemed that after the second schism in the union movement, which split the Red Unions, the party-obedient workers' interest groups were reduced to insignificance, and the modes of operation within the unions had to be radically changed if the Communists wanted to regain, at least partly, their former position in the union movement. The congress decided that ignoring the reformist unions, or showing only hostility to them, was not the best strategy. Instead, it recommended that party activists "approach sympathetically the membership and the lower-echelon functionaries" of these unions, and "take advantage through intensified factional activity of the growing dissatisfaction of the workers." Thus "revolutionary opposition groups" were to be constituted within the Social Democratic trade unions, which then would "cooperate as closely as possible with the communist unions."[5] As for the youth, and party work among the youth movement, the congress stressed that the Communists should not limit their attention to the young people organized in the Komsomol, which, in any event, was but a semilegal body, but broaden the scope of their activity. They should work on the young generations wherever they met them: in industrial enterprises, rural districts, schools and universities, and the army. All these directives and recommendations indicated that the party leaders were aware of the isolation into which the chronic internal crisis and power struggle had led the Czechoslovak Communist movement. The proposed solutions showed, however, that they were not prepared to step beyond the line of the "United Front from below," as delineated by Moscow, which amounted to little more than a rather clumsy attempt at subversion of the organizations to whom cooperation was being offered. It was obvious that these tactics were doomed from the very start.

Statistical data released at the Sixth Ordinary Congress concerning the state of the party organization suggested a net consolidation after the great shake-up of 1929. The number of organized members, which had reached the all-time low of twenty-one thousand at the previous Congress, had almost doubled—to forty thousand. These members were represented at the Sixth Congress by 97 voting delegates and 117 delegates with consultative status. The report on party property and other assets was rather discouraging: during the bolshevization and in its aftermath, because of numerous splits, secessions, defections, and expulsions, many of the party's possessions, especially real estate and operating funds, were lost. These losses considerably reduced the facilities available for daily party work.

The closer attachment of the CPCS to Moscow under the Gottwald leadership was reflected in the increased attention paid to the task of popularizing the USSR among Czechoslovak public. A new body, the Association of the Friends of the Soviet Union, created shortly before the Sixth Congress, took charge of this activity. Another new Communist-sponsored organization was the so-called Red Aid, which was part of a larger International Workers' Mutual Assistance Council. Red Aid had originally been set up to support unemployed and striking workers, but it gradually shifted its focus to Communist party members and officials condemned for violating the law through their political activity. The CPCS also took the initiative in the constitution of the Left Front, which was referred to as an "organization of progressive intellectuals." The Left Front showed more unreserved loyalty to the party and its Soviet sponsors than other, more spontaneously created groups of Communist intellectuals, such as the Czech Devětsil or the Slovak DAV; it also proved to be less prone to internal crises, and on the whole more viable.

The CPCS and Hitler's Third Reich

Besides the world economic crisis, another major element that was to determine the course of the party history in the 1930s was the rise of the totalitarian regime of the right in neighboring Germany. The evaluation of the Nazi phenomenon, whose significance had been perceptible several years before Hitler's final seizure of power, in the policy- and decision-making circles in Moscow betrayed an utter lack of understanding of power relations in the German Weimar Republic. Until the very eve of Hitler's *Machtergreifung* (seizure of power) in January 1933, the Komintern continued to identify the German Social Democratic party as the main enemy of the Communist movement, ignoring the very explicit dictatorial aspirations of the National Socialist German Workers' party (Nazis). The Communist Party of Germany (CPG) kept receiving instructions from the international headquarters that made any active participation in a united front against Nazism impossible. Such participation would have required at least a truce between the Communists and those whom the Third International labeled reformist renegades and social fascists, but already this very idea was interpreted as right opportunism in the Kremlin. The CPCS, which had become considerably more docile after the success of bolshevization, faithfully followed the policy line laid down by the Komintern, but it would be inaccurate to assert that no dissenting voices were heard among the leading party cadres.

No overdose of patriotism was necessary for a Czechoslovak Communist to recognize German National Socialism as a threat. The Nazi party had a branch among the German-speaking population in the border regions of Bohemia and Moravia and the spokesmen of this branch, like their counterparts in the German Reich, made no bones about their intention to do away with all political parties of the center and especially the left if they ever came into power. As early as 1933, the Czechoslovak government banned the National Socialist Workers' party and the National party in the border areas inhabited by ethnic Germans, but a newly created Sudeten German Home Front, led by Konrad Henlein, soon replaced the two outlawed parties. The experience of everyday politics showed some CPCS activists, especially those working among the German-speaking minority, that the Komintern's line on Nazism ignored political reality. This recognition created a crisis in the Communist ranks that broke out into an open conflict when Josef Guttmann, editor-in-chief of *Rudé právo* and a member of the Politbureau, chose to express his dissident views. As early as at the Ninth Plenary Session of the Executive Committee of the Communist International in Moscow in April 1931, Guttman criticized the policies of the CPG on the Nazi movement: this was tantamount to criticizing the general line of the Komintern on Germany.[6] He repeated his criticism, enlarged into a "serious warning" to the CPG, at the Twelfth Plenum in September 1932. This time, the Moscow center protested Guttmann's statements to the CPCS chairman, Klement Gottwald, and asked that Guttmann be disciplined. For a number of reasons, the Czechoslovak party leadership decided not to impose upon Guttmann the supreme sanction of expulsion, but to give him another chance. It should not be overlooked that Guttmann had been one of the most outspoken representatives of the new left during the bolshevization campaign and at the Fifth Party Congress in 1929. He was also the author of the famous party booklet condemning the so-called opportunists and liquidators. Whatever the reasons for the party's cautious action, the intervention from Moscow did not silence Guttmann. When Hitler took power in Germany on January 30, 1933, Guttmann published a series of articles in *Rudé právo* in which he placed the blame for the demise of the German constitutional regime on the German Communist party, and implicitly on the Komintern. His differences with the Komintern leaders reached a peak when Guttmann refused to carry in *Rudé právo* the resolution of the Third International on the Nazi take-over in Germany. Guttmann was summoned to Moscow, but he could not go because at that time he was serving a short prison term for a flagrant press offense. Thus the Guttmann case became a point on the agenda of the Thirteenth Plenary Session of the Executive Committee of the Komintern in October 1933. The committee requested Guttmann's immediate expulsion, and the CPCS Politbureau complied on December 31, 1933.[7] Obedience to Moscow once more seemed to be restored within the ranks of the CPCS.

It could be concluded from the manner in which the Guttmann incident was settled that the fictitious image of the political and social world, as entertained by the international Communist headquarters, would continue to dominate the Communist movement in all countries, including Czechoslovakia, for a long time to come. While this actually was the case at the level of decision-making bodies, pressure for a more realistic assessment of the situation slowly built up among the wider circles of the membership. The leadership never stopped identifying the Czechoslovak Republic as an imperialist polity that was bent on an aggressive war against the USSR, in collusion with England and France, while ignoring the expansionist speeches and military preparations in Hitler's Germany and only occasionally condemning the persecution of German Communists by the Nazi regime. Nevertheless, significant events in international politics were in preparation that would compel the Communists to revise their positions, though perhaps not immediately.

The Nazi triumph in Germany wrecked an important diplomatic initiative, the project of the Pact of Four, which would have modified the relations between Germany and its three former war enemies in Europe: England, France, and Italy. Communist historians later argued that the pact had been devised to strengthen conservative forces and to further isolate the USSR, but it had been intended primarily to protect the status quo in Europe and the interests of the victors of the First World War. Whatever the merit of this dispute, the failure of the Pact of Four created an opening for the Soviet Union. When, after the unsuccessful talks in Rome, Nazi Germany quit the League of Nations in the late summer of 1933, a new world conflict became a real possibility. In this situation, French diplomacy began to look for solutions that would help restore the balance of power on the continent. On the initiative of the French foreign minister, Louis Barthou, the Soviet Union was invited to participate in what was supposed to be the Eastern Pact, a regional agreement guaranteeing the peace and the integrity of the borders in Central and Eastern Europe. A preliminary condition of a positive outcome for the French plan was the normalization of relations with the most important prospective partner, Moscow. Thus Czechoslovakia, which had not maintained any official contacts with the USSR since the conflict with the Soviets over the evacuation of the Czechoslovak Legion and the occupation by the Czechoslovak troops of the Trans-Siberian Railroad in 1918, recognized the Soviet Union de jure and de facto on June 9, 1934.

It was characteristic of the views then prevailing among the leaders of the CPCS that less than two weeks after this event, the plenary session of the Central Committee held on June 20, 1934, adopted a resolution in which the danger of a fascist dictatorship in Czechoslovakia was singled out as one of the main subjects of concern of the working class. The continuing intransigence of the Communists was also reflected in the line they adopted concerning the presidential elections of May 1934. As in 1927, the CPCS presented its own candidate who, this time, was none other than Klement Gottwald, but in contrast to 1927, this nomination was not later revised, so that no intervention by the Komintern was necessary to make the party maintain the "only correct" course. The slogan launched at this occasion, "Not Masaryk—but Lenin!" and vehement, indiscriminate attacks on the incumbent of the supreme state office gave the authorities a cause for prosecuting some of the party's spokesmen, and this in turn provided the Communist media with welcome evidence in support of their claim about "mounting fascist oppression."

About half a year later, in November 1934, the Central Committee heard a report by a Politbureau member, Jan Šverma, on the prospects of a united front in Czechoslovakia. In agreement with the basic line of the Third International, it voted a resolution refusing all cooperation, or even ad-hoc action, with the bourgeoisie, which in this case included the two socialist parties and their "reformist and renegade" trade unions. As before, the only united front conceivable to the CPCS, in view of its obedience to the Komintern, was so-called common action from below with the rank-and-file members of the socialist organizations—in other words, the subversion of these parties and unions by siphoning away their membership base. It was only natural that under these circumstances the non-Communist components of the Czechoslovak left lacked enthusiasm for any such joint struggle. Thus an open letter of the Central Committee of the CPCS released in July 1934, addressed in typical fashion "to all members and local organizations of the socialist parties"—that is, over the heads of the leaders of these parties—and inviting the recipients to a "joint action against the menace of open fascism" (in Czechoslovakia), met with little or no response. The democratic left in its quasi-totality refused to minimize the external threat to the nation or to be scared by the bugbear of an allegedly imminent fascist putsch.

Meanwhile, the political situation in Europe deteriorated further. At the end of 1934, Germany reintroduced obligatory miliary service, and on March 7, 1935, Hitler's troops marched into the demilitarized zone on the left bank of the Rhine. Although the Komintern headquarters at that time still expected a proletarian revolution in Germany and the collapse of the Third Reich, it was obvious to all objective observers that successful defiance of the Great Powers had benefited Hitler considerably in the eyes of the German public, including the working class. The Nazi regime, far from breaking down, became more consolidated. It was equally obvious that by early 1935, the repressive apparatus of the Nazi party (NSDAP) state had succeeded in almost completely annihilating the underground network of the CPG, an operation that would be repeated, with comparable success, in occupied Czechoslovakia during the forthcoming war. Yet a change in the image of Czechoslovak democracy, as seen by the official leaders of the CPCS and their Moscow sponsors, and a more balanced view of the various non-Communist parties and movements that Communist propaganda had indiscriminately lumped together as reactionary and fascist was slow in coming. Even after Czechoslovakia signed the Tripartite Mutual Assistance Treaty with the Soviet Union and France, a compromise formula of the originally wider Eastern Pact, Czechoslovak Communists were reluctant to revise their stand on the Czechoslovak state and society. "You have concluded a pact with the Soviet Union, gentlemen, not with the Communist Party of Czechoslovakia," commented the party theoretical and ideological weekly *Tvorba* on the speculations that the event might make the CPCS more amenable.[8]

Nevertheless, a new assessment by the Communists of the world situation, and by implication of the domestic one as well, became inevitable. Their hand was partly forced by the systematic anti-Communist campaigns of the Nazi regime, which did not leave much room for neutrality. The Komintern itself was not left with much more choice when the political justice of the Third Reich attempted to exploit the fire in the Berlin Reichstag as a "cause celèbre" against the head of the West European Bureau of the Komintern in Berlin, Georgi Dimitrov. Thus, after some last minute hesitation, the Komintern joined the antifascist front in a major policy shift that was formally endorsed at the Seventh World Congress held in Moscow from July 25 through August 20, 1935. Dimitrov's speech and the congress's resolution made a clear distinction between "mere bourgeois nationalism" and "fascism," especially German fascism, which Dimitrov called "a form of bestial chauvinism." Communist parties in the whole world were exhorted to promote the idea of the united front as part of the defense against fascism, and some were criticized for alleged "sectarianism," for unwillingness to cooperate with other movements in the "struggle for the protection of the remainders of bourgeois democracy—in other words, for having faithfully obeyed previous Komintern instructions.[9]

The Komintern congress, which was actually the last gathering of this kind before the demise of the Third International, also marked a turning point in the position of the CPCS. Prior to the congress, the party had received a hint about the support it enjoyed among the population that gave it good reason to re-examine the validity of the ideological and general political assumptions on which it had based its program and its strategy. This hint came in the form of the results of the national elections held on May 19, 1935. The CPCS obtained a hundred thousand more votes than in the previous elections, which had been held in 1929, shortly after the bolshevization crisis. This extremely modest gain in absolute figures actually represented no real gain in electoral following, since the population of Czechoslovakia had in the meantime increased by about 10 percent.[10] The fact that after six years of Bolshevik leadership and the pursuit of Komintern-sponsored policies of Facing the Masses and Class against Class, the Communist share in the popular vote had not increased, pointed to an incomprehensible failure: the party was unable to profit from the most disastrous economic depression in the history of capitalism. It seemed, after all, that the cherished principle of the bolshevik leadership embodied in the slogan "The worse—the better!" was not paying the expected dividends.

The outcome of the 1935 general elections also belied the constant Communist assertions that an imminent fascist coup d'état was threatening Czechoslovakia. Not only did the party carrying the name Fascist remain an insignificant sect; a much more broadly gauged attempt to constitute a new party of the radical right also failed. The so-called National Unification (Národní sjednocení) party was formed from a merger between the conservative National Democratic party chaired by Dr. Karel Kramář and a radical right splinter of the Czechoslovak National Socialist party, the League against Closed Ballots, headed by Jiři Stříbrný. This National Unification party ended by polling fewer votes than the two constituting groups had obtained in the previous parliamentary elections.[11] The CPCS ascribed the defeat of the radical right to the "vigilance of the revolutionary proletariat," thus obstinately refusing to see in it what it really was: a proof of solid entrenchment of democratic values in the Czechoslovak political culture.[12]

The Party's Patriotic Stance:
The Seventh Congress

The first signs of a change in the attitude of the CPCS leadership to the established political order in Czechoslovakia were noticeable at the National Party Conference held in Prague on May 25, 1935. Significantly, unlike the previous national conference, in January 1934, it was not taking place in conditions of semilegality. The conference registered with satisfaction the collapse of the efforts of the extreme rightists to build a wide base of electoral support and stated that fascist aggression had finally been repelled in Czechoslovakia. The party also declared at this meeting that "while opposing all forms of capitalist rule and fighting for a proletarian democracy, i.e., for the dictatorship of the proletariat, working people cannot be indifferent to the political form in which capitalist rule is being implemented. . . . The working class therefore cannot passively watch the replacement of bourgeois democracy by a brutal fascist dictatorship."[13] This more positive attitude was strengthened especially after the Seventh World Congress of the Komintern, which modified Moscow's original position on eventual participation of Communist parties in coalition governments. The concept of the united front was broadened to include the possibility that individual parties might join other socialist groups and assume governmental responsibilities or give parliamentary support to what could be identified as "workers' governments" even though these governments need not necessarily include Communist ministers. A prominent case where this new policy line of the Third International was applied was the government of the Popular Front in France in 1936 headed by the socialist leader Léon Blum. The CPCS's attempt at a similar experiment in Czechoslovakia, however, failed completely. A Popular Front cabinet in Czechoslovakia would have required the participation of more parties than the three socialist ones. To elicit the support of other groups of the center-left would have been very difficult because by the mid-1930s the CPCS had lost all credibility with the public, on account of the incessant conflicts, internal crises, and purges, which had not stopped with the successful bolshevization. Moreover, not even the socialist parties were particularly keen on sharing executive power with the Communists.

A more salient symptom of greater political realism than the united front rhetoric was the action taken by the Communist party in the presidential elections of December 1935, which were made necessary by the resignation of T. G. Masaryk for reasons of health. The candidate of the democratic center-left, Eduard Beneš, deputy of the Czechoslovak National Socialist party and minister of foreign affairs, was opposed by the candidate of the right, the chairman of the Czech National Council, Dr. Bohumil Němec. The Czech parties of the right could not hope to elect their candidate by their own votes alone, nor to prevent the election of Dr. Beneš, even on the assumption that the CPCS and the conservative parties of the ethnic minorities would abstain from voting or run their own candidates. However, the right coalition speculated, with some reason, that the strongest party of the center, the Agrarian and Smallholder party, might eventually be drawn over to its side. Such a combination of forces, along with possible support from the Sudeten-German Home Front (the second strongest parliamentary group) could have changed the prospects of the two candidates radically. In this situation, the CPCS, following the modified Komintern line on possible cooperation with other progressive forces, offered its votes to Dr. Beneš. It was a very successful move. Although in terms of plain arithmetic the thirty deputies and fifteen senators of the Communist party could not yet guarantee the election of Dr. Beneš, they were sufficient to render the victory of his opponent in the first round impossible. The caucus of the

Agrarian party was aware of this fact and conscious, too, that a good part of its electorate disapproved of Němec and of eventual voting combinations with the right. Supporting a candidate who could not win easily would have signified a sure loss but only an uncertain benefit. Thus, curiously, "as the CPCS went, the whole of Czechoslovakia went." Dr. Němec resigned his candidacy and Eduard Beneš was elected practically unopposed.

The Communists expected, or at least professed to expect, that the parties who had supported Beneš from the beginning would "draw the consequences" from the experience of the presidential election.[14] By this they meant that the Agrarian party should be excluded from the government and a new coalition set up, more to the left, presumably with Communist participation. If the Communists hoped for anything of the kind (it is to be doubted that they actually did), their hopes were soon dashed. Nevertheless, after the new ruling of the Third International and the episode of the presidential elections, the issue of cooperation between the CPCS and other components of the left once again became an important problem within the party itself. Even under a Bolshevik leadership, the danger of "social-democratic opportunism" connected with the united front policy line did not seem to be completely banished. As early as 1936, the way some CPCS officials implemented the resolution of the Seventh World Congress of the Komintern began to cause apprehensions both in Prague and in Moscow. There was a certain irony in the fact that among the names cited in connection with what the party leaders and their supervisors in the Kremlin saw as another right deviation were those of the once most devoted representatives of the new left who had carried the day at the Fifth Party Congress in 1929. The criticism of them concerned their allegedly too eager cooperation with the "top organs of the reformist bodies" and the "neglect of patient work at the grass-root level, with the simple members" of these organizations. This definition of the situation by the leadership betrayed its unchanged intention eventually to subvert other socialist parties and workers' movements from below.

We may assume that the feeling of uneasiness about too deep an involvement with the reformist rivals was quite strong, since this issue occupied a prominent place on the agenda of the Seventh Ordinary Congress of the CPCS held in Prague April 11–14, 1936. This congress, deliberating publicly in the National House in Smíchov, a southern industrial and residential section of the capital city, assembled 559 delegates, among whom 495 had the right to vote and 64 held consultative status. According to party records, the membership at that time was about seventy thousand. The central point of the program was "the task of rallying the working class for the struggle against fascism, war and the capitalist offensive," with Klement Gottwald as general reporter. The major internal problem of the party, directly connected with this theme, was that in fulfilling the task of "rallying the working class," certain party activists, so went the report, had committed a new grave mistake of "rightist opportunism" because they had taken the instructions of the Third International too literally. Their mistakes were then examined by a special party commission and found serious enough to call for disciplinary measures. The two most prominent officials among the accused were Jan Šverma and Rudolf Slánský, both erstwhile lads from Karlín, who were later to gain great influence in the party and eventually meet premature death under dramatic circumstances. The Seventh Congress removed them from the Secretariat of the Central Committee, but allowed them to retain their positions as members of the Politbureau.[15]

The remaining major matters of concern at the Seventh Party Congress were the trade unions, recruitment of new members, and party work among the youth. The report on activities among the trade unions, submitted by Antonín Zápotocký, carried an ambitious title: "The Struggle for the Unity of the Trade Union Movement in Czechoslovakia."[16] In reality, the reporter had little to say on the subject. At the time of the Seventh Congress, truly red unions, that is to say, unions under effective control of the Communist party, constituted a small fraction of the Czechoslovak trade union body. The only way the CPCS could gain influence among the unions was to engage in occasional joint actions with the more powerful reformist unions, in the hope that some of their following could be converted to the Communist cause. The growth of the organized party membership was a more satisfactory situation. Although membership had not yet come back up to the pre-bolshevization-supercrisis level, it had increased by almost 75 percent since the Sixth Congress.[17] The report on party work among young people was presented by Václav Kopecký, a member of the Politbureau, who had been editor-in-chief of *Rudé právo* during the period after the expulsion of Josef Guttmann. According to party historians, the quality of youth work in the Communist organizations at that time left very much to be desired. For a long time the leadership had criticized the left radicalism of the Communist youth sections and suspected that the banned Trotskyist faction might have retained some of its influence among the youngest party members.[18] The shortcomings of the youth sector had also been scored by the Sixth Congress of the Communist International of the Youth, an organization affiliated with the Komintern, in Moscow in the fall of 1935. The activities of the Czechoslovak Communist youth leaders and youth leaders of other Communist parties in Europe had been found wanting because they appeared to be too élitist, intellectual, sectarian, and often "entirely detached from the masses." The immediate consequence of this criticism had been a thorough reorganization of the Komsomol, after which it was renamed the Youth Union. The new body was set up as a federation in which all ethnic groups were represented by autonomous sections.

When the Seventh Party Congress adjourned, hardly anyone, whether in the CPCS or outside it, could suspect that this had been the last meeting of its kind during the period between the two world wars. Ten long years were to elapse before the supreme organ of the party would convene again, in radically altered circumstances. Although this major hiatus in the series of party congresses was largely due to causes over which Czechoslovak Communists had no control, it was nevertheless true that the intervals between these meetings had already gradually lengthened before the war. Originally held almost every year, these conventions took place biyearly between 1927 and 1931, and five years elapsed between the Sixth and Seventh Congresses. A similar trend occurred in the Soviet party and the entire international Communist movement. The practice introduced by Stalin, and finally adopted by the Secretariat, of ruling by means of the Politbureau was slowly taken up by the Komintern and the CPCS, among others. Thus the Seventh Congress of the Czechoslovak party, not unlike the Seventh World Congress of the Komintern, was a milestone on the way from bolshevization to Stalinization.

The Seventh Ordinary Congress was the first party congress to be preceded and followed by the conferences of the regional Slovak organization, which was constituted in 1935. This new procedure underscored the new internal structure of the CPCS. The peculiar position of the Slovak ethnic component in the party structure, which it was to retain with little change up to the present day, was already evident; within the party it enjoyed neither equality nor genuine autonomy. The most unusual aspect of the party's internal arrangement, however, was its inconsistent application of the principle of self-government. The centralist character of the national party organization remained intact even after the Slovak units obtained more authority in matters concerning Slovakia. No corresponding concessions were made to other ethnic groups, even though the German-speaking minority, for example, was numerically equal to the Slovak group and indisputably superior to it from the viewpoint of the "maturity of class consciousness." Ethnic individuality was not recognized, either, in the largest nation-building partner, the Czechs, who continued to be amalgamated into the national party framework. What emerged after the agreements of 1930 was a solution that basically contained all the elements of the present formula known as asymmetric centralism. The absence of consistent reforms in the internal party structure made the limited gains of the Slovaks rather precarious. Slovak Communists were aware of this instability, and were prepared to show their discontent more forcefully should general conditions change.

In view of the current ethnic problems within their own ranks, the leaders of the CPCS surprised the Czechoslovak public when, in the fall of 1936, they launched a legislative initiative resolving the same situation on the national level. On November 6, 1936, the parliamentary caucus of the Communist party submitted a detailed memorandum to the government containing proposals of a "settlement of the question of the nationalities in the Republic." The proposals pertained not only to what was then known as the problem of the German-speaking minority—apparently the most pressing one since it had been correctly assumed for a long time that the Nazi regime in neighboring Germany would raise the issue to the level of an international dispute with the intention of neutralizing a potential obstacle to its expansionist policies—but also to the positions of other minorities, such as the Hungarians and Poles, and of the smaller nation-building ethnic groups, the Slovaks and the Ruthenians.[19] Comments in the non-Communist media pointed out that it was relatively easy for a party of "principled opposition," such as the CPCS, to suggest far-reaching constitutional changes and to devise seemingly perfect political arrangements since the responsibility for these changes would have to be borne exclusively by the parties of the government coalition. Some observers believed that the Communist step was dictated by the urgency of the ethnic problem in the party itself, that it was an "externalization of internal dilemmas." Discounting these criticisms, we can see the initiative of the CPCS as a remarkable gesture, especially from the proper historical perspective. In the interests of the truth, the party had to be credited with insight and perspicacity that did not then prevail in other political quarters of the country. If the CPCS, which only shortly before had discovered the worth of Czechoslovak bourgeois democracy, wanted to express its opinion in this way on the order of urgency of the various problems of the state, the point was very well taken. The events at the end of the decade vindicated its view in the most dramatic manner.

The Spanish Civil War

After the 1936 congress of the CPCS and the last world congress of the Communist International (both of which, incidentally, carried the same sequence number and took place at about the same time) the European and world political situation began to take on a very disquieting aspect. The unpunished Japanese aggression against China in the early 1930s had seriously undermined the authority of the League of Nations; now, in the wake of the Italian attack on Abyssinia, the Kellogg-Briand Pact and the system of collective security were put to a new test and were found deficient. The war in East Africa, in 1935 and 1936, had a special significance for Czechoslovakia, since the decision of the League of Nations to apply economic sanctions against Italy was taken while the Czechoslovak minister of foreign affairs and later president of the republic, Eduard Beneš, chaired the General Assembly of the Geneva organization. Although it was completely ineffective as a brake on Italian war efforts, this decision made fascist Italy into a mortal enemy of Czechoslovakia. Thus, after the two key powers, France and England, abandoned the policy of resistance to Mussolini, Czechoslovakia was one of the political losers in the Abyssinian conflict. The outcome of the East African war was undoubtedly a new blow to the League of Nations; this institution would be given one more opportunity, before its final demise, to demonstrate its impotence, in connection with a major crisis concerning Czechoslovakia.

The CPCS took no decisive stand in the face of these alarming developments despite its recent pledge to resist fascism and to recognize distinctions between various types of non-Communist systems and regimes. The Communists did not compromise on the negative position toward Italian fascism and German National Socialism that they had been so slow in adopting. They saw in Mussolini's colonial adventures a "desperate self-preservation attempt of capitalism in its most highly developed and most precarious stage." However, their scorn for what they called the "predatory peace settlement of Versailles,"[20] in other words the political order established in Europe after World War I, was boundless and it did not spare any institution or system of alliances connected with this order. This rejection of the status quo, which was partly due to the fact that the Soviet Union, as a successor to the Russian empire, had been one of the losers of the First World War and had been obliged to relinquish many territories previously held by czarist Russia, seemed to align the Communists with the most rabid elements of the extreme right and discredited the professed "common struggle with other progressive forces against fascism." The Communist world only slowly moved away from total lack of discrimination among all political factions to the right of the extreme left.

The Communists' perceptions of the impending confrontation between the aggressive forces of the fascist powers on the European continent and the Western liberal democracies were crystallized by an important historical event that occurred in an area remote from Central Europe but had repercussions throughout the world Communist movement: the Civil War in Spain, fought from 1936 till 1938. It broke out after a military coup led by General Francisco Franco against the coalition government of the Popular Front in July 1936. This government, which had succeeded the dictatorship's cabinet of rightist and monarchist groups following the general elections of February 1936, was another example of the practical implementation of the united front line laid down by the Komintern insofar as it included representatives of the Spanish Communist party. However, the Communist Party of Spain constituted a very special case among its sister parties. Strongly permeated by anarcho-syndicalist elements, which seemed to be endemic in the Iberian peninsula, it had always been a problem for the Communist International. It had resisted domination by Moscow more staunchly than many other sections of the Komintern, and this resistance increased along with Stalin's efforts to streamline the international Communist movement. The Spanish Communists, who were now in the strategic position of a government coalition partner, were anything but a dependable tool of the Kremlin. The consequences of their proclivity to follow an independent course risked becoming even more serious when the Civil War broke out. After a long wait, a new opportunity to prepare for a Communist take-over in an important European country had appeared, but the principal agent in this process resisted the control of the world Communist headquarters: the strategists of revolution in Moscow were not likely to accept this situation passively.

The problem was further compounded by the active participation in the Spanish Civil War of the various sympathizers with the cause of the Spanish Republic. These volunteers were by no means all Communists; they came from all progressive and leftist backgrounds, beginning with left liberals and ending with anarchists and Trotskyists. The organizational platform of their involvement was the International Brigade, or as it was called in the leftist jargon, the Interbrigade. The Communists, who constituted an important contingent of this unit, tried from the very beginning to gain and to maintain control over the recruitment, organization, and actual combat engagement of the volunteers. They had at their disposal an international structure that was relatively easy to coordinate and to subject to uniform policies. Communist parties enjoying legal status played a key role in the recruitment process; an extremely important function was assigned to the CPCS, which, since the Nazi take-over in Germany and the Dolfuss putsch in Austria, had been the only Komintern section east of the Rhine operating within a constitutional framework. The Secretariat of the CPCS thus became the clearinghouse for all those in Central or Eastern Europe who wished to enlist for service in the Interbrigade. On the other hand, the disparate political orientations of the volunteers was a source of permanent tension and conflict that was added to those already existing among the national components of the Komintern as well as within the individual Communist parties. Thus the Spanish Civil War laid bare deep-seated conflicts and divisions of the European extreme left and at the same time provided an arena for these conflicts to be fought out. The confrontation between the various chapters and trends of the international Communist movement took particularly appalling proportions and eventually became one of the reasons for the defeat of the republican government in the Civil War. The consequences of this struggle continued to plague many Communist parties long after the Second World War: the positions taken by individual Communist leaders and groups during the years of the Spanish civil strife marked their party careers for the rest of their lives and thus became bases of permanent cleavages. The CPCS was a prominent case in point.

The Czechoslovak participation in the Interbrigade was very significant in relation to its size. According to official Communist statistics published in the 1950s, more than twenty thousand volunteers from all countries fought in this corps during the three years of the Civil War, and of these no less than twenty-five hundred were recruited in Czechoslovakia: thus the Czechoslovak contingent formed about 12 percent. The Czechs and Slovaks fighting in Spain were organized in the battalions "Jan Žižka" (named after the military commander of the Hussite reformation forces in the fifteenth century), "T. G. Masaryk," and "Divisinario." There was also a smaller unit of artillery bearing the name of CPCS Secretary-General Klement Gottwald.[21] The choice of the names suggests that only a part of the Czechoslovak component of the Interbrigade was composed of orthodox Communist party members. However, the party secured an influence far exceeding the participation of its followers in the combat actions because it was the only Czechoslovak party that put its entire organization behind the Spanish republican cause. The socialist parties of the governmental coalition were bound by the commitment to nonintervention made by all member states of the League of Nations, a shameful compromise reached on the initiative of Great Britain and France that not only opened the door for massive intervention by the nonmember powers Italy and Germany, but also placed the Soviet Union and the various European Communist movements in a unique position of political and moral advantage. In Czechoslovakia, where public opinion, with the exception of the extreme right, deeply sympathized with republican Spain, this advantage was of particular significance.

Thus the Civil War in Spain became both a great opportunity and at the same time a trial for the CPCS. But because world communism in the second half of the 1930s was no more than an appendage of Stalin's personal power, the opportunity proved to be of little worth. On the contrary, through its involvement in the Spanish campaign the party became hopelessly enmeshed in the complicated internal struggles, both in the Kremlin and in the international Communist movement, that came into the open in the Spanish war arena. As early as the end of 1936, the Presidium of the Executive Committee of the Komintern, in a declaration concerning the situation in Spain, stated that there were Trotskyists who "worked as fascist agents and as stooges in the interest of Hitler and General Franco" and that they "undertook a slander campaign against the USSR, in order to prevent by all means the defeat of fascism in Spain." The declaration explicitly exhorted all Communists to a "complete and final annihilation of Trotskyism."[22] This instruction was widely followed. Indeed, the Spanish Civil War became an occasion for the physical destruction of individuals and whole groups who, for various reasons, had displeased Stalin or constituted a potential threat to his absolute rule. This destruction was achieved partly by selecting allegedly unreliable subjects in the Interbrigade for especially risky missions, where the vicissitudes of war were likely to take care of the problem (a method later repeated by Stalinist Kapos, or elected representatives of political inmates in the Nazi concentration camps) and partly by so-called direct disciplinary actions, which meant mass executions of Interbrigadists under the indictment of high treason. These hecatombs decimated many national contingents of the Interbrigade, especially the French and the German. The terrifying casualty rate among the Czechoslovak group—according to official Communist statistics, two thousand of the twenty-five hundred Czechoslovak volunteers lost their lives in Spain—can to a large extent be explained by this bloody showdown between the Stalinists and their opponents.[23] However, the death toll was not the only price the party paid for its involvement. The feuds and disputes generated among the Communists during the Spanish Civil War survived the dissolution of the Interbrigade and played a significant role in many later conflicts within the world Communist movement and in the CPCS. At the height of Stalinist terror in the 1950s, for example, a party member with an Interbrigade record was almost certain to be suspected and to suffer persecution. The so-called Španěláci ("Spaniards") were at that time counted among unreliable minorities, which also included bourgeois nationalists and Jews. Even as late as 1969, a year after the Soviet military intervention in Czechoslovakia, the Spanish past was a part of the blame put on Dubček's minister of the interior, Josef Pavel, when the latter was purged.

The Munich Crisis

When in October 1938, as a one-sided gesture of the Spanish republican government, the Interbrigade was pulled out of combat and the Czechoslovak detachments were interned in the south of France, the great European crisis leading to the Second World War was already far advanced. This crisis provided the CPCS with a new opportunity to present itself to public opinion as an uncompromising antifascist force and to appear as a guardian of democracy, liberty, and other progressive values and traditions of Czechoslovak history. The party made a serious effort to take advantage of this opportunity. Its task was not always rendered easy by the policies of the Soviet Union, especially at the outbreak and during the first two years of the war. On the other hand, it was greatly facilitated by the political debacle of the Western powers responsible for maintaining the political order on the European continent established by the Treaty of Versailles. The lamentable show of opportunism and impotence on the part of France and England at this critical juncture, which entered the annals as the "policy of appeasement," considerably detracted from both their claim to world leadership and the principles by which they had reconstructed Europe after 1918. It was this last consequence that the CPCS chose to exploit for maximum political capital and that has ever since been its ideological stock-in-trade and an indispensable part of the argument by which it has justified the existence of the present socioeconomic system in Czechoslovakia.

The Communists have not succeeded in substituting their value system for the one that was threatened or placed in doubt during the "appeasement" years of the late 1930s, nor have they achieved the desired transfer of the Czechoslovak population's allegiance to the Soviet Union. The events immediately preceding the Second World War have considerably shaken the confidence the Czechs and the Slovaks had placed in the West European democracies, but the anticipated "renversement des alliances" did not take place. Nevertheless, the CPCS has based a good deal of its claim to absolute power and unconditional obedience to the Soviet Union on the failure of the West to defend Central and Eastern Europe against German and Italian imperialism in 1938. The Communists have interpreted this failure as a proof of the nonviability of the social and political system associated with liberal democracy. In fact, the events of the fall of 1938 have played a greater role in the justification of the present regime than the arguments of classical Marxist sociology, economics, or philosophy of history. The most succinct expression of this line of reasoning is to be found in the current slogan "With the Soviet Union Forever—And Nevermore Otherwise!" The collapse of the system of alliance with Western democracies, so goes the argument, made the further existence of the Czechoslovak state— even the plain survival of the Czechs and the Slovaks—dependent on an indissoluble partnership with Communist Russia. The internal political form, the type of ownership of the means of production, and the cultural orientation of Czechoslovak society follow logically from this irreversible dependency. In other words, in the terms of this argument, the Czechoslovak Republic can exist either as a Communist party-state or not at all.

As has been suggested, this is not the view of the majority of the Czechoslovak population, or even of all party members. The USSR and its servants in the Communist movement have had recourse to it in times of crisis, whenever there has been the need to justify actions aimed at the restoration of Soviet control, such as the military intervention of 1968. Nevertheless, it would be a grave mistake to minimize in any way the impact of the experience, now known to history as Munich 1938, upon the perceptions the two nation-building ethnic groups have formed of their identity, the meaning of their past, and their place in world politics. Munich, without the slightest doubt, was an agonizing crisis of legitimacy of the entire system of social and political values that had been vindicated by the victory of the West in the First World War and upon which Czechoslovak independence had been based. The crisis was resolved only through a new global conflict, but a new dilemma arose in the end, that of resisting the challenge, this time from the left, to the open society. The Czechoslovak political culture proved to be resilient enough to withstand the pressures and temptations of fascism, despite the bitter disappointment about the indifference of the great democratic nations to the fate of Czechoslovakia. It was considerably less impervious to the totalitarian danger under the guise of socialism. The reasons for this weakness may be sought partly in the deep-seated leftist traditions, reinforced by the peculiar social structure discussed earlier in this volume, and partly in what can be called the Munich trauma. The effects of the latter will probably be felt for many years to come. The Communist party grasped the significance of this trauma from the beginning and used it as a stepping-stone to absolute power, which it eventually acquired in 1948. It may be seen as an irony of history that the so-called Munich complex—that is, the perception of the risk of isolation in moments of crisis that the Czechs and the Slovaks had developed in 1938 and that had for so long brought political dividends to Czechoslovak Communists—was exploited, thirty years after the actual event and twenty years after the February coup d'état, by the Soviet Union against the leadership of the CPCS. The circumstance that at the moment of military intervention by the Warsaw Pact armies against Dubček's course, no gesture of organized resistance, even on a token scale, was made by the group in control can be ascribed in part to the image of a hopeless international situation, very similar to that of the autumn months of 1938, that was shared by the whole Czechoslovak public, Communist and non-Communist alike.

To be sure, it would take more than one generation for the Czecho-slovak Communists themselves to experience the paralyzing effect of the Munich complex. In 1938, they could see themselves simply as bene-ficiaries of the political and moral bankruptcy of the West. Thereafter they gradually established themselves as champions of the independence and territorial integrity of Czechoslovakia, a nation that barely five years earlier they had vowed to destroy and whose ethnic minorities they never tired of inciting to exercise their right of self-determination "to the point of secession." This major shift in policy was made easier for the CPCS by the fact that the external enemy of Czechoslovakia happened to be a dictatorship of the extreme right that was persecuting all other political groups and parties, including the Communists, and at that point behaving, at lest verbally, like a militant opponent of the Soviet Union. The scenario was to change radically at the outbreak of the war, but in 1938 the patriotic posture of the Czechoslovak Communist party was in no serious contradiction with its allegiance to the "Fatherland of Workers and Peasants." This posture bore immediate political gains. In the municipal elections of May 1938, the Communist candidates were very successful in many industrial and urban centers except in the border regions inhabited by ethnic Germans. Their success was particularly pronounced in the capital city, where they polled about a hundred thousand votes—an increase of 66 percent over their total in the previous municipal elections. They became the second strongest party in Prague.

It is not easy to decide whether the more attractive public image of the CPCS was only a temporary phenomenon or whether it marked the beginning of a long-term trend. Similarly, it is difficult to evaluate today the Czechoslovak Communist movement's chances, in 1938, of maturing under the impact of the Nazi threat and hence of emerging as a more constructive element of the Czechoslovak left. The non-Communist components of the socialist and workers' movement repeatedly rejected Communist initiatives for a Popular Front or united front, arguing that the actual goal of the Communists was the subversion and ultimate control of all groups and organizations that would consent to a collabora-tion with them. In fact, the chances that the CPCS would be spontane-ously converted into a partner respectful of the rules of the democratic game did not appear very great at the end of the 1930s considering that the leadership was in the hands of officials unconditionally loyal to Moscow and to its international tool, the Komintern. Moreover, the continuing purges since the Fifth Party Congress, of which the years 1937 and 1938 had seen several, eliminated from the leading positions all individuals who had exhibited any independent judgment.

Speculations of this kind are certainly interesting, like all conjectures about the alternative courses history could have taken if certain events had not happened and others had; but they can never become more than speculations. What was certain during the European crisis of the late 1930s was the determination of the CPCS to build up its reputation as a force resolutely opposed to the Nazi aggressor and committed to the protection of Czechoslovakia's security. The real significance of these efforts, however, can only be measured if they are understood as a part of a master plan sponsored by the Soviet Union. After all, it was the international balance of power that the Kremlin wished to modify, not so much the image the Czechoslovak public at large had of the patriotism of the CPCS. The redemption of the Czechoslovak Communist movement from the charge of hostility to the Czechoslovak state which the previous twenty years of party policy appeared to justify was, to be sure, one of the preconditions for the success of Soviet designs, but in itself this would not have amounted to very much. Thus the stand taken by the Czechoslovak Communists on Munich in 1938 can be properly appreciated only if due attention is paid to parallel Soviet moves on the international political chessboard.

As the ultimate showdown in Central Europe approached and the "final abdication of France and Great Britain from the rank of great powers," aptly diagnosed by a perspicacious French columnist,[24] became a real possibility, various conjectures about the Tripartite Pact (France, the Soviet Union, and Czechoslovakia) to be substituted for the increasingly unreliable system of alliances based on the Western Entente began to spread in the international press and among political observers. Commentators tried to fathom the real intentions of the Soviet Union in the eventuality of a German attack on Czechoslovakia. They were aware that in the terms of the 1935 treaty the USSR was under no obligation, explicit or implicit, to provide assistance to Czechoslovakia if France did not recognize that a "casus foederis," an emergency requiring French intervention, had occurred. Soviet spokesmen remained uncommitted on this issue until the crisis reached its peak, in September 1938. On the other hand, the military preparations of the USSR, occasionally impaired by purges of the officer corps, and the vociferous anti-Nazi propaganda in the Soviet media left room for speculations of all kinds. It certainly is interesting to a historian to guess what the Soviet Union would have done if Czechoslovakia had had to fight alone against the Third Reich. However, in the context of our discussion, it is more important to evaluate actual Soviet behavior and its possible motivation during the Munich crisis.

Some Soviet diplomatic steps undertaken in the decisive week before the Munich conference could have been interpreted as signs that Moscow was preparing for a possible unilateral involvement in the eventual conflict between Czechoslovakia and Germany. Among them, the move by the Soviet vice-commissar of foreign affairs, Vladimir P. Potemkin, who on September 23, 1938, summoned the Polish chargé d'affaires Janowski and threatened the revocation of the Soviet-Polish nonaggression treaty should Poland participate in a military action against Czechoslovakia, stimulated much speculation in the world. Many understood it as an attempt to create legal conditions for moving Soviet troops via Poland to the Czechoslovak territory with which the Soviet Union did not at that time have a common border. However, the most authoritative source on Munich, Czechoslovak President Beneš, in his memoirs and in another volume dealing with the events of the fall of 1938, credits the Soviets with little more than the willingness to fulfill their explicit contractual obligations. This admittedly was more than France, for example, was willing to do, but it could not change the situation as it developed in September 1938. The Czechoslovak Communist party leaders, especially Klement Gottwald, then claimed that the USSR was prepared "to go it alone" for the sake of Czechoslovakia, and pressed the head of the state to "accept Soviet help." However, Beneš in his presentation of the events asserts that no such assurance was ever given to him or to any other member of the Czechoslovak government by the official Soviet representatives.[25]

Yet, seen from today's perspective, the stand taken by the Soviet Union was far more than just a beautiful gesture of a power whom the pitiful behavior of the leaders of nations responsible for the world order and peace put into a morally strong position. It was a deposit on very essential benefits to be collected in Central Europe a decade later. The "unselfish Soviet offer" of which the Czechoslovak government allegedly failed to take advantage became a legend with powerful psychological and propagandistic effects. The ingredients of this legend were many. In addition to ambiguous statements by Soviet politicians and diplomats in their dealings with the Czechoslovak government, Soviet conduct in the international arena at the time of the Munich crisis helped to build up the image of the Soviet Union as an objective and responsible partner in the community of nations, devoted to the cause of peace and security, and willing to take the inevitable consequences. The most memorable instance of this conduct was the initiative of Soviet Foreign Minister Litvinov in the General Assembly of the League of Nations, which was in session while the conference of the four European powers in Munich decided the fate of Czechoslovakia. "We live up to our treaties and honor our signatures," declared Litvinov, reiterating the Soviet readiness to fulfill the obligations of the Tripartite Pact. He then completed his statement with what might have seemed a very concrete proposition but was actually only an impressive gesture. According to Litvinov, the Soviet Union was prepared to go beyond the explicit commitments of the treaty and assist Czechoslovakia even if France did not recognize the existence of a situation requiring her intervention. This would be possible, the Soviet foreign minister declared, under either of two conditions: (1) An eventual German military action against Czechoslovakia would be tabled in the appropriate organs of the League of Nations as a threat to world peace and Germany would be identified as an aggressor by either the Security Council or the General Assembly or both. (2) The indictment of Germany would be tabled in the General Assembly without any action taken by the Assembly.[26] It appeared that the USSR really had gone a long way to help Czechoslovakia. From the purely theoretical viewpoint of international law, the Soviets indeed went to the limit. Under a more careful scrutiny, however, and taking into consideration the situation at the time, the Soviet move was basically a political demonstration calculated to enter the historical record.

It is obvious that neither of the two alternatives that Litvinov suggested as conditions for Soviet assistance to Czechoslovakia without French participation was realistic at the end of September 1938. About the fate of an eventual motion introduced in the Security Council, with the purpose of declaring Germany to be the aggressor, there could be no doubt once the Munich treaty was signed: it would have been vetoed by France and Great Britain. The chances that the motion would have been accepted in the General Assembly, that is, passed by a qualified majority over the double French and British veto, were equally illusory. Many of the lesser powers represented in Geneva in 1938 would have followed the French and English lead, not necessarily out of sympathy with Hitler or because of a grudge against Czechoslovakia, but rather because of the simple facts of international politics. The rest would have abstained. The alliance with the Soviet Union, too, had an adverse effect upon the Czechoslovak cause. Even among the small allies of Czechoslovakia, especially Rumania, the prospect that the endorsement of the motion would bring the Red Army west of the Curzon Line was truly frightening. There remained the second alternative: the possibility that the motion would be submitted to the General Assembly but not acted upon. This eventuality too was ruled out by all who realistically assessed the circumstances at that time. It was inconceivable that the League of Nations, an almost exclusive domain of the two European victors of the First World War, would disavow the architects of the Munich treaty, even by default. Thus we can safely assume that the initiative suggested by Litvinov would have failed in both instances: it would have been first thrown out of the Security Council and subsequently defeated in the General Assembly. Considering these facts, the Soviet offer appears to have been a very well-calculated risk. As history later showed, it brought in all the anticipated returns.

Moscow in 1938 was not really willing to become involved in a major conflict in Central Europe, and it is not difficult to see why. Although the conservative governments of France and England pursued a policy of extreme appeasement, they did not find the idea of an eventual war between the Third Reich and the USSR too repulsive. They did their utmost to avoid a military confrontation with Germany, sacrificing their influence, prestige, and finally their own security. However, should a collision between Hitler and Stalin have nevertheless occurred, it would have taken care of two dangerous rivals at the same time. The Entente could reasonably hope to stay out of the conflict or, a still better alternative, to act as an arbiter in its final phase. The Soviet leaders knew this well, and it is to the credit of their statesmanship that they did not want to oblige. As subsequent events showed, they were prepared to go a long way to avoid political and military commitments that they felt would have benefited the Western "plutocracies." Actually, they may have gone too far for their own good. In the immediate context of the Czechoslovak crisis of the fall of 1938, however, there was little they could be blamed for, either as signatories of the Tripartite Pact or as partners in the European concert of great powers.

The clean record of the Soviet Union, earned at the time of the fateful Munich conference, is one thing, but the internal political use the CPCS made of the Soviet gesture in Geneva is quite another matter. To paraphrase a familiar statement made in a different context, "never has so much been achieved by so few at such little cost." The exploitation of Litvinov's initiative, which now has continued for over forty years, has been a masterpiece of propaganda. Skillful hints and properly edited references to this brief and cheap show of goodwill became a very important element in the political ammunition that successfully lowered the defenses of Czechoslovak democracy against Communist totalitarian subversion. Shortly before its temporary demise, the CPCS acquired a political asset that would pay considerable dividends once the European and world holocaust was over.

During the weeks of the Munich crisis, the party was very active and appeared very patriotic. The emotional words that Secretary-General Gottwald spoke to the president of the republic on the eve of the capitulation to Hitler and in which he extolled the heroism of the Abyssinian Negus as an example for Czechoslovakia to follow, might not have been in agreement with Marxist principles, but they were meant for a broad audience and surely were heard.[27] What was even more important, they could be recalled with advantage by the Communist propagandists after the war. Vociferous statements by Communist leaders were accompanied by mass rallies in the whole country that, given the general mood prevailing at that time, had no difficulty in attracting the participation of people otherwise unconnected with or even hostile to the Communist cause. The main effort was directed at presenting to the public a situation in which Czechoslovakia was capable, with the help of the Soviet Union, of defeating the Nazi enemy but was betrayed by the "bourgeois establishment" because of its fear of socialism. In the fall of 1938, the party made considerable progress toward this goal. The image of the Soviet Union as the only reliable ally of Czechoslovakia was further reinforced by the vehemence of the anti-Soviet language used by the Nazi media and by the condition incorporated into the Munich "Diktat" that Czechoslovakia should sever all ties based on the Tripartite Pact. These perceptions still fell short of the actual Communist objective, which was to equate the survival of Czechoslovakia with a Communist revolution, but a change favoring the Communist movement was undeniable.

Chapter Four

From Munich to Liberation

The German Occupation and the War

The immediate consequences of the Munich crisis did not permit Czechoslovak Communists to enjoy the fruit of their new policies. Nor was the patriotic image of communism to last very long. The change in Soviet diplomacy on the eve of the Second World War and the conclusion of the Soviet-German nonaggression pact, which the CPCS unreservedly endorsed, deprived the party of the credit it had accumulated in 1938. However, the position it had taken at the time of national emergency at least made possible a gracious exit into political hibernation. It was obvious, once the mutilated Czechoslovak Republic fell into the power orbit of the Third Reich, that its pluralist political system was doomed. The road to the ultimate authoritarian order passed through the halfway house of a simplification of the political party spectrum, and the Communist party became the first casualty of this process. It cannot be said that this development caught the CPCS unprepared. On October 9, 1938, three days after a regional conference in Žilina, the party organization in Slovakia suspended its activity. One of the consequences of the Munich agreement had been the introduction into Czechoslovakia of a dualistic political form whereby Slovakia was granted autonomous status. Since the political groups in control of Slovak local government were right conservatives with fascist leanings, the climate there could not be expected to have been very favorable to the Communists. In the Czech provinces, Bohemia and Moravia, the internal situation was somewhat different: the Socialist party continued to exist under a different name, but the pressures from Berlin were very strong. Hitler wished Czechoslovakia to align with other fascist and authoritarian regimes in Central and Eastern Europe and to outlaw the Communist party, among others. The CPCS organizations in the western provinces therefore followed the Slovak example on October 20, 1938, and voluntarily stopped all activities. Identical measures were taken in Ruthenia. Also in October 1938, the Red Unions merged with the nationwide "reformist" Association of Trade Unions. A committee of trustees headed by Antonín Zápotocký was constituted in Prague to protect the assets and the legal interests of the party. Thus when the Czechoslovak government, on an explicit request from Berlin, dissolved the CPCS on December 27, 1938, the party was already well advanced along the passage from open activities to conditions of illegality. The Communist movement began to adapt to circumstances it had not earlier experienced. The first era of the history of the Czechoslovak Section of the Third International had come to an end.

The "Imperialist" Phase of World War II

On March 15, 1939, German armies occupied what was left of the Czech provinces after the amputation of the border regions, and a German protectorate was proclaimed over these territories. Slovakia (which in November 1938 had had to cede the southern districts inhabited by the Hungarian-speaking population to Hungary) became a puppet state of the Third Reich. Ruthenia had been incorporated into Hungary after twenty-four hours of independence. The new regimes in both Slovakia and Ruthenia started immediately to persecute all persons and groups suspected of left leanings: among these the Communists became the primary target. The government of the Protectorate of Bohemia and Moravia did not join in this campaign, but since matters of political security there were reserved to the jurisdiction of the Reich and entrusted to the German Secret State Police (Gestapo), leaders and activists of the CPCS experienced no less persecution than their comrades elsewhere in Central and Eastern Europe. The so-called Legal Representative Committee of the party, created in Prague in the fall of 1938, was soon decimated by arrests and internments. The underground political activity then passed into the hands of the First Illegal Central Committee, composed of Emanuel Klíma, Otto Synek, Viktor Synek, Eduard Urx, and Jan Zika. This secret party organ continued to operate until the fall of 1940, but the Gestapo succeeded, relatively early, in penetrating the underground network and it was merely a question of time until it identified and located the top leadership.[1] A certain delay in the action against the Communist organization was caused by developments of the international situation during 1939, which considerably improved the relations between the Soviet Union and Nazi Germany. As the Kremlin gradually but unmistakably moved away from a possible involvement in the now inevitable world conflict and the hostilities in Europe became imminent, the German political police in Czechoslovakia saw more urgent tasks to attend to than wiping out the surviving remnants of the Communist movement. This in no way signified that the Communist party was considered harmless by the authorities of the occupation, but it was spared, for the moment, the full impact of Nazi repression.

The records of party transactions from this period indicate that neither the significant propaganda achievements during the Munich crisis nor the passage from legal status into the underground had changed in any appreciable way the internal problems inherited from the era of the First Republic. On the contrary, during this period of illegality important new cleavages began to emerge that later engendered or aggravated a number of serious crises. The most portentous of these cleavages was ethnic. Ethnic tensions had been one of the weak spots of the Czechoslovak state, undermining its otherwise solid foundations. We have seen that although the CPCS took an uncompromising stand in favor of the principle of self-determination, it did not escape the dynamics of the unresolved problem of the nationalities. The political catastrophe of Munich and the territorial disintegration of Czechoslovakia sharpened the ethnic dilemmas of the Communist movement. This difficult situation was not much eased by the Komintern's position on these issues. Faster than the CPCS itself, the Komintern abandoned the positive attitude toward Czechoslovakia that it had exhibited during the crisis of 1938 and acknowledged, as early as January 1939, the territorial status quo created by Hitler in Central Europe. In a special recommendation by the Executive Committee, it sponsored the constitution of separate Communist parties of Slovakia and of the regions annexed to Germany under the Munich treaty under the name of Sudeten Province (Gau Sudetenland). The encouragement it gave to the Slovak chapter of the former CPCS especially helped to promote tendencies that long after the war and the seizure of power by Czechoslovak Communists were to result in a deep and protracted internal dispute.

Even without the initiative of the Third International, the centrifugal forces would probably have thrived in the conditions of illegality and isolation, and in the absence of a visible central leadership. In Slovakia, the responsibility for the underground organization was entrusted to a secret regional committee including, among others, Ludovít Benada, Július Ďuriš, and Ján Osaha. The last named was a dyed-in-the-wool Slovak nationalist who did not dissimulate the goals of Slovak communism as he saw them: to work for "an independent, Soviet Socialist Slovakia."[2] An external sign of the new course was the establishment, in a secret meeting in May 1939, of a Communist Party of Slovakia (Komunistická strana Slovenska or CPS), which comprised the underground segments of the CPCS in Slovakia and was to be on a par with all other national Communist parties affiliated with the Communist International. The course toward independence had a strong following among the lesser party officials in Slovakia. However, the illegal center in Bohemia and Moravia and the exiled leadership in Moscow, with a branch office in Paris, both preserved the name and the organizational form of the CPCS, thus claiming—implicitly and explicitly—the right to represent the entire Communist movement on the former Czechoslovak territory. It did not seem to disturb anyone that this claim contradicted the Third International's official ruling of January 1939. Ironically, too, many of those who were then most in agreement with the Komintern line became, a decade and a half later, the first victims of Moscow-sponsored purges, under the indictment of Slovak bourgeois nationalism.

With its ethnic problem anything but resolved, the party in the underground and in exile had to face a grave crisis soon after the dismemberment of Czechoslovakia, this time affecting all leaders of all parties in the world, as well as their rank-and-file memberships: the psychological and moral effects of the Soviet "renversement des alliances," which shattered the painstakingly built-up image of communism as a vanguard of the antifascist struggle. Stalin's volte-face—or at least what appeared to be a volte-face in the summer of the fateful year 1939—had far-reaching consequences everywhere. Some of these consequences were to become permanent, such as the estrangement of prominent individuals and whole groups from the Communist cause. It can be asserted that the temporary defection of the Soviet Union from the anti-Nazi coalition dealt the final blow to what was left of the Komintern's prestige. The indifference Stalin showed to the feelings and the interests of the Communists in areas threatened by Hitler demonstrated the brutal fact of the priority of the Soviet "raison d'État" over all considerations of international proletarian solidarity. The shock was exceptionally hard for the CPCS. In a way it was to the party's advantage that at that point it did not need to think of any elections, since it is almost certain that Stalin's diplomatic somersaults would have exacted a very heavy toll. We will never know exactly how much support the party lost on that occasion, but it can be safely assumed that the psychological effects of the Soviet-German pact nullified all the gains of the last prewar years. Party historians later admitted that at the beginning of the war the illegal CPCS had faced a very difficult situation and the necessity to engage in a two-front fight: against the German occupational power and against the Western-oriented Czechoslovak bourgeois anti-Nazi resistance. As the official party sources reveal, there were signs of wavering and hesitation within the party ranks, but they claim that all these problems were duly overcome. Party annals even take credit for having never lost sight of the specific interests of the working class and claim that the occasional salary and wage raises granted to the Czech labor force by the Protectorate authorities were enforced by a strike movement directed by the underground Communist organization.

The truth is that the image of the CPCS was then at its lowest. The illegal party leadership's unreserved acceptance of and faithful obedience to the new Moscow line of neutrality in the war and of partnership with Nazi Germany in the partition of Poland did not do much to improve this image. The non-Communist public occasionally caught a glimpse of the way the party elites thought from the underground Communist press, whose circulation in the first years of the war did not seem to alarm the German secret police. Most of these publications either engaged in antiwar propaganda, in which all belligerent powers and their respective political systems were lumped together as imperialist (but England and France got particularly harsh treatment as "rapacious Western plutocracies" bent on imposing a "new predatory peace of the Versailles style" on Germany) or they focused on systematic denunciation and defamation of the non-Communist resistance and the activities of the Czech and Slovak liberal leaders in exile, especially of those participating in the Czechoslovak National Committee in London headed by Dr. Eduard Beneš. They blamed the resistance movement and the liberation campaign abroad, among others, for "inciting the Czech workers to a hatred of their German brethren in uniforms."[3] Considering the tenor of these periodicals, it is easy to see why the Gestapo did not deem it essential to silence the Communist underground press.

As for the CPCS components outside the country, these offered a rather confused picture. There was the exile Presidium in Moscow, constituted in November 1938, and including Secretary-General Klement

Gottwald; Politbureau members Rudolf Slánský, Josef Krosnář, and Václav Kopecký; the CPCS representative in the Executive Committee of the Komintern, Čeněk Hruška; and two leaders of the German-speaking group in the party, Rudolf Appelt and Robert Korb. After the outbreak of the war, Slánský moved to Paris where he joined two other prominent CPCS members, Vlado Clementis and Jan Šverma. Thus a Paris center came into existence, although it led only a semilegal existence and was disbanded after the defeat of France in July 1940. Another group of Communist officials worked in London, under appreciably more favorable conditions: the British government, unlike its French counterpart, never outlawed Communist activities. The most prominent personality in the London branch was Karl Kreibich, whom we have seen as the organizer of the German section of the CPCS in 1919 and one of the founders of the Czechoslovak Communist movement. The three exile centers, Moscow, Paris, and London, worked without much coordination, although the Presidium in Moscow was recognized as the formal head of the party in exile. All three blindly followed the line on the war laid down by the Soviet Union. Their attitude to the action for the liberation of Czechoslovakia remained hostile until the invasion of the USSR by Hitler in June 1941. The London group conducted a very intensive campaign against Dr. Beneš and his associates, whom it singled out, in a pamphlet published soon after the Munich treaty, as "The Guilty Men of Czechoslovakia" for their alleged refusal to accept Soviet aid in September 1938 and the "betrayal of the Czechoslovak working people."[4] After the conclusion of the Soviet-German nonaggression pact, this approach was abandoned, only to be replaced by invectives against the National Committee as a "tool of plutocratic imperialism." The only exception in the records of the exile CPCS of that time was the condemnation by Vlado Clementis, in Paris in August 1939, of the Soviet-Nazi agreement, and his temporary withdrawal from Communist ranks. Clementis's gesture seemed to have been forgotten when, after the outbreak of hostilities between the Third Reich and the USSR, he found his way back to the fold; but it had never been forgiven, and Clementis eventually had to pay for it with his own head, during the Stalinist purges in the 1950s.

In an effort to justify the Soviet Union's cooperation with Nazi Germany, party underground workers and party media encouraged the membership to hope that the USSR might take advantage of its position and press for an improvement of the situation of the small nations within the German power orbit. However, the division of Poland between Germany and the Soviets in October 1939 and the occupation of the Baltic countries by the Red Army indicated that Moscow had its own ideas about how to put to the best use whatever edge the new international relations in Europe may have provided. The Finnish Winter War of 1939–40 and the annexation of Bessarabia by the USSR were quite consistent with this impression. A realistic interpretation of the Soviet foreign policy line appeared even more necessary when at the end of 1939 the Soviet government closed down the Czechoslovak legation in Moscow, expelled the plenipotentiary minister Zdeněk Fierlinger, and recognized de jure the Slovak state, a satellite of the Third Reich. The progressive implementation of the various clauses of the Soviet-German nonaggression treaty and of the secret protocol attached to this treaty, both of which were scrupulously observed by Stalin, signified that the USSR intended to abstain from all actions, even symbolic, that could be understood as support or sympathy for the populations under Nazi domination. This course created a difficult situation for those detachments of the Czechoslovak army that had fled to Poland and thence to the Soviet Union after the German occupation of Prague. The history of these units is pertinent to that of the CPCS insofar as their commander, Colonel-Lieutenant Ludvík Svoboda, a career officer with a rather conservative background, later joined the party and played an important role on two crucial occasions: in February 1948 and in August 1968. Following the Soviet-German agreement, these troops were interned and their position seemed to be rather precarious. Although their worst fears did not materialize, they could not be certain of their future, especially when they considered the fate of the former Interbrigadists who had found asylum in the USSR or of the German Communists whom Stalin, after a series of purges, had extradited to his Nazi treaty partner.

Despite all these individual agonies, the CPCS, like all other Communist parties, kept supporting the general Soviet line without reservation until the Nazi attack on the USSR, in June 1941, changed the situation. Stalin's dream of becoming the *tertius gaudens* in the world conflict and of preparing for the West the same fate that Chamberlain and Daladier had wished for the Soviet Union in 1938 came to nothing. Instead of profiting from the imperialist war, the Kremlin now had to bear its main brunt. Faced with implacable facts, Stalin chose to make a virtue out of a necessity. The imperialist war overnight became the Great Patriotic War.

Although this metamorphosis implied an admission of the failure of the policies adopted since 1939, nevertheless it gained a net psychological advantage for the Communist parties in occupied Europe. It made the blind Communist obedience to the Soviet Union, now the principal belligerent on the continent, less objectionable in the eyes of the populations suffering Nazi oppression. The Communists could again argue that the interests of the occupied nations and those of socialism converged. On the other hand, the outbreak of hostilities between Germany and the USSR caused the German repressive apparatus to focus its attention on the illegal Communist organizations, resulting in frightful losses for the Communists.

When Hitler launched his offensive against the Soviet Union, the various Communist groups organized on the territory of the former Czechoslovak Republic were relieved of a serious equivocation that had inhibited their political activity. It was then that the Communist underground made its first contacts with the non-Communist resistance organizations. The exile leadership of the party approved of these contacts on the condition that eventual cooperation with these organizations would in no way imply a surrender or a substantial modification of Communist goals or ideology. This restriction greatly limited the chances of a common action: indeed, with the exception of the Slovak uprising in 1944, no such action ever materialized. The illegal party network had one more reason to proceed with caution: a legitimate concern with guarding the underground units against discovery by the German political police. Even with the extreme care the leadership had shown, the losses were alarming. The First Illegal Central Committee, as the underground governing body is presently called in the official history of the party, was discovered as early as February 1941 and gradually liquidated by the Gestapo. Only Jan Zika was able to escape arrest. He later established the Second Illegal Central Committee, composed of Jan Černý, Julius Fučík, Miloš Krásný, Karel Lukeš, Václav Mařík, Bohumil Pokorný, Cyril Šumbera, and Jan Vyskočil, which the Germans discovered in the fall of 1941; all its members were arrested, although Václav Mařík committed suicide before he could be apprehended. For some time, the illegal party organization in Bohemia and Moravia was without leadership. In the summer of 1942, the Third Illegal Central Committee was set up by Karel Aksamit and Jan Molák; it also included Stanislav Brunclík, Josefa Fajmanová, Josef Košťálek, Václav Kůrka, and Antonín Vidim. The Moscow exile center sent Rudolf Vetiška to Prague in the spring of 1943, to join this third committee, but it fell victim to the vigilance of the Nazi secret police that very summer. Most of its members were arrested; Aksamit, Košťálek, and Fajmanová committed suicide, and Molák was shot to death by the Gestapo. No new attempt at setting up a leading organ of the Communist underground was made until December 1944, when the Fourth Illegal Central Committee was created, with Lumír Čivrný, Václav David, Vladimír Koucký, Josef Smrkovský, and František Šiška as members. In this instance, too, the ingenuity of the CPCS underground workers could not match the detecting skills of the Gestapo agents: even in the short time that was left to the occupying power to rule over Czechoslovakia, the Germans were able to trace and arrest the entire Central Committee. Šiška was executed before the end of the war and his fellow members were sent to various concentration camps.[5]

To sum up, the party paid a heavy price for relatively insignificant activity, if we judge the latter by the impact it had upon the course and the outcome of the war. In addition to losses among the leading cadres, thousands of rank-and-file members were arrested or taken hostage during the occupation, often without being charged with any crimes, and many of these perished in German prisons or extermination camps. Some twenty-five thousand people in Czechoslovakia are thought to have lost their lives during the Second World War because the Nazi regime associated them in some way with the Communist party. Possibly not all were organized party members, but if these figures are even fairly reliable, we have to conclude that the Nazi persecution seriously affected the very substance of the organized Communist movement. In the light of this fact, the circumspection the Communist underground exhibited in its contacts with other resistance groups appears justified.

The reservations of the CPCS about eventual cooperation with non-Communist elements in the liberation movement, however, were also dictated by purely political considerations. With the Soviet Union as the sole power opposing the German forces on the European continent, the possibility that Czechoslovakia would in the end be liberated and occupied by the Red Army was a real one, and it gradually became more likely as the war continued. In such an event, it was highly probable that the Communist party would play an important role in the constitution of the new political order after the liberation. Thus the Communists were not anxious to allow the non-Communist components of the resistance to siphon away any of the anticipated prestige that would accrue to them as the ideological representatives of the war victor and liberator, the Soviet

Union, or to overshadow their role in the antifascist struggle. Although all these claims were formally vindicated only in Yalta and at Potsdam, at the very end of the war, they had played an important role in the party strategy since 1941.

After the USSR entered the war, some official contacts and political cooperation developed between the party centers in exile and the leadership of the national liberation action in the West, where the requirements of security and secrecy were not as stringent as in the occupied countries. In the summer of 1941, the CPCS group in London, in accordance with instructions from Moscow, recognized the Czechoslovak National Committee in Great Britain as the provisional government of Czechoslovakia and the official representative of the Czechoslovak Republic abroad. The CPCS then sent its own delegation, composed of Anežka Hodinová-Spurná, Karl Kreibich, Václav Nosek, and Bohuslav Vrbenský, to the committee. This new positive attitude of the CPCS toward the London provisional government headed by Eduard Beneš, whom the Communist underground press in Bohemia and Moravia had identified a few months earlier as a "servant of Western capitalism and imperialism," was by no means out of tune with the official policy line of the Soviet Union. Actually, Soviet diplomacy moved faster than the Czechoslovak party. The USSR recognized the National Committee as a government before a Communist delegation was seated in it. It was also unambiguous in supporting the reconstitution of Czechoslovakia according to its pre-Munich borders. Since it had never participated in the abject capitulation of 1938, it was in a relatively good position to denounce the Munich treaty. This step, however, had significant repercussions in the Czechoslovak Communist movement.

The Great Patriotic War

The change in the Soviet stand on Czechoslovakia, which was merely a consequence of the sudden mutation of the Soviet view on the world conflict, implied a re-evaluation of various trends and tendencies that had been manifest in the Czechoslovak party since the disintegration of the First Republic. It was particularly significant for two components of the CPCS: one operating among the German-speaking population of Czechoslovakia and the other organized on the territory of what had become in March 1939 the Slovak state. The return to the pre-Munich geopolitical arrangement, which the USSR now advocated, also suggested the return to a centralized, single organization of the Communist party. The years after Munich, however, had seen the development of more or less independent, or at least autonomous, party organs in the Sudeten-German and Slovak regions, and the corresponding new parties had even received the explicit approval of the international headquarters in Moscow; by the summer of 1941, this trend toward diversification had gained momentum, especially in Slovakia. Nevertheless, the Soviet policy line, as spelled out in the official recognition of the London provisional government, called for its reversal. As far as the Sudeten-German group was concerned, the new policy was symbolized by the presence in the National Committee of Karl Kreibich, the most prominent leader of this group and the founder of the German Communist Party of Czechoslovakia in 1920. In fact, the new Soviet position signaled a much more fateful change for the German-speaking population than just the submission of its Communist movement to a centralized leadership: it provided the necessary muscle for a wholesale transfer of Sudeten Germans from Czechoslovakia to Germany, a project that the London provisional government had entertained for some time and that was implemented during the first postwar years. Soviet support for the transfer idea was very well calculated: as history later proved, the unprecedented social upheaval caused by this sudden forced mass migration considerably benefited the Communist cause.

Although the obliteration of the heretofore vigorously asserted rights of the German-speaking minority did not seem to stir much resistance within the party, the pressures for recentralization of the party body led to frictions with the local Communist organization in Slovakia. It was not the first time that friction had occurred, but the difficulties in maintaining the authority of the exile leadership over the illegal party groups in the Slovak state had been merely a weak foretaste of what was in store for the Czechoslovak Communists. The domestic Slovak party leaders had an advantage, since contacts with Moscow were irregular and could be preserved only at great risk. Furthermore, there were virtually no means of enforcing the will of the exile center. The Illegal Central Committees of the Slovak Communist party were not much more successful in avoiding systematic persecution than their counterparts in Bohemia and Moravia: all four of these committees, formed in 1939, 1941, March 1942, and August 1942, were broken up and destroyed by the secret police of the Tiso regime. On the other hand, the Slovak group's collaboration with the non-Communist elements of the antifascist resistance went farther and took more significant forms than was the case in the western provinces. The single most important joint action of the Communists and the liberal opponents of the satellite Slovak government was the Slovak uprising of August 1944.

Slovak liberals and even some conservatives of the center who had been loyal to the Czechoslovak Republic between the wars and had refused in 1939 to participate in the government of the Slovak puppet state or had suffered persecution at the hands of the fascist regime had felt for a long time the need to demonstrate publicly President Tiso's failure to attract unanimous support in Slovakia. This need became more urgent after the major German setbacks in the Soviet Union—especially after Stalingrad—and after the defeat of the forces of the Berlin-Rome Axis culminated in the capitulation of Italy in September 1943. It was evident, by then, that the future political order in Central Europe would depend, to a large extent, on the agreement between the USSR and its Western allies, and that this agreement, whatever its ultimate form, would reserve for Moscow considerable influence in this area. The situation of the non-Communist Slovak resistance was morally more delicate than that of its Czech counterpart, since the pro-Nazi regime in Slovakia had involved itself in Hitler's war by committing a special Slovak expeditionary corps composed of two divisions to the Eastern front. This active participation had greatly compromised the future political chances of Slovakia and threatened to bring on the Slovaks the fate of other small nations associated with the Third Reich. The Czechs had been spared this dilemma because the German occupational authorities had assumed that Czechs conscripted against their will would display a poor combat morale and would most likely defect, at the first opportunity, to the enemy, as their ancestors in the Austrian army had done in the First World War. Their assessment of the Slovaks as more reliable allies, however, proved to be incorrect. Whole detachments of the Slovak army corps in the Soviet Union had voluntarily constituted themselves prisoners and later joined the Czechoslovak Brigade led by General Svoboda. Nevertheless, the Slovak non-Communist resistance believed that it must bring about a change of regime on its own initiative if it was to avoid the unenviable role of a defeated people. This action was to be synchronized with the advance of the Soviet troops towards Slovak territory, but it had to occur early enough to establish the right of the new Slovak government to sit among the representatives of the Allied countries.

In 1943, the conspirators made first contact with the Slovak Communist underground. Slovak Communists, who at that time lacked a unified leadership and maintained only irregular contacts with the exile party center, agreed to participate in preparing an antifascist revolt. Although they did not perceive any particular need to exonerate themselves from the crimes of Tiso and his associates and were far from apprehensive about the prospect that the Soviet Union might become the dominant power in Eastern Europe, they too favored an armed action in which they saw an opportunity to strengthen their influence. To a sizable segment of the Slovak Communist leadership, a successful revolution seemed to be a chance to save the independent Slovak state, naturally in a new, Soviet-sponsored guise. Thus, paradoxically, they became heirs to the system they had conspired to destroy; it was not an accident that this group in the party became ironically labeled "Červení ľudáci" or "Red Populists" (the Populist party was the backbone of the pro-Nazi Slovak state). The negotiations between the liberal resistance and the Slovak Communists resulted, in the summer of 1943, in the constitution of the Slovak National Council, a secret top organ to coordinate all antifascist activities in Slovakia. These activities gradually multiplied and sometimes took the form of acts of sabotage and partisan warfare. Yet in 1943, such acts were mainly symbolic. Only with the approaching front did this kind of resistance begin to cause concern in Nazi headquarters. More important were the preparations for the overthrow of the satellite government and the take-over of the Slovak armed forces, which continued for another year. On December 25, 1943, all political groups represented in the Slovak National Council met in a secret session in Banská Bystrica, in central Slovakia, and adopted the so-called Christmas Agreement, a blueprint for the removal of the satellite regime and the restoration of "independence, liberty, and democracy."[6]

The Christmas Agreement testified to the clear commitment of the Slovak resistance to the idea of the Czechoslovak Republic, the future home of the Czechs and the Slovaks where both nations would live together on the basis of equality. This aspect of the agreement is of interest to anyone who wishes to understand the development of the "Slovak question" within the Communist movement after the liberation, and especially after the February coup d'état of 1948. The records and the testimony of the participants in the December 1943 meeting indicate that there were as many partisans of complete Slovak independence among the non-Communist groups in the Slovak National Council as there were among the Communists. The Communist separatists, however, were more prominent and their position proved to be of greater consequence. The radically nationalist stand of some of the Slovak party leaders was then visibly out of tune with the general line laid down by the exile Moscow center, but the relative isolation of the Communist underground organization did not allow these differences to come to the fore. Moreover, some of the Slovak officials whom the exile leadership succeeded in sending to Slovakia, such as Karol Šmidke, turned out to be nationalists themselves. In the winter of 1943–1944 the nationalist wing of the Slovak party organization still seemed to believe that the new political order would meet its expectations. The nationalists could think so because they did not have an accurate idea of what was going on in the relevant decision-making centers, in Moscow and in London.

The year 1943 saw a major diplomatic initiative on the part of the Czechoslovak provisional government in Great Britain that reflected, and also helped determine, the new relations of power in Central and Eastern Europe. President Eduard Beneš had been aware, since the outbreak of the German-Soviet hostilities, of the key position the Soviet Union would occupy in world politics after the war, especially in the area critical for Czechoslovakia; thus he concluded that only a formal system of treaties could save for the future Czechoslovak Republic the amount of independence necessary to preserve an internal pluralist democratic order. This was why he had insisted, prior to 1943, that a number of specific agreements be reached between the London State Council, which was the executive organ of the provisional government, and Soviet authorities. These agreements regulated diplomatic relations between the two countries; support of the Czechoslovak independence struggle; recruitment, training, and command of the Czechoslovak army units in the USSR; the jurisdiction of the provisional government over these units; the nonvalidity of the annexation of Czechoslovak territory by Germany, Poland, and Hungary in 1938 and 1939; and other issues. Since the beginning of 1943, Beneš had been negotiating via the Soviet embassy in London for a new Soviet-Czechoslovak alliance. All these agreements and transactions remained within the scope of classical diplomatic operations; they caused few changes in the then-prevailing international and national order. On the occasion of the signing of the new treaty, however, Dr. Beneš took an unusual and fateful step.

While he was in Moscow in December 1943, President Beneš initiated talks with the exile leadership of the CPCS, on Stalin's recommendation, concerning the organization of political life in Czechoslovakia after the war.[7] Formally, there was little that even a scrupulous partisan of constitutional rules could have objected to. The Soviets did not make the signing of the treaty in any way contingent on these talks. Indeed, the Soviet-Czechoslovak pact was concluded before Beneš first met with Klement Gottwald and his associates. There seemed to be nothing irregular, either, about an exchange of views between the president and the representatives of one of the political parties of the nation. Nevertheless, although the form might have been preserved, the actual content of these negotiations and their results were quite unusual and testified to a completely new situation. In his later writings Dr. Beneš indicated that some Western politicians, especially the British, had counseled caution and had doubted that the time was propitious for any comprehensive arrangements with the Soviets. He pointed out, however, that they had been unable to suggest an alternative course that could have saved the Czechoslovak national liberation action from the fate suffered by the Polish exile government in London. The latter, as we know, was not allowed to return home and was replaced by a government of Soviet choice.

The December 1943 talks in Moscow between the president of the State Council and the top officials of the CPCS did not immediately lead to concrete decisions, but they were significant in terms of the amount of ground covered and the issues addressed. Actually it was then and there that the foundations were laid for the postwar political system of Czechoslovakia; these principles were explicitly incorporated into the Košice Program of the National Front of April 1945. One such principle, calling for a considerable simplification of the political parties in the liberated country, marked a signal victory for the Communists. The Communist negotiators succeeded in making Dr. Beneš accept the rule excluding from participation in political life the parties and movements that, in the opinion of the Communists, "in the time of imperilment betrayed the Republic and collaborated with the enemy." Although the second criterion was relatively clear and would have applied chiefly to small parties and splinters of the extreme right, the first one was vague and could be extended to practically any party. According to the Communist interpretation, the conditions of national peril had existed since the Munich treaty, and any party that had in any way been active after Munich was to be viewed as an "agency collaborating with the enemy." A strict adoption of this yardstick would probably have excluded all parties except the CPCS. The exile center in Moscow did not insist on a rigid implementation, however, but preferred a more vague reading. Although the Agrarian party and the two socialist parties had participated in the political life of the second post-Munich republic, and although all three had merged into "Národní souručenství" ("National Solidarity Movement") after the Nazi occupation of Bohemia and Moravia, the Communists, in their negotiations with Dr. Beneš, only requested the elimination of the Agrarian Party. It was not the punishment of traitors they were seeking, but the removal from the political arena of a rival who could attract the bulk of the peasant vote and foil the plans of the CPCS to capture if not the majority, then at least a sizable portion, of the whole electorate.

Another point on the agenda of the Moscow talks on which the Communists scored considerable success and gained important advantages for the development of their postwar strategy was the establishment of the principles that were to govern the so-called retribution—that is, the legal procedure by which crimes committed by, in the name of, and in collaboration with, the occupying power would be prosecuted and punished. As in the case of the simplification of the party system, many aspects of these principles were either deliberately formulated vaguely or left unexplained, to permit politically expedient interpretations. Not war criminals, but rather individuals hostile to, or judged dangerous by, the Communist party were to be rendered harmless by the retribution. Thus a cleansing campaign like those carried out in all Nazi-occupied European countries after the war became in Czechoslovakia an instrument promoting the interests of the Communist movement. The term collaborationist came to be used very widely, but also very selectively, after the liberation. It was often paired with the claim that an individual was asocial, a charge usually brought up against employers and entrepreneurs whose record of political behavior during the Nazi occupation had been spotless, but whose property the party wished to confiscate.

A very important issue discussed by Dr. Beneš and the exiled CPCS leadership was the fate of the German-speaking minority in Czechoslovakia. Dr. Beneš considered the expulsion of this ethnic group, with the exception of those who had not been converted to the Nazi cause during the Munich crisis (some 11 percent of the population, chiefly Social Democrats and Communists), to be an indispensable condition of Czechoslovakia's future security. The desire to see this plan endorsed had helped to motivate Beneš to seek a global agreement with Moscow.

Here the president might have overestimated the difficulties. In reality, Stalin found Beneš's initiative rather welcome since it paved the way for an even more extensive plan to transfer German-speaking populations from the territories ceded to Poland and to the Soviet Union, as well as from Hungary and Yugoslavia. The eleven million expellees to be poured into Germany after its military and economic collapse seemed to assure that this key nation of the European continent would be brought to despair and would opt for Communist revolution. As for the Czechoslovak Communists who had abandoned the principle of self-determination without many conscience pangs, they espoused the idea of the transfer very eagerly. They only made sure that the distribution of the assets of the expelled minority would be firmly in the hands of Communist ministers and would thus become another vehicle of party influence.

Finally, the Moscow talks were an important step on the way to a new organization of the Czechoslovak economy. The basic principle of the nationalization of the key industries, energy resources, and mineral deposits was accepted by both parties. The agreement was only 'general and the Communist leaders did not seem to attribute much importance to the detailed timing of the nationalization program once the principle had been accepted. On the whole, the main preoccupation of the CPCS at that point was to ensure that the party would occupy a sufficiently strong initial position in the liberated state. The precise strategy of the conquest of power was to be worked out later. Much of the available evidence seems to support the belief that the Communists were prepared to observe the rules of the democratic game in December 1943, or, to be more exact, to take maximum advantage of these rules. The professed goal of obtaining the support of the majority of the voters in free elections was probably more than just propagandistic window dressing. However, the decision about the ultimate course to adopt was not entirely in the hands of the Czechoslovak party.

The Slovak Uprising of 1944

The Slovak Communists, who had hoped, at the time of the Moscow talks, that a successful overthrow of the fascist regime would eventually lead to the establishment of an independent Slovakia under Soviet sponsorship, were ignorant of the fact that the Kremlin had decided on a united and centralized Czechoslovakia. The planned uprising, as they and all the other parties and groups represented in the Slovak National Council were to discover, could not change this choice. The Soviet Union was determined to liberate the occupied countries of Central Europe on its own terms: the interests of the populations to be liberated played only a secondary role in these considerations. Stalin's order of priorities was demonstrated to the whole world in the summer of 1944 when the Red Army passively watched from Warsaw's suburbs as German troops massacred Polish patriots and totally destroyed the city. In the Slovak case, the Soviet indifference was not so salient, although Moscow's attitude was about the same and yielded similar results. Since it was doubtful whether the revolt would serve Soviet purposes, even if the Communists captured the leadership, the Soviet response to the uprising was one of benign neglect, only poorly camouflaged by rhetoric.

In early April 1944, the Red Army reached the former northeastern boundaries of Czechoslovakia and the territory of what before 1939 had been the province of Ruthenia. Retreating German units temporarily succeeded in consolidating their lines in this mountainous region, but it was obvious that the next Soviet offensive would—or at least could, if such were the intention of the top command—penetrate into Slovakia. In view of the military situation, the Slovak National Council immediately began preparations to overthrow the regime. One of the main issues was to secure Soviet assistance—that is, to coordinate the uprising with the future operations of the Red Army. The underground Communist party was only one of the components of the revolutionary organization, but its supposedly intimate links with Moscow put it in a key position. Slovak Communists were fully aware of this fact and prepared to take full advantage of it. They seemed to overlook the fact that the success of their ambition, which was the seizure of the initiative in the uprising, largely depended on the cooperation and support of the USSR, which they mistakenly took for granted.

By the end of June 1944, the Slovak National Council had succeeded in winning over to its side a considerable part of the Slovak officer corps in command of the troops stationed in home garrisons. The military aspect of the uprising thus seemed to be satisfactorily prepared.[8] It remained to make sure that a German intervention, which could be expected with certainty, would be either checked or rendered ineffective by an instantaneous attack of the Red Army at the critical German positions near the theater of uprising. To ensure this coordination, a delegation of the Slovak National Council was sent to Moscow on August 4, 1944.[9]

The Slovak satellite government was warned relatively late of the impending revolt. It proclaimed martial law in Slovakia on August 12, but it could no longer change the course of events. On August 28, the Slovak National Council was reconstituted in Banská Bystrica and exhorted the Slovak people to shake off the collaborationist fascist regime and to "join the Allies in the fight for a democratic Slovakia in a free Czechoslovakia."[10] Slovak army and police forces either actively supported the uprising or remained passive. Within twenty-four hours the whole of Slovakia was in the hands of the rebels, with the exception of the capital city, which could easily be occupied by German troops because of its extreme western position, only thirty miles from Vienna. The leaders of the uprising hoped that the major political goal—to cleanse the Slovaks of the stigma of pro-Nazi collaboration and to find a place for Slovakia among the future victors of the war—was now within reach. Everything depended on the next move by the Soviets. The uprising provided the Soviet command with a significant strategic opportunity: the Red Army had the chance to penetrate, practically without resistance, the formidable barrier of the Carpathian Mountains into the vital Hungarian plain, with key cities, such as Budapest and Vienna, as certain prizes. The eyes of the rebels and, indeed, of all the Allies were turned to Moscow to see whether the Soviets would avail themselves of this unique opportunity.

Unfortunately for the uprising, the signs were not favorable. The headquarters of the Red Army was not willing to modify its plans to assist the rebels. It seems plausible that the Soviet forces were not ready for a major offensive at that point, but there is enough evidence to support the theory that Stalin did not consider the success of the uprising politically desirable. The delegation of the Slovak National Council returned from Moscow empty-handed. During the fighting with the German expeditionary force in Slovakia, which lasted about two months, the Soviets took no military action, strategic or tactical, to relieve the Slovak troops. Moreover, they refused permission to the Czechoslovak Air Force, stationed in England, to land behind the Soviet lines for refueling and aircraft repair. Thus only a limited supply of light arms and ammunition could be delivered to the hard-pressed rebel units in the Slovak mountains. Several thousand partisans, chiefly from the

Czech provinces, joined the uprising, but it was hardly enough to save Slovakia from defeat. By the end of October 1944, the Germans had conquered Banská Bystrica, the political center of the revolt. The Slovak National Council had to retreat underground, and the Communist party returned to a state of illegality.

Soon afterward, the Red Army broke through the German positions at the Dukla mountain pass, at the Slovak border. This was a very costly operation, in terms of casualties; the German units, after having quelled the Slovak uprising and occupied the whole province, had built very strong positions in this sector. The Czechoslovak army unit in the USSR, commanded by General Svoboda, participated in this offensive. It, too, suffered heavy losses. The way in which the Soviets conducted their military activities in the southwestern part of the front at that time suggested that the Kremlin was prepared to forego even a major strategic advantage rather than make any political concessions or modify its political plans for the postwar period. To a careful observer this must have seemed a bad omen for the nations that were to enter the Soviet orbit of power in Europe.

On the whole, the uprising left bitter feelings about Soviet behavior among the liberal and socialist groups in Slovakia. In the Slovak chapter of the Communist party, it sharpened the complex cleavage that had been inherited from the First Republic and further deepened during the period of illegality. This cleavage was to affect the entire Czechoslovak Communist movement for many years to come. On the one hand, the divisions between the partisans of a centralist course based on a strong national party organization in a unitary Czechoslovak state and those of a separate party in an independent Slovak socialist state were accentuated because the uprising was oriented towards the reconstitution of the Czechoslovak Republic, however much the need for recognition of the Slovak right of self-determination was stressed in the uprising's program. These divisions were ideological as well as geographic: outside Slovakia, in the exile centers of Moscow and London, the restoration of a unified Czechoslovakia found its strongest advocates, whereas at home the situation was much less clear. On the other hand, many of the emissaries of the exile leadership themselves became involved in this dispute and failed to maintain loyalty to the centers that had dispatched them to Slovakia. The most serious aspect of the nationalist current was that it ran counter to the global policies of the Kremlin at that time. Now that there was a realistic prospect that the Communist parties in Central and Eastern Europe would either seize control or share significantly in governmental power in their countries, Moscow was not prepared to relinquish its grip on these parties. Stalin viewed the emergence of what later became the world Communist system—that is, a plurality of nations under Communist rule—as a mere extension of Soviet power, or a stretching of the concept of Socialism in One Country, however paradoxical this notion might have seemed.

It is easy to understand, in the light of the USSR's concern about the preservation of its dominant position, why the Slovak uprising was given only lukewarm support. Had Slovakia successfully shaken off the pro-German regime, this would not have served Soviet interests. The nationalist current would probably have gotten the upper hand in the Slovak Communist party and aggravated the problems of the international Communist movement. The experiences of Yugoslavia, Albania, and China later demonstrated the cogency of Soviet apprehensions. The Communist parties that established their rule over nations liberated by domestic forces, without Soviet assistance, in the end all rejected the Soviet claim to supreme authority over the world Communist system. Stalin showed considerable realism when he insisted, at the end of the war, that Communist power in Europe be a delegated power, power "by Moscow's grace," the material expression of which was liberation by the Red Army. Only in this way could unqualified obedience to Big Brother be ensured. A model case of the application of this principle was that of Slovakia's immediate neighbor, Ruthenia. After the liberation of this former easternmost province of Czechoslovakia by Soviet forces in October 1944, the Communist Party of Ruthenia was constituted at a conference in Mukačevo in November. The party that had once been a founding group of the CPCS did not lose any time in performing the act expected of it by Moscow: at the subsequent congress of the Ruthenian National Council, held on November 26, the Communist delegation obtained the endorsement of a resolution calling for the incorporation of Ruthenia into the USSR. An agreement to this effect, concluded with Czechoslovakia in June 1945, merely rubber-stamped this fait accompli. In addition to the "return of the Ruthenians to the family of the Ukrainian people, within the fatherland of Socialism,"[11] this move had the significant advantage for the Soviet Union of advancing the western Soviet borders deep into the Hungarian plains.

Chapter Five

From Liberation to the Coup d'Etat

Reconstruction to the February 1948 Take-over

After the hapless episode of the Slovak national uprising, the drama of the Second World War entered its final phase, for Czechoslovakia as for the rest of the world. Because the breakthrough at Dukla and the subsequent progress of the Red Army in Slovakia took place only after the defeat of the Slovak revolt, the liberation scenario in this part of Europe was set precisely as the Soviets had wished it: the Russian Big Brother came to relieve the oppressed populations who had been shown, shortly before, how powerless they were by themselves. In retrospect, Stalin seems to have been more anxious to teach Slovak Communists this lesson than to impress the Slovak population at large since it was the Communists who had ultimately caused problems for the Moscow center. Late in 1944 and early in 1945, however, these problems were not yet fully in sight. The Red Army moving west and southwest through Slovakia accorded the Slovak Communist party special privileges in the liberated areas, although this procedure contradicted the agreement between the Czechoslovak provisional government in London and the Soviet Union signed in May 1944. This agreement had recognized the sovereign authority of the provisional government over the entire territory of the Czechoslovak Republic within its pre-Munich borders, including Ruthenia. In fact, however, Ruthenia was ruled by the Communists long before its formal inclusion in the Soviet Union. Even in Slovakia the local governmental authority was often reduced to a passive role: the Communist party organizations held most of the administrative power and were recognized by the military commanders as the only representatives of the civil administration. These irregularities not only undermined the position of the Czechoslovak provisional government, but also, ironically, supported the separatist tendencies in the Slovak Communist party. The favor Red Army officers granted to various Communist function-aries and groups appeared to many Slovak nationalists to be signs of Soviet support for the idea of an "independent socialist Slovakia," which Moscow seemed to prefer to the Czechoslovak alternative. This rather confused situation was further complicated by the disorderly behavior of some detachments of the Soviet army who made little distinction between enemy territory and areas inhabited by allied populations. Looting, rape, and arson were daily incidents in Slovak territories occupied by the Soviets. The experience of the "passage of the front" contributed to much less successful electoral results for the Communist party in Slovakia in May 1946 than in the western provinces, especially Bohemia.

As the Red Army advanced, the Communist movement gradually emerged from its position of illegality. This process was rather disjointed because in Slovakia, as in the Czech part of the country, the collabora-tionist regime and the German police had succeeded in wiping out almost the entire underground leadership of the Communist party. To facilitate the reconstruction of the party's organizational network, the exile center in Moscow sent special representatives to the liberated areas. The first public meeting of the Communist party in these territories was the regional conference held in Košice, in eastern Slovakia, on February 28 and March 1, 1945. At that time, the delegates concentrated mainly on the military operations in Slovakia, and the conference identified assistance to the war efforts of the Soviet Union as the most important task for the Communists. Nevertheless, the pattern of the future distribution of influence among the various groups and currents within the Slovak party organization, especially the nationalists and centralists, had already begun to take shape. Although the responsibility for the organizational work was in the hands of Karol Bacílek and Marek Čulen, both loyal supporters of the Czechoslovak course, it was the Slovak nationalist wing represented by Gustav Husák and his associates who got control of the most important positions in the party apparatus.

In Moscow, too, the preparations for the return of the exile party leaders to Czechoslovakia were about to be completed in March 1945. The CPCS Bureau Abroad, which had been set up in 1943 after the dissolution of the Komintern and comprised Klement Gottwald, Jan Šverma, Rudolf Slánský, Josef Krosnář, Bruno Koehler, Václav Kopecký, and Rudolf Appelt, now awaited the most propitious moment to transfer its activity to Czechoslovakia. Šverma, one of the bureau's members and one of the most prominent characters of the bolshevization era, had died under somewhat mysterious circumstances during the Slovak uprising in 1944. Nevertheless, the continuation of the prewar course seemed to be assured, with everything that this course implied: above all, blind obedience to the Soviet power center no longer camouflaged by the now-defunct Third International. To be sure, the party faced the task of integrating into the renewed structure all the groups and tendencies that had grown apart during the six years of war and illegality, but with Soviet backing the exile leadership felt confident that this task would be accomplished satisfactorily.

More immediate in early 1945 was the need to assure the CPCS of the best possible position in the political institutions of Czechoslovakia to create favorable conditions for the deployment of a strategy aiming at eventual take-over. The necessary concessions to this end had to be obtained from the London provisional government whose head, Dr. Eduard Beneš, had held preliminary talks with the CPCS officials in Moscow in 1943 and had already accepted some of the principles advocated by the Communists. The fact that the country was liberated from the East put the Communist party into an excellent bargaining position. The members of the London provisional government, the overwhelming majority of whom represented non-Communist parties and tendencies, had to return to Czechoslovakia via Moscow and to receive power from the hands of the Soviet troops; this was a heavily symbolic circumstance. Actually, the non-Communist Czechoslovak politicians who arrived in Moscow on March 17, 1945, had no diplomatic or political resources to draw upon except the fact that in 1941 both the USSR and the CPCS had recognized the London State Council as the official representative of the Czechoslovak Republic. Later CPCS historiography recognized one additional reason, a more political and tactical one, for the Communists to acknowledge the authority of the London provisional government: since this body was presided by Dr. Eduard Beneš, who enjoyed undisputed popularity among all segments of the Czechoslovak population, including the working class, it was expedient to come to terms with it. Even so, the leverage available to the non-Communist component of the future Czechoslovak government was not very impressive. Compared with that of the non-Communist politicians of other nations in the area to be liberated by the Red Army, especially Poland, it might have seemed stronger, but in retrospect, even this advantage has to be viewed with skepticism since it did not save Czechoslovakia from ultimately sharing the fate of its Polish neighbor. As one of the liberal members of the State Council later observed, the provisional government brought home from London via Moscow "an almost accomplished communist revolution."[1]

The Košice Program: "Democratic Way to Power"

The conditions that greatly facilitated the success of the Communist strategy in the postwar years were formally spelled out in the Košice Program. This program resulted from the talks held in Moscow, at the end of March 1945, between the State Council and the CPCS, before the constitution of the first postwar cabinet with Communist participation. It determined in detail not only the political form of the liberated republic— a curious kind of restricted plurality—but also the political process it would employ. The Moscow talks and the Košice Program completed the evolution begun in December 1943 with the first negotiations between Dr. Beneš and the exile center of the CPCS. A pivotal aspect of the Košice Program was the explicit listing of the political parties to be admitted to the renewed Czechoslovak state. The Moscow and Košice agreements recognized six such parties, four Czech and two Slovak. The Czech parties included besides the CPCS, the National Socialist party, the Social Democratic party, and the Czechoslovak Populist party (which was Catholic in inspiration but actually interdenominational). The two Slovak parties were the CPS and the Slovak Democratic party, a new organization whose leadership had been recruited mainly from political circles that had belonged to the Slovak center-left before the war: agrarians, liberal-nationals, and populists. This arrangement exhibited several inconsistencies, if not contradictions, that all benefited the Communists in the long run. Thus, for example, the Czech parties were not allowed to nominate candidates or poll votes in Slovak constituencies, and vice versa. Although this limitation actually deprived the non-Communist parties in both regions of potential following, it left the field entirely free for the Communists since there were separate Communist party organizations for the western provinces and for Slovakia. The existence of a formally distinct, but in reality completely dependent CPS brought an additional advantage to the Communist cause: in the distribution of governmental seats, the CPS was considered a self-contained unit, equal to each of the remaining five parties, a ruling that assured a substantial enlargement of Communist representation. The fact that the parties running in the Czech provinces all carried the designation "Czecho-slovak" but were not allowed to recruit Slovak members later prompted the quip that the republic was composed of two parts, "Czechoslovakia" and "Slovakia." The fact that the non-Communist majority accepted such a flagrantly discriminatory arrangement may indicate the extremely narrow room for maneuvering it had had during the Moscow and Košice talks. Also surprising today is the acquiescence of the liberal parties in the restriction on the number of the parties, despite the patent weakness of the Communist argument. The requirement that collaborationist and traitor groups must be excluded could easily have been satisfied by dissolving these organizations, but there was no ground for limiting political competition a priori, much less for preventing new political parties from being constituted. Yet nobody seriously objected to this illogic; thus the Communists achieved their aim without much difficulty.

Ambiguity of principle working to the advantage of the Communist party also characterized other points of the Košice Program in which the preliminary agreement of 1943 between Dr. Beneš and the exile leader-ship of the CPCS was finalized, especially the regulations for the punish-ment of war criminals and collaborators—the so-called retribution issue—and the project for the transfer of ethnic minorities, German and Hungarian, from Czechoslovakia. As in the case of the streamlining of the party system, the liberal partners in the talks leading to the Košice agreement accepted a legally highly objectionable solution even though a much better alternative was obvious. The retribution was a legal mon-strosity, a penal law with retroactive effect. This situation could have been avoided if the continuity of the Czechoslovak Republic and its legal order had been postulated for the entire critical period 1938–45, based on the nullity of the Munich treaty, the protectorate of Bohemia and Moravia, and the Slovak state. Under this assumption, any person or organization who voluntarily assisted the foreign occupation force could have been tried for high treason. In endorsing the retribution, the non-Communist politicians considerably speeded up the eclipse of Czechoslovak democracy. The retributive legislation of 1945 not only tarnished the reputation of Czechoslovakia as a civilized legal state, but also became an important instrument for the liquidation of individuals and institutions the Communists perceived as dangerous. In combina-tion with the expulsion of most of the German-speaking populace, the cleansing action led to enormous shifts in property ownership, from which the Communist party profited amply. It partly bribed land-hungry peasants, poor artisans, and shopkeepers from the Czech and Slovak hinterland into joining the CPCS, and partly promoted additional nationalization of the means of production, beyond the framework provided for in the Košice Program.[2]

The program was promulgated on April 4, 1945. At the same time, the first coalition government of Czechoslovakia was constituted. The rules governing the form and the composition of this government and all future ones were also an important part of the Košice agreement. This coalition was more rigid than those Czechoslovakia had experienced in the past. There was no opposition: all parties were represented in the government, which called itself "The National Front of the Working People of the Cities and the Countryside." The Košice Program referred to Czechoslovakia as a "People's Democracy," a pleonastic term that was applied to all countries in Central and Eastern Europe (with the exception of the USSR) and that even became current in the Western press, especially during the first phase of the Cold War. The National Front included the parties listed above. Within it, the Košice Program identified a distinct subcoalition of parties under the name the "National Bloc of Working People," which was intended to link the two Communist parties with the National Socialist and the Social Democratic parties. On the whole, the first postwar government appeared to be highly structured, unlike the pragmatic, ad-hoc groupings that had characterized the pre-Munich cabinets. The only classical democratic aspect of the political mechanism introduced in 1945 was the separate ballot for each of the parties represented in the National Front. Although this did not in itself permit measurement of the strength of support for the Košice Program—all parties without exception had subscribed to this program—it allowed an observer to assess the distribution of electoral following between the Communists and their coalition partners.

The non-Communist parties had a majority in the government established in Košice, but the ministerial posts they held were not very influential, with the exception of the portfolio of justice that came to the National Socialist party. The office of prime minister was entrusted to Zdeněk Fierlinger, the former ambassador to the USSR, who was by affiliation a Social Democrat but in reality a staunch partisan of close cooperation, if not fusion, with the CPCS. The Communists, thanks to the existence of the CPS as an independent member of the National Front, controlled two vice-premierships and three vital governmental posts: interior, information (mass media), and education. The Ministry of Agriculture, under a Slovak Communist named Július Ďuriš, normally not a key cabinet position, was to play a very important role in the exceptional postwar situation in view of its authority to distribute land confiscated from the German-speaking minority group and the collaborationists; it became a priceless resource in the Communist campaign for membership recruitment. An objective picture of the distribution of executive power in the first postwar government must also take into account the ministries allocated to so-called nonpartisan politicans and to the representatives of mass organizations. Two important portfolios were given to people in these categories: foreign affairs to Jan Masaryk, former ambassador to London and son of the first president of the republic; and defense to Ludvík Svoboda, who claimed not to be affiliated with any party and drew on his popularity as the commander of the Czechoslovak army corps in the Soviet Union, but actually had strong pro-Communist leanings. Jan Masaryk was undoubtedly a supporter of the pluralist liberal regime and enjoyed a good deal of reflected charisma because of his family name. Svoboda, on the other hand, gradually drew closer to the Communist party and was later to contribute to the success of the Communist take-over.

This situation, which could satisfy the most optimistic expectations of the Moscow leadership, was evaluated in detail by the party chairman, Klement Gottwald, in his address to the joint session of CPS and CPCS officials in Košice on April 8, 1945. His presentation left no doubt that the ultimate political objective of the party was to assure for the CPCS full control of the country, although the party's intention to strive to obtain an absolute majority of votes at the forthcoming election was stressed at that time. In 1945, it seemed, the Communists were still willing to give democracy the chance to vote itself out of existence. The April 8 meeting was an important landmark in the postwar development of the CPCS. The various components of the Communist movement were organizationally welded into a new leadership represented by a seventeen-member Provisional Central Committee. Klement Gottwald was confirmed in his function of party chairman; the Slovak Karol Šmidke became vice-chairman, and Rudolf Slánský became secretary-general. Šmidke's election was an obvious concession to the aspirations of Slovak autonomists, although Šmidke himself did not come from the domestic party ranks but had been sent to Slovakia from Moscow during the last months of the war. To what extent this compromise satisfied the expectations of the Slovak nationalist group may be seen in the explicit reference in Klement Gottwald's report to the "independent function of Slovakia in a reconstructed Czechoslovakia," which seems to indicate that this issue then was a very topical one.[3]

The Making of a Myth

While the provisional government of Czechoslovakia, now called the Revolutionary Government of the National Front, prepared in Košice for its immediate postwar tasks and while the Communist party mapped its next series of moves in its bid for power, the Second World War was rapidly approaching its end. It was virtually in the last hours of the conflict in Europe that unexpected military events, combined with lack of political understanding and imagination on the part of the Western allies, permitted the Czechoslovak Communists to gain an additional important advantage. It had appeared all through the winter of 1944–45 that the advance of the Red Army, however costly and slow, would be fast enough to bring not only Eastern and Southeastern Europe, but also Central Europe under Soviet control before the Allied expeditionary force could occupy Germany. At the end of March, 1945, however, the American troops engaged in the "Battle of Germany" scored a sudden spectacular success and moved swiftly east. Among them, the Third Army commanded by the dynamic Gen. George S. Patton swept through the industrial areas of northern Bavaria and Franconia, both bordering on Bohemia, the westernmost province of Czechoslovakia. At the beginning of April, as the Soviet troops prepared for the final assault on Berlin, the supreme command of the hard-pressed German armies decided to adopt the strategy of retreat in the West so that it could offer more resolute resistance in the East. This decision was in part politically motivated, since Hitler's last hope was to divide the Allies by demonstrating to the Western powers that Germany was "containing the Bolshevik tide." Under these circumstances, Patton's armored units were able to advance rapidly eastward, and reached the Czechoslovak border near the Bavarian town of Tirschenreuth in the latter half of April. After a short halt and regrouping, the American advance continued east and northeast, unhampered by the Czechoslovak system of border fortifications, which the German troops failed to utilize. Soon Patton's reconnaissance detachments penetrated into western Bohemia, and at the beginning of May, the Third Army took firm possession of the city of Plzeň (Pilsen), an important center of the armaments industry. The

American positions were now deployed some fifty miles west of Prague, with about a third of Bohemia under U.S. control.

This situation created a delicate political problem. Nobody in the top command of the Allied expeditionary force seemed to pay much attention to the possible international implications of General Patton's advance until Prague was within the reach of his tanks. At that point the Allied Supreme Command realized that Patton had been moving in a rather sensitive zone. The belated reaction of Patton's superiors, Generals Marshall and Eisenhower, can be understood if we consider that, contrary to a widely held belief, no detailed agreement between the Soviet Union and its Western allies then existed concerning the areas of military occupation by this or that power. Patton's image as an impetuous enfant terrible messing up a carefully prepared division of Europe into zones of influence, however popular, is therefore false. Since the Yalta conference, there had been an understanding of principle among the members of the anti-Nazi war coalition that certain definite regions of Europe would be recognized as being of vital interest to the Soviet Union. Czechoslovakia was one of these regions. Nevertheless, it was a long way from this general agreement to the detailed plan of the various demarcation lines that was actually finalized only after the German surrender. The ambiguity resulting from the absence of such a plan produced in Czechoslovakia a sociopsychological effect that was to have the most serious consequences for the development of political life during the crucial period after the war.

The uncertainty in early May 1945 about the liberation of the most industrialized and most populated Czechoslovak territories and, above all, of the capital city of Prague, was unsettling and contained a strong potential for serious political complications. Yet it took a catalyst to turn this uncertainty into an acute crisis whose outcome considerably reinforced the psychological and propagandistic position of the Communist party. This catalyst was supplied by the uprising of the population in Prague, stimulated by a series of uncoordinated actions of various resistance groups, including the underground Communist organization. Not unlike the Slovak uprising of 1944—a much larger, better planned operation—the Prague revolt expressed the general mood of the Czech population, regardless of political leanings, and it only gradually slid under Communist influence. Also like the Slovak uprising, the Prague revolt was later expropriated by Communist party historians and presented to the public as a popular movement under Communist leadership, occasionally backed by "patriots and progressive elements from all walks of life."[4] It began on May 5, 1945, with a take-over of the main broadcast station and the studios of the Czechoslovak Radio Corporation, in a lightning move supported by the police corps of the former protectorate Bohemia and Moravia. Taking control of this sector of the mass media was a clever operation that guaranteed the spread of the revolt over the whole country and indicated a significant innovation in modern insurgency techniques. Incidentally, the same technique would be applied twice in the subsequent history of Czechoslovakia, once during the seizure of power by the CPCS in February 1948, and again during the Soviet military intervention in August 1968, in each instance against a different opponent.

The Czech National Council, a cultural organization that could point to an earlier revolutionary tradition, before and during the First World War, identified itself as the leader of the uprising. Only one member of the council, Josef Smrkovský, claimed to represent the CPCS. The goals of the National Council were primarily political, not military. After the death of Hitler and in view of the rapid advance of the American troops in western Bohemia, the rebels counted on a relatively smooth passage to a new order. An unsubstantiated but widely believed report, which the council took advantage of in its contacts with the German military garrison in Prague, asserted that the head of the new German government in Flensburg, Admiral Doenitz, had given orders to the German units in Bohemia and Moravia to capitulate and to hand over all heavy war equipment to the Czech authorities in exchange for the guarantee of a free withdrawal west into American captivity. The military commander of Prague, General Toussaint, showed a willingness to negotiate such a settlement, but there were also Nazi diehards, especially the elite SS-troops officers, who were not prepared to give up and planned to make Bohemia the place of their last stand against the Red Army. The Soviet troops at that point were still a good 150 miles east and northeast of the Czechoslovak capital, and the immediate prospects of the civilian population in the regions not yet occupied by the allies looked bleak.

The refusal of the SS troops to surrender put the uprising in a precarious position. The rebels were poorly armed and equipped; they were no match for the professional Nazi soldiers strengthened by the courage of despair. In this situation, saving Prague from destruction and its citizens from mass slaughter seemed to depend on a quick action of the Allied armies. Considering the location and the readiness of the

American units on the one hand and of the Red Army on the other hand, the U.S. Third Army Corps appeared to be the logical candidate to carry out this rescue move. At that point Patton's tanks had advanced east of Plzeň, so the occupation of Prague would have been a relatively easy maneuver. The commander of the Third Army was not only an insightful strategist, but also a man endowed with a good sense of political judgment. He could not help seeing the unique opportunity for the West to score in the forthcoming contest with the Soviet Union by making the population of Prague and of Czechoslovakia associate its liberation from Nazi oppression with the help given by the U.S. troops. Aware that a decision of this magnitude could not be taken by a commander of his rank, Patton referred the Czech plea for help to the Supreme Headquarters of the Allied Expeditionary Force. The appeal had been transmitted to him by a U.S. intelligence unit stationed in Plzeň that on May 5, late in the evening, had made a lightning trip to Prague without encountering German resistance, and thus had proved that an eventual American advance to the Czechoslovak capital would have been no major military problem. As Patton later indicated in his memoirs, he was ready to move unless an explicit counterorder was given by his superiors—that is, he was prepared to interpret the absence of a reply as approval of the proposed action.[5] Secretly, he may have hoped that the decision, whatever its content, would be slow in coming so that the liberation of Prague could meanwhile become a fait accompli. However, the allied military machine, usually as cumbersome when confronted with political issues as all military machines, proved exceptionally swift in this case. Patton was ordered to stop his troops by his immediate boss, Gen. Omar Bradley, who in turn had received this instruction, in no un- certain terms, from the commander-in-chief himself, Dwight D. Eisen- hower.[6] The Allies brilliantly succeeded in destroying a unique historical chance and in providing their future adversary with a tremendous political advantage. In retrospect, the comments of the British Field Marshal Montgomery on Patton's proposition to assist Prague, stressing that "war is not politics" and endorsing the decision by Eisenhower, reveal especially clearly the incapacity of the West to measure up to the political perspicacity and propagandistic skill of the Soviets.

Thus the officers and soldiers of the Third Army had to watch helplessly, from a distance shorter than that separating Baltimore from Washington, as the rebels in Prague waged their uneven battle against the tanks and the airplanes of the German SS. The Czechoslovak Air

Force in Britain, ready to relieve the Prague uprising, never received the permission to start.[7] Close to three thousand lives were lost and irreparable damage was done to several historical monuments in the city during the subsequent four days of fighting, which could have been avoided. Although the regular German garrison of Prague capitulated on May 7, isolated elite SS units continued the war against the population. Senseless killing went on even after the general armistice in Europe, which was signed on May 8. From the point of view of Communist political strategy, however, what happened was not all that meaningless. The scene was set for a new legend that would help paralyze future efforts of the non-Communist leaders to strike a balance between the East and the West: the legend that Soviet troops had saved Prague in its darkest hour or, as an election poster of the CPCS put it in 1946, had come "just on time." The historical truth—that the drama of the Prague uprising was over before the Soviet army corps under Marshal Konyev reached Prague on May 9—mattered little. It was the Red Army, not the Western allies, whom the citizens of the Czechoslovak capital saw marching down the Václavské Square, an experience that appreciably influenced the first postwar elections and made them the last opportunity for political choice.

The Emergence of a Mass Party

The period of war and enemy occupation formally ended for Czechoslovakia when the revolutionary government and the president of the republic moved from Košice to Prague in the first half of May 1945. For the Communist party, the period of reconstruction then began. The balance of the war was grim: according to estimates, there were only twenty-seven thousand party members left in Bohemia and Moravia and no more than ten thousand in Slovakia when the Provisional Central Committee first met in Prague on May 18, 1945. This was about half the number of effectives reported at the Seventh Ordinary Congress in 1936. The subsequent session of the top party organ, held May 31, 1945, elected a new party Presidium into which the leaders of the former underground Communist organization were co-opted. At the same time, the Central Committee was enlarged by a number of activists who had returned from Nazi prisons and concentration camps.

The reorganized leadership immediately launched a wide recruitment campaign, which soon marked good progress. Now the CPCS was a party in power: in contrast to its past situation, now it could not only make promises but also distribute benefits of all kinds, land to farmers, civil service positions, profitable posts of so-called national administrators (národní správci) to manage property confiscated from Germans and collaborationists, and more. Some of the new candidates to party membership did not seek immediate material advantage but hoped, by becoming followers of the movement sponsored and supported by the Soviet Union, to gain immunity from eventual punishment for their unpatriotic behavior during the Nazi occupation. Thus the party profited in two ways from the retribution action: on the one hand, it used the confiscated assets as bait for prospective adherents; and on the other hand, it frightened minor collaborationists into membership, which they believed to be a protective shield against the consequences of their failure, real or alleged, to behave like loyal citizens of the Czechoslovak Republic during the six years of foreign rule. A significant proportion of the postwar aspirants to party membership was composed of those who anticipated expropriations and nationalization of property on a large scale and hoped that a party card could save their possessions. Among these freshly baked Communists the peasant element was very strongly represented. The inroads the CPCS made into the middle and upper classes of farmers confirmed the correctness of the assumption that the exclusion of the Agrarian party from the political spectrum of the Second Republic would work to the benefit of the Communists. Finally, a considerable portion of the recruits stemmed from previously unorganized and politically indifferent circles and had been impressed by the Soviet Union's victory in the war. Nothing succeeds like success, and the Czechoslovak party leadership very adroitly exploited the implicit equation, however simplistic, between the USSR and the CPCS, so that Soviet achievements were mostly perceived as those of the Communist movement. The standards and criteria applied during this period were very flexible; the openness of the postliberation era was equalled only by the mass recruitment after the 1948 take-over.

There can be little doubt that this policy constituted a radical departure from the conception of the Communist party as an elite revolutionary body, the avant-garde of the proletariat, originally shared by all sections of the defunct Komintern, including the CPCS. There was a good deal of irony in the fact that the leadership that had the successful bolshevization of 1929 to its credit now presided over the transformation of the CPCS into a mass party. It brought about a change that has never again been reversed, one that became the source of many chronic difficulties. Much of this apparent indulgence, as opposed to traditional Communist selectivity, was prompted by a concern for maximum possible gains at the forthcoming elections. In 1945 and later, the CPCS intended, and believed it possible, to acquire decisive influence over Czechoslovak politics by means of the popular vote. Although Communist intentions concerning the use of an eventual electoral majority, once secured, were not purely constitutional, the first step on the road to absolute power was to remain within constitutional channels. In the interim period, before the voting support for the CPCS reached the desired majority—51 percent was often quoted as a magic figure—the party sought to implement its policies in cooperation with the other two socialist parties, the Social Democrats and the National Socialists. To this end, a new platform was created on June 5, 1945, called the National Bloc of Working People and including the latter two parties as well as the CPCS. It was to become a special coalition within the framework of the National Front. In the late spring of 1945, no one dared to predict with any certainty the outcome of the parliamentary elections slated for May 1946, despite an impressive growth of the CPCS membership, which soon attained a six-digit figure. Thus, the National Bloc was a safeguard for the Communists to maintain the initiative in the political process. It was already evident, however, that the two socialist partners could not be depended upon to be docile instruments of the CPCS. The Communists seemed to be able to count on the Social Democrats more than the National Socialists for support. Among the top officials of the Social Democratic party, there were several outspoken partisans of close cooperation with the CPCS, to the point of eventual fusion, and many backers of the Soviet Union. As subsequent events showed, though, not even this advantage was sufficient to guarantee that the Social Democratic party would lend unqualified support to the policies promoted by the CPCS under all circumstances.

A significant event in the early postwar history of the Czechoslovak Communist movement was the formal constitution of the CPS at a regional party conference in Žilina on August 11 and 12, 1945. This conference endorsed the principle of an autonomous Slovak party body within a centralist national party organization, whose elements had already been spelled out and implemented in the late 1930s. In its new edition, however, the Slovak chapter was to express, explicitly and implicitly, the changed image of the Slovak ethnic group. It was to be "the party organization of the Slovak nation."[8] This nation was seen as an equal of the Czech nation, but since no initiative developed toward the constitution of a Czech counterpart of the CPS, the Žilina conference of 1945 actually endorsed what would be known twenty years later as the curious solution of asymmetric centralism. It was an absurd state of affairs, in which the dominant nation-building ethnic group, the Czechs, recognized the distinct personality of the Slovak people without, however, being themselves represented by a separate structure in the central framework. The formula adopted in 1945 was an uneasy compromise between two conflicting principles: federalism, still incomplete but in progress, of the polity, and centralism of the Communist party organization. To a careful observer, the dealings in Žilina suggested that serious difficulties lay ahead. The leaders of the Slovak Communist party faced a painful dilemma: they had to profess federalism in everyday political life—if for no other reason than to profit from the nationalistic mood of their constituencies—but they had to accept a hybrid centralism-cum-autonomy whenever they dealt with the party's internal problems. This was the essence of the Slovak question as it presented itself in the summer of 1945; it has never ceased to plague the Czechoslovak Communist movement, and asymmetric centralism, institutionalized at that time, has remained with the party as a costly mortgage until the present day.

On the other hand, the power position of the CPCS in the state continued to grow all through the first year following the liberation. Its dominant position in the economy, through control of the key ministries, such as industry, trade, and agriculture, was reinforced by the Communist hold over other important areas, including information, education, and interior. Furthermore, the party pursued an energetic drive for influence in the semipolitical zone, among the so-called mass organizations. The success of this drive depended on the adoption by the other parties of the National Front of the principle of one organization only in each vital sector (trade unions, youth, agricultural cooperatives, and so on). This principle was never unequivocally accepted by the non-Communist majority, but on the whole, the CPCS made remarkable inroads into the world of the voluntary organizations that traditionally had been the domain of the liberals and conservatives. This was particularly true of the Communist influence in the trade union movement, which soon became an unofficial branch of the Communist party. Consistent with the principle of one monopoly national organization for each sector, the CPCS did not reconstitute its own youth union (Komsomol) or the Red Unions after the liberation. The centralization of the voluntary bodies had a double advantage for the Communists: it laid the foundations for the totalitarian structure of Czechoslovak society that was to be completed after the 1948 coup d'état, and it further increased the de-facto representation of the Communist party in the National Front. Even where the CPCS did not exercise full control, the existence of single national organizations was more profitable to the Communist cause than the prewar spectrum of various trends, tendencies, and colors: constrained by the requirement to be "all things to all people," these mass organizations were ideologically neutralized and could not become sources of rival ideologies or alternative political ideas.

Thus the long-term political goals of the Communists were already visible to a careful observer during the first months following the liberation. The commitment to operating through the existing structures—or, as the party spokesmen put it, to the "democratic way to Socialism"—appeared to be serious. The absolute power necessary for carrying out the party program was to be obtained through a majority vote in the first election or in one of the subsequent ones. It took a series of failures and crises, internal as well as international, before this policy was revised, and it is doubtful whether it would have been revised had not the Soviet power center adopted a clearly aggressive line in the wake of the Cold War. In 1945 and 1946, the CPCS expected a rather slow, gradual progress toward its ultimate aim: hence the attention paid to voluntary organizations and the considerable effort expended in the search for various new coalitions with the Social Democrats and the National Socialists. This view of the situation was explicitly confirmed in a resolution of the Provisional Central Committee at its meeting on December 18, 1945. The same meeting voted to call the first postwar congress, the eighth in sequence, to be held in Prague March 28–31, 1946. It was to be the first supreme party assembly in nearly ten years.

The Eighth Ordinary Congress presented a completely different picture of the CPCS from the one the public had been used to before Munich. The Communist movement in Czechoslovakia was no longer a small sect-like membership core occasionally mobilizing the support of various disaffected segments of the society. The party itself was now a mass body; the number of organized followers was unprecedented in history. No less than 1,159,164 members were registered at the time of the Eighth Congress, and they were represented by 1,166 delegates. The congress resembled a mass rally rather than the working session of a conspiratorial radical group that had been characteristic of the First Republic period. Secretary-General Rudolf Slánský submitted a report on party activities since the Seventh Ordinary Congress in 1936, and Chairman Klement Gottwald dealt with the immediate situation and the tasks in the near future. Gottwald pointed out that the most important goal at that time was to "preserve the accomplishments of the national revolution" and to "prevent the bourgeoisie from regaining the power." The party was to "strive towards strengthening the position of the working class, in order to make possible the final victory of the proletariat over the bourgeoisie."[9] This analysis of the given situation and the delimitation of the objectives in the years to come were also built into the closing resolution of the congress. They merit special attention since they testify to the leadership's idea in the early spring of 1946, of the party's prospects for attaining absolute control in the state, and to the tactics it planned to employ for this purpose. The congress also put an end to the provisional status of the various party organs, since it partly confirmed the leading officials in their functions and partly elected new governing bodies. On the whole, the members of the former exile centers, especially of the Moscow center, maintained their firm hold over the party. Klement Gottwald remained party chairman and Rudolf Slánský secretary-general. The Central Committee set up by the congress comprised 101 full members and 33 candidates to committee membership. It was a considerably larger assembly than the Central Committees of the prewar years, but the growth of the party membership appeared to justify this increase.[10]

For several reasons, the Eighth Party Congress was a milestone in the party's history. It marked the end of the period of internal polycentrism during which several foci of initiative, created as a consequence of the dismemberment and foreign occupation of the country, had co-existed and sometimes even competed with each other. These foci had been the domestic illegal party organizations in the German Protectorate and in Slovakia, and the party leadership in exile, which in turn was divided between the Moscow and the London centers. The most significant element in this polycentric network was the CPS, as we have seen earlier. The congress integrated all these centers in one organization, although this did not necessarily mean that the problems resulting from the polycentric tendencies had been resolved. Another reason why the Eighth Congress has to be viewed as a milestone is the radically changed character of the party membership: the composition of the rank and file had been modified drastically compared with the membership before the war. Many of the changes were qualitative—different class background, age, and motivation—but equally conspicuous were the quantitative ones. With more than a million party cardholders, the CPCS was the largest party in Czechoslovak history. The dream of the founders, who had been gradually eliminated from control and influence, became reality under the leadership of the erstwhile promoters of bolshevization, which was actually a principle incompatible with the notion of a mass party. Thus the situation was not devoid of irony. This change in the party concept seems to have been consistent, however, at least in 1946, with the general political line. It is difficult to tell how much the party leadership at that time was convinced that the mass character of the party organization was only temporary and how firmly it believed that at some point in the future a return to a more Leninist formula was possible. In the immediate postwar period, a broad popular base of support, as the large membership was officially referred to, played an important role in what then appeared to be the Communist strategy in the struggle for power. The seven-digit figure seemed to indicate that the goal of obtaining an absolute majority of the electoral vote, repeatedly spelled out by the party leaders, was not impossible to reach.

The 1946 General Elections

Considering the general political course endorsed by the eighth congress, the elections to the Constitutional National Assembly held in May 1946 were of particular significance as a means of getting feedback. Before the vote was cast, political analysts expected that the outcome of the elections would be determined by the then-undecided population segments. It was argued, for example, that none of the competing parties could be sure of getting the bulk of the peasant vote. The size of the Communist membership was recognized as impressive, but some observers pointed out that in Czechoslovakia organized following had never reliably indicated actual electoral support; the Communist party needed more than one million votes if it was to become really influential, and many more still if it wanted to achieve an absolute majority or, as the party spokesmen used to put it, to "acquire power by democratic means." A significant but at that point uncertain element was the mood of the Slovak electorate. This was not thought to be very favorable to the

Communists, if only because of the traumatic experience a considerable part of the Slovak rural population had suffered through at the hands of the Soviet troops at the end of the war. Slovak Communists, who like their Czech counterparts capitalized on the fact of Czechoslovakia's liberation by the Red Army, had to expect Slovak voters to identify the Communist party with the Soviet Union and express their sympathies—or antipathies—accordingly. On the other hand, many observers assumed that the industrial working class would prove to be a safe stronghold of the CPCS. They pointed to the particularly successful reconstruction of the party among workers and the firm Communist control over the powerful monopoly national trade union organization.

When the vote was counted, the CPCS came out as the strongest party, but its main bastions turned out to be in unexpected places. The Communists polled 38 percent of the total national vote. Their following was especially large in the Czech provinces, where it amounted to some 40 percent, and in several districts in the border regions, formerly inhabited by the Sudeten Germans, where they polled more than 50 percent. In Slovakia, however, only 30.7 percent of the vote was cast for the CPS; since only two parties competed there for electoral support, the Communists found themselves in the minority, with the rival Democratic party receiving about twice as many votes. Another surprise was the lopsided vote in favor of the Communists in rural precincts in the western provinces, whereas the vote in the industrialized urban centers and the capital city was much more balanced (see Table 2).

In itself and by all objective standards, the outcome of the 1946 elections was very successful for the CPCS; by the normal yardsticks of a pluralist system, it has to be viewed as a model electoral victory. However, the situation in Czechoslovakia one year after the war was not quite normal. That is why neither the public nor the party appreciated the remarkable Communist performance as it would have some ten years earlier. After an intense political mobilization stimulated by the party's use of all means of persuasion, bribes, pressure, and threats, the Czechoslovak polity had become unusually polarized. It could be claimed that any vote not cast for the CPCS was actually cast against the party. In a way, the general election of May 1946 was a referendum, but in that light, the 38 percent polled by the Communists was hardly a triumph. Also, in the context of the Communist party's goal to achieve an absolute majority, the election results were at best inconclusive. On the one hand, they argued for maintaining the adopted strategy because they could be

TABLE 2

COMMUNIST VOTE IN SELECTED DISTRICTS DURING
THE GENERAL ELECTIONS OF 1946

District	Ballot Run By	Percent of Vote
Banská Bystrica	CPS	39.3
Brno	CPCS	33.8
České Budějovice	CPCS	42.7
Hradec Králové	CPCS	39.5
Jihlava	CPCS	38.6
Karlovy Vary	CPCS	52.2
Košice	CPS	20.0
Liptovský S. Mikuláš	CPS	27.2
Mladá Boleslav	CPCS	43.4
Moravská Ostrava	CPCS	37.9
Olomouc	CPCS	32.4
Pardubice	CPCS	35.7
Plzeň	CPCS	44.9
Praha	CPCS	36.1
Prešov	CPS	28.1
Trnava	CPS	33.0
OVERALL NATIONAL COMMUNIST VOTE		37.9

interpreted as a proof that the objective was within the realm of the possible. On the other hand, they could also support the claims of those who advocated a change in tactics; after all, had not the popular support fallen far short of the desired mark even in ideal national and international conditions that probably could not be replicated in any future elections? The Presidium of the Central Committee, at a meeting held three days after the elections, admitted that the CPCS alone "was not yet in the position to implement its political goals." The Central Committee plenum endorsed this view on May 30, 1946, and stated that it would be the party's task to achieve an absolute majority in the next elections, slated for May 1948. Judging by official pronouncements, then, it could be inferred that the acquisition of full control "in a democratic way"— that is, the suspension of the pluralist system by its own mechanism— remained the policy of the party after the first postwar vote.

Analysis of the 1946 Vote

An analyst of the voting pattern in the first and only free postwar elections would have to consider the extraordinary conditions, ethnic, demographic, and economic, in which the elections took place, since these in addition to the unusual psychological climate of extreme polarization, influenced the vote. Prior to the elections, the ethnic

composition of the electorate underwent a radical change. The largest
ethnic minority, the Sudeten Germans, was in the process of being
transferred to Germany, and those Germans who still remained in
Czechoslovakia were denied the right to vote. Ruthenia had been ceded
to the Soviet Union in the summer of 1945. An exchange of population
with Hungary—that is, a transfer of Hungarian-speaking inhabitants of
southern Slovakia to Hungary and of Slovak-speaking inhabitants of the
Hungarian Plain to Czechoslovakia—was under way, and although it was
never to reach the proportions of the German ethnic-group transfer, it
significantly influenced participation at the polls. Therefore it can be said
that in the 1946 elections, the only cleavages that mattered were those
within the Czech and Slovak society. Yet these cleavages determined the
results of the elections only to a limited degree. After the traumatic
experience of the dismemberment of Czechoslovakia in 1938 and 1939,
and after the Nazi occupation, six years of war, the Slovak uprising of
1944, the liberation by the Soviet and American armies, and the
tremendous upheaval caused by the population transfers, the Czechs
and the Slovaks lived in abnormal conditions, to say the least. Large
segments of the Czech population (up to 20 percent in the western
border areas) had been uprooted by the resettlement following the
expulsion of the German minority. Old community and kin ties had been
severed and new ones not yet formed. In these circumstances, the bases
of typical social and cultural cleavages were absent. Instead of a society a
considerable part of the Czechoslovak population was an atomized social
mass, homeless clusters of people who had nothing in common except
the fact of having lived in the same place for a short time.

We may come nearer to the truth about the rather complex voting
motivation in 1946 if we duly consider the sociopsychological consequences of mass migrations. We know from observation of other
pluralist polities that under normal conditions, issue voting—and the
vote for the Communist party out of gratitude for the country's
liberation by the Red Army and for the redistribution of property would
in fact be an ex-post-facto issue vote—is rare. Factors such as socioeconomic status, ethnic origin, religion, and area of residence invariably
inhibit the switch in allegiance that such a vote might require and also
determine the relatively stable pattern of an individual's voting over a
long period of time. Of the four factors listed, two were rendered
completely irrelevant in the case of the recent migrants into the border
regions. Area of residence obviously ceased to be a factor and the

political significance of ethnic origin—that is, the significance for party choice of being a Czech or a Slovak (and those were the only ones to vote)—had been very much reduced by the expulsion of the Sudeten Germans and the hope, still plausible in May 1946, that the problem of the Hungarian minority could be disposed of in a similar manner; the quality of belonging to a nation-building group thus could no longer in itself determine voting choices. Moreover, the remaining two factors, religion and socioeconomic status, have always been closely tied to stable residence. Religion and religious affiliation have never played a prominent role in the politics of the western Czechoslovak provinces because of the laxity the forced recatholicization after the Thirty Years War produced. Whatever was left of meaningful religiosity depended on church membership and community for maintenance and reinforcement; but community life was by definition nonexistent in the critical frontier regions. Socioeconomic status, especially its subjective perception by the voters in these areas, was the most unstable influence on voting behavior precisely because of the uprooting of these people and the unprecedented shifts in property distribution.

Thus it was chiefly the very fact of the mass migration, with the attendant gigantic transfer of wealth, that had nullified the traditional social alignments and resulted in the atypical voting behavior in the border districts that in turn assured the leading position of the Communist party on the national level. However, the core regions of the country, too, experienced a notable shift in political allegiances. An important factor in this shift was the streamlining of the political spectrum, the restriction on the number of parties imposed by the Moscow and Košice agreements of 1945. It made politically homeless a considerable portion of the Czechoslovak electorate, especially in the countryside where the Agrarian party, the largest party before the war, was banned. Thus the traditional cleavage between agriculture and industry lost one of its main instruments of articulation. Part of the former left wing of the Agrarians joined the Catholic-inspired but now virtually interdenominational People's party, especially in Moravia. In Slovakia the bulk of the prewar supporters of the Agrarian party voted for the Democrats. Nevertheless the Communist leaders' expectation that the dissolution of the largest peasant party would benefit the CPCS was on the whole confirmed. In Bohemia, for example, whole electoral districts that had been solid Agrarian bastions for fifty years, since the time of the Austro-Hungarian empire, went Communist in the elections of May 1946. Yet, theoretically, the choice then open to the voters was broad enough, even within the framework of the National Front; a vote for the Communists was not the only option, although many voters did not find in the new spectrum the party of their traditional preference. The political homelessness of a substantial part of the electorate cannot fully explain the success of the Communist party, especially in view of the fact that the CPCS also siphoned away a good deal of support from the Social Democrats, a party that was not subject to any formal restrictions.

Two others factors merit our attention because they contributed to the Communist triumph in May 1946. For one, the Communist party had become a partner in the ruling government coalition. Gone was the climate of semi-illegality and extremist rhetoric that had frightened and repelled the moderates and the conservatives before the war. Some of the previous Communist objectives had been shelved, some were now presented to the public as national, suprapartisan concerns, for example, the nationalization of the industries or loyalty to the Soviet ally in matters of foreign policy. The middle-class citizen's experience with the Communist party in the postwar years differed considerably from that of his counterpart in the First Republic. We should not disregard, either, the appeal that a party holding considerable governmental power had for weak elements and opportunists. The second factor worth examining is the strong pro-Russian sentiment that prevailed in Czechoslovakia, again chiefly in its western provinces, after the war. Many saw the Red Army as the sole liberator. The fact that this impression was the result of rather unsentimental horse-trading between the Allied powers on a world scale could not change the genuine nature of pro-Russian sympathies. Since the CPCS had always been viewed, for better or for worse, as representing the Soviet Union, a vote for this party appeared a logical choice to those who wished to express their gratitude for liberation. Not all pro-Russian and pan-Slav sympathizers made such a plain connection between their feelings and the act of voting, but the number of those who did was statistically significant. The Communist electoral campaign, far from scorning this simplistic equation, exploited it to the maximum.

To sum up, the Communist electoral victory of May 1946, which did not immediately lead to the seizure of power but considerably facilitated this seizure at a later date, was caused by a number of coinciding factors: these factors—mass migration and resettlement of the population, large-scale transfers of wealth, artificial restrictions on political competition, a radical change in the image of the Communist party after its entry into the government, and the deep impression of the Soviet victory in the war—all contributed to the shift in, or to the suspension of the effects of, the traditional social cleavages. The strikingly atypical voting behavior of the Czech and Slovak population can be traced back to this political anomie. It may also suggest that the relation between social cleavages and the voting alignment is possibly more complicated than one of an independent versus a dependent variable. It may well be that just as social cleavages determine party choice, a party is a mirror helping the voter to perceive the critical cleavage. If this surmise is correct, then sudden changes in the party spectrum would not necessarily prompt him to rationally shop for the next best party to cater to his particular interests. Instead, we should expect the voter to lose his sense of political orientation and become much more susceptible to radical propaganda. This seems to be one of the lessons the Czechoslovak parliamentary elections of May 1946 could teach a political sociologist.

Election Results and the CPS

Soon after the first postwar elections it became obvious, even to the most optimistic observers, that the party's preference for the democratic way of acquiring power was motivated by considerations of expediency rather than by a commitment to constitutional principles. This was illustrated by the course the Communists adopted in the regions where the election results had placed the CPCS in a minority position—that is, in Slovakia. Because two non-Communist parties in this province, the Labor party (the Slovak counterpart of the Czech Social Democracy) and the Freedom party (the replacement for the prewar Populist or National party), had set up their organizations and launched their electoral campaigns only after a considerable delay, practically the entire non-Communist vote went to the Democratic party, which won twice as many votes as the Communists. There was some irony in this situation: the triumph of the Democratic party was largely made possible by the adoption of the Communist-sponsored principle that no Czech parties would be allowed to run in Slovakia and no Slovak parties in Bohemia and Moravia. The Labor and Freedom parties had been latecomers in the electoral contest and thus had failed to divert more non-Communist support from the Democrats because Slovak Communist officials had deliberately obstructed their efforts to establish themselves. Whatever the reasons, the Central Committee of the CPS, in its plenary session on

May 31, 1946, registered the election results with much less equanimity than the party's national headquarters in Prague. It was clear that the CPS would not accept the situation as it evolved and would look for ways and means to restore the privileged position it had enjoyed since the end of the war. Apparently inspired by the "salami tactics" employed by the Communists in neighboring Hungary against their political opponents, the Central Committee of the Slovak Communist party called for the dissolution of the Democratic party, which it denounced as a protector of traitors and collaborationists and a poorly camouflaged new edition of the fascist Hlinka's People's party. It appealed to the Slovak working class to enforce the ban on the Democrats by "direct action," that is, a general strike. However, the situation in Slovakia in 1946 was somewhat different from that in Hungary. Here again, paradoxically, the success of the Communist initiative in streamlining the party system weakened the Communist argument. It was in the very logic of the Moscow and Košice agreements that only untarnished political movements could operate in the liberated republic. Consequently the Democratic party, established on these principles as an heir to the tradition of the Slovak uprising of 1944, could not be disposed of so easily. Therefore the Communists adopted a different approach. In the session of the Slovak National Council on June 17, 1946, they tabled a proposal to revise the relationship between the Slovak regional and national legislative and executive organs that had been established by the Košice agreement. The revision marked a perceptible retreat from the principle of federalism. It was interesting to see Slovak Communists, who had been staunch champions of Slovak self-government during the war and immediately after the liberation, aligned in the defense of the new restrictions with the centralist elements, Communist as well as non-Communist. Undoubtedly they hoped that the power that had been denied them by the vote of their own people could be acquired in an indirect way, via the national government in Prague. The talks in the National Council at Bratislava at that point simply laid the foundations for the actual changes in the authority of the various autonomous organs that were made a year and a half later, but it was clear that a new wind had already begun to blow in the Slovak chapter of the Communist movement. Needless to say, in the ranks of the CPS the leadership's policy reversal only deepened the controversy between the nationalists and the partisans of a strong, unified party organization.

Although the Slovak party's unwillingness to bow to the verdict of the people in the parliamentary elections clearly indicated that the Communists "played the constitutional game" only when they found it profitable, several concrete steps taken at that time by the national party headquarters strengthened rather than weakened the impression that the CPCS continued to believe absolute power could be achieved by means of a popular vote. Six weeks after the elections, the Central Committee set up a special commission to prepare the draft of a new constitution. The commission submitted the first version of the draft to the Central Committee as early as July 25, 1946: its speed suggested that the CPCS assumed the project of the constitution would have to be discussed with the coalition partners in the National Front. The fact that the commission had to report to the party chairman, Gottwald, indicated that this issue probably ranked high among the current political problems perceived by the Communists in the summer of 1946. In the early fall of 1946, Gottwald sharply criticized "the main promoters of a sectarian and dogmatic line." These words, uttered at the September 25 and 26 session of the Central Committee, were accompanied by an explicit endorsement of the principle of a "specifically Czechoslovak road to Socialism.[11] The criticism of sectarianism and dogmatism had a double edge: it defended the current line of cooperation with non-Communist parties in the government and the distinct political entity of the Czechoslovak Republic against those who advocated the annexation of Czechoslovakia by the Soviet Union as "the eleventh Union member," and it also implicitly rejected the aspirations of certain Slovak party leaders to autonomy. These leaders found themselves in a rather complicated, if not contradictory, situation. As nationalists and autonomists, they sought to enhance the individual personality of the Slovak Communist party and of the Slovak ethnic group; however, since they looked to the Soviet Union for eventual help in their struggle, they also supported Moscow's tutelage and dominance in Central and Eastern Europe. Compared with their position, that of the national leadership was then more consistently Czechoslovak.

The Marshall Plan Episode and the Kominform

The decisions the party leadership made in the first postwar years concerning the political form of the Czechoslovak state and the participation in the race for power with other parties would have been of momentous significance if the CPCS had been the sole judge in these matters. However, Czechoslovak Communists had never, at least not since bolshevization, determined their policies independently. The dismemberment of Czechoslovakia at the end of the 1930s promoted various centrifugal forces, as did the Second World War, but as we have seen, autonomism and separatism were not synonymous with emancipation from control by the international center in Moscow. Moreover, the exile leadership succeeded relatively soon in neutralizing these trends. On the other hand, the commitment to the Czechoslovak Road to Socialism professed by the leadership and declared on various occasions proved to be an insufficient guarantee against the party's ultimate subjection to the pressures and interests of Soviet global politics. When the real crisis came, the strategy of the acquisition of power by constitutional means was replaced by a more aggressive approach. This crisis actually did not occur in February 1948: it only became more salient at that point. It had been under way since 1946 and its character was international. The problem was whether a pluralist experiment had a chance in a country within the Soviet power orbit while the climate between the East and the West was rapidly deteriorating toward Cold War in the wake of the conflict over Germany. History soon gave a negative answer to this question. This was also the real cause of the change in Communist tactics. The failure to capture the absolute majority of votes in the May 1946 elections and a pessimistic assessment of the party's prospects in the forthcoming 1948 general elections would hardly have forced a reversal in themselves; only in combination with the growing rivalry between the Soviet Union and its Western allies did they make inevitable what later Communist historiography called "the revolutionary option."

In Czechoslovakia, the effects of the European crisis had been felt since 1947. As the political head-on collision among the victors of the Second World War inevitably approached, it was only logical that the Soviet Union had little use for Communist parties participating in coalition governments. This was true of all nations in the Soviet sphere of influence, but it was demonstrated especially dramatically in Czechoslovakia, where the attempt at a symbiosis between parliamentary democracy and pro-Soviet orientation had been most serious and was allowed to last the longest. Czechoslovak non-Communist politicians in the postwar period often referred to their country as to a "bridge between

East and West." However, Stalin was interested in pulling down bridges rather than in building them at that time. The year following the elections for the Constitutional National Assembly brought several events in international politics that testified to a rapidly increasing tension among the Allies. Signs multiplied, too, that this tension would not fail to influence deeply the international relations of the states within the power orbit of Moscow as well as the entire world Communist movement. Among these indicators two in particular merit singling out because of their bearing upon Czechoslovak politics and on the development of the policy line of the CPCS. These were the reception of the Marshall Plan (U.S. Secretary of State George C. Marshall's European Recovery Program) in Central and Eastern Europe, and the foundation of a new body for the coordination of the activities of various Communist parties, the so-called Kominform.

The events relating to the Czechoslovak government's decision to participate in the Marshall Plan and to the subsequent reversal of this decision are particularly interesting to the historian of the Czechoslovak Communist movement: they demonstrated not only the extent of Soviet control over Czechoslovak foreign politics but also the degree to which the CPCS then depended on the power center in Moscow. On July 4, 1947, the Czechoslovak government (at least, all the Communist ministers) voted unanimously to accept the invitation of the American Department of State to participate in the preparatory conference of the European Recovery Program in Paris. The CPCS spokesmen and mass media justified this step as "the only right course counselled by enlightened self-interest" in view of the fact that Czechoslovakia was an advanced industrial nation whose high standard of living could be regained and maintained only through an international division of labor and trade involving other developed industrial economies.[12] A few days later, however, the Soviets forced Czechoslovakia's withdrawal from the impending conference. Moscow handled the issue in a rather high-handed manner: Stalin took advantage of the visit of the Czechoslovak cabinet delegation, which included the prime minister, CPCS chairman Klement Gottwald, and the foreign minister, Jan Masaryk, to dictate this step. He insisted that the new decision be taken while the prime minister and foreign minister were still in the Soviet Union.[13] Apart from serving as proof of the reduced international status of Czechoslovakia, Stalin's intervention showed that the Kremlin dictator did not have any more consideration for the image of the Czechoslovak

Communist party than he had for the sovereign rights of the Czecho-slovak nation. The Marshall Plan incident, which was echoed in neigh-boring Poland, demonstrated to the world the clearly demarcated limits of any independent initiative by the national chapters of the interna-tional Communist movement (in Czechoslovakia in the 1940s such initiative was not exhibited very often). It was a bad omen for the future development of Czechoslovak domestic politics.

If Czechoslovakia's forced retreat from the European Recovery Pro-gram spelled a new form of vassal relations in the Soviet-controlled areas, another event in the late summer of 1947 underscored the tightening grip of the Moscow power center over the various European Communist parties. At the end of September 1947, Communist media announced that an international conference of Communist party officials had been held September 22–27 in Szklarska Poremba in Polish Silesia. Delegates of the Soviet Communist party and the Communist parties of all European "people's democracies," as well as of France and Italy, had been present. The conference had deliberated behind closed doors and decided that an "Information Bureau of Communist and Workers Parties" would be set up to "facilitate the exchange of information and experience among the various national communist organizations" and "help coordinate their activities." The need for such an agency was seen in the "reactionary and subversive maneuvers of the capitalist powers aiming at the destruction of Socialism," an alleged example of which had been an almost successful attempt to include Czechoslovakia and Poland in the Marshall Plan, "a plan for the domination of Europe by U.S. monopoly capitalism."[14]

It was not difficult for any informed observer to understand the real purpose of the new international Communist clearinghouse devised in Szklarska Poremba. The Information Bureau of the Communist and Workers Parties (Kominform) was obviously to succeed the defunct Komintern as the Kremlin's tool for steering the policies of the indivi-dual Communist parties. The new body was far more restricted in scope, however, than the Third International: the Kominform was exclusively European, and it was constituted only by a selected group of the Communist parties of the continent.

Among the Western delegations, only the French and the Italian parties were represented; for the rest, the bureau's representatives were recruited exclusively from Central and Eastern Europe. The regional character of the Kominform suggested the focus of interest of the Soviet sponsors. In 1947, Stalin still hoped for Communist gains in Europe, beyond the demarcation line drawn at the end of the war. France and Italy were two very promising targets, prey to chronic social unrest and agitation. On the other hand, the Soviet zone of influence had not yet been completely stabilized. Moscow could not be absolutely sure of all the people's democracies even though the importance of the Communist share in the government of these countries was growing steadily. Czechoslovakia was a vital and sensitive component of this system, and soon the Kominform began to show concern for the course of events there.

The CPCS was represented at Szklarska Poremba by the secretary-general, Rudolf Slánský, the secretary of the CPS, Štefan Bašťovanský, and Politbureau member Bedřich Geminder. The report submitted by Slánský on September 23 stood out from other contributions from Eastern European delegations by virtue of its relative objectivity and moderation of tone. Slánský voiced the apprehensions of the Czechoslovak party about the increasing resistance to Communist policies shown by the non-Communist members of the National Front, but he expressed the hope that the CPCS would nevertheless be able to carry out its program with the support of the Social Democrats, by majority rule within constitutional limits. Other speakers at the conference condemned with particular vehemence the willingness of some Communist parties— but it was obvious that only the French and Italian comrades were the subjects of this criticism—to cooperate with other parties and their rather positive stand on the question of U.S. aid to Europe. Indeed, the indictment of the Communist parties of France and Italy seems to have been the main point on the agenda, next to the constitution of the information bureau. French and Italian delegates later confessed that they had felt at Szklarska Poremba as if they were sitting "on the defendants' bench."[15] Rudolf Slánský also criticized these parties, but it was evident that this part of his presentation had been prepared in cooperation with the Soviet initiators of the conference, because the line of argument and occasionally even the wording were identical with these of other, especially Yugoslav, participants.[16] Slánský's position was somewhat delicate; he spoke for a party that, not unlike the French Communists in 1945 and 1946, sat in a governmental coalition with other, non-socialist and bourgeois partners. It was assumed, of course, that the Czechoslovak Communist party was ruling, or would soon avail itself of decisive influence. Purely formally, however, the situation in September 1947 had not yet reached that stage. Condemning cooperation with bourgeois elements thus meant that Slánský implicitly committed his party to a more radical course.

The Gathering Storm

The hot summer of 1947—hot climatically as well as politically—was followed in Czechoslovakia by an eventful autumn. The "obstruction and the sabotage of the idea of the National Front" by the non-Communists, as perceived by the CPCS leadership and denounced by Slánský at the constitutive meeting of the Kominform, continued. The charge of sabotage was addressed to what the Communists labeled "reactionary circles" that allegedly had found their way into other parties of the coalition, especially the Czech Populist and the Slovak Democratic parties. However, the wrath of the Communist spokesmen descended with equal force upon the more outspoken individual critics of Communist abuse of power, who could be found all along the political spectrum, even on the left and among former Communist party members. These latter were considered to be ideological enemies, just as dangerous as class enemies. During the autumn of 1947 a serious conflict was in the making between the CPCS and its erstwhile mother party, the Social Democracy, whose cooperation Rudolf Slánský had taken for granted in his speech at the Kominform conference.

The Czechoslovak Social Democratic party, theoretically the closest to the CPCS on the political scale, polled only 15 percent of the vote in the general elections of 1946. Even if the modest following given to its sister party in Slovakia, the Labor party, is added, Social Democrats gained barely half of the votes given to the Communists. Nevertheless, the Social Democratic party occupied a key position in Czechoslovak political life for several reasons. Although it had been unable to regain its prewar strength among the working class, the party still retained the vote of what is called the worker aristocracy: automobile and steel workers, some miners, and so on—in short, the most skilled, best organized, and best paid segment of the labor force. It also attracted many liberal intellectuals who, while they subscribed to the basic idea of social solidarity and of the supremacy of collective interests, were keenly aware of the threat to democracy represented by a mass Communist party subject in major issues to the will of a foreign power. That was why the Social Democratic party was sometimes called, half jokingly, "the party of decent people," a connotation that stressed not only the ethical stature of its members, but also a possible lack of political acumen and realism among them.

In the Communist strategy, especially in the policy of a democratic road to power, the party's relationship with the Social Democracy played a very important role. The Communists' ambivalent attitude toward this party originating before the war, persisted in the postwar period despite the fact that the CPCS now was no longer the smaller of the two. Mistrust and rivalry continued for a number of reasons. Both parties vied for the sympathies of the same population strata, and the only alternative to Communist rule capable of winning the endorsement of the bulk of the working class was democratic socialism. This made the Social Democrats the chief challengers of the CPCS. On the other hand, an eventual political pact with the Social Democrats could assure the Communists of what they could never be certain of achieving by themselves in the electoral contest: an absolute majority in the legislative organs and in the government. The 15.6 percent of the popular vote and the corresponding number of assembly seats controlled by the Social Democrats would have enabled the Communists to reach the 51 percent necessary for the enactment of the various parts of their program. Joining forces with the Social Democrats would have also reduced the risk of the fluctuation of votes, since a shift in the following away from the CPCS would probably bring gains to the Social Democrats and thus maintain the total majority. The Communists were aware of this possibility: that was why they had always striven, since the liberation, to conclude such an alliance, in one form or another. One such attempt was the 1945 agreement with the Social Democratic and the National Socialist parties about the constitution of the "Socialist Bloc of Working People," which largely remained a dead letter. Communist efforts to revive the bloc in September 1947 were not very successful. The leadership of the National Socialist party rejected the Communist initiative out of hand. A provisional agreement with the Social Democratic leadership raised a wave of protest from that party's rank and file, who considered it unauthorized, and it was annulled by the subsequent national party congress.

In fact, the attempts to put the Social Democracy at the service of Communist politics had already started before the liberation. They were not always as straightforward and official as the project of the Socialist Bloc, but they were at times more rewarding. Among the most significant of these moves was the implantation into the Social Democratic party of units of activists who sympathized with the Communist cause. Many were Social Democrats of long standing, supporters of the left wing or people whom the experience of Munich and foreign occupation had converted to radicalism. Many such conversions had occurred in Nazi prisons and concentration camps, where Social Democratic and Communist inmates had often shared the privations and perils of prison life. In such a psychological climate, the differences between various shades of socialist creed were not perceived as very important, and feelings of loyalty and solidarity among otherwise very heterogeneous individuals and groups flourished, outlasting the war. Some of these attachments gave the Communist party the opportunity to subvert the Social Democratic organizations, because several Social Democratic ex-internees consented to become Communist undercover agents ("vtyčky"). Some functionaries of the Social Democracy became allies of the Communists without ever making any agreement, tacit or explicit, by taking the position "pas d'ennemi à gauche" ("there can be no enemy to the left of us"), a position that paralyzed the party at the moment of ultimate crisis. It is difficult to assess the extent of the penetration into the Social Democracy of pro-Communist elements but, as was apparent during the dramatic days of the Communist take-over, Communist lines of communication and control reached the highest echelons of the Social Democratic party.

Considering the important place the Social Democratic party occupied in the Communist plans, it is not hard to understand the lively concern of the CPCS leadership over the distribution of power and influence among the various groups and currents within this party. The general trend of development since the 1946 elections, however, did not give the Communists grounds for optimism. The majority of the rank-and-file members of the Social Democracy felt that too close relations between the two parties would be detrimental, and called for a better articulated and more independent policy line. It was only a matter of time until the new course would prevail. At the Twenty-First Party Congress in Brno, held November 14–16, 1947, the wartime party chairman, Zdeněk Fierlinger, who had been an ambassador to the Soviet Union and was closely associated with the exile center of the CPCS, was replaced by Bohumil Laušman, a representative of a more independent course.[17] The CPCS immediately recognized the sign of change and Communist media sounded the alarm. It was obvious that under its new governance the Social Democracy could not be counted upon for unreserved support of Communist policies. The road to majority via an alliance between the

Communist and the Social Democratic parlimentary factions did not seem a realistic option any longer. The failure of the Social Democratic party to live up to the expectations of its Communist partner was probably the single most important internal factor in the change of Communist tactics.

Another serious crisis in the autumn of 1947 broke out in the relations between the CPS and the Slovak Democratic party. Tensions had continued in this area since the 1946 elections, in which the Democratic party had polled twice as many votes as the Communists. After launching a vain call for the dissolution of the Democratic party, the CPS, with the assistance of the CPCS national headquarters, pressed for changes in the Košice Program relative to the status of the Slovak regional legislative and executive organs, changes that implied curtailment of the powers of these organs. On the same occasion, the Communist national leadership in Prague tightened the reins on the Slovak Communist party. The 1946 crisis had sharpened the opposition between the centralist and autonomist groups within the CPS to the point that Secretary-General Rudolf Slánský was forced to admit in his report to the first Kominform conference the fact of "a large number of Slovak comrades opposing a reinforcement of the Czechoslovak national government" and "endorsing views promoted by the Slovak bourgeoisie." Now, in their dispute with the Democratic party in the fall of 1947, Slovak Communists did not question the institutions of Slovak self-government, but asked for a larger share in power. The confrontation took a very sharp form in October and November 1947, when the CPS mobilized factory workers and Communist-front organizations against the politicians of the Democratic party. While these self-appointed spokesmen of the Slovak working people harassed the non-Communist local government members and impeded the function of the Slovak executive, the chairman of the Board of Commissioners for Slovakia, Communist deputy Gustav Husák, arbitrarily dissolved the board without consulting the Democratic party majority or the Slovak National Council. Since the Democratic members of the board refused to acknowledge the dissolution, the matter was submitted to the Executive Committee of the National Front in Prague.

The issue under dispute was the distribution of seats between the Communists and the Democrats in the Slovak regional cabinet, not the application of the principle of autonomy in Slovakia (as in the 1946 crisis); thus there were no significant differences of opinion among the various groups in the Slovak party or between the Slovak leadership and the national headquarters of the CPCS. Party Chairman Klement Gott-wald went to Bratislava in his capacity as prime minister of the national government and obtained some concessions from the Democratic party in the reconstituted Board of Commissioners. However, the CPCS planned to take even greater advantage of the opportunity. Profiting from the fact that the controversy between the two Slovak parties had been referred to the National Front, the CPCS proposed to introduce a new element into the rules governing the assignment of posts in the legislative and executive bodies. This reform would have changed the nature of the ruling coalition known to that point. At first sight, the proposal appeared to be a compromise between the demands of the CPS for a larger representation in the Board of Commissioners and the Slovak National Council, and the opposition to those demands by the Democratic party supported by all non-Communist parties in the national government. Instead of an enlargement of the CPS's share in the Slovak regional cabinet, the proposal called for the participation in the board of delegates of the so-called mass organizations—trade unions, the youth movement, farmers' associations, and so on—that up to then had been included in the National Front but not allowed to send representatives to the National Assembly or the Slovak National Council. This new cri-terion for the selection of candidates to government posts, according to the proposal, was to be used by political organs at all levels.

Although the representation of the Communist party in the legisla-ture and in the administration would have remained formally unchanged under this reform, subject only to fluctuations in electoral support, the proposed reform would actually have strengthened the Communist position considerably, since most of the mass organizations were con-trolled by the CPCS. It was not difficult to see the significance of the Communist initiative. If it had been successful, this project could have secured for the CPCS what it could not have achieved in the elections: an absolute majority. The idea must have seemed particularly attractive to the party leadership in the fall of 1947, when another substitute democratic road to power threatened to close on account of the change in the top positions and the policy line of the Social Democracy, which was now less than ever prepared to enter upon an alliance with the Communists. After having tabled their proposal, the Communists in-vited officials of the mass organizations to the meeting of the Executive Committee that was to deal with the Slovak crisis, as if the reform had already been approved. However, the partners of the CPCS in the government coalition recognized the real objectives of the Communist maneuver and refused to sit in the Executive Committee of the National Front with representatives of organizations other than political parties. The CPCS bowed to the resistance and withdrew its proposal.[18]

The Party Seizes Power

Regular confrontations between the Communists and the rest of the National Front, a group composed of all the non-Communist parties in the front, rendered increasingly tense the internal political situation in Czechoslovakia at the end of 1947. The tension was considerably aggravated by external factors. Indeed, it was the contemporary international crisis of polarization between the Soviet Union and the Western powers that made the relationship between the Communists and the non-Communists a very sensitive issue, and in the end prevented the establishment of any basis of cooperation. It notably reduced the flexibility of the CPCS: the party could not easily retreat or make concessions, even on issues that in themselves were not essential, for fear that such a policy might be interpreted as a capitulation before the forces of reaction and perceived as a defeat of the entire Communist bloc, including the Soviet Union. Occasional pronouncements by the leaders of "fraternal" parties made this point very clear. For example, at the first regular session of the Kominform in Belgrade, in December 1947, Anna Pauker, a member of the Politbureau of the Rumanian Workers' party, severely criticized the Czechoslovak comrades for what she felt to be an unduly tolerant attitude toward their coalition partners. By all objective standards, the criticism was greatly exaggerated. The CPCS had hardly sinned through an excess of conciliation, but the attack indicated what was in store for the Czechoslovak Communists if they did not fall in line with the current intransigent Soviet position. On the other hand, the uncompromising stand of the Czechoslovak party, reinforced by external pressures, had as its consequence a further stiffening of resistance from all members of the National Front coalition. In the long run, a collision was inevitable.

The final showdown, although impossible to avoid, required a precipitant. Either the Communists or their opponents, or both at the same time, had to see the situation as mature for a major confrontation and make a move. There was also, of course, the possibility that the conflict might be escalated to the point of no return, without either of the two rival groups actually intending it. This outcome was made more likely by the growing irritation of the non-Communist public about the frequent abuse of power by the Communists, which reduced the maneuvering room of the other parties of the National Front coalition. It was a very risky alternative for the non-Communists because successful resistance to Communist pressure required very careful preparation and a clear and dependable strategy. Because the forces opposing the Communists constituted a very heterogeneous group, despite their unanimity on goals, faultless coordination among them was indispensable. No chance could be given the adversary to divide them, an attempt the Communists were sure to make in a crisis situation. A spontaneous, unexpected outbreak of a major conflict in an emotion-laden climate could mobilize the sympathies and support of the non-Communist "silent majority," but without a preconceived plan of how to harness this valuable energy for concrete political action, the odds favored the better organized Communist minority. This, indeed, was the way in which the ultimate showdown developed.

The final crisis was triggered by a dispute between the Communist-controlled Ministry of the Interior and the non-Communist majority of the cabinet over a concrete case of the misuse of police power.[19] The Service of Internal Security, which was subject to the minister of the interior, had attempted to bribe some minor Nazi war criminals awaiting trial in a Prague prison to testify to an alleged collusion between certain non-Communist leaders of the resistance movement and the Gestapo during the occupation. They also tried to construct a case of espionage, implicating several prominent non-Communist politicians, for the benefit of Western intelligence. These moves strongly resembled the tactics applied in neighboring Poland and Hungary, where all independent groups and leaders had been gradually eliminated by the use of the police and the judiciary. However, these machinations became known to the non-Communist government members before they could lead to the expected results. A well-documented interpellation concerning this misuse of power was submitted by the representatives of the National Socialist party to the minister of interior, Václav Nosek, but the minister failed to carry out investigations and to report to the cabinet plenum as requested, under the pretext that the confidential nature of the work of the Service of Internal Security made such an investigation impossible. The non-Communist majority nevertheless pressed for an action against those responsible for the abuse of authority. The tension that resulted from this unsettled controversy dominated the climate of the cabinet deliberations from the end of 1947 until early in 1948, when it was escalated to the point of an imminent break: at that time, the Ministry of the Interior replaced police commissioners in eight vital regions with members of the Communist party. The function of the commissioners was very important. They had the power to provide the police units with arms and ammunition and to supply the members of the uniformed security forces with the kind of firearms they considered necessary in any given situation. It was obvious that the Ministry of the Interior wanted to assure full control of the police by the Communist party in case of an emergency.

The non-Communist members of the government would not permit this under any circumstances. Thus the conflict over the illegal activities of the security service and the personnel policies of the Ministry of the Interior became the most immediate cause of what has been referred to since then as the February crisis, which put an end to the pluralist system in postwar Czechoslovakia. For the coalition majority, who were anxious to preserve the basic elements of the constitutional order, this situation was a most unfortunate one. Although the misuse of power by the security service was flagrant enough to stir strong resistance, it did not directly involve any of the core issues dividing the Communists from the rest of the nation. In itself, it could have been settled by a compromise in which the Communist minister could have saved face. The question of the appointment of the police divisions commissioners was even less clear-cut from the legal standpoint. Although the intention of the Communists in this case was patent, and although every cabinet minister was obligated, by the letter of the constitution, to answer to the rest of the cabinet for any measure taken by him or his officials, the tradition of leaving decisions about civil service personnel to the discretion of the respective portfolio holder had been established in Czechoslovakia for a very long time. Therefore it would have been better for those who wanted to stop the Communist abuse of power if matters had come to a head over an open-and-shut case. A simple and salient major issue might not have impressed or influenced the Communists, but it would have much more readily rallied the majority of the nation behind the non-Communist leaders—an indispensable condition for the success of the move.

However, the defenders of the constitutional system actually had little choice. As a consequence of the tactics they had adopted since the liberation, things had now come to a point from which no retreat was possible.[20] Equally serious was the fact that they had not taken, or even considered, any measures aimed at coordinating their policies in the case of a crisis. An understanding in principle on this subject among the four major non-Communist parties should have been reached as soon as the first government of the National Front was established in Prague in 1945; it became necessary after the elections of 1946. In reality, no systematic consultations of this kind ever took place. Even when the leaderships of these parties decided individually to take a stand against the Communists and risk a cabinet crisis in February 1948, no clear plan of action was devised. The last-minute agreement was merely an improvisation that did not even include all parties in question: the Social Democracy had not been invited to the crucial talks among the National Socialists, the Populists, and the Slovak Democrats on February 20. Little effort, too, was made to assure the cooperation, or at least to ascertain the position, of the nonpartisan government members, the foreign minister and the minister of defense. Nor did anyone inform the head of state, President Beneš, ahead of time to obtain his support. As for Beneš, permanent contact and an exchange of views between him and the non-Communist majority had been vitally important since the ominous episode of the Soviet-imposed withdrawal from the Marshall Plan conference in 1947. Instead, the non-Communist politicians let things take their course and mustered only a makeshift resistance to the well-conceived and detailed Communist strategy.[21] Under these circumstances, the Communist triumph was easy.

The timing of the showdown between the Communists and their coalition partners was far from optimal for the non-Communists. It should have occurred much earlier. Once the best chances had been missed, however—or not even perceived—the end of February 1948 was again too early. If by more perspicacity or skill the ultimate confrontation could then have been avoided or postponed, two events that were then in the making might have greatly improved the chances of the non-Communist leaders. One of these events was the general election slated for April or May 1948. There were valid reasons to expect that the Communist party would lose some of the support it had mustered in 1946. Informed observers estimated the probable loss at about 10 percent; this would have left the CPCS in the position of the strongest party in the nation, but it would have notably reinforced the non-Communist majority, which then held close to two-thirds of the seats in the National Assembly and in the cabinet. A 10 percent reduction in the Communist vote would also have brought about a redistribution of the ministerial posts, since the Communists would have been obliged to relinquish at least one of the key portfolios they had held. Even more important, however, would have been the psychological effect of the elections: the results would have indicated that acquiring an absolute majority was not a realistic alternative for the Communists and that the pluralist system was there to stay. It is often claimed that precisely the prospect of an eventual loss of votes made the Communists carry out the February coup d'état, and that the party would have never allowed the elections to take place. No one can tell, of course, what the CPCS might have undertaken between February and May 1948 to prevent an electoral defeat if the crisis had not occurred. The fact is, however, that the showdown was initiated by the non-Communist majority and only aptly exploited by the Communists. The majority had legitimate reasons to consider itself a potential victim of Communist subversion, but following the classical principle of von Clausewitz, as a victim it had the option to decide whether and when the conflict would materialize.

Another imminent event that could have modified the outcome of the confrontation if it could have been postponed was the split between Moscow and Belgrade. The Tito-Stalin controversy actually came into the open only three months after the Prague coup d'état. Therefore we may ask whether the Soviet power center would have been eager to precipitate another crisis within the area of its influence while it was still absorbed with the problem of Titoism. Naturally, it can also be argued that the uncertainty produced by the dispute with the Yugoslav Communists might actually have speeded up the Communist take-over in Czechoslovakia. In this case, the assessment of the risks, costs, and benefits by the Soviets rather than by Czechoslovak Communists would have played the crucial role. Whatever the probabilities, salvaging the pluralist polity under these circumstances and ensuring its survival until the advent of a more favorable internal and international situation would have required exceptional skill and insight, as well as a good deal of luck. The coalition majority opposing the Communist party possessed none of these.

Thus events took their course, which turned out to be fatal for Czechoslovak democracy. On February 17, 1948, when it became certain that the minister of the interior would only submit a report about the action already accomplished instead of suspending the nomination of the police commissioners as the majority vote in the cabinet session of February 13 had recommended, the government members representing the National Socialist, Populist, and Slovak Democratic parties obtained authorization from their respective party Presidiums to abstain from further cabinet meetings until the issue was settled to their satisfaction. If this did not happen, they were empowered to hand in their resignations. As I mentioned earlier, no explicit agreement was reached with the governmental faction of the Social Democratic party. This omission was a grave mistake. An error of comparable gravity was the failure of the non-Communist parties to coordinate their efforts with the stand and the possible action of the two "nonpartisan" ministers, Masaryk and Svoboda, and to consult the president of the republic about the appropriate steps to be taken after their resignations were submitted. The latter was a real blunder, one that is nearly incomprehensible if we consider that the head of state played a key role in the strategy of the three parties. He was expected to refuse to accept their resignations and thus either oblige the Communist minister of the interior to comply with the request of the cabinet or enforce the dissolution of the National Assembly and bring about premature general elections. The cooperation of the president became even more crucial when, because of the lack of preliminary agreements, the number of resignations turned out to be short of an absolute majority. Such a partial cabinet crisis could be resolved by a simple reconstruction of the government if the top State executive formally acknowledged the walkout of the minority group of ministers. Yet the three parties did nothing but simply inform the president of their intention to abstain from cabinet deliberations and to resign if their conditions were not met. Actually, they tendered their resignations on the afternoon of February 20.

The Communists met the crisis with an original mixture of force and manipulated public support, a method that subsequently became typical of the Communist regime's reaction in emergency situations and that has been used against opponents outside as well as inside the party. The use of coercive means was to be legitimated by popular will. The technicalities of the crisis left some room for constitutional window dressing. As only twelve cabinet members out of twenty-six had resigned, the truncated government was theoretically still capable of making decisions. Under normal conditions, of course, a withdrawal of this scope would have caused any ministry to fall. The Communist party, however, was not prepared to respect the established norms of the political process.

Even when the minister of foreign affairs and the Social Democratic ministers, Laušman and Blažej Vilím, later joined the resigning group, the Communists refused to submit to the parliamentary rules. They made it clear that they viewed the resignations not as the exercise of a right vested in all members of the coalition, but as a "desertion from responsibility," "deliberate creation of chaos," and "sabotage" of the then-unfolding Two-Year Economic Plan. Mass meetings of "working people" (that is, members of the Communist party) and of "voluntary" (Communist-sponsored and Communist-controlled) mass organizations, were called to Prague and to other major urban centers where these hand-picked "representatives of the Czechoslovak population of all walks of life" applauded the determination of the CPCS leaders to respond energetically to the alleged "provocations of the right" and to "restore the spirit of loyalty and cooperation within the National Front."[22]

The real meaning of the latter objective, spelled out with emphasis by Gottwald in his speech to "the people" at the Old City Square in Prague on February 21, soon emerged. It became evident, soon after the outbreak of the governmental crisis, that the Communist party judged the moment propitious for the implementation of its plans for the reform of the National Front, which it had already unsuccessfully attempted in 1947. Now representatives of mass organizations under Communist control were to be seated in the coalition next to the delegates of the political parties. The fact that the formula of a broadly based government involving the participation of various mass movements had been strongly recommended to all Communist parties at the Kominform session in Belgrade in December 1947 indicated that the Regenerated National Front was by no means a specifically Czechoslovak concept.

While this solution of the crisis—according to Klement Gottwald, a democratic and constitutional one—was receiving endorsement by various meetings and gatherings called by the Communist party, the CPCS took full advantage of its control of the key portfolios, especially those of information and interior. The mass media were immediately put at the disposal of the Communists and broadcasting personnel not obedient to them were prevented from resuming service. Press organs not directly dependent on the Communist party were made subject to harassment by Communist unions who instructed the printers not to set in type, reproduce, or distribute "anything oriented against the people," (with "the people" being understood to mean the CPCS). Later in that critical week, the police under Communist command began to round up, arrest, and intern many middle-echelon leaders of the non-Communist parties in the capital city as well as in the provinces. During the five days after the resignation of the twelve ministers, the non-Communist majority proved to be unable to counter the Communist-manipulated "manifestations of popular will" by any induced or spontaneous manifestation of its own electoral following, even though that following comprised millions of voters. Under these circumstances the linchpin of the resistance action was the refusal of the president of the republic to accept the resignations. Beneš's situation became increasingly difficult in the conditions of police terror and scantily veiled Soviet pressure. The Soviet government sent the former ambassador Valerian A. Zorin to Prague under the pretext of inspecting the process of the delivery of Soviet grain to Czechoslovakia. Zorin was received by the president of the republic, to whom he expressed the concern of the Soviet ally over "possible developments imperiling the interests and the security of the USSR" in connection with the ongoing cabinet crisis.[23] It will never be known with certainty whether, in a real emergency, the Soviet Union would have intervened militarily to install the Communist party in power. Stalin appears to have been less prone to adventures of this kind than his successors. Nevertheless, Soviet interest in the crisis was a factor that had to be considered by Beneš, who was the only remaining non-Communist decision maker of any importance. Even his room for maneuvering dwindled rapidly. When the Communist-dominated trade union association called a general strike to force the president to accept the resignations, Beneš made a last-ditch attempt to restore constitutional order by appealing to the army, of which he was legally the supreme commander. However, his effort was foiled by the minister of defense, General Svoboda, who was secretly in collusion with the Communists. The fate of Czechoslovakia as a parliamentary democracy was sealed.

On February 25, 1948, the president of the republic yielded to the pressure, validated the resignations of the non-Communist ministers, and approved a new cabinet list compiled on the principles of the so-called enlargement and revitalization of the National Front. In this new government, the Communists assured for themselves the majority of seats, and their control was further reinforced by the inclusion of the representatives of mass organizations, who were all staunch supporters of the new course. The minority of portfolios reserved for members of the non-Communist parties were assigned to hand-picked sympathizers with the CPCS, who were formally members of these parties, but in reality had long fostered pro-Communist activities among the rank and file. It came to light that the Social Democrats were not the only ones to have Communist undercover agents planted in their organizational network. Two weeks after the constitution of the government of the "Regenerated National Front," the minister of foreign affairs, Masaryk, who was the only non-Communist cabinet member to have retained his post, was found dead under the window of his apartment. Officially the case was explained as suicide, but rumors that Masaryk had been killed by special agents of the Soviet political police ("Beria's gorillas") never ceased.[24]

The leaders and functionaries of the non-Communist parties who had supported the policy of resistance against the CPCS were forcibly removed by "direct popular action," that is, by commandos set up by the Communists in the various governmental offices and industrial enterprises. Real or alleged sympathizers with the independent course in important posts of civil service, economy, armed forces, and education were purged en masse during the weeks following the cabinet crisis. This purge was carried out by self-elected bodies called Action Committees of the Regenerated National Front that were composed exclusively of Communists, Communist fellow travelers, or members of Communist-front organizations. Some of the victims of the purge were transferred to lesser positions, some were dismissed, some were arrested and tried at a later date, and some escaped to the West. The exiled leaders were soon joined by a large number of citizens who had not been directly affected by the purges or immediately threatened, but found life under the new regime intolerable. A very high proportion of these refugees were students, actually the only population segment that during the crisis days had showed enough courage to demonstrate publicly against the Communist take-over. It is estimated that approximately a hundred thousand persons left the country after the February coup d'état. The number would probably have been considerably larger had not the Communist power holders later transformed the hitherto purely political notion of the Iron Curtain into a palpable reality by building barbed-wire fences, minefields, and ditches all along the borders of the Federal Republic of Germany and Austria. This barrier was completed in the early 1950s, whereupon the stream of refugees dried up to a small trickle until a new mass wave began at the end of the 1960s.

The Communist victory was now complete. Historians, both Communist and non-Communist, have always had some difficulty in identifying the kind of process that took place in Czechoslovakia during the last week of February 1948. It certainly was not a revolution.[25] It was not comparable to any of the classical cases of mass revolutionary movements, and even comparison with the Bolshevik bid for power by a minute elite group of insurgents in the midst of general chaos was clearly not called for. The CPCS operated on a much more solid organizational basis than Lenin had ever established in Russia, so that its action had more popular support than the October Revolution in 1917. On the other hand, there can be no doubt about the unconstitutional nature of the event. In rather pedestrian language it could be defined as taking advantage of the resources accruing to a strong minority in a pluralist system for the purpose of acquiring power otherwise reserved only to solid majorities. Indeed, there seems to be no simple brief term in the vocabulary of political sociology for this type of system change. In the absence of a more appropriate expression, analysts and commentators have often chosen the label coup d'état, which may come closest to this specific case. The events that led to the establishment in Czechoslovakia of absolute rule by the Communist party will therefore be referred to as the February coup.

Chapter Six

From Victorious February to the Death of Stalin

The Peak Years of Stalinism

For students of the postwar history of the CPCS, it is interesting to find how strong the desire of the party elites for mass support was even after the coup had been accomplished and the goal of undisputed control of the state had been achieved. This concern might have been fostered by the results of the election of 1946: the party's success in that contest was too great to be underestimated by anyone, including its opponents, but too limited to qualify as attainment of the Communist goal of acquiring power in a democratic way. Once that power was firmly in their hands, the Communists may have believed that its transfer could be legitimated ex post facto by an enlargement of the party's popular following. The preoccupation with an endorsement by the nation, however, could also have been an outgrowth of the democratic education of the CPCS's leaders, who had served their years of political apprenticeship in a pluralist system and had assimilated, in contrast to members of fraternal parties with purely underground experience, some basic democratic principles. Whichever cause was more important, the wish to make the take-over appear to have been supported by the bulk of Czechoslovak working people seems the only plausible explanation for various methods the party used, after the February coup, especially to recruit new members.

Record Party Membership

As we have seen, the character of the Communist party organization profoundly changed in the first year after the war. By then the number of party cardholders already exceeded one million. No longer was the party a small militant avant-garde of the revolutionary industrial proletariat. In fact, if we consider its entire history, the CPCS met the orthodox requirements concerning the size of membership for a period of less than ten years, not taking into account the six years of illegality during the war when no party organization existed. Before the bolshevization of 1920 it had been too large to satisfy the Komintern's criteria, and after the liberation it became a mass party in the literal meaning of the word. If the unusually large membership base disturbed the party's mentors in the Kremlin during its formative years, its size must have alarmed Stalin and the Kominform leaders even more when the number of effectives reached a seven-digit figure. Yet membership had by no means peaked at the first postwar congress in 1946. Much faster and more spectacular growth was still to come, at a time when substantial streamlining would have been both possible and desirable. Several factors were responsible for the party's growth in the aftermath of the February coup. The success of the Communists induced many opportunists to jump on the bandwagon of the strongest party. Moreover, since membership in a political party had been an asset in civil service careers since the nineteenth century, a large number of state employees wishing to advance or simply to keep their posts also joined the applicants. In some offices and industrial enterprises, whole local organizations of the People's Socialist, Populist, and Slovak Democratic parties pronounced their dissolution and entered collectively the local unit of the CPCS. Often such apparently spontaneous decisions were prompted by suggestions: many hesitant followers of the non-Communist parties suddenly found on their desks application forms for CPCS membership, ready to sign. Others were told, in no uncertain terms, that their failure to join might jeopardize their promotion prospects or even the security of their jobs. It is hard to tell whether this more or less unofficial recruiting took place on the initiative of the top party leaders or only with their tacit approval, but there can be no doubt that they in no way opposed these methods. In addition, a separate membership recruitment campaign went on in the country, aimed chiefly at nonaffiliated individuals from all segments of the population.

The drive to enlarge the already impressive membership base undertaken in the first weeks of absolute Communist rule was paralleled by an attempt to dispose of the party's erstwhile most dangerous rival, the Social Democratic party. The Communists' refusal to settle for anything less than a fusion—that is, the absorption of the Social Democracy by the CPCS—surprised no one. Despite its shrunken size, the Social Democracy continued to be an intolerable rival of the CPCS. Its neutralization through absorption into a unified party dominated by the Communist component resembled the techniques adopted in the neighboring people's democracies, which claimed to be more advanced on their road to socialism than Czechoslovakia. Unlike its Polish, Hungarian, or East German counterparts, however, the new party retained the name Communist Party of Czechoslovakia. No explicit justification was offered for this choice. The grass-roots activists were told that the name was only natural since the CPCS had been the larger of the two constituting parts. Nevertheless, it is difficult to dismiss completely a more plausible explanation: that the CPCS feared the loss of its own identity and the possible resurrection of the "ghost of Social Democratism" in an organization bearing a name other than Communist. On the other hand, the manner in which the merger was carried out strongly indicates that the desire to increase the membership was the primary motivation. The fusion between the two parties was not effected simply by a decision of the supreme organs. Instead, the Communists insisted on individual affiliation: every single member of the Social Democratic party had to apply for admission to the new CPCS. Officially, this requirement was presented as a proof of the voluntary nature of the fusion. The decision of the Social Democratic party's Central Committee was supposedly not binding for the rank and file: each member was allegedly free to follow or to reject it for himself. In reality, it required a good deal of courage, in the climate after February 1948, to abstain from individual affiliation and thus to become politically visible in the crowd. Indeed, only a small minority of the organized following of the Social Democracy refused to join the CPCS.

The incorporation of the Social Democratic party and the official and semi-official recruitment campaigns of the post-February period led to the most significant increase of the CPCS membership in the party's entire history. Its ranks had swelled to two million by the end of the spring of 1948 and continued to grow. About a third of the whole economically active population was then organized in the CPCS. It would not be hard to see this unprecedented drive for support as an attempt to find a substitute for the representative political system the February coup had just destroyed. The new mass membership base, larger in proportion to the population than the following of any other Communist party in the world, might have replaced, in the eyes of the Communists, the body politic. Although all post-February elections could be open to doubt as genuine expressions of the popular will, since there was always a single ballot, the Communist leaders could argue that the size of the party membership was a convincing proof of the endorsement of the regime's policies. Since every fifth adult citizen of the Czechoslovak Republic carried a CPCS membership card and in most cases the cardholders were heads of households in which the same political alignment could be assumed for the rest of the family, the endorsement appeared quite impressive. Following this line of reasoning, a claim could be made that the party had the support of the quasi-majority of the nation.

On the other hand, the record increase in party effectives, whatever its purpose, engendered serious problems. The criticism by the spokesmen of the international Communist movement of the Czechoslovak comrades' failure to follow the Leninist principles of the party organization—limiting membership to a small group of picked elites—was but one of several sources of difficulty. It was obvious that the control of such a large and heterogeneous body was an almost impossible task. Among the new recruits, the proportion of those who had been forced to join and those who had had purely opportunistic motives for joining was very high. The disadvantages of indiscriminate growth were also reflected in the distribution of the new members by class origin, occupation, and age, which was completely unsatisfactory by all orthodox Communist standards: the middle class and white-collar workers were in the vast majority and youth was only very weakly represented. The membership had already shown signs of "embourgeoisement" since the end of the war, and the continuation and reinforcement of this trend could not but cause alarm. It was not until the end of 1948, however, that the first measures were taken to redress the situation. Until then, the number of organized followers continued to grow.

Single-Ballot Elections and the May 9 Constitution

By the end of 1948, the process of transformation of the Czechoslovak polity from a rather uncommon type of restricted pluralism during the short period after the war into a more standard type of people's democracy characteristic of most countries within the Soviet orbit was completed. The general elections had been scheduled for May 30. Now that all control was in Communist hands, the voting process lost much of its original significance, but it was necessary for the new power holders to ensure that their monopoly position would in no way be challenged by an expression of popular dissent. Thus, in a formula similar to those adopted by other people's democracies, a consolidated ballot was introduced in which the distribution of parliamentary seats was predetermined: the first two-thirds of the eligible places were reserved for the Communist nominees and their fellow travelers in mass organizations; and only the remaining posts could be divided among non-Communist candidates. The latter, as we have seen, were mostly obedient instruments of the CPCS: they could not be viewed as a genuine oppositional minority. For the voter who did not want to support this ballot of the Regenerated National Front only one alternative course was open: he could deposit a white (or blank) ballot. Since the white ballot was equal to an invalid vote, the Regenerated National Front could be certain of winning 100 percent of all available seats.

The consolidated ballot of the Regenerated National Front polled 89.3 percent of all votes, if we accept the official statistics.[1] This is not easy to do since the vote count was supervised by more or less self-appointed commissions, comparable to the post-February Action Committees, who interpreted the election rules in their own way. In addition, the opponents of the unified list were not allowed to conduct any organized campaign except by word of mouth: no media were allowed to carry their messages. On the other-hand, the regime used all means at its disposal, including propaganda, to obtain the approval of the electorate for the new political order. The pressure was increased by the abolition of the confidential vote; only those who expressed a wish to vote secretly could do so. Local organizations of the CPCS and party units in industrial enterprises organized trips of whole working teams to voting premises where everybody was expected to demonstrate his or her loyalty to socialism by voting publicly. This made mere abstention, let alone depositing a white ballot, an act of courage. Under these circumstances, the 10.7 percent outspoken protest vote and the relatively low turnout—in the terms of voting tradition in Central Europe—testified to a significant level of discontent.

Shortly before the elections of May 1948, the Constitutional National Assembly, from which all deputies allegedly hostile to the cause of socialism had been forcibly removed, passed a series of laws nationalizing all enterprises employing more than fifty persons and unconditionally expropriating certain "vitally important sectors of production and services." After this second wave of nationalizations, the structure of the Czechoslovak economy resembled that of the present East Germany, with only small industrial plants in private hands. In agriculture, a new phase of land reform was introduced: 50 hectares (123 acres) of arable land became the legal limit for private holdings. The Constitutional Assembly also attended to the principal task for which it had been elected; on May 9, 1948, it approved a new constitution previously prepared by the Communist party. This constitution, referred to in official documents as "the Constitution of the 9th of May" (May 9, the anniversary of the arrival of Soviet troops in Prague in 1945, became a national holiday under Communist rule), bore a clear imprint of the period of restricted pluralism during which it had been drafted. It spelled out legal principles and individual rights similar to those in classical Western liberal constitutions. There were no explicit references to the CPCS as the sole or privileged political group. The constitution was to remain formally in force for twelve years, but most of its civil and human-rights guarantees were already dead letters in 1948. Since some of its important clauses were imbued with the spirit of the Regenerated National Front and thus contradicted the rules of the democratic political process, the president of the republic refused to sign it and abdicated on June 7, 1948. He was succeeded in his office by the CPCS chairman, Klement Gottwald. With Gottwald in the Prague Castle, the last key executive post passed into Communist hands. The last vestiges of the Masaryk democracy had been wiped out.

Problems of the Party in Control

The first years of undisputed Communist rule in Czechoslovakia were marked by many serious problems. Among the major issues the new masters faced were internal party conflicts and the problem of the party's relation to the international Communist movement. With the USSR and other fraternal parties the CPCS shared the impact of the schism between Moscow and Belgrade that came into the open in June 1948. The second session of the Kominform, held on June 28, 1948, under normal conditions would have devoted a significant amount of attention to the recent events in Czechoslovakia. Czechoslovak Communists could have hoped for endorsement and praise by the information bureau as architects of a successful take-over. Instead, the session was dominated by the dispute between Stalin and Tito. For the CPCS the matter was rather embarrassing. The violent language of the Kominform resolution on Yugoslavia and the unqualified support given by the Czechoslovak delegation and the domestic media to the Kominform (that is, to the Soviet position), perplexed wide circles of the Communist party. Relations between Czechoslovakia and Yugoslavia had traditionally been very good; the fact that a Communist regime had been established in Yugoslavia made the pro-Yugoslav sentiment among the Czechoslovak party members even stronger. Slav solidarity mixed with political ideology when, for example, Czechoslovak Communists demonstrated in 1947 for the incorporation of the Italian Adriatic port of Trieste into Yugoslavia. It also impressed the Soviet-obedient Czech and Slovak comrades to see with what zeal the Yugoslav party emulated the Soviet model in all sectors of life; this example reinforced their own loyalty to the Soviet Union. The denunciation of Yugoslavia as a "renegade" nation and of Yugoslav Communists as "lackeys of imperialism" came as a surprise. Confusion among the rank and file, however, was not the only adverse product of the Kominform's anti-Yugoslav campaign. Soon the repercussions of the Moscow-Belgrade conflict were to affect the top leadership. On the whole, the nature of the external problems of the CPCS in the first phase after the seizure of power was determined by the fact that these years happened to be the last of Stalin's rule, when the totalitarian character of Stalinism became the most pronounced and Moscow's grip over the individual Communist parties was tightest.

As for internal party problems, the liabilities of the abnormal growth of membership after the February coup became quite evident. The plenary session of the Central Committee of November 17 and 18, 1948, imposed a stop on further admissions and introduced a new category of candidature to membership. Applicants were no longer directly accepted or rejected, but those against whom there were no major objections were first given the status of candidates. After a fixed period of time, usually not longer than two years, the final decision was made. Another internal problem, continued from the past, was the delicate relationship between the national party body and the CPS. We have seen that the unsatisfactory results of the 1946 elections in Slovakia had induced the national leadership to tighten the reins on the Slovak party. After the 1948 take-over this trend continued. The new political system was much more centralist than the earlier restricted pluralism, and the party operating this system had little use for genuine autonomy within its own organization. Gottwald and his group were determined to put an end to the state of affairs that had prevailed before February, wherein the national government in Prague could in many respects exercise its power only over the two western provinces because Slovak politicians, including the Communists, had jealously guarded their local and regional prerogatives. These were the conditions Secretary-General Rudolf Slánský had complained about at the Kominform meeting in Szklarska Poremba in 1947. Now that all the power had passed into the hands of the Communists, reimposing the authority of the national leadership over the CPS appeared to many to be the most promising avenue of attack upon what they perceived as centrifugal or separatist tendencies.

At a plenary session of the Central Committee of the CPS, held on September 27, 1948, the CPS defined itself as "a territorial organization of the CPCS in Slovakia."[2] This wording indicated a departure from the original principle anchored in the Košice Program of 1945, according to which Slovak local government organs and Slovak political parties embodied the will of the Slovak people, on an equal footing with the Czechs, to realize their political aspirations and identity. The Slovak party now described its mission in merely geographical terms. As for the national party leaders, it seemed that the CPCS, which had been a champion of Slovak nationalism and self-determination during the First Republic, had ended by becoming heir to what it used to label "petty-bourgeois Czech imperialism."[3] There can be little doubt that the actual reason for the increasingly hostile attitude of the CPCS leadership toward the national aspirations of the Slovaks was due to specific factors operating within the Communist movement, but it is difficult to overlook the circumstance that the high-handed manner in which the party dealt with the Slovak problem was approved and supported by a large portion of the Czech rank-and-file membership, whose feelings towards the Slovaks were just as prejudiced as those of the so-called bourgeois segments. This development was a bad omen not only for the Communist party but also for the whole intricate complex of relations between the two nation-building ethnic groups.

In addition to these controversial issues, Czechoslovak Communists had to wrestle with other difficulties that were more in the forefront of public attention. There was a continuing resistance to Communist rule among all population segments, although this dissent lacked coordination and unified guidance. To suppress this opposition, a very large police apparatus was set up and reinforced by an extensive network of spies and informers. During the first two years after the February coup, the Communist authorities claimed several times to have uncovered underground organizations and plots aiming at the overthrow of the regime. About three hundred death sentences were meted out by special state courts to individuals allegedly convicted of high treason between 1949 and 1956. Many of these trials were held in camera, but some were given considerable publicity. Among the latter, the show trial involving former leaders of the National Socialist party in 1950 drew the attention of the world because of the harsh verdict against its principal defendant, Mrs. Milada Horáková, a member of the National Assembly. Appeals for clemency made by prominent personalities of the West, many with radical leftist leanings, could not save the defendant's life. The execution at the same time of Záviš Kalandra, a renowned Communist intellectual with a long record of CPCS membership, indicated the gradual shift of the focus of political justice to a new circle of potential class and state enemies. As of early 1951, Communist officials, activists, and eventually top party leaders constituted the main body of those accused of, and prosecuted for, political crimes. This marked a major change in the internal climate of both the party and the nation: although this change took some time to assume its most appalling forms, some unmistakable signs were visible as early as 1950. Similar tendencies could be observed in the neighboring people's democracies. They were all stimulated by Stalin's campaign against Titoists and Titoism, but in the case of Czechoslovakia the search for spies and traitors had an additional motivation. The accused were also made to serve as scapegoats for the regime's failures, especially in economic policies.

Hand in hand with the repression of real and imaginary opponents went a campaign against religious organizations, especially the Roman Catholic Church. The government established a special National Office for the Affairs of Churches in 1949: this step was then justified by the necessity to regulate the material support of churches that had lost all their property through land reform and nationalizations. Actually, the new agency was a political instrument designed to limit all religious activities, especially religious education, to a minimum. It was to preside over the withering away of religion. As the withering away appeared too slow, repressive measures were applied. Religious orders were dissolved and their members reportedly integrated into productive work. Leading clergymen were harassed or imprisoned and show trials were organized against popular priests, with the help of informers and provocateurs. The persecution was particularly intense in Slovakia, but the archbishop of Prague and primate of Czechoslovakia, Cardinal Josef Beran, was also interned for several years in his episcopal palace at the Prague Castle. The effects of this pressure were on the whole questionable. Among the religiously lax, agnostic population of the Czech provinces, it led to a revival of religiosity; in Slovakia, where religious affiliation had always had political connotations, opposition to the regime only stiffened. The most disturbing fact for the party governance in the first years after the February coup was the continuing religious practice of many of its own members, regardless of their class background. Hundreds of thousands of organized Communists kept on attending masses, having their children baptized, and getting married in church.

As the sole power holder in the country, the Communist party also faced serious economic problems. The new wave of nationalizations that had followed the seizure of power in 1948 produced new disruptions and further aggravated the economic situation, which had not yet completely returned to normal. Especially harmful to the performance of the economy under the "regeneration of the constructive spirit of the National Front" was the replacement, in many cases, of non-Communist experts and managers with politically reliable but professionally incompetent members of the CPCS. Inefficient bureaucracy and constant political interference made the exporting branches of the Czechoslovak industry miss the unique opportunity to capture highly receptive postwar world markets before foreign competitors, especially West German, could recover from damages that Czechoslovakia had been spared. In 1948 it would have been possible to take advantage of these circumstances, since Czechoslovak import and export policies were still governed by more or less pragmatic criteria. In the following years, this businesslike approach was to become a casualty of political discrimination enforced by the Soviet power center, which was often at variance with the real economic interests of the nation. Owing to disastrous personnel policies after the coup, however, the promising trends of foreign trade were reversed during the first years of Communist rule. Since export had always been a vital requirement of Czechoslovak prosperity, shortcomings in this field could not fail to affect the whole economy adversely. The average consumer soon began to feel the consequences.

The Ninth Party Congress

These were the circumstances, internal as well as external, in which the CPCS convened for its Ninth Ordinary Congress, the first since its seizure of power. The congress, which met in Prague May 25–29, 1949 entered the party annals as the occasion at which the membership reached a peak that has not been attained since; 2,068 full delegates and 278 delegates with consultative status represented no less than 2,311,066 party cardholders. On the strength of absolute figures, the CPCS already belonged among the strongest parties of the international Communist movement (the CPSU, in 1946, had about six million members); in proportion to the total national population, it was the largest Communist party in the whole world and of all time. Close to 17 percent of the entire population carried CPCS membership cards: thus every sixth inhabitant of Czechoslovakia, regardless of age, was formally a Communist.[4] Although this unprecedented growth in membership was one of the highlights of the general report submitted to the congress, and although several speakers referred to it in their presentations, some voicing concern about the motivation and ideological maturity of those who had recently been admitted, little was done at that time to deal with the new situation. The Ninth Congress only endorsed the decision of the Central Committee Plenum of November 1948, confirmed the ban on new admissions, and incorporated into the party statutes a clause instituting the category of membership candidates. Another year elapsed before the Central Committee elected at the congress moved further and ordered what then was termed "party cards renewal," which purported to be a "purification of the party from opportunistic elements." This move may have been prompted by other considerations besides the desire to maintain ideological purity within the party ranks. It seemed consistent with the call for Bolshevik vigilance and the search for internal enemies that then characterized the party climate. The exchange of party cards lasted about eight months. When it was concluded, the secretary-general adjoint, Josef Frank, could report, at the plenary session of the Central Committee held February 21–24, 1951, that the number of cardholders had been reduced to 1,677,433. Almost a third of the entire membership had been eliminated, which made the operation the most extensive purge in the history of the CPCS.[5] Nevertheless, party membership remained at about 12 percent of the whole Czechoslovak population. A return to the Leninist model of an elite vanguard party appeared as remote a goal as before.

Considering the historical situation in which the Ninth Congress took place, it is natural to expect that it would focus, above all, on outlining the main tasks of the party in the first phase after the seizure of absolute power. These tasks were indeed summed up in the report by the Chairman Klement Gottwald as "ten points relative to the general policy line." Prominent among these tasks were "assuming the cultural and spiritual leadership of the entire nation," overcoming the "survivals of bourgeois ideology," and "restructuring the society according to socialist principles." Among the economic goals, a successful implementation of the First Five-Year Plan, adopted by the National Assembly in October 1948, was assigned top priority. It seemed that no further changes were planned in the ownership system now that about 80 percent of the production means in industry belonged to the public sector. No explicit references were made, either, to eventual agricultural collectivization projects. Gottwald's pledge, given in 1948, that "there will be no kolkhozes in our country!" still seemed to hold. An observer judging by the congress speeches and materials might have gained the impression that the party was chiefly concerned with bringing production and the standard of living back to their prewar levels, so that the party could consolidate its freshly acquired power monopoly.

This might actually have been the intention of the party leadership, which exhibited considerable continuity. The two men at the helm, Chairman Klement Gottwald and Secretary-General Rudolf Slánský, were confirmed in the offices they had held since the end of the war, and only normal turnover occurred in the top party organ, the Central Committee. The only innovations reflected the post-February growth of membership and the merger with the Social Democracy. Yet to conclude that a period of relative stability lay ahead would have been to ignore other significant factors that were then at work. Among these, the international situation at the end of the 1940s and developments within the Communist bloc, especially the relations between the USSR and the smaller Communist nations in Central and Eastern Europe, had a strong influence on the course of events in Czechoslovakia. Few delegates at the Ninth Congress suspected, for example, that of the two top leaders, neither would live more than four years, and that before the next congress had convened many of the members of the Central Committee and of the party Presidium would have passed away, often under highly dramatic circumstances. The fate reserved to the leadership mandated in 1949 strangely resembles that suffered by the Politbureau and the Central Committee of the CPSU elected at its Sixteenth Congress in 1935. Only a handful of the nearly 150 members of these party bodies survived until the next following congress met or died a natural death before then. The Central Committee of the Czechoslovak party was somewhat smaller than that of the CPSU, but the proportional losses during the five years after the Ninth Congress were comparable to those inflicted upon the Soviet party during the years of the Great Terror.

The chilling events that came to dominate party life after the Ninth Congress are usually referred to as the political trials of the 1950s. In a specific jargon used by official Communist commentators and historians, they are presented as the "mistakes of the personality cult era." This is both a strong understatement and too restrictive a label. It would seem to apply only to accomplished acts of repression by the police and the judicial apparatus. In reality, the impact of the punitive actions carried out during that period was much wider. We would not be able to assess their significance for the Communist party if we paid attention only to the most conspicuous cases, those of the top-level officials who sat on the defendant's bench. In addition to some two thousand prominent members and leaders of the CPCS who were tried and condemned during the 1950s, several thousand activists and functionaries at lower echelons were prosecuted and often punished only by party disciplinary sanctions: by the loss of party office or by expulsion, which almost invariably entailed dismissal from employment or demotion to a lower position. As in most cases involving the ruling Communist parties of Central and Eastern Europe, the Czechoslovak purge of the 1950s had more complex causes than the Soviet purges. Its origin was not exclusively domestic; the power center in Moscow had considerable influence in bringing it about. Had it not been for the ever-sharpening conflict between Stalin and Tito, the intensification of the Cold War, and the resulting need, as perceived by the Soviets, to close the ranks of the international Communist movement, the purge in Czechoslovakia probably would not have assumed the dimensions and the forms it did. Nevertheless, the purge also had clearly internal roots, both in the general make-up of the Czechoslovak party and in the economic situation at the end of the 1940s. Internal party struggles of some kind probably would have occurred at that point even without stimulation from the Soviet Union.

Political Terror in Communist Czechoslovakia

Purges in totalitarian systems are often explained as substitute mechanisms for circulation of elites. In the absence of an open market of ideas and of institutional provisions for the expression of dissent, the differences of opinion on theoretical and policy issues that inevitably divide the leaders in all types of government can be aired, according to this interpretation, only through violent confrontation. This confrontation is seen as a zero-sum game: it results either in the removal from positions of power of the decision-making group and in a change of policies or in the liquidation of the group opposing the current line. It would seem, however, that the disagreement need not always be about principles or concrete policies. We have often seen various cliques contending for control without submitting alternative propositions on policy. Historical experience teaches us, too, that purges usually do not take place in the very first stage of development of totalitarian systems. The German Nazi regime experienced its first purge about a year and a half after the 1933 take-over, but this case was an exception among the internal crises in modern totalitarian dictatorships. In the Soviet Union, serious conflicts in the core of the Bolshevik party started only some ten years after the October Revolution. This rather long lead time might have been needed because in the first period, during Lenin's lifetime and the years of the first collective leadership, organizational channels existed for the articulation of divergent views; this was the essence of the Leninist version of democratic centralism. When the experiment with democratic centralism later failed, the avenues of institutionalized policy change were closed. Then purges became the only means of leadership succession. Under Stalin as first party secretary, every subsequent purge reinforced his personal power. The purges finally ceased to reflect clashes on concrete policy issues and served as a means to remove Stalin's potential rivals. At this point, they were often deliberately induced and followed a preconceived plan.

The Czechoslovak purges of the 1950s coincided with the last period of Stalin's rule, when the terror took irrational and pathological forms. The extent of Soviet influence in these matters can be seen in the rapidity with which the repression spread into the ranks of the party. There had not been much lead time, even though there seemed to be every reason to expect it. On the face of it, the Czechoslovak Communist movement might have been a suitable medium for intraparty democracy, considering its experience in a pluralist polity and its heterogeneous character. It did not produce any individuals with Stalin's skill for intrigue and desire for uncontrolled power. True, all genuine elements of pluralism and nonconformity that had ever existed within the Czechoslovak party had been stifled in the successful bolshevization process of the late 1920s, but neither Gottwald nor Slánský could measure up to Stalin. The internal factors that favored the purges were of a different nature. Undoubtedly the suspension of the democratic decision-making process after the February coup created a climate in which political repression thrived. Also, the so-called dynamic (or politically biased) interpretation of the law, the class approach of the judiciary, engendered legal uncertainty, which is one of the basic components of terror. Of course, these factors operated in the USSR and the people's democracies of that time as well. Specifically Czechoslovak was the unqualified acceptance of the Soviet model: as a consequence, the Stalinist terror assumed the most appalling aspects precisely in that Central European country where it had been the least anticipated. Several students of totalitarianism have observed that only individuals or groups conscious of what is humane and dignified are capable of deliberate and systematically inhumane behavior. The assault on the rule of law and human dignity in Czechoslovakia after 1948 was as vehement as it was partly because respect for the law had prevailed in this part of Europe for a very long time. The Communist spokesmen knew what they were talking about when they voiced their contempt for legal formalism, such as the presumption of innocence or the requirement that the prosecution prove the defendant guilty beyond reasonable doubt.

It would be hard to overestimate the significance of the purges for the subsequent development of the party and the system. The terror of the 1950s shaped a new image of the regime in the eyes of both the Communists and their opponents, that of a monster devouring its own children. Within the Communist party itself, the purge produced deep-seated, lasting cleavages, and perpetuated or considerably reinforced already existing conflicts and contradictions, such as those between the national leadership and the Slovak regional organization. The events of the Prague Spring of 1968 and the Soviet military intervention often found confronting each other groups and individuals who had also taken opposite sides during the great purge. More than anything else, the reluctance of the post-1953 leadership to redress, or even to duly acknowledge and re-examine, the cases connected with the political trials speeded up the evolution that culminated in the brief episode of Socialism with a Human Face. Indeed, the impact of the purge has been felt in the party until the present day, as Soviet interference has slowed down and eventually stopped the process of rectifying the wrongs perpetrated in the 1950s. It should not be overlooked, of course, that the unwillingness shown by Antonín Novotný until 1968 and by the power holders imposed by the Soviet Union in 1969 to thoroughly revise this dark chapter of the past has not been unusual among the ruling Communist parties. The present Soviet malaise, too, can be explained partly by the failure of the various leaderships to finish properly the job of destalinization. However, the Czechoslovak Communists have shown unusual resistance to this task, although many of them were not directly implicated in the acts of terrorist justice. They were also the last to revise the verdicts of the political trials.

The First Phase of the Great Terror

Although the most spectacular phase of the great purge started only in 1951, the indications that the repression would not stop short of the party structure began multiplying right after the February coup. If we disregard the measures taken against the members and officials who had disapproved of the seizure of power or of the cleansing methods applied by the Action Committees of the Regenerated National Front, such as the journalists Michal Mareš and Jiří Lederer, the first case of the removal of an uncomfortable prominent party member was that of Arnošt Kolman, professor of philosophy at the Charles University in Prague. Kolman, a party member of long standing, had spent many years in the Soviet Union, where he had acquired Soviet nationality. In academic circles he passed for a representative of what could be labeled Marxist dogmatism of the Stalinist school. Nevertheless, he committed the imprudence of criticizing in the party press the "undemocratic, bureaucratic behavior and habits" of several top CPCS leaders, especially Secretary-General Rudolf Slánský. Taking advantage of Kolman's legal status as a foreign national, the Ministry of the Interior, after the case was discussed with Soviet authorities, ordered Kolman to be deported to the Soviet Union, where he was arrested and remained in prison for more than four years.[6]

As the CPCS leadership was dealing with the Kolman case in the summer of 1948, a careful observer could have noticed the first signs of the forthcoming purge. At the meeting of the Presidium on June 28, which coincided with the Second Regular Session of the Kominform, Presidium members Václav Kopecký and Július Ďuriš, speaking on the issue of the split between the USSR and Yugoslavia, uttered rather threatening words aimed at unnamed "petty bourgeois nationalists" who allegedly indulged their deviance in some important party quarters, especially in Slovakia. In the following years, this charge was to become one of the most serious indictments in the great purge. However, 1949 was the year that saw the first major wave of demotions, expulsions, and legal prosecutions of prominent party members. After the arrest of Záviš Kalandra, who, as we have already mentioned, was later tried and condemned to death for Trotskyist conspiracy, the Central Committee ordered a thorough investigation of what it termed "possible infiltration of the party by the class enemy." The first target of this investigation was the regional party organization in Karlovy Vary, in western Bohemia. As a result, almost the entire Central Committee of this organization was expelled from the party. The security official of the Regional National Committee in Karlovy Vary, A. Tannenbaum, was arrested in June 1949 for "condoning antiparty activities." Purges in other regional party sections followed, with similar results. Later in the year, the wave of persecution reached the highest levels: Vilém Nový, the editor-in-chief of *Rudé právo* and a Central Committee member, was expelled from the CPCS and arrested. In December 1949, Evžen Loebl, the minister of foreign trade and a member of the Central Committee of the CPS, was also deprived of party membership and arrested.[7]

While the reported offenses of all these officials were connected with their activities in Czechoslovakia, another broadly launched police action was directed against party elites who supposedly had participated in hostile, subversive, or intelligence work in other Socialist countries. This latter operation was started on the demand of the Hungarian secret service and the Soviet advisers delegated to this service. It was to establish proofs of presumed international ramifications of the alleged high treason of László Rajk, a leader of the Hungarian Communist party and the minister of foreign affairs. The Soviet security agents wished to demonstrate that Rajk, a "potential Hungarian Tito," had cooperated with the intelligence services of the Western countries, especially the

United States, with the help of Czechoslovak accomplices. To this end, evidence was fabricated against two American citizens, the brothers Herman and Noel Field, who were charged with having been Rajk's intelligence contacts. The information Rajk released had allegedly been transmitted to the brothers Field via "imperialist spies" operating from Czechoslovak territory. Upon the request of the head of Soviet Security, General Belkin, Czechoslovak security services discovered the head of this imagined spy ring in the director of the Slovak branch of the Czechoslovak State Travel Bureau ("Čedok"), Dr. Gejza Pavlík. Pavlík was arrested at the same time as Noel Field and a couple of Communist party members believed to have belonged to his intelligence network. The theory that the Field brothers were involved in intelligence activities played an important role in Rajk's trial, which was held in Budapest in 1949; however, the arrest of Pavlík and his interrogation in Hungary by Hungarian and Soviet security officers were to provide the evidence to justify another major purge, this time in Czechoslovakia. Pavlík was supposed to have supplied information about a "bourgeois nationalist conspiracy" among Slovak Communists.[8] With the identification of this new category of suspects, the terror entered a new phase.

In May 1950, a special Ministry of National Security—an agency independent of the Ministry of the Interior and the military counter-intelligence—was established. It seemed that the party was serious about what its spokesmen called the fight against subversion, sabotage, and infiltration by enemy agents. This new repressive apparatus was further expanded by the inclusion of specialists from the Soviet KGB. In the interest of historical truth, it should be pointed out that the experts from Moscow had joined the Czechoslovak security organs as the result of an explicit demand by the CPCS leadership. It is also interesting to note that when Stalin later wanted to recall the head of the advisory group to the USSR because he had found his work and his behavior irresponsible, Gottwald urged Stalin not to do so, since the help of the Soviet specialists was invaluable.[9] The presence of Soviet agents lent the purge an additional momentum: it was obvious that any accusations by these agents about various conspiratorial centers would be accepted at their face value by party and government officials, and that repressive means would be applied to any extent and in any direction they suggested. Moreover, Czechoslovak police and security services would vie with each other for Soviet support that would allow them to overrule unwelcome instructions from state and party organs and maintain uncontrolled freedom of action. For example, when Klement Gottwald, after a consultation with Stalin in July 1951, ordered an investigation into possible connections between the arrested party functionaries and Secretary-General Rudolf Slánský to be stopped, a group of security service officials who had conducted these interrogations complained directly to the Soviet embassy in Prague and simply ignored the order given to them by the party chairman and president of the republic.[10] The great purge became an operation that unfolded independently of all political and administrative influence. Party sanctions such as dismissals, demotions, and expulsions were imposed without any statutory requirement for preliminary examination. Arrests, interrogations, and trials were carried out in complete disregard of all valid laws and rules of legal procedure.

The campaign against the bourgeois nationalists was publicly launched with the speech of the Czechoslovak representative in the Kominform, Ladislav Kopřiva, at the enlarged plenary session of the Central Committee held February 24–26, 1950. Kopřiva announced that the party would "mercilessly destroy all those who serve bourgeois nationalism and anti-Soviet imperialism in international conspiracy with the capitalists and their agent Tito."[11] Although Kopřiva did not cite any such evildoers by name, the concrete targets of his attack became known soon after the plenum. On March 14, 1950, Vladimír Clementis, the minister of foreign affairs, was replaced in his function by Viliam Široký, secretary-general of the Slovak Communist party. Three weeks later, in a report to the Central Committee of the CPS, Široký singled out Clementis and two other prominent Slovak Communists, Gustav Husák and Laco Novomeský, as "promoters of nationalistic trends." The Presidium of the Slovak Communist party then relieved all three of their party functions and summoned them to "redress their errors through conscientious work and make themselves thoroughly acquainted with Marxist theory." Compared with what had previously happened to many a party leader, these disciplinary measures did not then seem very harsh. Soon afterwards, however, Husák and Novomeský were also stripped of their membership on the Board of Commissioners for Slovakia. At the Ninth Congress of the CPS, held in Bratislava May 24–27, 1950, Viliam Široký as general reporter again sharply attacked the bourgeois nationalists, whom he accused of having tried to isolate Slovak workers from their Czech comrades, "under the pretext of the defense of Slovak economic interests," and of having resisted the action of the national government in Slovakia. Široký thus defined as a serious deviation what was simply a legitimate concern of the Slovaks for maintaining the prerogatives of autonomous Slovak organs that had been instituted by the Košice agreement in 1945. In rejecting this concern as subversive, Široký actually declared war by the centralists on the autonomist majority. Following Široký's report, Husák and Novomeský submitted self-critical declarations that the congress found unsatisfactory and rejected. Vlado Clementis made a written statement to the Central Committee about a month later in which he confessed to all charges, but his self-criticism, however abject, was not accepted either. Clementis's unpardonable crime probably was his condemnation in 1939 of the Stalin-Hitler treaty. Because of this gesture, apparently, the Soviet stage managers had chosen him as a protagonist of the master show trial. When the Ninth Congress of the CPS elected the new Central Committee, the names of Clementis, Husák, Novomeský, and Karol Šmidke, a member of the Board of Commissioners and during the war an emissary of the Moscow CPCS center in Slovakia, were no longer on the list.[12] The extensive discussion of the issue of bourgeois nationalism at the congress indicated that the circle of those accused of this deviance would eventually become still wider.

Although the action against the Slovak bourgeois nationalists had started relatively early, a specific trial involving this group was held only at the very end of the purge period. In the meantime, the security apparatus worked with great zeal on the preparation of other show trials. Considerable attention had been paid since the spring of 1950 to the regional party organization in the Moravian capital city, Brno. Under the pretext of investigating complaints from members about partly inadequate, partly undemocratic, and "overbearing" methods of work of the regional secretary, Oto Šling, a special Control Commission set up by the CPCS Central Committee gathered and fabricated evidence, later turned over to the security organs, to support the charge that Šling had committed "grave errors in cadres work" and "deliberately introduced dangerous elements into important party functions." The goal was to show to the public a concrete case in which "spies and saboteurs" had been planted in the party organization. In October 1950, Šling was arrested.[13] The manner in which his case was presented at the moment of his apprehension suggested that the engineers of the purge might have chosen him to be the Czechoslovak counterpart of the Polish party leader Wladyslaw Gomulka, or even of László Rajk, with all the consequences that such indictment would entail. However, subsequent comments on the Šling affair in the party media pointed to a different plan. Frequent references to Šling's accomplices and to Šlingism as a more general phenomenon indicated that an eventual trial involving Šling would include more defendants of his rank or even higher. And indeed, by the end of the year another twenty party officials had been arrested in the Brno region in connection with the Šling case, among them high army officers, two generals, and one political commissar. They were all accused of having helped Šling in his "subversive activities," but they were probably arrested because of their past affiliation with some international organization, or simply because they had lived in the West at some point or had Western contacts. A more general theory developed in Moscow underlay this selection: it was assumed that Communists with such backgrounds were necessarily "infected" by so-called cosmopolitanism and thus less loyal to the Communist movement and to the Soviet Union. The adoption of this theory immediately made suspect whole categories of party members: former soldiers and officers of the Interbrigade in Spain, Communists who had spent the war in the West ("the Londoners"), workers in the prewar Communist-sponsored peace movements, and individuals of Jewish origin. The latter were sometimes explicitly connected with Zionism, a charge that often had no other basis than official contacts with the state of Israel at a time when such contacts had been legitimate and desirable from the viewpoint of the Communist governments and their Soviet supervisors. Often, however, Jewish background in itself was taken as a sufficient ground for suspicion and persecution.

Terror Reaches the Party Top

The public gradually came to understand that the phrase "destruction of the enemy within the party ranks" was intended to be taken literally. At the plenary session of the Central Committee of the CPCS held February 21–24, 1951, thirteen members and two candidates to membership of this supreme party organ were expelled. The expulsions included the four Slovak bourgeois nationalists reprimanded by the Ninth Congress of the Slovak party in 1950: Clementis, Husák, Novomeský, and Šmidke, as well as several Czech members of long standing, such as the former Interbrigadist Josef Pavel and Mrs. Marie Švermová, a Presidium member, the assistant secretary-general, and the widow of the Communist war hero Jan Šverma, who had died during the Slovak uprising in 1944. Not long before the disciplinary action of the Central Committee, Mrs. Švermová had participated in the commission investigating the various regional party organizations. It was characteristic of this stage of the purge that at the time the decision to expel these individuals was announced, it was admitted that they had already been arrested and would be subject to legal prosecution. This was a highly irregular procedure, since under normal conditions the explicit approval of the representative party organs would have been necessary before they could be apprehended. Many of the defendants also enjoyed constitutional immunity, so that an extradition by the National Assembly would have been legally required in their cases. Nevertheless, the mass arrest of the Central Committee members in February 1951 was only a prelude to a vast repressive action against the top leadership. Soon after the February 1951 Central Committee plenum, the Ministry of Defense announced the discovery of an "anti-state and anti-Soviet plot" in the army, which resulted in the arrests of several commanding officers, among them General Bedřich Reicin, the deputy defense minister and the chief of military intelligence.

The intention of those who organized these arrests and investigations obviously was to demonstrate that the enemy lay within the very core of the system. To substantiate the alleged linkages to "foreign espionage centers," they regularly made sensational announcements about the interception of Western and Titoist agents. Show trials were staged with foreign citizens and press correspondents. Even diplomatic immunity was often violated. The Yugoslav consul general in Bratislava was condemned to life imprisonment as a "Titoist spy ringleader" in the fall of 1950. In July 1951, the Associated Press correspondent in Prague, William N. Oatis, received a ten-year prison sentence because of alleged intelligence activity, although this activity actually had consisted of the usual everyday information gathering characteristic of a journalist. Hundreds of Czechoslovak citizens were arrested and tried for espionage because at some point, often before 1948, they had given the most trivial information to some Western diplomat or visitor. However, neither these individuals nor any Western nationals occasionally sentenced for subversive acts were meant to be the main protagonists in the great drama that was now being rehearsed. The pattern of the security service's investigation indicated that the intention was to parallel the show staged in Hungary and to organize nothing less than a trial of the Czechoslovak Rajk. If this surmise was correct, the circle from which a candidate for such a role would eventually be chosen was not large, and it was not impossible to guess to whom the role would be assigned.

An interesting question for the historian is who made the actual choice—an individual power holder or a clique—that is, who determined that precisely this and not another top party official would be immolated on the altar of the allegedly imperiled unity and safety of the socialist camp. The available data do not seem to be conclusive. Practically any hypothesis built on some of these facts can be refuted because of contrary evidence. This is true not only of the theory imputing the responsibility to domestic leaders, especially to Klement Gottwald, but also of the apparently most plausible guess, that the idea originated with Stalin himself. Although there is no doubt that the purges of the 1950s in the people's democracies were precipitated by Stalin's obsessive fear of the possible spread of "Titoism," other circumstances contradict the inference that he set up in advance the casts of the various show trials. Especially in the Czechoslovak case, we know that the first suggestions that CPCS Secretary-General Rudolf Slánský become the scapegoat had been rejected by both Stalin and Gottwald. Gottwald even went as far as to order all further investigation based on this suspicion to be discontinued. For his part, Stalin recalled the Soviet security specialist, Boyarsky, who had first voiced the charge. Only later did the dictator in the Kremlin change his position.[14]

All these facts make Slánský's selection as the main defendant in the master trial of the great purge something of a mystery unless we consider the possibility that no advance decision was made as to who would eventually be indicted as the presumed "head of the conspiratorial center." The various victims designed for political and physical liquidation may simply have emerged from the purge process: for example, the confessions extorted from the arrested officials of lower and intermediate levels may have led ultimately to Slánský. Even if we disregard the mental state of the interrogated prisoners, who were held for months in isolation and subjected to all kinds of privation and torture and thus capable of conceiving any fantasy, it seems only logical that, when asked who had given them orders to do this or that, these officials would most often cite the name of the highest executive functionary. Under these circumstances, no advance indictment was necessary. Once the name of Slánský was spelled out, the expected answer appeared to have been found and events took their inevitable course.*

The possibility that Slánský's guilt was not designated in advance but discovered in the process of the investigations seems to be substantiated by the honors that were bestowed upon him shortly before his arrest. The conspicuous celebration of his fiftieth birthday and his decoration with the prestigious Order of Labor on July 31, 1951, would have to be viewed as a monstrous and senseless comedy if he had already been picked as the principal defendant in the master trial. It seems more likely that the decision makers in Prague and Moscow had not yet made up their minds. Shortly afterward, however, events unfolded in rapid succession. On September 6, 1951, Slánský was relieved of the office of secretary-general, but the punitive character of this measure was masked by the Central Committee's decision to abolish this office altogether, so that Slánský formally had no successor. The executive responsibilities of the Secretariat were transferred to the party chairman. A similar change in the statutes was later carried out by the CPS. Slánský himself was appointed deputy prime minister, with the task of coordinating various state organs for economic management. Then suddenly, on November 24, 1951, he was deprived of his new function. Three days later, at a public meeting of the employees of the security services in Prague, the minister for the state security, Lubomír Kopřiva, referred to Slánský as an "enemy of the people." On the following day November 28, 1951, Slánský's arrest was publicly announced.

The Peak of Terror: The 1952 National Party Conference

The reaction of the wide party circles to the news of Slánský's fall shows yet again how historical events can be misunderstood by those who immediately experience them. A large number of resolutions emanated

---

*This procedure also seems to fit the established tradition of Soviet purges. It is said that Yagoda, one of the State Political Department (GPU, the official name of the Soviet secret service) chiefs under Stalin, started an investigation against himself as a potential foreign spy during the last years of his rule, and for that matter, of his life. This could have been a symptom of progressive mental disorder, but it could also be seen as a consequence of the literal application of the jigsaw-puzzle method of investigating political crimes. Since at that time no suspicion was thought fantastic enough to be dismissed offhand, the conclusions could not fail to be as fantastic as the premises on which they were based.

from grass-roots units endorsing the arrest and calling for "severe punishment of the culprit and his accomplices."[15] Most of these resolutions were probably "made to order," on the initiative of the top party leadership. Nevertheless, reliable witnesses and observers reported a genuine feeling of relief among the rank and file. Ironically, a considerable part of the public, Communist as well as non-Communist, believed, that Slánský's demise would stop the terror at its very source, that his arrest would put an end to all further arrests. Slánský's central position in the party apparatus and his harsh pronouncements on the cases of comrades who had previously been purged made this interpretation appear quite plausible. Also, the replacement in January 1952, a few weeks after Slánský's apprehension, of Ladislav Kopřiva, Slánský's confidence man, in the position of minister of national security by the secretary of the Central Committee of the CPS, Karol Bacílek, seemed to many an indication of a long-hoped-for change in the party's course. Hopes were now pinned on Party Chairman Klement Gottwald, who was expected to restore order and legality. Little did these optimists suspect that the nightmare had just started.

It took about a year of preparation before the show trial of the so-called Anti-State Conspiratorial Center of Rudolf Slánský and Associates was ready to be enacted. The parallel between Stalinist show trials and drama is fully justified. There were stage managers, script writers, actors and understudies, rehearsals and décors, even costumes and makeup. Now that the Czechoslovak Rajk had been found, the most important task before the organizers of the purge was to prepare the most appropriate "mix"—that is, to put the main defendant together with the co-defendants that would make the case most credible. The alleged accomplices of the secretary-general had to be comparable in rank, not simply recipients of orders who could have put all the blame on their boss; this would hardly have been a conspiracy. One such high-ranking prisoner was Vlado Clementis, the former minister of foreign affairs. His transfer to the Slánský trial must have considerably modified the original plans for the case of the bourgeois nationalists. It may also help to explain the curious fact that although the Slovak nationalists had been among the first to be rounded up, their custom-made trial was almost the last to take place, much later than Slánský's. However, the sponsors of the Anti-State Conspiratorial Center trial were not satisfied with bringing into the dock only the prominent duo of Slánský and Clementis. A perfect case of conspiracy required that partners in crime be found in all important sectors of political and economic life, and eventually they were. One of them was Bedřich Geminder, who was head of the International Department of the party secretariat and a former member of the Komintern's Executive Committee in Moscow. Geminder was of German-Jewish origin, and despite many years spent in the party apparatus, he had not completely mastered the Czech language. The nature of his functions in the secretariat, together with his origin and background, made him an almost ideal candidate for the role of an "evil-plotting renegade and traitor." André Simone-Katz, a former member and functionary of the CPG and since 1946 a foreign correspondent of *Rudé právo* and professor of international politics in Prague, had a similar profile. He was arrested several months after Geminder. Also of Jewish origin were another eight defendants whom the prosecution associated with the Anti-State Conspiratorial Center: Central Committee secretary Josef Frank; Ludvík Frejka, originally a member of the German Communist party and head of the Economic Department of the Office of the President of the Republic; the "pilot defendant" of the trial, Oto Šling; Deputy Minister of Foreign Trade Rudolf Margolius; Chief of Military Intelligence Bedřich Reicin, who had already been arrested in 1950; deputy minister of finance and a former ambassador to East Germany, Otto Fischl; the former deputy minister of foreign trade, Evžen Loebl, who had been under arrest since the end of 1949; and Arthur Gérard-London, a former Interbrigadist and deputy foreign minister, who had been apprehended in January 1951. Vlado Clementis and Evžen Loebl represented the bourgeois nationalist element of the Anti-State Center. The alleged group of conspirators was completed by Vavro Hajdů, who had held the post of deputy foreign minister after the ouster of Vlado Clementis in 1950, and Karel Šváb, Marie Švermová's brother and former deputy minister of interior and head of security, who had been arrested in the summer of 1951. It was an impressive gallery. With such positions in the hands of saboteurs and spies, it was easy to explain and excuse the sore state of the Czechoslovak economy and society. However, it is questionable whether this carefully prepared discovery of the anti-state plot actually led even a small fraction of the population to absolve the regime of its responsibility for the lamentable performance of the country in practically all vital sectors that had become manifest by the early 1950s.

The trial of the Anti-State Conspiratorial Center opened in Prague on November 20, 1952. It was given ample coverage by all mass media.

Again, as after Slánský's arrest, resolutions from party organizations at all levels poured in condemning the defendants before they had even been heard and calling for the most rigorous punishment. The accused repeated monotonously the answers they had been taught during the long solitary confinement. The artificial character of the entire procedure could not be dissimulated. For example, when at one point the prosecutor skipped a question contained in the original "script," the unprepared defendant replied to the question that had been left out. The sentences were prepared in advance by the party Presidium, which held consultations by telephone and did not even bother to meet, let alone to request the opinion of the Central Committee. With the exception of Loebl, London, and Hajdů, all of the accused were sentenced to death.[16] A particularly revolting part of the show consisted of the declarations of many close collaborators, friends, and relatives of the defendants, who explicitly endorsed the verdicts. The son of Ludvík Frejka came to the courtroom to request the death penalty for his father. On December 3, 1952, the eleven accused who had been condemned to death were hanged.

Those who had expected that the terror would now subside were in for a bitter disappointment. Another dozen major political trials were in preparation, of which seven were directly linked to the Anti-State Conspiratorial Center. Moreover, only a few initiated individuals knew that the Soviet security organs, shortly before the December 1952 trial, had attempted to connect the Slánský affair with a similar conspiracy that was presumably developing in Poland. Instead of ending, the wave of persecutions was thus reaching ever wider circles. The signs seemed to point to further intensification of the terror in all Communist countries of Central and Eastern Europe. In Czechoslovakia, the deliberations of the party's governing bodies immediately after the Slánský trial stressed business as usual; this policy should have applied to the security forces and the repressive apparatus as well. Nevertheless, the arrests of so many prominent people had left serious gaps in the leadership ranks that had to be filled. An overall assessment of the situation by a representative party body appeared indispensable. As early as October 25, 1952, the plenum of the Central Committee discussed this issue thoroughly, and it returned to the subject at its next meeting on November 7. However, both the Central Committee and the Presidium were apprehensive about the idea of convoking a party congress, although it was already overdue. They felt that the topic of the political trials could not be kept out of the transactions of the congress, and that the subject, once tabled, could hardly be discussed in an orthodox manner without causing embarrassment to the leadership. Therefore a substitute formula of a National Party Conference was chosen. Participation in national conferences, as past experience had shown, could be much more effectively controlled by the party's central organs.

The National Party Conference was scheduled for December 16–18, 1952. Of the two main points on the agenda, the drafting of new statutes and by-elections of members and candidates to the Central Committee, the second appeared to be the most important. Viliam Široký, a member of the Politbureau, served as the principal reporter, while Gottwald submitted an outline of further political and organizational tasks for the CPCS. Despite this routine program and the rather dry coverage of the national conference in the media, it was not difficult to imagine which topic occupied the minds of the delegates the most. The subsequent sessions of the Central Committee on January 8 and of the Presidium on February 4, 1953, implemented the decisions of the December meeting.[17] In the reorganized Secretariat of the Central Committee, besides Bruno Koehler, an apparatchik of long standing, were five new men, among them the former youth movement leader Vratislav Krutina, who was later to assume the portfolio of agriculture in the government. The reconstruction of the cabinet took place at the end of January 1953; it had been due for the same reasons as the by-elections into the various central party organs. On this occasion, Antonín Novotný, who in the following years was to climb up to the highest positions in the party and in the state, became deputy prime minister.

There were unmistakable signs that none of the changes carried out in the leading political offices at the turn of 1953 could be interpreted as symptoms of the end of the purges. On February 17, 1953, the Political Secretariat of the party awarded special recognition to the workers of the security services who had conducted the investigations into the Anti-State Conspiratorial Center. Sixty officers and agents were decorated with the highest state orders and received promotions and considerable cash payments. Václav Aleš, the deputy attorney general whose office had received the most credit for the discovery of the Slánský plot, was appointed attorney general. All of this indicated that no respite was in sight; the purges, arrests, and trials would continue as scheduled. Other, at that time wholly unanticipated but imminent, changes in the Soviet power center and in the leadership of the Czechoslovak Communist party could have given more hope. Klement Gottwald was probably not aware that the appointment of Aleš as attorney general would be his last constitutional act as president of the republic, indeed the last political decision he would ever make. On March 5, 1953, Stalin died in Moscow—a portentous occurrence for the whole world Communist movement, especially for the parties in control in Central and Eastern Europe. Gottwald traveled at the head of the Czechoslovak party and government delegation to the funeral of the Kremlin dictator. On this trip he reportedly contracted a mysterious illness that took his life on March 14. Thus within one week, the two top Communist officeholders who had the power to determine the course of Czechoslovak politics passed away. There was now a possibility that their successors might revise the current policy line because they saw the international situation in a different light and preferred to build relations with the people's democracies on a different basis from the one Stalin had chosen. This might have led them to the rejection of terror and to a return to rule based on law. As for the Soviet Union, definite changes seemed to take place in the general political climate. The emphasis Stalin's heirs placed on the need for a genuine collective leadership, as opposed to a one-man system, indicated that serious attempts might be made to introduce a different method of governing. Explicit references in the press (for instance in a *Pravda* editorial of April 6, 1953) to the concern of the new leaders of the CPCS about socialist legality reinforced this impression. The change in Moscow had its repercussions in the Communist countries in Czechoslovakia's neighborhood. No further show trials took place in Hungary, and the plan of the Polish security forces to exploit the Slánský affair for a monster trial in Poland was scrapped. However, those who expected that this new climate would soon spread to Czechoslovakia were to be disappointed. Curiously enough, the Czechoslovak Communists, who had always ranked among the most loyal partners of the Soviet Union since the bolshevization of the party in 1929, and had been the most eager among all the national parties to emulate the Soviet example, gradually fell out of step with the prevailing Soviet line. This state of affairs was ironic in that it was the previous "Stalinism à l'outrance" that prevented the CPCS from following the course set by Stalin's successors. This reluctance to change its ruling methods more substantially and to revise at least the most flagrant excesses of the past was to impede party and state politics in Czechoslovakia for many years to come.

Chapter Seven

From Stalin's Death to the Hungarian Uprising

Marking Time

The new top leaders of the Czechoslovak Communist party could not claim that they were unaware of the legal irregularities of the political trials that had been held up to Stalin's and Gottwald's deaths. Antonín Zápotocký, who was elected president of the republic on March 21, 1953, and Antonín Novotný, whose function in the party had not yet been formalized but who was in charge of the Secretariat of the Central Committee, became now the two supreme officials in the party and in the government. They had already participated in all important decision making before Slánský's trial. Moreover, in their new capacities they kept receiving petitions from condemned and arrested individuals or from their families protesting their innocence and complaining about the inhuman treatment they had to suffer from the police and the investigating organs. As early as in the spring of 1953, many imprisoned and detained individuals began to retract confessions previously made under duress. Reports on the behavior of the prospective defendants of the scheduled trials were regularly submitted to the Office of the President of the Republic and to the Secretariat of the Central Committee of the Communist party. The leadership thus was duly informed about the unwillingness of the accused to cooperate in their own destruction. All these facts notwithstanding, the terror continued.

Gruesome "Business as Usual"

On May 25 and 26, 1953, the first trial involving the presumed accomplices of Rudolf Slánský's Anti-State Conspiratorial Center was held in Prague. It included several prominent officials of the Foreign Ministry, among them Eduard Goldstücker, a former Czechoslovak ambassador to Israel, whom the prosecutor presented as a "Jewish bourgeois nationalist." Goldstücker was sentenced to life imprisonment. Also connected with Israel and Zionism was the trial of Mordechai Oren, an Israeli citizen and alleged Israeli spy who had testified against Slánský in the December 1952 proceedings. Oren was tried in camera and condemned to fifteen years in prison. The confession extorted from him was later used as evidence against several Czech and Slovak Communist leaders charged with "subversive activity for the benefit of Zionism." At the end of the year, there was another follow-up to the Slánský affair. A group of workers in the Ministry of the Interior and State Security sat on the benches of the accused as enemy agents. Although some of the defendants had participated in the early stages of the investigation of the Slánský case and had possibly helped to fabricate false evidence, they were obviously found wanting in zeal. This trial and another five dealing with the officials of the security services had been staged to prove that the enemy had succeeded in planting agents also in the organs responsible for the protection of the state and the socialist system. It should also explain why Slánský and his accomplices had remained undiscovered for such a long time. In the prosecution of the security workers, the main responsibility was imputed to the first postwar head of the security service, Colonel Osvald Závodský, who was a long-standing member of the CPCS and had been a Spanish Interbrigadist and a French resistance-movement fighter. Závodský had been arrested as early as 1951, presumably because he did not show enough enthusiasm for the cleansing action among party members or sufficient obedience to Soviet security experts. He was condemned to death on December 23, 1953, and executed in 1954, despite numerous appeals and the fact that the accumulated evidence based chiefly on extorted confessions of other defendants had already collapsed before the sentence was carried out. Other officials of the police and state security were condemned either to life or to long prison terms. At the turn of 1954, Josef Pavel, a former deputy minister of the interior and commander of the uniformed police, received a twenty-five-year sentence as another accomplice of the Anti-State Conspiratorial Center. Pavel, like Závodský, had been a prominent Spanish Interbrigadist and had participated during the Second World War in partisan units in France and Northern Africa. Such a background lent itself easily to the construction of the case against him as against a "cosmopolitan renegade and traitor."[1]

Neither the arrest of the Soviet secret service chief, Lavrenti P. Beria, in July 1953, nor the material Nikita Khrushchev put at the disposal of the Czechoslovak party leadership about the illegal methods and activities of the KGB under Beria, nor even Beria's conviction and execution in December 1953 seemed to impress the party officials in Czechoslovakia responsible for the purge. Nor did the news of the release and the rehabilitation in Poland of Herman Field halt these politically warped acts of justice, although with Field's acquittal, one of the principal pillars of the anti-state center theory had crumbled. The show trials continued well into 1954. The absurdity of the charges under which many of the defendants had been brought into court was particularly striking in the case of Marie Švermová and her supposed accomplices. Her trial was held January 26−28, 1954. No attention was paid to the fact that the evidence fabricated against Slánský in 1952 had already lost much of its credibility, and that since the guilt of the principal accused was subject to doubt, the crimes of his alleged accomplices must be even more questionable. The prosecutor indicted Švermová and her five codefendants of being "accessories of the conspiratorial activities of Slánský and Šling," precisely as planned and regardless of the new facts that had become known in the meantime. He requested the death sentence for Švermová, but the court condemned her for life, while the rest of the accused were given prison terms of up to twenty-five years.[2] From February 23 to 25, 1954, seven Communist party members with long membership records stood trial as supposed participants in a so-called Trotskyist Grand Council. The charge of Trotskyist conspiracy was mainly based on their past association, often as remote as the First Republic, with various CPCS factions that had later been labeled Trotskyist. Terms totaling 193 years in prison were imposed at this trial. One of the condemned died in prison shortly afterward, when he was denied medical help.[3] In the spring of 1954, a trial of high army officers and functionaries of military intelligence took place in which eight generals and other top-ranking military personnel were condemned to a total of 128 years of confinement.[4] This show trial obviously was meant to demonstrate that the Slánský plot had not stopped short of the headquarters of the armed forces. It was followed by a trial of Zionist nationalists that resulted in the condemnation to long jail sentences of a leading Slovak Communist of Jewish origin, Koloman Moškovič, and a prewar party activist and economic expert, Vojtěch Jančík.[5]

The trial of the Zionist nationalists was a prelude to the second most important trial of the 1950s, that of the Slovak bourgeois nationalists.

Actually, according to the original plans, this case was intended to be the master trial of the whole great purge. Only during the gradual unfolding of the whole operation did a better, or more impressive, choice of presumed culprits offer itself. The switch from the Slovak party elite to the circle around the secretary-general of the national party organization had caused a considerable delay in the actual court action against the former. The significance of the trial of the bourgeois nationalists was somewhat reduced by the inclusion of the highest situated member of this group, Vlado Clementis, in the Slánský trial. In the spring of 1954 the Czechoslovak party bosses believed that the time was propitious to deal with the Slovak autonomists. In a four-day court proceeding in Bratislava, April 21–24, 1954, Gustav Husák, the former chairman of the Slovak National Council, Laco Novomeský, former commissioner for education, Daniel Okáli, former special envoy to Budapest in charge of the population exchange with Hungary, Ladislav Holdoš, Slovak National Council member and former Interbrigadist, and former ambassador Imre Horváth, were all found guilty of "having conspired with the intention of separating Slovakia from the Czech working people and putting a wedge between Czechoslovakia and the Soviet Union." The second charge must have sounded strange to anyone who remembered that Husák, for example, had been criticized by the non-Communist politicians and reprimanded by the CPCS national leadership in 1945 for having advocated the establishment of a Soviet Slovakia, presumably as the eleventh union republic of the USSR. In contrast to the trial of the Anti-State Conspiratorial Center, most defendants in this case denied the accusations. Their refusal, however, did not change the preordained course of the court proceedings. Husák was condemned for life and his codefendants to long jail terms: Horváth to twenty-two, Okáli to eighteen, Holdoš to thirteen, and Novomeský to ten years in prison.[6]

However important this trial was in the history of political justice in Czechoslovakia, the verdict in the trial of the bourgeois nationalists did not mark the end of the great purge of the 1950s. Show trials continued until the end of 1954. In June 1954, a group of economic experts, members of the State Planning Board, was tried together with the former deputy minister of agriculture and the representative of the CPCS in the Czech National Council during the Prague uprising of 1945, Josef Smrkovský. The seven defendants were accused of "systematic economic sabotage in cooperation with the anti-state conspiratorial center of Rudolf Slánský" and condemned either to life imprisonment or to many years in jail.[7] Smrkovský was later to play a key role during the short period of liberalization in 1968. Another group of economic saboteurs was brought into the dock in August 1954; this time terms totaling 204 years of imprisonment were imposed upon the accused. The most prominent economic expert, the chairman of the State Planning Board, Eduard Outrata, was judged separately in November. In view of his ill health, he was condemned to only twenty years, but died fairly soon after the trial.[8] In November 1954, there was a show trial of the so-called illegal leadership of the Social Democratic party, which, as we know, had merged with the CPCS in 1948. In reality, the only crime most of the defendants had committed was to refuse individual merger— to fail to apply for membership in the CPCS. Simultaneously with these more spectacular model trials, many proceedings against less prominent party officials were held before the courts of lower instance; these received little media coverage, but resulted in long prison sentences for most defendants. In all, nearly ten thousand persons were condemned during the great purge. In this respect and in the severity of the sentences, especially the number of death penalties, Czechoslovakia appeared to be the most accomplished disciple of the Soviet Union.

Yet this last statement requires an important qualification. If the Czechoslovak Communists, in unleashing the terror of the early 1950s, demonstrated a degree of Stalinist orthodoxy unparalleled by any other people's democracy in Central and Eastern Europe, their zealous emulation of the Soviet example eventually led them to be at variance with the course set by the Soviet power center under the collective leadership. To fully appreciate this contradiction, it is necessary to put the great purge, especially its final phase, into the right historical perspective. The course of political justice in Czechoslovakia was not affected in any significant way by the events in the USSR and in the Soviet bloc countries following Stalin's death in 1953. The show trials, which had been carefully prepared and rehearsed prior to these events, had the purpose of demonstrating the extent and depth of the alleged subversion of the state and the party by hostile elements, and to channel the growing discontent of the population in a direction less dangerous to the system. Although this had not been their only motive, it was a very important one: therefore the trials continued without pause or change. It was characteristic of the Czechoslovak situation that the second master trial of the purge, that of the Slovak bourgeois nationalists, took place as late as April 1954, at a time when a substantial, if not yet public, revision of the status of the political police in the Soviet Union and in its subordination to the authority of the Communist party was taking place. When the defendants of the Czechoslovak political trials of 1954 finally appeared in the courts, many a Soviet security advisor and expert who had supervised the fabrication of evidence against them had already been demoted, imprisoned, or executed. Similarly, the rehabilitation of the victims of political trials in the neighboring Communist countries often weakened or invalidated the charges against the individual suspects in Czechoslovakia. This made the unrelenting pursuit of the trials appear even more absurd.

Posthumous Cult of Personality

The degree to which the Czechoslovak regime after 1953 worked itself out of tune with the general trend in the international Communist system and above all in the Soviet Union is perhaps best illustrated by an event that was not directly connected with the purge, but that nevertheless had a strong symbolic meaning: the erection in Prague of a giant memorial to Stalin. Above all, it is the date of the unveiling of the monument that is indicative. The oversize statue, an artistic as well as a technological monstrosity, was dedicated no earlier than May 1, 1955, only nine months before Nikita Khrushchev denounced the crimes of Stalin in his famous "confidential" report to the Twentieth Congress of the CPSU. The unveiling ceremony, which included obsequious eulogies to the defunct Kremlin dictator by prominent members of the Central Committee and the Presidium of the CPCS, also preceded by only a few days the "historical" visit of Khrushchev with the Yugoslav Communist leader Tito in Belgrade. The very fact of this visit, regardless of its political or diplomatic results, repealed the accusations, heaped upon Tito during Stalin's lifetime, that Tito was "an agent and a lackey of Western capitalism and imperialism." Nevertheless, these charges had played a pivotal role in the justification of the terror of the late 1940s and early 1950s all through the Soviet bloc, especially in Czechoslovakia. On this occasion, Khrushchev made some explicit statements that had a shattering effect upon the whole edifice of Stalinist ideology. Yet the Czechoslovak Communists hardly took notice of this event.

This peculiar lack of responsiveness of the Czechoslovak Communists to the change of course in the Soviet Union may seem a mystery. On the face of it, the objective conditions for some kind of revision of the general line seemed no worse in Czechoslovakia than elsewhere in

Central and Eastern Europe. Actually, they might have been better, since the CPCS had replaced its leadership almost at the same time the CPSU had done so. In view of the fact that the main decision maker in matters concerning political trials, party chairman Gottwald, was gone, it should have been easier for his successors to admit errors of this kind than it was for the Communist rulers in Hungary and Poland, for example, where the leaders responsible for political justice remained in positions of control after Stalin's death. The difficulty in overcoming the resistance to rehabilitation of those who had profited from the purges should not have been any greater in Czechoslovakia than elsewhere in the Communist bloc. Yet the Czechoslovak regime carried on the terror, and Stalinist practices in general, well into the post-Stalinist era. The significance of the systematic violation of legal principles in the 1950s for the history of the CPCS in more recent years has to be fully recognized. It can be said without exaggeration that the "unassimilated Stalinist past" (a term that comes close to the German "unbewältigte Vergangenheit," which was coined, of course, in a different context) has been the key to the peculiar dynamics of communism in Czechoslovakia for the last quarter of a century. The failure to overcome the legacy of the cult of personality has to some extent been a source of instability of all Communist regimes that are, or have been, part of the Soviet satellite system. In Czechoslovakia, however, this instability proved to be exceptionally acute.

What, then, were the specifically Czechoslovak causes of the unusual delay in adjusting to the new trend in the Soviet bloc after 1953? We will have to look for them within the idiosyncratic framework of Czechoslovak political culture. The Czechoslovak Communist leaders' experience with pluralist democracy may account for their apprehensions about the possible consequences of a major policy revision. Among the parties in control, only the CPCS was aware of the power of public opinion. The leadership of the Czechoslovak party may have believed that the most important segment of public opinion was that of the organized membership, but it is unlikely that it would have completely disregarded a possible reaction of the Czechoslovak population as a whole to an admission of a major error, if not of a crime.* Such apprehensions

---

*The perception of this problem by the leaders of other Communist parties, who unlike the CPCS leaders had never had the experience of political work in the conditions of constitutional democracy (especially the Soviet party bosses), has been radically different. The Soviet decision makers have always appeared totally insensitive to eventual repercus-

would have been well founded; as subsequent events showed, destalinization, despite its inconsistencies, led to a serious legitimation crisis, first in the neighboring people's democracies and eventually in Czechoslovakia.

The 1953 Workers' Riots and Resistance to Collectivization

Several major events during the initial phase of the post-Stalinist period testified to a widespread perception of the Communist system in Czechoslovakia as an illegitimate one. The most alarming aspect of this lack of acknowledgement was that it came chiefly from social strata on whose support the party had always counted: the industrial workers and the rural proletariat. As for the former, the mistrust of the working class found its most dramatic expression in the riots that broke out in the main industrial centers of the country after the monetary reform of June 1953. This was the second such reform since the liberation. The initially wholesome effects of the first reform, carried out in November 1945, had been nullified by radical and often ill-advised interventions in the Czechoslovak economy after the February coup, especially by a rapid reorientation of the traditionally diversified Czechoslovak production to heavy industry, following the Soviet example. Serious inflation resulted, since the purchasing power of salaries and wages was not balanced by a sufficient volume of consumer goods. It was rendered even more acute by the rationing system continued after the war. The excessive currency in circulation made a new reform indispensable. Unlike the first reform, this one affected very deeply all categories of the population. The new monetary unit was revalorized in the ratio 5:1, but savings above a very modest limit were exchanged only for one-fiftieth of their nominal

sions upon the mass following of sudden switches in political line. The famous exchange between Vyshinski and the Italian Communist senator Reale in New York, in 1946, in which Vyshinski stated that for a true Marxist, no such thing as public opinion can ever exist, is characteristic of this attitude. Soviet politics, domestic as well as international, have always lived up to this principle, braving opinion not only in their own country, but also in all fraternal parties around the world. The most notorious examples of this utter indifference to the negative impact of certain steps in states pledging allegiance to the Communist cause were the conclusion of the nonaggression pact with Nazi Germany in 1939 and the military interventions in Hungary in 1956 and in Czechoslovakia in 1968. On these and many other occasions, leaders of various Communist parties in countries with pluralist systems became very keenly aware of the reality of public opinion. It manifested itself in waves of resignations, splits in the parties, and electoral defeats.

value. The rationing system was abolished and commodities priced, on the average, at ten times their previous cost. Workers, especially in the best-paid categories—miners, steelworkers, and construction workers— lost about half their real wages and their savings were virtually wiped out.

Although the spokesmen of the regime affirmed that the measure had been aimed chiefly at the liquidation of the assets of rich bourgeoisie, or at a more equitable distribution of national income, the main losers were the salaried labor force and the small savings-account holders, the economic categories most strongly represented in Czechoslovak society. This was why the monetary reform sparked off stormy protests, demonstrations, strikes, and clashes with the police. The unrest, which was finally quelled with the help of the army, preceded the more famous, because geographically more visible, uprising in East Berlin by some two weeks. Although the Czechoslovak regime did not make any major concessions to the protesters, the riots of June 1953 were a signal of alarm to the party leadership. They showed how little confidence the system enjoyed among the working class, the supposed avant-garde of the socialist society. The claim of the CPCS to leadership of the industrial proletariat was again placed in doubt when later in the same year the workers of several large machine factories in Prague stopped work to voice their refusal to obey a new law intended to tighten labor discipline. This legislation would have made repeated absence from the work place a criminal offense ("sabotage") punishable by stiff jail terms. It had been inspired by the Soviet example. However, when the strike broke out and the workers sent a delegation with very definite demands to the president of the republic, Antonin Zápotocký, the party retreated and the law was repealed.

Moreover, it became evident in 1953 that the support of the regime among the peasantry also left much to be desired. The Communist party's loss of popularity in the countryside was mainly due to the policy of collectivization launched after the Ninth Congress, despite the assurances then given by party chairman Gottwald to the farmers that "there would be no kolkhozes in Czechoslovakia." Most of the Czech and Slovak peasants had been hostile to the new, socialist form of land ownership. The "haves" among the rural population—and these occupied a strategic place in the collectivization process since only they had something to contribute to the collective enterprise—felt that joining the Uniform Agricultural Cooperatives (Jednotná zemědělská družstva or

UACs) was not a genuine choice, but an act under duress. Thus they were looking for the first opportunity to free themselves from the enforced commitment. The collectivization program made progress as long as terror prevailed, but with the first signs of uncertainty on the part of the rulers, the campaign came to a halt, and the already established cooperatives began to disintegrate. This trend persisted until 1955. The leadership, in which Antonín Zápotocký then played a dominant role, adopted a rather pragmatic approach to the exodus from the collective farms. In his speech at the opening ceremony of a new dam at Klíčov in west Bohemia, on August 1, 1953, Zápotocký pointed out that membership in the UACs was in principle voluntary and that provisions would be made for possible resignations from the cooperatives.[9] Legislative regulations to this end were indeed enacted by the end of the year. Tens of thousands of farmers took advantage of this opportunity during the following two years.

Zápotocký was later severely criticized for his relative open-mindedness, which was seen in some party circles as a sign of social-democratic opportunism. Such charges may be dismissed as fabricated for the internal use of the Communist movement, especially since they were formulated only several years after Zápotocký's death. Instead, it could be inferred that it was the alarmingly low productivity of the agricultural sector—even as late as 1955 it had reached only 94 percent of the prewar level—that had dictated these concessions. Yet a different explanation of Zápotocký's position is also conceivable. His realistic attitude might actually have had some connection with his Social Democratic background, or more precisely, with his political education in a constitutional system. As Zápotocký's influence gradually dwindled in the following years and as Antonín Novotný's grew, however, manifestations of "social-democratism" became rarer. This might have put the minds of the Soviet protectors at ease: in April 1954, at a consultation between the CPCS Presidium and the representative of the Central Committee of the CPSU in Moscow, they had made Zápotocký engage in "self-criticism" and confess to "errors of the cult of the President's function." The Soviets then seemed to object to the fact that as the president of the republic, Zápotocký had capitalized on the prestige this office had enjoyed under its two prominent democratic incumbents, Masaryk and Beneš.

While they occurred, the presumed or real manifestations of "social-democratic mentality" contrasted strangely with the patently inflexible refusal of the entire party leadership to admit any criticism or need for revision of the political processes. Yet it would be possible to argue that this contrast was only an optical illusion, and that both relative flexibility in face of popular resistance and intransigence in matters of political justice had one and the same cause, the recognition of the real force of public opinion. Meanwhile, the unanimous refusal of the party leadership notwithstanding, the pressure from many quarters for the correction of the injustices perpetrated at the political trials continued. We can assume that these trials were an unofficial but all the more important subject of discussion in the party about the time the Tenth Ordinary Congress convened. It was noted earlier that the terror had affected the life of the Czechoslovak party much as the Stalinist purges of the last prewar years had affected the Soviet Communist party: it had paralyzed the mechanisms of control and feedback provided in the statutes. During the early 1950s, decisions not only about the life and death of accused party members, but also about major policy issues of all kinds depended on the Presidium, where, once again, power was concentrated in the hands of two or three individuals, usually the party chairman and his confidence men. This disregard for the will of the membership may also explain why more than five years elapsed between the Ninth and the Tenth Ordinary Congresses.

The Tenth Party Congress and the
Dissolution of the Kominform

The Tenth Party Congress deliberated in Prague June 11–15, 1954. It was preceded by the Tenth Congress of the CPS in Bratislava in May 1953. The unusually long time span between the CPS congress, which itself was already overdue, and the congress of the national party organization was most likely caused by unanticipated events immediately following the former such as the monetary-reform riots and the unrest in the countryside in connection with the failure of the collectivization drive. There are good grounds to assume, too, that the new leadership did not wish to convene the supreme party organ before obtaining comradely advice from the Soviets on most questions. Incidentally, it was on the occasion of these consultations, which were mentioned earlier in connection with Antonín Zápotocký's self-criticism, that Nikita Khrushchev informed the members of the CPCS Presidium about the role of Lavrenti Beria in the preparation of the various show trials in

Eastern Europe. As history later showed, this information was not to benefit the Czechoslovak leaders; this was not the kind of advice they had been seeking or were prepared to follow.

The Tenth Congress assembled 1,393 delegates with the right to vote and 117 delegates with consultative status. Josef Štětka, chairman of the Control Committee, reported that the membership totaled 1,489,234. This was a notable reduction from the all-time record figure of more than 2.25 million cardholders registered at the Ninth Congress in 1949 or even from the total released by the Central Committee in February 1951. Several hundred thousand members had been expelled because of "inactive behavior," which meant anything from the failure to participate in the meetings of the local organizations and in regular political schooling to simple default in the payment of membership dues. Although the effectives had shrunk by a good third since the previous congress, the CPCS was still the largest Communist party in the world in relation to the country's population. The general reporter to the Tenth Congress was Antonín Novotný, who by that time had been able to solidify his somewhat ambiguous position as the functionary "in charge of the Secretariat of the Central Committee," by becoming first party secretary. In adopting this new title for the chief executive official to replace the earlier secretary-general, as well as in abolishing the position of the party chairman, the CPCS followed the Soviet model.[10] Novotný was also able to reorganize the party apparatus following his own ideas. Several of the younger apparatchiki whom he then placed in key posts, however, would later make headlines as his opponents.

Officially the two main points on the agenda of the congress were the new party statutes and the situation in the agricultural sector. The latter issue certainly was a very topical one, not only in Czechoslovakia but all through the Soviet bloc, including the Soviet Union. The chief delegate of the CPSU at the Tenth Congress, Nikita Khrushchev, had only a few months earlier revealed that agricultural production in the USSR had not in 1953 reached the level of 1913. Agricultural problems were to remain a very serious headache for the CPCS leadership long after the Tenth Congress. Nevertheless, we may take for granted that the issue of the political trials, the last phase of which was actually still under way in June 1954, preoccupied the minds of the party elites even more, although no official report on this subject had been submitted. It is probable that the pressures behind the scene for a change in course were considerable, since the new Politbureau decided on January 10, 1955, to set up a special party commission to deal with the appeals and demands for an examination of the substance and procedures of the trials. Rudolf Barák, a former regional secretary from Blansko in Moravia who had recently been promoted to Central Committee membership and to a position in the Politbureau, was appointed chairman of this commission.

The Tenth Party Congress was held shortly after the elections to local government organs (National Committees). To create a climate favorable to the regime and conducive to a large turnout, as well as to an impressive victory of the single ballot of the National Front, the media carried a speech by Bohumil Laušman, former chairman of the Social Democratic party, who had gone into exile after the February coup. Laušman was kidnapped by the Czechoslovak secret service in the winter of 1953–54 from his apartment in Salzburg, Austria, and brought to Czechoslovakia. His case actually was part of the political justice of the 1950s. After he had fulfilled his task of publicly denouncing the cause of the anti-Communist opposition at home and abroad, Laušman was kept in custody for four years without trial. Although the Politbureau decided in May 1956 that he should be released, the responsible authorities simply ignored this decision, an indication that the secret-police apparatus still represented a state within the state. Only in September 1957 was a trial held in camera in Prague: Laušman was condemned to seventeen years in prison. The promise given to him that he would be allowed to meet his wife and children was not kept, and he died in jail in 1963.[11]

Although the internal politics of Communist Czechoslovakia did not change to any appreciable degree during the first three years after Stalin's death, the party could not altogether escape the new forces that had begun to make themselves felt in other Communist countries, above all in the Soviet Union. To an observer of the development of relations between the Moscow power center and its European satellites it was increasingly clear that the collective leadership of the CPSU was seeking new ways to coordinate the international Communist movement, different from those that had characterized the period of late Stalinism. Neither Malenkov as first secretary nor Khrushchev, who later replaced him in this office, made much use of the Kominform for this purpose. It might have been too closely associated, in their eyes, with Stalin's ruling methods during the last years of his life. Other, more immediate, considerations probably also militated against giving too much muscle to this peculiar substitute for the defunct Third International. The early and mid-1950s were among the years of a beginning international détente. The war in Korea ended in 1953, and there seemed to be a hope for an end to the war in Indochina also. In May 1955, the four wartime allies evacuated Austria. The Czechoslovak regime responded to this liquidation of a potential source of conflict in typical fashion by extending the Iron Curtain fortifications, hitherto limited to areas bordering on the Federal Republic of Germany, all along the Czechoslovak-Austrian frontier. The only conciliatory gesture the new Czechoslovak party leadership seemed capable of making in international politics was the declaration by the president of the republic, Zápotocký, on February 4, 1955, that the state of war had ceased to exist between Germany and Czechoslovakia. The peace moves and initiatives of the Soviet Union at that time appeared more systematic than those undertaken by the CPCS. This discrepancy might have been wilfully tolerated by Moscow. It is possible that the Soviet decision makers felt that undue stress on rigid discipline within the international Communist movement and on the dominant position of the USSR might not then be propitious.

It is also likely, however, that the reluctance to activate the Kominform was due above all to Khrushchev's desire not to spoil the slowly improving relations with Tito's Yugoslavia. In 1954 and 1955 the Soviet leaders might still have hoped that the damage to the unity of the Communist nations caused by Stalin's action against Tito in 1948 could be repaired and the status quo ante restored, with Yugoslavia returning to the fold. There was a certain paradox in these hopes: actually, Stalin's Soviet critics wanted to make the Yugoslav party obedient to the Soviet center, which had also been Stalin's goal. Subsequent events proved that these expectations were not realistic; nevertheless, they might have determined for some time Soviet policies on fraternal nations and parties. As a consequence, Stalin's and Zhdanov's creation of 1947, the Kominform, had led a dormant, if not plainly moribund, existence since the collective leadership had taken over in the Kremlin. Other ways of coordinating what official Soviet sources called "the world Socialist system" were progressively introduced: these included occasional Communist summits—meetings of party and state leaders held along with regular sessions of the Soviet-sponsored regional organizations, such as the Council for Mutual Economic Assistance (CMEA or COMECON), constituted in 1949, and the Warsaw Pact (Warsaw Treaty Organization), a counterpart to NATO, set up in 1955. It was in the 1950s, too, that the Soviets introduced the ultimate innovation in conducting the business of the world Communist movement, the consultative meetings of Communist and workers' parties. Two such meetings were held in Moscow before the decade was over. It is unlikely that many tears were shed, therefore, when the Kominform became a casualty of the destalinization line adopted by the Twentieth Congress of the CPSU in 1956.

The mourning over the Kominform's demise might have been more serious in Czechoslovakia. The CPCS leadership could not overlook the message implicit in the dissolution, a message that both the rank-and-file members and the public at large could not fail to read, each in its own way. Just as the constitution of this body in 1947 had marked a tightening of the control of the Moscow power center over the individual Communist parties, its disbanding nine years later suggested a possible return to more subtle and flexible policies. If this interpretation was correct, more responsibility would now accrue to the ruling parties in Central and Eastern Europe. And whether or not it was justified, this assumption could awaken hopes and expectations that would become a challenge to the Czechoslovak party leadership. Moreover, the Czechs and Slovaks had not yet forgotten that the Kominform had been born under the sign of a crusade against the deviation of national communism and against the thesis of national roads to socialism advocated at that time by Tito's Yugoslavia. Was its dissolution a tacit endorsement of such deviant theories? In Czechoslovakia, this interpretation could be uncomfortable for the leading party circles. That was why First Secretary Antonín Novotný, at the plenary session of the Central Committee on June 29 and 30, 1955, went to great lengths to discourage speculations of this kind. He stressed that the normalization of relations with Yugoslavia that now, after the visit of Nikita Khrushchev to Belgrade, would also be the policy of Czechoslovakia, had to remain strictly limited to the governmental and diplomatic levels. No contacts would be developed between the Communist parties of the two nations. Yugoslavia continued to be an unacceptable partner on ideological grounds. Such a rigid view might not have been identical with those of other Communist leaders in Central and Eastern Europe, but it was dictated by the internal needs of the CPCS.

Titoism had played a pivotal role in the indictments at all the major political trials of the 1950s. Slánský, in his confession before the court, had declared that his crime consisted of promoting a Czechoslovak road to socialism. If the course the USSR embarked upon in 1955 meant the departure of the Soviet power center from the position that had justified the excommunication of Yugoslavia in 1948, many of the charges formulated against the defendants would have been open to doubt. The CPCS leadership was not prepared to admit any such uncertainty. Although this stand gradually became an anachronism in the international Communist movement, the party continued its efforts to contain the mounting pressure for a revision of the political trials. The Central Committee's Commission of Inquiry headed by Rudolf Barák might more aptly have been called a commission for the prevention of inquiry. During the two years of its activity, it reviewed only 300 verdicts, although it had received no less than 6,678 demands for re-examination, and of these 300 investigated cases it found a mere 52 meriting revision.[12] Even then, the solution adopted in this small number of cases was usually a recommendation to release the convict by means of clemency procedure or by a special pardon from the president of the republic. Only a handful of victims were actually rehabilitated. While the commission was at work, the Soviet leaders were involved in its dealings only once: when the CPSU was informed by the Politbureau of the CPCS of its intention to submit an interim report on the inquiry to the plenary session of the Central Committee scheduled for February 6–8, 1956, the CPSU advised its Czechoslovak comrades not to air the problem of the trials at that occasion, "as no useful purpose would be served by such a move." Rather, they were advised to discuss it with the CPSU officials at the forthcoming Twentieth Party Congress in Moscow.[13]

We certainly can ask what useful purpose this postponement was to serve in the minds of the Soviet advisers. At first sight, their recommendation might appear to be an implicit approval of the Czechoslovak party's negative position on the revisions. However, another explanation is possible, and it seems plausible if we consider the time at which the Czechoslovak-Soviet consultation took place. We can assume that when the CPSU's Politbureau sent its letter suggesting a delay in the presentation of the Barák commission's report, the agenda of the Twentieth Congress was already more or less set. The critical comments of Anastas Mikoyan on Stalin's rule and, above all, the "secret report" of First Secretary Khrushchev about the "mistakes of the personality cult era" had already most likely been approved and included in the program.[14] It may therefore be inferred that the CPSU did not wish to stop the investigation of the show trials, but rather to synchronize it with a similar process to be launched in the USSR. The Czechoslovak party leaders followed the Soviet advice. The February Central Committee plenum, instead of considering the interim report of the Barák commission, heard a report by Viliam Široký on the international situation and the comments of Minister of Agriculture Vratislav Krutina on the thorny problem of insufficient food production. On the same occasion, a National Party Conference was called for June 6, 1956, in Prague. Few Central Committee members suspected that before the conference met, the action taken by the Soviet leadership would introduce a strong destabilizing element into the world Communist movement, an element whose impact would eventually also affect the CPCS.

Containing Destalinization:
The 1956 National Party Conference

The attack on the Stalinist legend launched by Khrushchev at the Twentieth Congress of the CPSU, in his confidential speech on February 24, 1956, came at the most inopportune moment for the internal situation in the CPCS. Taken even in its narrow meaning as an ex-post-facto rejection of Stalin's personality cult—and it actually meant more than this—it hardly suited the needs of the Czechoslovak regime. The Czechoslovak party could ill afford a destalinization. More than in any other country of Central and Eastern Europe, Czechoslovak Communist propaganda and indoctrination had been based on the presumed perfection of the Soviet model and the infallibility of the Soviet decision makers. The image of Stalin as an unparalleled many-sided genius and a paragon of statesmanlike virtue—the very essence of his personality cult—had been the keystone of the justification for the Communist system in Czechoslovakia. Although abject adulation of the Soviet party boss had flourished in all Soviet-controlled nations, the exaggeration of his reputation in Czechoslovakia had broken all records. Under these circumstances, an open admission of Stalin's crimes threatened to shatter the legitimacy of the regime.

However, by far the riskiest aspect of the Soviet drive for the correction of the mistakes of the personality-cult era in the eyes of the Czechoslovak Communists was the condemnation of the form that political justice had taken during Stalin's lifetime, and the implicit call for a reassessment of the trials. To the party leaders, besieged by the protests of thousands of victims and their families and desperately trying to keep in check the growing movement of discontent, the initiative of the Twentieth Congress of the CPSU came as an unexpected assault from the rear. It is easy to imagine the consternation of the Central Committee members who received the account of Nikita Khrushchev's secret speech from Antonín Novotný at the plenary session on March 29, 1956, even though his report was only summary and failed to convey the true severity of Khrushchev's denunciation. Yet, coming like lightning from a blue sky, it had a devastating effect. The party leadership made a great effort to keep the details of the Stalinist terror from the knowledge of the rank-and-file membership. It distributed a limited number of copies of an expurgated version of Khrushchev's speech to individual members, who were to return each copy after reading it to the respective local party organization. Considering the fact that not long after the Twentieth Congress of the CPSU, unabridged versions of the report in various translations, published in Western periodicals, became available to many higher-echelon party functionaries and even non-Communists in certain governmental positions, and that tens of thousands of the Czech and Slovak versions, printed in the West, were smuggled or dropped by balloon into Czechoslovak territory, these precautions proved futile. Returning to the subject of the excesses of the personality cult at the plenary session of the Central Committee on April 19 and 20, 1956, party First Secretary Novotný was forced to acknowledge that the secret speech had meanwhile become something of an open secret. As the CPCS leaders had feared, it had had a damaging effect. Disappointment, despair, and indignation spread through the party ranks. The Presidium and the Secretariat kept receiving numerous resolutions and petitions from party groups at all levels requesting a thorough investigation of the crimes and violations of legality committed after February 1948. Some of these resolutions demanded the demotion and expulsion of all culprits, "regardless of their position in the party hierarchy"—an unambiguous hint to the party leaders of what might be in store for them should the movement acquire further momentum—or called for the immediate convocation of an extraordinary party congress. Other resolutions suggested that concrete political reforms be implemented, such as the restitution of the multiparty system as it had existed prior to the February coup or the renewal of the Social Democracy as the party of socialist opposition. In view of the fact that these appeals came from the various party units long after they had been supposedly cleansed of all rightist and opportunistic elements, it is not surprising that the movement caused alarm in the party headquarters.

It soon became evident to the leadership that it would have to make some minimum concessions to this wave of discontent. It was impossible to deny completely the commission of terroristic and criminal acts by the holders of power in the 1950s, especially after such admissions had already been made in the Soviet Union. The first casualty of this mass demand for change was the minister of defense and Politbureau member, Alexej Čepička. Čepička was particularly suitable for the role of scapegoat because he had been generally disliked by both party members and the public, and because of his family ties to the former party chairman and president of the republic Klement Gottwald, whose son-in-law he was. Čepička was stripped of his state and party functions at the April 1956 Central Committee plenum, and shortly after expelled from the party. The official charge against him was that he had indulged in the cult of personality. In reality, indicting and expelling Gottwald's close relative was a smart move intended to redirect the wrath of wide strata against a dead party leader and thus to neutralize the impact of popular dissatisfaction. As for the mounting pressure from the membership for a thorough discussion of the evils of the Stalin era at a larger party forum, preferably at a congress, the top officials chose to temporize. The call for an extraordinary party congress was probably the most dangerous challenge of the moment since it could be resisted only with difficulty, while the demands for far-reaching political reforms, such as the return to pluralism, were not realistic and could have been relatively easily dismissed as "bourgeois-idealistic illusions." Yielding to the pressure for the convocation of a congress could well be a disaster not only for the ruling group, but also for the system as it had been established since 1948. In the end, the leadership avoided this risk by including some of the issues opened by the Twentieth Congress of the CPSU in the agenda of the pending National Party Conference, which for this purpose was postponed for a few days. This was an adroit move, since the delegations to national party conferences had always been hand-picked by the party's executive organs: it would have been much harder to keep critical and dissident voices out of a party congress. Paradoxically, too, the new pattern of relationships between the Soviet power center and the Communist periphery helped the Czechoslovak leaders in their predicament: the destalinization embarked upon in Moscow implied less direct interference and consequently strengthened the position of the Stalinists in Prague.

The National Party Conference opened on June 11, 1956. It was attended by 694 delegates, 28 of whom had only a consultative vote. In addition to the points contained in the original agenda, such as the discussion of economic questions (especially those related to agriculture), the reorganization of the governmental structure (the abolition of certain ministries and the introduction of new portfolios), and the extension of the competence of the autonomous Slovak organs, the conference heard a concise report on the findings of the Commission of Inquiry in matters concerning the political trials. This report was included in the cumulative report on the situation and the tasks of the party presented by First Secretary Novotný. The decision to include the Barák document in the main conference report had been made previously by the party Presidium, with the obvious intention of reducing the profile of the issue. Novotný also promised the delegates that a final report on the trials would soon be made available.[15] Except for this point and a few cursory remarks on the resolutions of the Twentieth Congress, which were also included in the presentation by the first secretary, the national conference of June 1956 hardly reflected the thaw presently gaining ground in other Communist countries, especially in Hungary and Poland. With a certain stretch of the imagination, the concessions made to Slovak demands for more autonomy—that is, the power awarded to the Slovak National Council to nominate the members of the Board of Commissioners, a power that until then had been held by the central government in Prague—may be seen as symptoms of the climate of destalinization. It would be difficult to overlook, however, the limitation of this decentralization to a governmental level only; asymmetric centralism continued to prevail in the party organization.

The Party and the Intellectuals during the Thaw

If the party leadership could maintain its grip over the restive membership largely unchallenged, on the one hand, it could not, on the other hand, completely silence the voices of dissent. This dissent made itself heard through channels that were formally connected with the system but were not immediate components of the party structure. Among these, youth organizations and the various professional organizations of intellectuals (writers and artists) proved to be the most outspoken. This was not a phenomenon limited to the Czechoslovak scene; everywhere in Central and Eastern Europe the intelligentsia played an important role in the 1956 crisis. Nor was its involvement of a temporary nature: once engaged in the struggle for change, it remained the spearhead of the drive.

The relationship between Communist parties and intellectuals had never been an easy one, especially during the formative years of the movement. However, much of the current mistrust of this social segment by the Communist power holders dates precisely from the period of the thaw. The intellectuals have often been blamed by the party leaders for the crises that shook the Communist world in the wake of destalinization or liberalization, as if these crises had been deliberately brought about by the intellectual elites. The view that the dramatic events of the late 1950s were contrived is undoubtedly exaggerated, since it credits the intelligentsia with more influence than it has ever had. Nevertheless, it is true that in the societies built on the Soviet model certain institutional factors have been at work that have favored a more significant role for the intellectuals in the process of social and political change. Although often unwelcome to the party apparatus, this influence has stemmed from the very organization of public life in the Communist systems.

One of the changes the Communist parties carried out in the social structure of the individual nations after the seizure of power was the introduction of the principle of "transmission belts." This is a Communist term for the type of relationship between the political decision-making center and other areas of social life that is characteristic of a Communist party-state. In such a relationship, all initiatives and goal setting by the various organized groups—professional and interest groups, as well as groups known in pluralist systems as voluntary organizations—are reserved for the monopoly decision-making source, the Communist party, which thus "propels" the entire social life, just as one single steam engine in a typical nineteenth century industrial plant used to propel all machines by means of a system of wheels connected by leather belts. Communist regimes, wherever they became established, partly took over the existing network of professional and voluntary organizations and partly created new bodies. Organizations retained or newly constituted always enjoyed a monopoly position in their particular area of activity or interest.

This arrangement resulted in a streamlining of the pattern of public life. Many voluntary organizations disappeared because they had been following similar objectives, although recruiting their membership from different strata, and thus were found to be duplicating the same purpose. The centralization that often wiped out the voluntary character of the various associations, however, also provided them with power and material resources that they had never controlled before. This was the case of the artists' and writers' unions. Novelists, poets, painters, and sculptors first joined these unions because they felt they had no other choice if they wanted to see their creations published, exhibited, or marketed. They soon realized, however, that membership gave them a good deal of economic and, to the great surprise of the party leaders, political muscle. The intelligentsia began to wield this power when the protracted crisis of destalinization set in. It became obvious that the parallel of transmission belts had but a limited application. In certain situations, the belts proved ineffective, or even threatened to turn in the opposite direction.

Czechoslovak intellectuals, like the intellectuals in other people's democracies, had been both instruments, voluntary or involuntary, and victims of the political and ideological subjection of the culture. Even those who had supported the system, party members of long standing or of recent date, could not escape the effects of this subjection. The tight control of all cultural activities exercised especially during the last, or "Zhdanovian," period of Stalinism was tolerable only to artists who were willing to obey slavishly political directives concerning their choice of topics and styles. It was at that time that the most mediocre literature and works of art of the most appalling taste were created, sad monuments of so-called socialist realism. A great many personalities of cultural life, regardless of their party affiliation, tried to steer clear of these abominations. They either focused upon areas more remote from the immediate interest of political supervisors, or pretended lack of understanding of political guidelines, at the risk of occasional reprimands; or else they simply wrote, painted, and sculptured for restricted audiences. There can be little doubt that this "mimicry"—or, as a Czech poet of the time called it, "hibernation"—was, despite the ingenuity it fostered, a poor substitute for freedom of artistic expression. Thus the discontent with political tutelage of culture never ceased to grow.

By coincidence, the National Conference of the CPCS of June 1956 was held shortly after the second congress of the Union of Czechoslovak Writers. The disenchantment of the intellectuals over the revelations about Stalinist crimes made at the Twentieth Congress of the CPSU was on the whole much keener than that of the political cadres. The commitment of the intelligentsia to the Communist cause had had chiefly ethical and philosophical roots. Many believed that they had subscribed to a better world, free of oppression and exploitation, more respectful of human dignity, and allowing uninhibited self-fulfillment. They prided themselves on being part of the vanguard of mankind. The political and economic reforms spelled out in the Communist party program, which were at the center of the party leaders' interest, appeared to the intellectuals only as means to these lofty ends. The explosion of the Stalinist myth therefore hit them very hard. It was not surprising that many of them used the writers' congress as an opportunity to voice their disillusion. Their sharp criticism of the moral failure of the Communist movement was paired with protests against political interference in the autonomy of the intellectual sphere. Several speakers at the congress also recalled the great traditions of Czechoslovakia's past and recommended that the party take its inspiration from these democratic traditions in its attempt to correct the deformations of the personality cult era. Some made concrete suggestions about ways in which the system could be reformed; they proposed the abolition of censorship, a return to the multiparty system, free elections, and many other steps whose implementation had already been requested by certain local and regional party groups in the period preceding the National Party Conference. This development took the party leadership by surprise. It required two personal interventions of the president of the republic, himself a member of the writers' union, before the mounting temper of the congress could be contained.[16]

Unlike the situation in Hungary and Poland, the outburst of the critical spirit at the writers' congress was not followed by any sustained action aimed at liberalizing the regime. Writers rapidly rejected the constraints of socialist realism, and thus satisfied their most immediate aspirations. However, no movement headed by intellectuals, with a strong response among the general public, was launched in Czechoslovakia at this time. The party leadership, apprehensive of change, could once more believe that it had the situation in hand.

The new equilibrium, however, was a rather precarious one. The party continued to wrestle with the problem of the reassessment of the trials—a major element of uncertainty, which grew as the rehabilitation of the victims emerged as the only logical course to adopt. Yet the power holders preferred to avoid the issue. The Commission of Inquiry, whose members, after the consultations in Moscow in February 1956, could have no doubts about the rejection by Khrushchev and his associates of the findings of Stalinist justice, kept on seeking excuses for inactivity. Desperate efforts were made to uphold the charges against the defendants, although many security officials who had been arrested in the meantime had confirmed that the charges had been fabricated and the confessions extorted. Where original indictments crumbled, new accusations were formulated, ex post facto, that were grave enough to justify the verdicts. In this context, a statement made in 1961 by Antonín Novotný concerning the condemned in the Anti-State Conspiratorial Center may be recalled. Novotný then claimed that Slánský and his associates had "become victims of a machine which they themselves helped to build." Other members of the Politbureau put it more succinctly, saying that "Slánský was rightly hanged for a wrong cause."[17] In the eyes of the rank and file, and even of many anti-Communists, such pronouncements were plausible, but it was characteristic of the peculiar sense of legal perception at the top of the power pyramid that they should be accepted as arguments against the rehabilitation in general. Therefore, nothing, or next to nothing, was done to redress the wrongs, except for occasional releases of individual prisoners, carried out in a very discreet way. By mid-1956, some of the defendants of the trial of the Slovak bourgeois nationalists (Novomeský and Okáli) and of the anti-state center (Hajdů and London) were set free. In no case was a public rehabilitation made.[18]

Meanwhile events in the Communist countries north and south of the Czechoslovak border took their fateful course. The ferment in Poland and Hungary that preceded the radical change in leadership at the Fifth Plenum of the Polish United Workers' party in October and the Hungarian uprising in November 1956 was soon perceived by the Czechoslovak power holders as a new threat to internal stability. As the Polish and Hungarian media became more outspokenly critical of the Stalinist heritage, the authorities forbade the circulation in Czechoslovakia of newspapers and periodicals from those two countries. It was an inefficient measure, since Hungarian and Polish broadcasts could be received unjammed, but it testified to the keen feeling of insecurity among the CPCS leaders. This insecurity was aggravated by lack of clarity, real or imagined, in the indications of the long-term intentions of the Soviet Union. The Czechoslovak party was not at all certain how far the CPSU would allow the policies initiated at the Twentieth Congress to be followed in the USSR and in the satellite countries. It must have been with considerable relief that a change toward a tougher course, announced by Nikita Khrushchev at the Central Committee session in August 1956, was registered in Czechoslovakia. However, Soviet reaction to the decisions of the Fifth Plenum of the Polish party, initially forceful but ending in concessions to the reform trend, suggested Moscow's willingness to compromise. When the crisis in Hungary later escalated, Czechoslovak leaders watched Soviet behavior very closely and with great apprehension.* The consequences of the Hungarian liberalization experiment seemed to vindicate the extremely cautious Czechoslovak line on the policies initiated by the Twentieth Congress of the CPSU. For the CPCS leadership there appeared to be a reasonable hope that these issues would once more be viewed in a similar, if not an identical, way in Prague and in Moscow. This hope was reflected in the report on the international situation that First Secretary Novotný presented to the plenum of the Central Committee on December 5 and 6, 1956.[19] A short but turbulent period of reappraisal in the international Communist movement came to an end before it could stimulate any significant changes in the Czechoslovak system.

---

*If students of Soviet relations with other Communist parties and countries, examine in detail the coverage of the Hungarian events in 1956 by the Czechoslovak media, they might find an interesting clue to what they have taken as a puzzling contradiction in Soviet policies during that memorable year. At the very peak of the crisis (October 30, 1956), when the Central Committee of the CPSU released the declaration recognizing the right of the individual socialist nations to choose their own form of government and their own road to socialism, a declaration to be violated only five days later by the Soviet military intervention in Hungary, the Czechoslovak party's central daily, *Rudé právo*, carried an editorial in which it implicitly admitted the possibility of Hungary's secession from the Communist bloc. The author of the article was then in error, like many of his counterparts in the West; however, conveyed by the official press organ of the Soviet Union's most loyal satellite, the message carried much weight. It indicated that the leadership of the Czechoslovak party took the Soviet declaration seriously. Thus it seems to support the theory that the Soviet intervention was of one of several options, chosen only at the last minute. This interesting aspect of the Czechoslovak coverage of the Hungarian crisis probably does not change the fact that the supression of the Hungarian drive for independence was most welcome to the Czechoslovak Communist leaders. Incidentally, the CPSU resolution of October 30, 1956, was to reappear on the front page of the Czechoslovak newspapers twelve years later, under comparably dramatic circumstances, but serving an entirely different purpose.

Chapter Eight

From the Hungarian Uprising to the Crisis of the 1960s

The Party Leadership on the Defensive

Immediately following the restoration of a Moscow-obedient regime in Budapest, signs of stabilization became visible all through the Soviet bloc. However, there were also indications that the good old times of uniform policies under a single undisputed command, mourned by the conservatives, were not about to return very quickly. In the very foci of the crises, in Poland and in Hungary, some of the reforms achieved during 1956 survived. János Kádár himself soon showed that, despite his Soviet sponsorship, he did not plan to pick up where Rákosi had left off. The name of Gomulka had, from the beginning, been associated with the spirit of reform, even though many of the hopes pinned on his nomination were eventually to be dashed. As for the Soviet party, where the 1956 thaw had originated, it was not possible to speak of a complete reversal of course as long as the group responsible for the debunking of the Stalin cult remained in control. In the aftermath of the Hungarian uprising there was little likelihood that a change in leadership would soon occur. On the contrary, Khrushchev appeared to be firmly in the saddle, especially after the unsuccessful attempt of the Old Guard to make him pay for the failures of the liberalization at home and abroad. The Czechoslovak leaders could not ignore these facts, but the relationship between them and the Khrushchev group never became trustful and problem-free. They seemed unable to espouse the basic idea underlying Khrushchev's criticism of Stalin's rule—that the police terror and rigid centralism that had characterized Stalinist times were unsuitable for the successful operation of a modern industrial state. The disagreement may not have been one of principle: it was dictated by the specific conditions in which the CPCS had to conduct political business. Zápotocký, Novotný, and their associates felt that a thorough revision and open criticism of past policies would be the most pernicious course on which the CPCS could embark. Thus their attitude to many initiatives undertaken by Khrushchev in 1956 and later was more than cautious. By an irony of circumstances, the CPCS became the party most committed to Khrushchev's line only when Khrushchev was about to be ousted. Thus the Czechoslovak party remained out of tune with the power center of world communism for many years to come, even though it sometimes lagged behind its Soviet model and sometimes moved too quickly ahead of it.

Impact of the First World Communist Conference— Novotný's Power Grows

The late 1950s and the early 1960s were the years when the CPCS showed the most circumspection, in the belief that the 1956 thaw had been merely an episode and that the Communist world would eventually return to what the Czechoslovak party officials considered a more realistic approach. Undoubtedly, some of the Soviet moves during that period could be interpreted in this way. The convocation in Moscow in November 1957 of an international conference of Communist and workers' parties might plausibly have been seen as a new formula to replace the previous instruments of coordination, such as the Komintern and the Kominform. The stress put by the organizers of the conference (officially named "Consultations of the Representatives of Communist and Workers' Parties") on the necessity to "thwart the intensifying efforts of international imperialism to weaken and to disintegrate the world revolutionary forces" seemed to indicate that Moscow indeed was striving to close the ranks of world communism. As subsequent developments showed, the real goals of the Soviet sponsors of the conference were to formalize, as much as possible, the rapprochement with Yugoslavia that had recently been imperiled by the impact of the military intervention in Hungary, as well as to maximize the political benefits the active policy adopted by the post-Stalin leadership in the Kremlin had reaped in the Third World. The simultaneous pursuit of these two objectives was not without problems. To facilitate Yugoslavia's gradual return to the fold, certain concessions had to be made in formulating common goals for the rather heterogeneous alliance of the world Communist and radical left parties. These concessions were to reassure the prospective adherents that no threat was posed to their independence by affiliation with the socialist camp headed by the Soviet Union. Although such guarantees were also useful in the overtures to the developing countries, Soviet concern for a closer association with Yugoslavia caused mistrust in the Communist Party of China, which at that time was anxious to see the central authority in the world Communist movement reinforced. The final declaration of November 19, 1957, turned out to be a compromise.[1] The critical passage calling for cooperation among nations and parties "on the basis of equal rights, respect for national sovereignty and interests, and in consideration of mutual advantages and comradely help" was too vague to cause the League of the Communists of Yugoslavia to take a resolute step toward eventual reintegration in the system of Communist powers of Central and Eastern Europe under Soviet leadership.[2] On the other hand, those who favored a more structured cooperation among the Communist movements and regimes in the world did not consider it firm enough. By an irony of history, the affirmation of respect for independence and sovereignty that had been meant for, but did not pacify, Yugoslavia was later often invoked by the parties of the smaller nations of the Soviet bloc, such as Albania and Rumania, in their disputes with the USSR. In brief, the Moscow conference of November 1957 and its transactions reflected all the cleavages in the international Communist system, but did not close, or even bridge, any of them.

In the fall of 1957, however, many of these cleavages were still only latent. Therefore, the Czechoslovak party leadership could read the message of the conference as a promise of a gradual return to greater stability and better coordination of the policies of the Communist regimes in Central and Eastern Europe. The perilous destalinization experiment seemed to have been shelved and the trend towards polycentrism reversed. It was in a way paradoxical that the CPCS leaders, who were afraid of change, should take a negative stance on polycentric tendencies; it was precisely because of the greater autonomy they enjoyed as part of the destalinization process that they could develop into an island of Stalinism in a changing European Communist orbit. Shortly before the Moscow conference convened, the Barák Commission of Inquiry submitted its concluding report to the plenary session of the Central Committee held from September 30 through October 2,

1957. This report, and even more its uncritical acceptance by the party's supreme executive organ, reflected the spirit of hostility to any reform that then dominated the Czechoslovak Communist organization. We have seen earlier that the record of action taken or recommended by the commission was very meager indeed in proportion to the number of cases calling for reassessment. The failure of the Barák group to make any significant progress in this matter would later be held against the commission's chairman and become one of the arguments for his liquidation. In the interest of historical truth, however, it is necessary to point out that even recommendations by the commission for a mild revision of this or that case often were not followed up by any action by the Central Committee or the Politbureau. We may safely assume that opposition to any move that would imply an admission of serious faults, if not crimes, committed in the past unified all top-echelon party cadres. This assumption is further supported by the fact that the party took harsh disciplinary measures against members and officials who either criticized the inconsistency of the rehabilitation or pressed for further inquiry after the final report of the Barák commission had been adopted by the Central Committee. Several prominent individuals, among them the wife of the German ethnic-group Communist leader Karl Kreibich, were stripped of their functions, expelled from the party, and dismissed from their jobs because they had taken this course of action.

This alliance for immobility, as we could well call the quasi-unanimous determination of the CPCS top officeholders to let the matter of the political trials rest where it stood in the fall of 1957, was not broken up but actually seemed to be further cemented when shortly after the Moscow conference important changes occurred in the incumbency of the highest party and state functions. The Presidium chairman and president of the republic, Antonín Zápotocký, died on November 13, 1957. The distribution of power that had existed until then between the surviving group of Communists of long standing—those with records dating back to the period of bolshevization, represented by Zápotocký—and the younger generation of leaders recruited from the party appara-tus around Antonín Novotný ceased with this event. Novotný proved to be strong enough to prevent the emergence of a potential rival to fill the vacant office of the head of state. Instead, he himself was elected to this position. Since the office of party chairman had not been renewed in the new version of the statutes adopted by the Tenth Congress in 1954, and had been dormant since the death of Klement Gottwald, an unprecedented cumulation of power ensued from Novotný's election to the presidency. This concentration had no parallel in any country of the Soviet bloc, not even in the USSR itself. Only years later was it replicated in Rumania and, eventually, in the Soviet Union. In Czechoslovakia, although it was to be severely criticized by Novotný's opponents and to become one of the justifications for his removal, it would not remain an isolated case.

Some observers in 1957 were inclined to assert that organizational bases had been erected for an unrestricted one-man rule similar to the cult of personality. The process seemed to culminate about two years later, when Novotný was also elected chairman of the National Front. Novotný was not the type of dictator Stalin had been, but his influence in the party grew enormously, and he could make many decisions virtually unchallenged. This was often unfortunate for the party, since Novotný, for all his shrewdness and skill at intrigue, was on the whole a narrow-minded person, characterized by a number of prejudices from his lower-class Czech background. This character trait of the first secretary proved to be especially harmful in the delicate relationship between the two main ethnic groups, the Czechs and the Slovaks, both in the party and in the state. Not unlike many Czech petty bourgeoisie on the right of the political spectrum before the February coup, Novotný viewed the Slovak search for national identity as artificial, a luxury that a country building socialism could ill afford, and perceived Slovak nationalists as a group of quarrelsome separatists who should be put back in their places.

An equally serious handicap of the new powerful party boss was his recent political past, especially his somewhat equivocal role in the purges and the terror of the 1950s. Novotný's star, truly enough, had begun to rise only after the deaths of Stalin and Gottwald; until then he had belonged to the not-too-visible staff of the party apparatus, and his name had not been widely known. On the other hand, it is difficult to imagine that he could have had no knowledge of the misuse of the judiciary for political purposes in the early years of Communist rule. Some party and government functionaries, who had been officially responsible for the show trials, for instance Karol Bacílek, who at one point was minister of national security, attempted to implicate Novotný directly, asserting that he had participated in "the evaluation of the relevant materials making possible the neutralization of the Anti-State Conspiratorial Center headed by Slánský"—that is, in the fabrication of fake evidence against the defendants.[3] This point has never been fully clarified. Whatever the facts may have been in Slánský's case, it remains indisputable that Novotný bore major responsibility for the continuation of the political trials after he took over the party Secretariat, first on an interim basis and later as the first secretary. This hard line and the subsequent reluctance to redress the wrongs of the Stalinist era made him an unwitting promoter of the reform movement that would sweep him off the political stage a decade later.

At the end of 1958, however, the brief dramatic period of liberalization still belonged to a fairly remote future. It seemed, on the contrary, that with the personal triumphs of Novotný the road would be open to a dogmatic restoration of Stalinism without Stalin. The overall international situation, but especially the conditions within the Communist bloc, appeared to favor a conservative backlash. Belgrade's cold reception of the invitations of the 1957 Moscow conference to the resumption of full membership in the Soviet-led system of Communist nations, and the explicit rejection by the League of the Communists of Yugoslavia of the principles on which the Kremlin had believed the reintegration of Yugoslavia possible, made the Soviet power center temporarily abandon the policy of rapprochement with Tito. As a consequence, the campaign against revisionism was relaunched. The Czechoslovak leaders joined in without hesitation. In Czechoslovakia, the idea of revisionism was given a special connotation and it was combated by very broad measures. A new mass purge of civil servants and employees of the nationalized industries was launched in the summer of 1958. This time it affected both deviant party members and unreliable non-Communists with reactionary class backgrounds. Many experts who had been able to maintain their positions in the state administration or in the economy because of their experience and special skills were now ruthlessly dismissed and replaced by Communists with dependable (that is, unreservedly docile) attitudes, but a complete lack of professional competence. This purge testified to the regime's feeling of insecurity and hardly lent any more legitimacy to the Communist system in the eyes of the population. It also seriously compromised the chances that the new methods of economic management introduced in 1958 would be successful.

The drive toward the collectivization of agriculture, which had been resumed and intensified after a few years of relative inactivity, could be seen as yet another form of the preventive campaign against revisionism. By the end of the 1950s, about 90 percent of all arable land had been incorporated into the Uniform Agricultural Cooperatives. However, the problem of insufficient productivity did not cease to plague Czechoslovak agriculture; indeed it became even more serious. Output continued to lag behind prewar levels, and the new form of ownership in no way increased efficiency. The party experts admitted that the yields from the 10 percent of land cultivated by private farmers and from the private plots of the members of the cooperatives (1.5 acres per family) greatly exceeded the yields from the jointly worked land. Despite this fact, the collectivization was pursued to its end, according to the original plan. It was, above all, a political measure: the regime's spokesmen often quite openly stated that the existence of individual property to any significant extent in the countryside would in the long run imperil what they defined as socialism.

The 1958 Economic Reform and the Eleventh Party Congress

The shortcomings of the socialized agricultural sector were not the only economic difficulties preoccupying the party after Antonín Novotný assured himself of undisputed primacy in the power structure. The low productivity in industry, inferior quality of goods, and unsatisfactory state of services of all kinds had not improved since the take-over in February 1948. Neither the sacrifice of selected scapegoats in the great purge of the early 1950s nor the drastic monetary reform of 1953 could change the situation in any appreciable way. That was why, at the end of the decade, new means were sought to improve the economy, including a reform of the system of industrial management. The proponents of this reform were inspired by the examples of the organization of economic management in the neighboring Communist countries, especially in Poland and in Hungary, that had been implemented in the aftermath of the 1956 crises. In part, these innovations were modeled on the industrial decision-making structure previously introduced in Yugoslavia, but in view of the continuing ideological dispute between the Soviet and the Yugoslav parties, this fact was usually passed over in silence. Although the 1958 blueprint was much less radical than the one adopted eight years later, both shared with the Yugoslav system the principle of vesting in individual enterprises the power to make decisions on micro-economic issues.

The economic reform of 1958, like its more pervasive sequel in the

1960s, recognized the utopian character of the Stalinist model of management—that is, the impossibility of establishing a central agency capable of correctly registering all the needs of the population and translating them into detailed production tasks for individual enterprises. However, in contrast to the later New Economic Model, the 1958 reform attempted to resolve the problem merely by decentralizing the decision-making process, but it did not take any explicit steps toward restoring the regulative role of the market. The central planning board relinquished its right to determine the entire production programs of the industrial plants and retained only the power to set target figures for products considered vital. As the rest of the enterprise's capacities could now be employed where its own management thought it profitable, namely, for the manufacture of goods that were in demand, the laws of the marketplace were nevertheless implicitly, albeit only partly, restored. Another important aspect of the reform was the introduction of the principle of material interestedness—a hybrid term denoting a new system of incentives, including premiums, bonuses, special rewards, and so on, for both management and employees. Whereas before, an enterprise achieving an output higher than the imposed target had had good reason to fear that its unusual performance would become a norm in the subsequent economic plan, after the 1958 reform it could be sure of substantial compensation if it voluntarily accepted higher production assignments for vital products than those foreseen by the top planning authority.

The decentralization considerably reduced the bureaucratic workload, both for the central planners and for plant-level managers. However, as a consequence of the new approach, another problem emerged: that of adequate evaluation of the overall accomplishments of the various enterprises. As long as the national planning board specified, to the minute detail, how much of what each plant was to produce, it was easy to measure the fulfillment or the overfulfillment of the quotas. In the new system, in which only some of the production goals were determined centrally, this became much more difficult. It was hard, too, to decide which commodities in a highly diversified line of products were "socially important" enough to merit special reward for their increased production. It was already difficult enough to set up a list of vital products for the purpose of the national plan; this list could never be exhaustive, regardless of the imaginative power of the planners. Any product left off the list on the assumption that it was plentiful could become rare and thus vital if not enough enterprises included it in their programs. Considering that the immediate demand, as perceived by the managers, was the main criterion for such inclusion, less profitable articles would not be manufactured. These then would become scarce and would be added to the list of vitals, which would never cease to grow. With it grew the volume of production imposed by the central planning agency upon the individual enterprises, leaving less and less room for autonomous decisions by the plants' directors. Thus, the innovation contained built-in elements ensuring its own progressive nullification. The failure of the reform prepared the way for a more extensive project seven years later. In 1958, of course, only a few insightful experts anticipated this outcome. The principles of the reform were submitted to the plenary session of the Central Committee on February 25, 1958, the tenth anniversary of the seizure of power by the Communists. The Central Committee approved the project and referred it to the Eleventh Ordinary Party Congress for discussion.

The Eleventh Congress met in Prague from June 18 until June 21, 1958; 1,425 delegates were present, of whom 1,327 had the right to vote and 98 enjoyed consultative status. The publications of the congress stated that the CPCS had at that time 1,422,199 members and 47,478 candidates to membership. The number of party effectives thus had not changed appreciably since the Tenth Congress in 1954. The Czechoslovak Communist party still held first place in the entire world Communist movement: 10 percent of the total population of Czechoslovakia carried party cards. The master report to the congress was submitted by the first secretary, Novotný. Officially, all issues that could divide the party were kept out of the congress's agenda. Following the reports and the published minutes, the main problems of the CPCS discussed were those connected with the organization of the national economy. It was at the Eleventh Party Congress that the claim was first made that the conclusion of the "phase of the construction of Socialist society" was near.[4] Since a similar claim could be heard, time and again, from the Soviet Union, where it was eventually made into the main theme of the Twenty-First Congress of the CPSU in January 1959, the Czechoslovak Communists seemed to be better attuned to the Moscow power center than they had been before. According to the pronouncements of their spokesmen, both parties were bound to soon enter the "era of developing communism."

As for the composition of the party leadership, the Eleventh Congress did not introduce many changes. The election of Alexander Dubček to the Central Committee for the first time was an important event, but hardly a surprising one. Antonín Novotný was confirmed in his position as first party secretary. The Politbureau was enlarged to include eighteen members and three candidates. Despite official statements that the period of the construction of socialism was basically concluded, the stagnant, and from some points of view even declining, living standard of the population was a very real issue. It was to dominate the agenda of all plenary sessions of the Central Committee that followed the Eleventh Congress. The hopes pinned on the new system of economic management that was implemented after the congress did not materialize. Many promoters of the reform felt that it was not consistent enough to remedy the faults of the previous system; that it had been watered down too much while the project was making its way through the various organs and special subcommittees of the party and the government. Interestingly enough, this complaint was echoed about ten years later by the advocates of the second, much more extensive, reform of the structure of economic management.*

An additional source of difficulty in the system of economic management applied in 1958 was, as has already been suggested, the purge in the civil service and industry to eliminate unreliable elements. The last survivors of the old reserve of experts became its casualties. The consequences were disastrous. Far-reaching changes in the methods of operating the industrial sector were attempted at the same time that inexperienced, and often incompetent, party-sponsored managers were beginning to act in their new roles. This indicated the absolute priority of political over economic criteria in the policies of the Czechoslovak party leadership. It helped to explain the failure of the 1958 reform, but it was also a bad omen for all future efforts to improve the performance of the economy by decentralizing decision-making power.

---

*The charges that the decision makers in the party had tended to restrict the impact of both reform formulas may have been well founded. The observers and commentators on the Communist scene, and sometimes Communist economic experts themselves, overlooked the implications of these reforms for the power monopoly of the party. To a certain extent, the decentralization of economic authority required that the party leadership and apparatus relinquish the grip on the industrial work organizations that had previously been assured to them by the "double-track" nature of the Stalinist model (that is, by the existence of various party sections that duplicated the economic decision-making centers and were superordinated to them). A success of the economic reforms would thus amount to a "closing-down," virtual or formal, of the "second track"; it would entail a radical change in the whole party design, hardly compatible with Stalinist principles.

The 1960 Constitution and
the Second World Communist Conference

The failure of the new methods of industrial management was inevitable if we consider the major trends in the development of the Czechoslovak political regime at the end of the 1950s. Instead of decentralization, which the project would have required, everything pointed in the direction of greater centralization and cumulation of power. The message of the Twenty-First Congress of the CPSU, the slogan about the incipient stage of communism, only reinforced these tendencies. Curiously enough, the Czechoslovak rulers, in patent disagreement with Marxist theory, associated the idea of communism as the ultimate form of social order with ever-increasing political control. It seemed to be a peculiar form of the "leap from the realm of necessity into the realm of freedom" that Karl Marx had postulated. The stress on "more power to the party" at this historical juncture fit in with Stalin's claim about the intensification of the class struggle in the period of maturing socialism, a tenet that had been explicitly condemned by the Twentieth Congress of the Soviet party in 1956. Given the thoroughly Stalinist structure and spirit of the CPCS at the end of the 1950s, this position is not surprising. The quest for more control found its expression in a new constitution that replaced the document of 1948, which had been enacted shortly after the February coup. It was modeled on the Soviet constitution of 1936 ("The Golden Book of the Soviet Peoples"), which in turn had been a product of the peak period of Stalinism. Although the Czechoslovak constitution of 1948 (The Constitution of May 9), had strongly resembled similar documents in countries with pluralist democracy both in form and in content, the new constitution was more in tune with the political reality of Communist Czechoslovakia. It listed basic civil rights in only very general terms and referred in every instance to "the law," which was to "determine the details," that is, to guarantee the exercise of these rights; it was a convenient way of making possible various restrictions while acknowledging the principles. Where the previous text had made only ambiguous references to the Communist party and its privileged position in the state, the new constitution made no secret of the unchallenged and unchallengeable authority of this party, to whose interests all others were to be subordinated. It also explicitly stated the monopoly right of the CPCS in nominating candidates to political functions at all levels. The thesis about the then imminent completion of the construction of socialism was reflected in the new designation given to the state: the Czechoslovak Socialist Republic.

In the new constitution, the institutional symbols of the autonomy of Slovakia were maintained, but a simultaneous territorial reform abolished the provinces, replacing them with smaller units called regions. For Slovakia, this meant that whereas it kept the rudimentary organs of self-government, it completely disappeared as a self-contained geographical unit. The new constitution also perpetuated the anomaly of the Czech ethnic group's lack of representation and its rule by the national political organs. This asymmetric centralism, which had characterized the Czechoslovak system since the end of the Second World War, was to continue for another eight years. In its new form, it was less palatable than ever before to the Slovaks, both party members and the unorganized, who felt that the system did not sufficiently respect the rights of the Slovak ethnic group to self-expression and self-determination. It thus added to an already existing tension and compounded the problems with which the party had to wrestle.

The draft of the new constitution was approved by the National Party Conference in Prague, held July 5–7, 1960. The conference was attended by 505 voting delegates and 47 observers. According to the report of the party's Central Control and Auditing Commission, the CPCS at that point had 1,379,441 members. This represented a slight decrease in effectives from the figures quoted at the Eleventh Party Congress in 1958; on the other hand, the large number of candidates to membership, 179,641 in all, more than compensated for the apparent loss. Aside from the proposal of the new constitution and the territorial reform, the agenda of the National Party Conference of 1960 included the Third Five-Year Plan, to be implemented from 1961 through 1965. The plan had been in preparation since the plenary session of the Central Committee of September 23 and 24, 1959. It was on this occasion that Oldřich Černík, minister of industry and Politbureau member, stated the goals of Czechoslovak industry "in the period of the completion of Socialism." The claim that the conclusion of the construction of socialism was imminent was also the leitmotiv of the conference. The Third Five-Year Plan was supposed to bring this construction to a successful end. Neither the delegates at the conference nor the members of the National Assembly who later approved the new constitution and the Five-Year Plan suspected that the plan they voted for would soon be suspended because of major difficulties, and that the crisis resulting from these difficulties would be one of the factors that would eventually bring about a radical change in the political course.

The developments in the international Communist movement in 1960 did not allow a simple interpretation, comparable to that made by the Czechoslovak leadership in 1957 after the first Moscow conference of Communist and workers' parties. The position of the Soviet Union could not be seen, even by wishful thinkers, as a commitment to simple restoration of the conditions that had prevailed before 1956. The disagreement on many theoretical and practical issues between the USSR and the People's Republic of China deepened considerably and became visible to any careful observer. To maintain a minimum of cohesion among the countries of the Communist bloc, Soviet leaders pushed forward a project of a new world conference. This conference was preceded by consultations held in Bucharest, in June 1960. The choice of the Rumanian capital for the consultations was a gesture symbolizing the recognition of the equal status of all ruling Communist parties, but it was also a concession to the party that was most apprehensive about the impending split between Moscow and Peking and about the Soviet expectation that all parties would align with the CPSU should the split become irreparable. The preliminary talks in Bucharest did nothing to reconcile the conflicting positions of the two Communist giants, and further escalation of the dispute appeared inevitable. Other disagreements, too, came to the fore. Yugoslavian Communists chose not to participate in the scheduled world conference. A latent but persistent conflict threatened the relations between the Soviet Union and Rumania: the latter resented what it perceived as an infringement upon its sovereignty implied in a Soviet project of a jointly-operated industrial complex on the Danube river near the Rumanian port of Galati. Last but not least, the break between the Soviet Union and Albania was about to be consummated.

When the second world conference of Communist and workers' parties finally convened in Moscow on November 26, 1960, the Czechoslovak party delegation led by Antonín Novotný and the chief ideologist Jiří Hendrych could not fail to see that the situation in the world Communist system had profoundly changed since 1957. The hope of a return to the earlier unanimity and stability now appeared more remote than ever. The question is whether the CPCS leadership also fully grasped the consequences for the future policy line of the nearly complete split with China. It must have been evident to any objective analyst that after giving up Peking as lost to the concert of Moscow-oriented Communist powers, the Soviet party would be much less inhibited in pursuing policies that were more in accordance with the internal needs of the bloc, as Khrushchev and his associates saw them. These policy options included a return to the spirit of the Twentieth Congress and a renewed emphasis on the need to overcome the consequences of the personality cult. This was what actually happened; the Twenty-Second Congress of the CPSU launched a new wave of destalinization in October 1961. The Czechoslovak party, for whom this turn was highly inconvenient because of the unresolved problem of the revision of political trials, was again in danger of falling out of line with the rest of the Soviet bloc. The inseparable connection between destalinization and the need to redress consistently the misuse of justice was an inexorable fact of life. Jiří Hendrych, who had represented the CPCS at the Twenty-Second Congress along with First Secretary Novotný, pointed out in his report to the Politbureau that the concern for the restoration of socialist legality and the desire to prevent a possible repetition of the Stalinist terror had been among the most important topics on the congress's agenda.[5]

The reassessment of the political trials in Czechoslovakia had in principle been shelved since the final report of the Barák commission to the Central Committee in the fall of 1957. Nevertheless, a certain number of cases were still acted upon even after the official conclusion of the investigations. A great majority of these cases were settled on an individual basis, by applying the clemency procedure or by presidential pardon. The largest contingent of prisoners was released through a general amnesty that also benefited common law criminals, proclaimed on the fifteenth anniversary of the liberation in May 1960. Among these was the alleged head of the group of Slovak bourgeois nationalists, Dr. Gustav Husák. Clemency, however, did not entail rehabilitation, but rather underscored the guilt of the convict. Moreover, amnesty was an ineffective means to rectify the injustice done to those who had been executed or died in prison. It was to be expected that the pressure for a renewed, more thorough revision would again make itself felt as soon as conditions favored it. The course adopted by the CPSU at the Twenty-Second Congress provided such an opportunity.

The chances that the trials would be revised became more real after 1960 also because the Czechoslovak leaders had concluded, on the evidence supplied by the Twenty-Second Congress, that Khrushchev's position was stronger than they had originally estimated and that the policy of removing the heritage of the personality-cult era would be a long-term one. Assuming this, Novotný and his associates decided, belatedly and somewhat reluctantly, to jump on Khrushchev's bandwagon. It is ironic that their diagnosis was no more accurate in 1961 than it had been five years earlier, when they had anticipated that the thaw would be a brief episode without lasting consequences, possibly followed by a powerful backlash that would put an end to all liberalization experiments. Whereas in 1956 they had erred in their evaluation of the Soviet policy line, in 1961 they assessed wrongly the political future of the first secretary of the Soviet party. Consequently they were in for another unpleasant surprise.

The Barák Affair

The Czechoslovak realignment with the Soviet course after the Twenty-Second Congress initially brought about an internal crisis within the CPCS. This crisis did not originate from any basic disagreement about the realignment itself, but from personal rivalries and power struggle. The long-delayed thaw, which in Czechoslovakia meant, above all, a more systematic revision of the political trials, seemed to some ambitious individuals in the top party offices an opportunity for personal advancement. In the case of the minister of interior, Politbureau member Rudolf Barák, who had chaired the Commission of Inquiry on the misuse of justice, personal intrigue grew into a major intraparty conflict. The so-called Barák affair is a very interesting chapter in the history of the CPCS, and one that so far has not been satisfactorily elucidated. It need not astonish us that the main protagonists in this conflict, especially Novotný, have given only an incomplete and unconvincing account of what actually happened and what, precisely, Barák's crime—if there was any crime—was. The way the case was handled by the Novotný leadership resembled uncomfortably the very methods and actions that Barák at one point had been charged to investigate and for whose insufficient rectification he would eventually be blamed. However, even the sources that never had any immediate interest in obscuring the issue often left a number of questions unanswered, although they had firsthand information and data at their disposal; among these was the Commission of Inquiry of 1968, presided over by Jan Piller.[6]

In the explanations given by Novotný, as well as in the versions submitted by his most determined opponents, Barák is depicted as a saboteur of the reassessment of the political processes. Although it seems credible that Barák and his commission conducted the business that had been entrusted to them rather halfheartedly—but hardly with any more distaste than that with which the entire leadership viewed this intricate issue—it is not impossible that Barák recognized the advantages of an eventual thorough revision of the trials and of the exposure of the main culprits. There could be no doubt that such a course would have been popular with much of the party rank-and-file membership and even more popular with the non-Communist public. Barák probably realized that a consistent reassessment of the political justice of the 1950s would inevitably lead to the demise of most of the top party officials. Since Barák himself had a clean record as far as the trials were concerned—he had been only an intermediate-level apparatchik at that time—this would have meant a unique opportunity for his promotion. Novotný, for his part, saw that the only way he could escape an untimely end to his political career was to prevent anyone else in the leadership from taking the initiative and appearing as a champion of the restoration of socialist legality.

Rudolf Barák was one such potential champion, in fact probably the most dangerous of all to Novotný. Some of the available evidence indicates that he actually intended to turn the matter of rehabilitations to his own benefit. Before he could do so, however, he was stripped of his offices, expelled from the party, arrested, and tried in camera by a military court in February 1962. The charges against Barák included misuse of power and embezzlement of state funds, for which he was condemned to twelve years in prison. The embezzlement reportedly consisted of his failure to account for a sum of foreign currency, very modest by Western standards, that he had received as a travel advance for one of his official trips to Italy. It seemed to be a trumped-up indictment characteristic of Communist justice. However, certain circumstances of his liquidation appear to substantiate the theory that Barák had planned to profit, politically and personally, from the anticipated psychological and moral impact of his disclosures about the political trials. After Barák's demotion, and before his condemnation in court, Jiří Hendrych accused him in the Central Committee of "illegal possession of secret party documents concerning the attitudes and the behavior of the Politbureau members during the past years." This charge, made in the plenary session on November 27, 1961, was based on the fact that the police had found some material concerning the political processes of the 1950s in the safe of Barák's secretary. The most important of these papers were the minutes of the Politbureau sessions since 1954, in which the issue of the trials had been discussed. They documented the positions of the individual Politbureau members on the question of political justice.[7] In combination with the original material from the police and court archives to which Barák had had unlimited access in his capacity as the inquiry commission's chairman, these papers, if aptly used, could have put Novotný and his associates in a very awkward situation. This indeed might have been Barák's intention. His expulsion and imprisonment might have saved the ruling group in the CPCS from downfall.

Interestingly enough, Novotný's group, which shared the responsibility for the crimes of the past and therefore had every reason to show maximum cohesion, did not do so. Thus, as we have seen, Karol Bacílek, who during the most crucial period of the trials had been the minister of national security, seized the occasion of a public speech in Bratislava in early 1962 to praise Antonín Novotný for his part in the conviction of Rudolf Slánský and his codefendants in the prosecution of the Anti-State Conspiratorial Center in December 1952. Bacílek's intention was clear to everyone who knew the history of the rehabilitation controversy during the previous decade: it was a stab in Novotný's back, a transparent maneuver intended to cut off possible lines of retreat for the first secretary when a systematic revision of the trials could no longer be postponed. Novotný survived this intrigue because, as became evident later, he already had a plan of his own.

Novotný understood that if the rehabilitations became a serious concern of the party, only a few, if any, of the top leaders associated with the organization of the trials stood a chance of maintaining their positions. He was determined to be one of those few. The situation did not call so much for closing the ranks of the past prosecutors as it did for finding the ones to whom the blame could most readily be attached. Novotný had probably had a fairly precise idea, since the end of the 1950s, who these individuals should be; at that point, however, he did not judge it opportune to name them publicly. Instead, he found a scapegoat among the dead, the former party chairman, Klement Gottwald. Such a move appeared clever: since the general line of the new policy was to criticize and rectify the evils of the so-called personality-cult era, Gottwald was a very suitable subject to present as a Czechoslovak edition of Stalin. Unaware of Novotný's scheme, many of the party leaders of the Old Guard chose to express open dissent. Shortly after the critical statement by the first secretary on Gottwald's responsibility for the terror of the 1950s, made to the Central Commitee in November 1961, the majority of the Politbureau commemorated with great pomp the sixty-fifth birthday of the late party chairman. At the Gottwald mausoleum in Prague, a ceremony was held that was strangely out of tune with the trend in the Soviet Union: Stalin's body had only recently been removed from the mausoleum at Red Square in Moscow. Novotný was conspicuously absent from the ceremony. He also shunned the unveiling of a monument to Gottwald in the industrial city of Gottwaldov-Zlín in Moravia, at which Politbureau member Jaromír Dolanský eulogized the deceased party boss as "the greatest revolutionary fighter of the Czechoslovak communist party."[8] Almost all the party leaders who participated in these celebrations would eventually be sacrificed when the major violations of justice committed at the political trials were exposed.

Chapter Nine

Belated De-Stalinization

From the Twelfth Congress to Novotný's Demise

The removal of Rudolf Barák from the party leadership gave First Secretary Novotný two tactical advantages. On the one hand, he was rid of a potential rival who, because of his key position in the rehabilitation procedure and the popularity the rehabilitation issue enjoyed in wide party circles, might actually have ousted him. On the other hand, Barák served as a convenient scapegoat who could be blamed for all the delays and inconveniences in redressing the past wrongs of political justice. Novotný now found it safer to respond to the increasing pressure for a new revision of the trials. At the meeting of the Politbureau on August 30, 1962, Novotný tabled a recommendation to "re-examine the trials of individuals who formerly occupied important political functions."[1] A special commission charged with the task of studying this proposal reported to the Politbureau, on November 21, that a new examination of the trials was justified because new facts had come to light that proved that the Barák commission had handled many cases inconsistently. Novotný made sure that the responsibility for the unsatisfactory work of the commission was given entirely to Barák; he kept coming back to this issue in all his subsequent comments, especially in his report to the Twelfth Party Congress in December 1962. In the meantime, a new investigative body was set up by the Central Committee. Its mandate covered all trials held from 1948 till 1954. It was chaired by presidium member and Central Committee secretary Drahomír Kolder. Among its members were prominent figures of the later liberalization period of 1968 such as Alexander Dubček and Václav Prchlík. The commission received its general instructions from the Politbureau on September 11,

1962. Everything seemed to indicate that the party meant business this time.

The Kolder commission submitted its preliminary report to the Central Committee via the Politbureau on November 27, 1962. This course was chosen because Novotný and his associates feared the effects of the report upon the Central Committee's plenum and wished to edit or censor it before it was released. Their fears appear to have been justified: despite several unclear or ambiguous passages, the report left no room for doubt that the trials of the 1950s had on the whole been gross violations of justice, based on fabricated or extorted evidence. It also contained some definite indictments of individuals responsible for these violations and called for their removal from the Central Committee. The recommendation was not carried out, but the report caused considerable alarm among the Old Guard. After a thorough discussion, which more than one member found embarrassing because of his role in the political trials, the Presidium decided that the report to the impending Twelfth Congress should refer to the matters of rehabilitation in accordance with the decision of the Central Committee's meeting. The meeting in question was the plenary session of November 2, 1962, at which the main items on the agenda for the forthcoming party congress had been discussed. The issue of the rehabilitations had been discussed only in very general terms, since the Central Committee could not yet have known the contents of the preliminary report. The committee only determined the form in which the expected report was to be presented to the delegates to the congress. This gave the leadership sufficient leeway to manipulate the document so that eventually only a brief passage in the main congress paper was devoted to the problem of the revision of the trials. Even so, the report of the Kolder commission had a considerable impact both upon the apparatus and the rank-and-file membership.

The Twelfth Party Congress

The Twelfth Ordinary Congress, which convened in Prague December 4–8, 1962, assembled 1,568 full delegates and 94 delegates with consultative vote. These represented 1,588,589 members and 92,230 candidates. In comparison with the Eleventh Congress held in 1958, the number of followers had increased by some 15 percent. In addition to the thorny, and potentially explosive, question of the overcoming the deformations of the personality cult era, which had been allocated little official space but was quasi-omnipresent at the meeting, the congress had to deal with a very difficult economic situation, a topic that in the congress transactions was listed under the title of "Main- Trends of Further Development of Our Socialist Society." The party's supreme organ had to make decisions on both issues. As for the rehabilitation, the leadership ruled that all investigations related to it must be completed within four months after the congress. In the matter of the crisis of economic growth, it launched some important initiatives that later led to the most radical reform of the system of economic management in the Communist orbit thus far. By contrast, the ruling party organs elected at the Twelfth Congress, the Central Committee and the Secretariat, did not reflect much change. Antonín Novotný was reconfirmed as first secretary. Among the 97 members and 50 candidates of the Central Committee there were few new faces.[2] Yet significant events were to follow, almost on the heels of the congress.

The plenary session of the Central Committee held on January 4, 1963, dealt with "the conclusions for the work of the party and the government to be drawn from the decisions of the Twelfth Congress." These included not only the efforts to resolve the current economic crisis, but also the need to bring a speedy and satisfactory end the investigation of the political trials. In compliance with the directive of the congress, the Kolder commission presented its final report to the next following Central Committee plenum, on April 3 and 4, 1963. Again, the report had first been filtered through the Presidium, where the commission's inferences about the responsibility of individual party officials for the misuse of justice had been considerably diluted. This expurgated report nevertheless had a powerful impact upon the party's top governing body. The April session of the Central Committee decided that the attorney general should be advised to proceed immediately to formally nullify the verdicts and to introduce measures aimed at the rehabilitation of the victims. Also, the Central Committee agreed that "consequences should be drawn on the party level from the findings of the investigative commission."[3] It was clear what consequences the Central Committee had in mind: then and there the powerful leader of the Slovak party organization, Karol Bacílek, the minister of national security in the early 1950s, whom the congress of the Slovak party had only recently reconfirmed in his office of the CPS first secretary, was relieved of his seat in the Presidium of the national party organization. At the same time, another two members of the Old Guard, Bruno Koehler and Václav Slavík, lost their positions in the Secretariat of the CPCS Central Committee. The plenary session of the Slovak party Central Committee, held four days later, stripped Bacílek of his Secretariatship and other offices in the CPS executive. Bacílek was succeeded, both in the CPS and in the CPCS, by Alexander Dubček.

These measures were but a prelude to much more significant changes in the party leadership. On August 22, 1963, the Supreme Court made public its findings in the matter of the revision of the political trials. From the legal point of view, practically all the verdicts were declared invalid. None of the defendants were found guilty of any violation of the law. Their rehabilitation in court called for a parallel action by the party: restoring the rank and the status to the victims and assessing the responsibility among the power holders for the misuse of justice. Reaction to this second stipulation was swift. At the plenary session of the Central Committee of the CPCS on September 20, 1963, the Old Guard paid the price for the terror of the 1950s. Its members virtually disappeared both from the Presidium and the Central Committee. Among the losers were prominent party members such as Július Ďuriš, Ludmila Jankovcová, Jaromír Dolanský and Viliam Široký. Novotný's long-planned scheme worked: he saved his position by sacrificing the majority of his collaborators. It was but a temporary victory, however. The issue of the trials continued to undermine the first secretary's power, mainly because he was not willing, or not able, to draw all the consequences from the investigations and to rehabilitate the condemned as party members and officials. Moreover, the spectacular changes in the party executive and apparatus brought into leading positions individuals who no longer were bound to Novotný by the tie of joint culpability in the crimes of the Stalinist period, and therefore were less malleable than the Old Guard. Some later turned out to be his outspoken enemies. Thus the initiative of the Twelfth Congress in the area of overcoming the mistakes of the personality cult era considerably affected the party leadership, but it did not contribute in any way to its stability.

The second major concern of the Twelfth Congress, the state of the national economy, was dictated by reasons as serious as those that had put the rehabilitations on its agenda. Since 1961, signs of a new crisis in the production and distribution of capital and consumer goods had multiplied. The performance of both the industrial and the agricultural sectors had been very unsatisfactory; the target figures of the national plan had not been met. As early as the plenary session of the Central Committee on April 12, 1962, Novotný had to admit that the goals of the Third Five-Year Plan were no longer attainable. The plan had to be scrapped, and for several years to come the Czechoslovak economy operated on the basis of individual yearly planning. The declining living standard of the population inspired critical voices among economic experts. It was widely acknowledged that the new system of management instituted in 1958 had failed. Some saw the reason for the failure in the inconsistency of the system itself; some believed that it had not been applied with sufficient vigor or that it had been deliberately sabotaged by party officials jealous of their power over the economy. All agreed, however, that the blame belonged to political decision making. The legitimacy of the regime, which had been tenuous from the start, faced a new challenge. The source of dissatisfaction had to be attacked.

The leadership, which had initially rejected and resented the criticism of economists, decided to change its approach and to turn to these critics for help. This change was not easy, nor was it unanimous. As on all other important issues, opinions on how to best respond to the economic crisis were divided. Rather than speak of a position shared by the entire leading team, it would be more accurate to say that the unorthodox, mostly the younger, critics and innovators found sponsors in certain members of the top party hierarchy and that the rest of the leadership acquiesced because of a lack of substitute solutions. This absence of unanimity, or even of a solid majority, may explain why certain reforms that were apparently encouraged by the party decision-making center encountered serious opposition when they were implemented. This had been the fate of the blueprint for decentralized economic management in 1958, and it did not spare the much more ambitious project of the 1960s. Thus the green light given to economic theoreticians in 1962 was only partial and conditional. The project they prepared was never really safe, even when it was approved and formally adopted by the party governing organs.

It was characteristic of the equivocal situation of the reform proponents, whom the power holders viewed as both useful and potentially subversive, that they had often been denied access to the media and prevented from making their ideas publicly known. They often had to use unconventional channels. Critical articles concerning the problems of the economy frequently appeared in literary and artistic reviews, with obvious complicity on the part of the editorial boards of these periodicals.

Among these, the semi-weekly *Literární noviny* ("Literary News") soon gained notoriety as it gradually broadened its field of coverage to include all subjects of topical interest, whether artistic, economic, or political. The party grudgingly tolerated this trend and thus helped to create an alliance that later played an important role in the reform movement. Halfhearted and ineffective attempts to restrict the cultural press to the topics in its own area, undertaken in the second half of the 1960s, only further cemented this alliance.

The party leaders, who, pursuant to the resolution of the Twelfth Congress, set up a commission charged with the task of working out a proposal for the reform of the economic system, had expected this commission to proceed in a way comparable to the methods of other party commissions, above all to deliberate behind closed doors. They soon were forced to admit that they had been mistaken. The commission was presided over by Ota Šik, who was known to the public through a number of theoretical analyses concerning Communist economics, especially the role of the market in a planned economic system. It was unrealistic to expect Šik to insulate himself from the rest of the community of economists or to help silence the voice of this community. Individual participation and initiative, stimulated by adequate incentives, were in his eyes the principal ingredients of satisfactory production and distribution in a system of public ownership and central planning. He wished to restore to the market its regulative function, and consistent with these views, he believed as firmly in the wholesome effects of an open market of ideas as in the benefits of the market of commodities. Instead of remaining an internal, more or less confidential affair of the party, economic reform with Šik in command became a public issue. It provided a new platform for the promotion of unorthodox ideas, not only in economics, but in political matters as well.

The Anti-Novotný Coalition

The unrest stirred by the rehabilitations of 1963 persisted long after the rulings of the Supreme Court and the ensuing cadre changes in the CPCS had been made public. Partly by its own momentum, because of the monstrosity of the crimes the party now admitted to, and partly because even in this second phase the leadership continued to adopt only half-measures, the general uneasiness did not subside. Moreover, the inconsistency of the rehabilitations, which stopped short of restoring the victims to their party membership and offices, called forth another hostile force, Slovak nationalism. Although political rehabilitation was denied to practically all defendants of the political trials, the refusal to reinstate those condemned in the proceedings against the Slovak bourgeois nationalists provoked a much more lively reaction in the party because in that case a whole ethnic group appeared to have been unjustly indicted and discriminated against. Also, the protagonists of the 1954 Bratislava show trial were all still alive, whereas there were few survivors of, for example, the Anti-State Conspiratorial Center of Rudolf Slánský and Associates. Many Slovak Communists felt that their indignation over the party leadership's refusal to rehabilitate politically their fellow comrades whom the courts had found innocent was equally justified on grounds of ethnic pride. The reluctance of Novotný and his collaborators was seen as a manifestation of Czech chauvinism and centralism, an insult to the right of self-determination of the Slovak people. What was left of the Novotný clique after the September 1963 shake-up acquired a new and formidable enemy.

The hostility of Slovak party circles towards Novotný further increased after the first secretary neutralized yet another attempt at the political rehabilitation of the bourgeois nationalists. In June 1963, two months after the Kolder commission presented the final report on the investigations of the political trials, a new body was set up by the Presidium to formulate "an impartial political and ideological opinion on the justification for the criticism of bourgeois nationalism voiced at the Ninth Congress of the Communist Party of Slovakia and afterwards."[4] This group, called the Barnabite commission because it met in the former Barnabite nunnery at the Prague Castle, was constituted as a concession to the pressure from Slovak party circles. Although it was composed of both Czechs and Slovaks and presided over by a Czech, its findings fully exculpated the alleged bourgeois nationalists. In December 1963, the Barnabite commission stated that "the charge of bourgeois nationalism had no justification."[5] The road was now free for the party rehabilitation of Husák and his codefendants. However, the Central Committee yielded to Novotný and resorted to an inconsistent, opportunistic solution. Although the victims were formally restored to membership, their tenure in various party offices was declared to have expired with time. To regain their previous positions they would have had to run as candidates at the subsequent Slovak and national party congresses. That meant a waiting period of at least three years, but with Antonín Novotný at the helm, the chances of a comeback of the rehabilitated Slovak Communists were rather slim.

In the decision of the Central Committee, not only the feud between the first party secretary and Gustav Husák, but also very plain and practical considerations probably played a role. The offices that the victims of the trials claimed were not vacant, and it would have required a number of highly unpopular personnel shifts to satisfy the requirements of justice. Nevertheless, the failure of the party to make these changes considerably speeded the demise of the Novotný regime. In the time following the rehabilitation of the victims of Stalinist terror, an entire anti-Novotný coalition began to take shape. In addition to adversaries among the unjustly condemned, their families and friends, and partisans of Slovak autonomy enraged by Novotný's narrow-minded view of the issue, there emerged a kind of a united front of intellectuals and artists who were equally critical of Novotný's policies, albeit for different reasons. At the time of the Twelfth Congress, this union, as we have seen, began to acquire new allies among important party economists and specialists in economic management who were concerned about declining productivity and living standards in Czechoslovakia. Unorthodox political scientists and innovative Marxists completed the spectrum of the opposition. The solidarity among its individual components was fostered by the perception shared by all these intellectual and cultural elites that the rigid approach to pressing problems and the aversion to change manifested by the Novotný leadership were at the root of all recent setbacks, economic and otherwise. The cohesion of the anti-Novotný coalition grew when the regime, after an initial hesitation, began to censure indiscriminately entire professional groups and to impose ideological control over cultural life. The regime found itself in a difficult position, since the threat to orthodoxy came from the very centers that the party had established to preserve the purity of Marxist thought, or of what officially passed for such but was actually only Stalinism of Czechoslovak vintage.

The need to revise the system of production and management aggravated the conflict. It was nearly impossible to draw a line between the now-legitimate criticism of the economic order and the political implications of this criticism, which were not welcome to the party. The connection between the two was the nature of the whole reform enterprise. Furthermore, the improved system of industrial management the Šik commission was in process of devising had been inspired to a significant degree by the system applied since the 1950s in Yugoslavia. There the reform had been understood from the start as a vehicle for increased participation and decentralization, that is, for redistribution of power. Šik himself never denied this source of inspiration, but kept pointing out that the Czechosovak conditions were different from those in which the Yugoslav model had been implemented. Yugoslavia was one of the developing Balkan countries, whereas Czechoslovakia had already been a fairly advanced industrial society when the CPCS took control. The principles of decentralization of planning and increased responsibility of individual production units for profits and losses were the main elements taken over from the Yugoslav system. In the Czechoslovak draft, too, the central planning board was to retain only the authority to determine the most basic, the so-called macroeconomic, conditions, such as the volume of investment in the extraction of raw materials, the production of energy, the import quotas, the exchange rate of the currency and the amount of foreign monies to be spent, and the interest rate on loans granted by the state banks to the various enterprises. Decisions on the actual target figures of the plan—the scope and amount of commodities to be produced and the allocation of profits to investment and reserve funds—were to be left to the managers of the individual plants or corporations. Personnel questions such as hirings, dismissals, promotions and transfers, and salary and wage policies were equally entrusted to first-level managers and to their partners in the bargaining process, the local trade unions. The introduction of the principle of workers' participation in management, an innovation that was to be fully implemented only in a later phase of the reform, was also inspired by the Yugoslav example.

Some important theoretical underpinnings of the new system, however, were quite original: these had consequences for the whole structure of Czechoslovak society that were not paralleled in the Yugoslav experience. The changes were felt most in the political sector. Unlike the Yugoslav model, the Czechoslovak reform of industrial management engendered an initiative, unique in Central and Eastern Europe, that aimed at a change in the prevailing distribution of power. Although this initiative was launched somewhat later, by a different group of experts, the proponents of the new economic model recognized, at an early point, the need for a political counterpart to the economic reform. The call for a reform of the political order completed the concert of voices demanding a thorough change in the regime. It was the last wave of the innovative movement, but from the point of view of the monopoly position of the party, it represented the most direct and most dangerous challenge to the established interests, especially to those of the group around First Secretary Novotný. The coalition of the forces of dissent that had begun to take shape at the beginning of the 1960s picked up a formidable momentum from the structural crisis in the national economy. It made Novotný's adroit escape from the consequences of the rehabilitations merely a temporary reprieve.

The Roots of the Reform Movement

The intellectual ferment that culminated in the Prague Spring of 1968 can be traced far back into the history of Communist Czechoslovakia. Its spiritual and moral roots have to be sought still farther in the past. Thanks to these foundations, the reform movement could engender a penetrating critique of the existing social and political order and indicate, at least in theory, alternative solutions. The charge of spreading antisocialist ideology that was subsequently leveled against the reformers by the spokesmen of the Soviet power center must have seemed well substantiated to the Soviets, who had always equated socialism with their own system. Indeed, the Czechoslovak model of socialism was incompatible with the image of socialist society that Stalin's successors entertained and endeavored to make other Communist parties accept. It could hardly be otherwise, since it grew from entirely different traditions. The passionate search, undertaken in Czechoslovakia during the 1960s for new answers to the universal problems of the Communist party-states, not only was one of the most important dramas of the Communist movement, but also exemplified the resilience and vitality of the Czechoslovak political culture. In view of the significance of this unique phenomenon, its origins should be paid special attention. Here, we shall take a close look at how it evolved, survived, and developed in the hostile conditions of a totalitarian system. Investigating the nature of the social vehicles that helped carry the reform thought into the very heart of the Communist establishment is as fascinating as identifying the sources of this thought.

It is easy to see that unorthodox ideas in a totalitarian environment have to employ different channels of articulation from those in a pluralist society. Many political scientists have long held that divergent views cannot be openly voiced in a one-party system, and that this is one of the essential characteristics of totalitarianism. However, a more thorough scrutiny will reveal that this restriction is valid for the Soviet-inspired types of government only during certain definite periods of their history. Articulate opposition seems to have been impossible in the USSR and in the people's democracies during the mature stage of Stalinism. When the worst persecution frenzy subsided and the power of the repressive apparatus (which was never formally anchored in the party statutes or in the state constitution) was curbed, it became evident that Communist systems were not completely impervious to deviant thinking. This deviance, however, could thrive only within the frame-work of the state and the party; the hopelessness of all opposition unconnected with the power structure has appeared to be an axiom in all totalitarian regimes of right and left. Nothing could prevail in society that had not previously been accepted by the ruling party, but with these restrictions, dissident spirit could and can prevail.

This has been true, above all, for the Communist systems of Central and Eastern Europe, of which Czechoslovakia is a particularly illuminating case. Partly because of the Western origin of the political theory underlying the Communist political order, with its democratic and populist elements (however emasculated in practice), and partly because of the nature of the party as an organization "doing politics," these systems have stimulated political thought in many segments of the population, including those that did not share the orthodox creed. Communist regimes also pursue deliberate political mobilization of the whole society through ideologized mass media and politicized education. Since political power and thus activity in a party-state are reserved to the party membership, which ideally remains a small elite, this mobilization leads to a paradox. If successful, it cannot be consummated because the opportunities for public participation in politics are severely restricted. Individuals to whom access to positions of real power has been denied have to seek substitutes. They find them usually in professional or mass organizations—trade unions, youth movements, writers' and artists' associations, and scientific institutes. Here, on the periphery of politics, ideas and groups that are not subject to close party supervision, can emerge as potential foci of dissent.

In the case of the CPCS, two more facts have to be considered. First, the exceptionally large organized party following, mocking the Leninist ideal of a select avant-garde, offered wider opportunities for participation, but at the same time increased the risk that unorthodox currents of thought could penetrate to the party core. In 1948, for example, the CPCS absorbed the bulk of the membership of the Social Democratic party. However involuntary such adhesions might have been—or perhaps precisely because they were involuntary—the Communists thereby imported an ideologically alien element of considerable magnitude. The rather indiscriminate admissions criteria that generally characterized CPCS recruitment further aggravated the danger of contamination by ideas the ruling group and its Soviet sponsors considered undesirable. The second fact to take into account is the coincidence of the regime's crisis with an intergenerational change in the control of the party. The Communist elites who began to assume leading functions in the party apparatus in the early 1960s could not be blamed for the deformations and crimes of the personality cult, committed fifteen years earlier, and therefore had little stake in preventing public discussion of this subject or, for that matter, of any thorny issue facing the party. The leadership experienced a difficulty common to all revolutionary movements: the near-impossibility of passing on to the members of the upcoming generation, who were prone to take the Communist ideals and goals literally, the skills of "double-talk" and "double-think" that were characteristic of arrived revolutionaries—that is, the ability to read between the lines of the theory whenever it served the interests of power. It was not an accident that the communication barrier between the two generations closely resembled the one that was to separate the new CPCS leaders from their Soviet counterparts later in the decade.

These were the historical circumstances and social mechanisms that facilitated independent thinking among younger party elites. The actual content of the new thought was a peculiar blend of purified Marxism, akin to what the West has known as neo-Marxism (attempts at correcting the deformations of theory by a return to the theses of the young Marx contained in his early work *Economic and Philosophical Manuscripts*), on the one hand, and elements of Czechoslovak progressivism, liberalism, and populism on the other. The mix was in no way uniform: sometimes the national value system came out very strongly and only the rhetoric was Marxist. Not even the messianic ingredient, characteristic of all important political currents in Czechoslovak history, was missing. The opinion that the Czechoslovak reform would show the way to the entire socialist world was not voiced too often, but the confident tone was unmistakable. Yet the continuity of the reform with the mainstream of socialist thought cannot be denied. In the history of this thought during the 1960s, an important place must be reserved for the Czechoslovak contribution. The Soviet rejection in toto of the Czechoslovak model implies the rejection of much of the Western socialist heritage and shows the extent to which Stalinism and its superficially revised Brezhnevian variant themselves constitute a deviation from the universal socialist tradition.

In the unique synthesis that later would be referred to as Socialism with a Human Face, the input of the Czechoslovak political culture was dominant, supplying the ethical and philosophical basis, as well as the organizing principle. In its turn, the crisis of the regime provided an opportunity for a brief but very intensive revival in virtually all fields of intellectual pursuit. It seemed as if the fruitful exchange and confrontation of ideas, which had been arrested after the Communist take-over, had taken on a new momentum now that the guardians of dogmatism had lost their assurance and faced serious conflict in their own ranks. Inventiveness and originality marked most of the intellectual products of that time. In philosophy, Karel Kosík offered an example of creative Marxism in his *Dialectics of the Concrete*.[6] With a degree of objectivity until then unusual in Communist scholars, Milan Machovec examined the humanist foundations of democracy, the legacy of pre-Communist Czechoslovakia and its prominent statesman T. G. Masaryk.[7] Some philosophers, such as Ivan Sviták, traveled far from orthodox Marxism seeking the "human meaning of culture."[8] Several brilliant writers and publicists, not all of them philosophers by profession, completed the wide spectrum of those concerned about the quality and purpose of life in modern industrial society. Radoslav Selucký reminded the official advocates of the Communist order that the acid test of a socialist state was its ability to make its citizens happy, to "give somebody bread and to somebody roses."[9] In his popular travel reports, he pointed out that the mentality and the expectations of the people in the East do not differ from those in the West as much as Communist doctrine claims.[10] A student of modern technological civilization, Radovan Richta, emphasized that the "scientific-technological revolution" of the second half of the twentieth century poses problems that cannot be resolved by mere application of the classical Marxist recipe for the organization of political power and the ownership of the means of production.[11]

Many asked questions more directly related to the existing political order, a subject that had been strictly taboo for a long time. The interest in the performance of the political system came naturally to economists; indeed they could not avoid touching upon the matter if they wished to come to grips with their own problems. Thus they constituted a link, as it were, between the philosophers and cultural analysts on the one hand and the social and political scientists on the other. The latter, too, were very active. Slovak Miroslav Kusý tried to resolve the problem of successful popular control of the state by the separation of party functions from those of the government and by the democratization of the decision-making process in the Communist party.[12] His compatriot Július Strinka went a step further and called for the "institutionalization of criticism" as an indispensable condition of satisfactory performance by the state; this could mean only creating an organizational basis for opposition in the form of another political party.[13] Another Slovak social scientist, Michal Lakatoš, expressed the opinion that the system would not function properly until elections to the various political bodies were genuine—until voters were offered a choice among several candidates to the same office, rather than simply being permitted to approve a choice already made by a central authority.[14] The chorus of these critics was joined by several prominent literati, novelists and poets, a category of intellectuals that had always played an important role in Czech and Slovak politics; these included the Czechs Ludvík Vaculík, Antonín Liehm, Milan Kundera, Ivan Klíma and Václav Havel, and the Slovaks Ladislav Mňačko and Dominik Tatarka. They all pleaded, either explicitly in public speeches and editorials or indirectly but none the less urgently in their artistic works, for a thorough change in the society and the polity. It was from this rich variety of ideas that the well-rounded Czechoslovak Model of Socialism gradually emerged, to the dismay of the defenders of the status quo in the Kremlin, at the end of the decade.

Novotný's Leadership and the Change
in the CPSU Secretariat

The belated alignment of the Czechoslovak party leadership with Soviet policy in matters of destalinization took visible form after the Twelfth Congress. The huge monument to the defunct Kremlin dictator in Prague was demolished in 1962; the official reason given was an "unanticipated collapse of the foundations." Names of places, streets, squares, and mountains connected with Stalin were changed. Textbooks containing passages of praise for Stalin's genius were withdrawn or expurgated. None of these outward symbols was as significant as the issue of the political trials and rehabilitations, but they all testified to the decision of Novotný and his associates to adopt without reservation the course set by Nikita Khrushchev. It was hardly a matter of conviction or conversion, but rather one of necessity. With domestic opposition gradually growing, Soviet support appeared more vital than ever to Novotný. The first secretary of the Czechoslovak party was prepared to repay this support not only by joining the efforts aiming at "overcoming the survivals of the personality cult" but also by unreservedly backing all Soviet initiatives in the world Communist movement and international politics. Czechoslovakia, in the first half of the 1960s once again lived up to its reputation as the most docile Soviet satellite. It took the Soviet side when the CPSU broke off with its Albanian counterpart and favored the Soviet Union without reservation when the latent Sino-Soviet conflict finally came into the open. In both cases, the almost total break with the fraternal parties and governments was very costly to the Czechoslovak economy, freezing indefinitely claims from foreign trade and loans amounting to several hundred million dollars. The Novotný leadership enthusiastically endorsed Khrushchev's idea of a new world conference of Communist parties although the obvious purpose of such a gathering, the excommunication of the Communist Party of China, made almost all other members of the world Communist movement reluctant.

An example of the unrestricted loyalty of the CPCS leading team to the power center in the Kremlin in the early 1960s was the way in which Czechoslovak representatives in COMECON subscribed to the project of the so-called International Socialist Division of Labor. The project had been launched by an article written by Nikita Khrushchev himself and published in the September 1962 issue of *World Marxist Review*. In this context, the term division of labor was used in a much narrower and more precise sense than in the current economic language. It denoted a centrally planned and geared specialization of production among the individual member nations of the council, to the point of creating one single supranational economy operating under one supranational management. The political benefits that the implementation of this project would have brought to the Soviet Union are easily seen: it would have ensured Moscow's control over the economies of the smaller COMECON countries, and the political impact of this control could well have paralleled, if not surpassed, that of the former Komintern or Kominform. On the other hand, the price the member nations of the council were expected to pay for this purportedly more efficient organization of production was very high. The specialization proposed by the project required closing down not only individual plants that were judged to be inefficient, but even entire production sectors. Khrushchev's International Socialist Division of Labor would thus have raised some national economies to the level of advanced industrialization and reduced others to the status of purely agrarian societies or providers of raw materials. Opposition to the project, therefore, was very strong in almost all COMECON countries.

Czechoslovak economists, both conservative and less orthodox, were particularly apprehensive about the consequences the implementation of the project could have for the privileged position of the Czechoslovak automobile industry in the Communist markets. Soviet experts commenting on the International Socialist Division of Labor often suggested that "no car production could be considered economical which has not attained a turnout of at least one thousand per day," a rather ominous remark for the Škoda plant, where the MB 1000 cars, "the Volkswagens of the East," were assembled at a daily rate of six hundred to seven hundred.[15] However, the CPCS leadership paid little attention to the cautious voices of Czechoslovak industrial circles and gave the idea of the supranational integration of Communist economies its full support until the final defeat of the project by the Rumanian veto at the COMECON meeting in Bucharest in December 1962. The motives behind Novotný's policy, in this matter as in all other questions concerning Soviet initiatives, stemmed from the given situation of his group in the party: unreserved loyalty toward the USSR was to buy Soviet backing in the event of a serious challenge to Novotný's position.

Unqualified Czechoslovak approval did not save Khrushchev's project. Worse, it proved in the end to have been wrongly invested. A year and a half later, Khrushchev lost his position as first secretary of the CPSU. To his dismay, Novotný found that the change in the CPCS's stand on destalinization had been made too late to yield benefits.* Khrushchev's fall in October 1964 did not signify a complete reversal of his policies,

---

*It is reported that on receiving the news about the change in the top executive function in the Kremlin, which came as unexpectedly to the fraternal parties as had most news about major changes in Soviet politics in the past, Novotný openly voiced his displeasure about the manner in which the Soviet leadership presented its counterparts with a fait accompli. If this is true, it was quite an unusual reaction on his part and showed how upset he must have been. However, the fact of Khrushchev's downfall and its possible consequences for his own position probably disturbed him more than the form in which the demotion of the top Soviet leader had been communicated to the world Communist movement.

but it brought about a new, more conservative approach by the CPSU to various problems. Leonid Brezhnev showed considerably less predilection for change and innovation than his predecessor. Actually, the new, more cautious, climate in the Kremlin was more congenial to Novotný, but he could not take advantage of it. The forces released by the Twelfth Congress and during the period following it had already gained momentum. Novotný's leadership nevertheless adopted the same obedient attitude to the new Soviet top team as it had shown to Khrushchev before his demotion. For the time being, the position of the first secretary of the Czechoslovak party appeared unchallenged. Novotný was re-elected president of the republic on November 12, 1964, and thus continued to occupy the two most important positions in the power structure.

At the preliminary consultations of the Communist and workers' parties in Moscow, March 1–5, 1965, the Czechoslovak delegation supported the Soviet proposal of a new Communist summit despite the patent unwillingness of the majority of represented national sections and groups to participate. Few seemed to be enthusiastic about the prospect of presiding over the expulsion of the Chinese comrades from the world Communist movement, but the CPCS was one of these few. After having heard at its session of March 16, 1965, the report of the CPCS delegation to the Moscow talks, the Central Committee reaffirmed its unreservedly pro-Soviet position. The Central Committee's resolution urged an early convocation of a world conference for the purpose of settling the dispute between the Communist Party of China and the Communist Party of the Soviet Union. It must have been clear to any informed observer at that point that such a conference could lead only to a formalization of the break that had already become irreparable. The Central Committee's stand on this issue, therefore, was little more than a pious wish. Nonetheless, it met the purpose that had motivated it—that of demonstrating its unqualified approval of the Soviet line in the hope that Moscow would reciprocate in an eventual crisis faced by the Czechoslovak party leadership.

The Thirteenth Party Congress

As the Novotný team continued to support all Soviet initiatives, including the problematic cause of a new world Communist summit, it came under increasing fire from the various centers of domestic opposition, among which the Slovak nationalists were the most outspoken. The Slovaks seemed determined not to accept without protest the manner in which the CPCS leaders had acted, or rather failed to act, on the recommendation of the Barnabite commission. In the spring of 1965, the official daily of the CPS, *Pravda*, published an editorial in which Milan Huebl, a lecturer at the School of Political Science in Bratislava, declared that the charge of bourgeois nationalism had been sheer fabrication and identified First Secretary Novotný in rather explicit terms as the author of the plot. The article caused a scandal and cost the author his teaching post as well as all party offices. Yet it was clear that Huebl had only said aloud what many others had been thinking for a long time. In addition to the pressures from the Slovak side, the system became a target of criticism by economists who participated in the discussion about the reform of industrial management. Nonconformism also reared its ugly head among other academicians, especially social scientists, who after a long period of Stalinist repression celebrated their reinstatement as recognized members of the scholarly community. The unrest and discontent in the circles of artists and writers dated back even earlier, and further complicated the situation for the CPCS leadership. Because of the urgency of the economic problems and because of the interdependence of these problems with other issues under public discussion, the ideological guardians in the party hesitated to take drastic measures against the dissenters. Instead of nipping in the bud the deviant ideas and views, the spokesmen of the regime had to content themselves with occasional refutations that did not greatly impress the opposition. One young Slovak scholar labeled this official response "apologetic or embarrassed dogmatism."[16]

By the time the Thirteenth Ordinary Party Congress convened, the divisions of opinion in the CPCS on the most important political and ideological questions had widened considerably. The supreme party gathering took place in Prague from May 31 to June 4, 1966; 1,477 voting delegates and 50 delegates with consultative status participated in the deliberations. According to the report by the Control and Revision Commission, the membership figure had reached 1,698,002 by January 1, 1966. Of this total, 1,638,695 were full members and 59,307 were candidates to membership. Party membership in proportion to population had not increased much since the Twelfth Congress in 1962, when it had already achieved a record level among all Communist parties of the world. Officially, the central topic of the congress was "further general development of the socialist society in Czechoslovakia." Concretely, the congress's resolutions dealt with the reform of economic management, with the special problems of agriculture, and with "new unfolding of socialist culture." Of these three subjects, economic reform was by far the most important. The discussion clearly revealed the disagreements within the party ranks between those who accepted the idea of a thorough reform of the economic structure and those who were hostile to the proposal because they put the preservation of the power monopoly of the party above all else. The latter correctly anticipated that a decentralization of decision-making authority in economic matters would not fail, sooner or later, to necessitate changes in the political process itself. Their anticipations were reinforced by some statements of the partisans of the reform. For example, Ota Šik concluded his report to the congress on the reform project, on June 3, 1966, with a call for a "new political model" to complete the currently tabled New Economic Model.[17] It was characteristic of the situation then prevailing in the party that this passage of his speech was carried by radio and television, but was deleted from the printed records of the congress.

It would be difficult to determine with authority the relative strengths of the two contending groups, the reformers and the conservatives, but the reform-inclined elements seemed to be in the majority. On the other hand, the conservatives retained their influence and, on the whole, enjoyed the support of the Novotný leadership. There was also an important percentage of the party functionaries who did not come out strongly in favor of either of the two positions, the so-called centrists. The distribution of these three tendencies persisted all through the second half of the 1960s and became manifest at frequent intervals during the various crises of the Dubček regime, before and after the Soviet military intervention. As for the remaining two issues addressed by the congress's resolutions, the shortcomings of agricultural production and the concern for maintaining the socialist character of cultural activities, these were not so much in the forefront of attention, but they were not unimportant. During the two following years, the conflicts about party policies in these areas were to contribute significantly to the change of the political course. Other matters also occupied the minds of the rank-and-file membership as well as of the party elites in the late spring of 1966, such as the still-unresolved question of the party's rehabilitation of the victims of Stalinist justice or the Slovak party organization's unsatisfied aspirations to greater autonomy, but these were not openly discussed at the Thirteenth Congress.

The congress elected the largest Central Committee thus far, composed of 110 full members and 56 candidates. This committee, and the later constituted party Presidium, included a small number of younger party officials who were new to these responsibilities. But, on the whole, the top organs of the party appeared to remain firmly in the hands of the Novotný establishment. Novotný himself was reconfirmed, for the fourth time, in his key executive office. Among the theses of the congress, however, one indicated a change in the overall ideological climate, the re-election of Antonín Novotný notwithstanding. It stated that "the working class dictatorship has fulfilled its main historical function" and should give way to "a system of socialist democracy" that should develop "hand in hand with an emphasis upon a scientific and professional approach to social management."[18] The immediate purpose of the thesis was to stress the importance of expertise over party background, especially in the economy, but at the same time the thesis closed the door on the dictatorship of the proletariat and the Stalinist claim, implicitly contained in many policies of the Novotný leadership, that the class struggle intensifies as a society approaches the stage of socialism. The call for a broad socialist democracy, on the other hand, was theoretically unassailable, since the team in control had already proclaimed, in the constitution of 1960, that the construction of socialism had been completed in Czechoslovakia.

The plenary sessions of the Central Committees of both the CPCS and the CPS held through the rest of 1966 were dominated by economic questions, especially those connected with the project of economic reform. At the plenum of the Central Committee of the CPCS on December 19 and 20, 1966, the details of the New Economic Model and the technicalities of its implementation were made public and approved. The plenary session of the Central Committee of the Slovak party on December 28 took analogous steps. As the blueprint for the reform had foreseen, the new methods of industrial management were to be tested, in the course of 1967, in a hundred selected enterprises. In this preliminary, experimental phase, the issue was already becoming strongly politicized. Both the partisans and the opponents of the project were mobilized: the former with the intention of proving that the reform would work, the latter in the hope that either it would fail or its impact could be restricted so that it would not challenge the power monopoly of the party. At the close of 1966, however, there was not much opportunity for either side to establish the cogency of their respective positions. The discussion, more or less a theoretical one, on the merits and the disadvantages of the new model continued. This discussion was by no means a detached academic exchange of opinions, but a rather animated confrontation in which the proponents often accused their adversaries of dogmatism and the critics charged the proponents with revisionism. One typical objection to the new system of management raised by the opponents was that it amounted to reconstitution of capitalism without capitalists. The heat of the debate indicated how alarmed the party establishment was about its possible loss of control over the economy as a result of the reform.

The End of Novotný's Rule

Nonconformism in economic thought of the second half of the 1960s was paralleled, as we have seen, by ideological deviance in other areas, especially in the arts and in literature. The events of 1967 appreciably deepened the conflict between the party guardians of doctrinal purity and the dissenting intellectuals. The Czechoslovak public had for a long time watched with mistrust and disapproval the uncompromising support given by the party and the government to Soviet policies in the Near East, especially to the hard Soviet line on Israel. Although the official Czechoslovak position in these matters was but one of many instances of blind obedience to Moscow, this issue was more sensitive than any other. Some of the pronouncements of the regime's spokesmen about Israel uncomfortably resembled the Nazi vocabulary and arsenal of arguments. They recalled the shattering memories of not-so-distant history, the German occupation and the "anti-Zionist" tenor of the political trials of the 1950s. Except in the most backward areas of the Slovak countryside, anti-Semitism had never had much currency in Czechoslovakia. On the contrary, the rejection of racial prejudice had a long tradition among the Czechs. The official comment on the Near East developments slavishly echoing the Soviet views irritated the cultural and intellectual elite, but the government position on the Six Days War in 1967 brought things to a head.

By coincidence, the Fourth Congress of the Union of Czechoslovak Writers took place only three weeks after the military operations. All conventions of Czechoslovak writers had the reputation of also being platforms of political criticism. This time, the mood was near the boiling point. Prior to the congress, some purely internal subjects of controversy had already created considerable tension between the writers' union and the party leadership: for example, the new press law, which the writers perceived as a new subtle form of censorship. When the congress opened, on June 27, 1967, the speakers condemned, among other things, Czechoslovakia's unreserved endorsement of the Soviet stand on the Near East conflict, especially the zeal with which the Czechoslovak government had met Moscow's request to break off diplomatic relations with Israel.[19] They pointed to the example of Rumania, which showed that a Soviet ally could adopt a different course. Above all, however, they protested against the thinly veiled anti-Semitic propaganda contained in the official reports on the Six Days War and in the statements of the Ministry of Foreign Affairs.

In the eyes of the party leaders, this amounted to political mutiny. The situation was aggravated by the fact that some newspapers and other mass media carried the controversial views aired at the writers' congress even though the party did not want these publicized. The most outspoken critics of the regime among the union members even used the foreign press to voice their opinions. Thus, for instance, Ludvík Vaculík published an article in the Swiss weekly *Die Weltwoche* in which he made West European audiences familiar with the aspirations of Czechoslovak intellectuals to independence and free expression.[20] One of the young Slovak novelists who for a long time had enjoyed the protection of the party leadership, Ladislav Mňačko, protested in the West German daily *Frankfurter Allgemeine Zeitung* against anti-Semitism in the party and the government, and went to Israel as an exile.[21] Novotný realized that he had to curb this movement before it got completely out of control. The nonconformism of the writers set a dangerous example. On September 3, 1967, the *Sunday Telegraph* of London printed a "Manifesto of Czechoslovak Writers" complaining of Communist party interference in all creative activities and calling for moral support of Czechoslovak novelists and poets in their plight. The police succeeded in identifying and arresting the author of the manifesto, historian Ivan Pfaff. An energetic response to all these manifestations of disobedience appeared indispensable if the CPCS leadership was to retain its authority.

All things considered, this was not the most propitious time for Novotný and his associates to wage a major battle against the intellectual opposition. At the same time, they had to repel the attacks from the Slovak nationalists. In 1967 the relations between the first secretary of the CPCS and the majority of the leaders of the CPS were worse than ever. The unresolved issue of the party rehabilitation and reintegration of the bourgeois nationalists continued to poison the political atmosphere. Voices from completely different quarters criticizing the poor performance of the regime in the economy further added to the problem. It was obvious that the anti-Novotný coalition of intellectuals, Slovak autonomists, and unorthodox economists ("the triple alliance") could be rendered harmless only by a simultaneous move against all three groups. A successful showdown of this kind required a solid unity at the center of the party and full support from the Soviet leadership in case a serious crisis developed. Novotný hoped that he could count on Brezhnev's backing in view of the spotless record of obedience to the will of the Kremlin his team had established, especially in matters of foreign policy and those concerning the international Communist movement. It was precisely the year 1967 that saw the CPCS hosting an important meeting of European Communist parties in Karlovy Vary, at which problems of European security were discussed. However, subsequent events showed that Soviet interest in the Czechoslovak party was not vested in any particular leadership group or person, not even in Antonín Novotný.

The counterattack against the triple alliance began with a sharp invective against the writers by Novotný on June 30, 1967, in his speech in the Political Academy of the Central Committee. Punitive measures against the writers' union followed. Its main organ, *Literární listy*, was subordinated to the jurisdiction of the Ministry of Culture, and the Writers' Fund, a symbol of the union's independence and the source from which publications of the members were subsidized, became subject to governmental supervision. The most outspoken critics of the regime among the participants of the fourth writers congress were expelled from the party. In an obvious allusion to the dissent among the intellectuals, Novotný in his address to the graduates of the Military Academy in Prague on September 1, 1967, declared that "some individuals do not seem to realize that our democracy is a class democracy and that, as well, our freedom is a class freedom."[22] It did not seem to disturb the first secretary that this statement contradicted the final resolution of the Thirteenth Party Congress, which had defined the dictatorship of the proletariat as a thing of the past. His position was supported by the Presidium member and chief party ideologist Jiří Hendrych, who at the celebration of the hundredth anniversary of the birth of poet Petr Bezruč in Opava on September 6 warned the writers that the party would not tolerate any liberal tendencies in Czechoslovak cultural life.

Right after this first round of Novotný's counteroffensive, however, the first complications arose. The Central Committee, which on the whole endorsed the disciplinary measures requested by the first secretary against the recalcitrant writers, showed some reluctance to take further, more radical steps to restore the undisputed control of the party over intellectual and cultural life. Members attending its plenary session, held on September 26 and 27, 1967, felt particularly uneasy about Novotný's recent violent attack on Slovak comrades for their alleged petty-bourgeois nationalism. The attack was felt to lack good taste since it had been made on Slovak soil, on the centenary of Matica Slovenská, a cultural organization that had played an important role in the Slovak struggle for national liberation. It appeared that the Central Committee would not unreservedly back Novotný's general action against his adversaries even if he were able to conduct it on all fronts at the same time. The session also dealt with other delicate issues, such as economic shortages, and this further complicated Novotný's situation since the responsibility for these difficulties was automatically given to him as the head of the party executive. The deliberations ended with these issues unresolved, and they were referred to the next plenary meeting.

The following Central Committee plenum convened on October 30 and 31, 1967. It turned out to be even more eventful than the preceding session. A main point on its agenda was the draft of a document "Theses about the Tasks of the Party in the Present Phase of the Development of Our Socialist Society," which was submitted by the first secretary. The draft contained a number of Novotný's personal views on the current state of the party and echoed many of his invectives against the intellectuals and the Slovak nationalists. Negative remarks about the latter provoked a vehement response from the Slovak members of the Central Committee and the Presidium. A stormy exchange between the first secretary and his Slovak counterpart, Alexander Dubček, ensued. In this controversy a great number of Czech Communists supported Dubček. This was an alarming discovery for Novotný, especially when it became clear that the Czech majority was receptive to a proposal from Slovak quarters to separate the two supreme functions in the state and in the party, which was aimed at eliminating Novotný either as first CPCS secretary or as president of the republic. Of the two offices, the former was the most significant in the power structure, but the function of the president was also very influential in the Czechoslovak political tradition. Whichever the Central Committee chose, the result would be a perceptible reduction in Novotný's power.

Novotný recognized the gravity of the situation and decided to neutralize the domestic opposition with the help of his Soviet protectors. The way he chose to demonstrate the support he believed he enjoyed in Moscow was not very subtle, however, and the maneuver backfired. Without previously informing his colleagues, Novotný invited the Soviet party boss, Leonid Brezhnev, to Prague and asked him to participate in the session of the party Presidium on December 9, 1967. The unexpected appearance of the prominent guest elicited mixed feelings in many party leaders, but failed to have the effect Novotný had anticipated. Brezhnev refused to give any explicit endorsement to his Czechoslovak counterpart or to take sides in the internal conflict of the CPCS. His reluctance to back Novotný might have been due partly to his unpleasant memory of the hostile reaction of the Czechoslovak party leadership to the demotion of Nikita Khrushchev in October 1964. At that time the Czech reaction had been understood in Moscow to mean that Novotný and his associates had not welcomed the arrival to power of the Brezhnev-Kosygin team.

After the unsuccessful attempt at mobilizing Soviet support for his personal cause, Novotný became more isolated than ever. At the plenary session of the Central Committee beginning December 18, 1967, he had to consent, after three days of stubbornly resisting, to a temporary solution of the "function cumulation problem" whereby the next Central Committee plenum would decide which of his two top offices Novotný would be allowed to retain. A major change was in the making. From hindsight, it may appear a unique coincidence that the December 1967 session of the Central Committee, which prepared the agenda for the historic meeting of January 1968, dealt also with the Soviet project of an international consultative conference of Communist and workers' parties to be held in Budapest in February, and unanimously approved the Soviet initiative. Few could have suspected that one of the major issues that would occupy this conference, and half a dozen other Communist summits, would be developments within the CPCS.

Novotný, a shrewd party apparatchik with unparalleled experience of intrigue, was perfectly aware of what awaited him at the Central Committee plenum called for January 3, 1968. He knew that unless he succeeded in turning the tide, the loss of either of the two key posts he had held for so long in the party and in the state would be but the first step toward his complete ouster. A reversal of his bad fortune, however, was difficult to achieve. He had become, in the eyes of many of his comrades, a major obstacle to any reasonable arrangement of relations between the Czechs and the Slovaks. His feud with the intellectuals, after the action against the spokesmen of the Fourth Writers' Congress, was beyond conciliation. The support he lent to the opponents of the economic reform irritated the majority of industrial management experts. And the "unassimilated past" in which his name was connected with the political trials of the 1950s estranged him from most younger party leaders, even from those he himself had favored and placed in positions of influence. Only an impressive display, if not an actual use, of force, Novotný thought, could save him from the fate of the members of the Old Guard whom he had sacrificed four years earlier. The absence of the most important ingredient of such a display, implicit or, even better, explicit Soviet support, did not make his prospects very hopeful, but Novotný nevertheless attempted a last stand. In his capacity as president of the republic and supreme commander of the armed forces, he approached some officers of the army general staff with the request to prepare a military demonstration, a kind of march on Prague of the armored units, on the eve of the Central Committee plenum. The response was not enthusiastic; the officers did not wish to be involved in internal party struggles. In 1948, through its inactivity, the army had sealed the fate of the pluralistic political system. Twenty years later, by failing to act, it helped to overthrow the most prominent conservative of the CPCS leadership and contributed to a temporary eclipse of the regime as it had been known since the February coup.

Novotný's desperate act not only failed; it worsened the situation of the first secretary still further. The suspicious role in the abortive plot of Lieutenant-General Jan Šejna, the Czechosovak liaison officer to the headquarters of the Warsaw Pact, which has never been fully elucidated and which became even more mysterious after this officer had defected to the West, seriously harmed Novotný's reputation. Now even an orderly and dignified retreat from glory seemed denied to him. The discussion about Novotný in the January 1968 session of the Central Committee was very lively. On the third day of the meeting, January 5, the Central Committee made a decision whose consequences might not have been evident to all members concerned. It relieved Novotný of the post of first secretary, the office he had held unchallenged for more than fifteen years. His successor became the Slovak party secretary, Alexander Dubček.

Chapter Ten

Spring Without Summer

Socialism with a Human Face

Many observers assessing the change in the CPCS leadership carried out by the Central Committee plenum of January 5, 1968, drew the logical conclusion that the change reflected a victory of the Slovak autonomists over the Czech centralists represented by Novotný and what was left of the Old Guard. This was one aspect of that event, but certainly not the only one. Several groups and segments, each for its own reasons, had been involved in the struggle against Novotný, had contributed in various ways to his eventual fall, and had considered themselves, each on its own specific grounds, to be the victors. In spite of a great heterogeneity, they all had had a common stake in the confrontation: all had felt a long time that a major policy change was necessary and realized that there was no hope for any such change as long as Novotný remained in control. Therefore, when the office of the first secretary passed into the hands of Alexander Dubček, the party was filled with great expectations. It was also evident that the various interest and power groups would now press for a speedy realization of their specific goals. The gradual process of eliminating Novotný and his associates from the top positions continued to divert the energies of their opponents for some time; but when it was accomplished and Novotný had also lost the offices of president of the republic and chairman of the National Front, the attention of the individual components of the anti-Novotný coalition turned in new directions. On March 30, 1968, the National Assembly elected the former minister of defense, Army General Ludvík Svoboda, to the chief executive post in the state. The subsequent expulsion of Novotný from the Central Committee and the suspension of his party membership passed almost unnoticed amidst many important personal and policy changes that followed each other at a rapid pace. The elements identified as conservative were in retreat; the reformists were advancing. The brief but eventful period later referred to as the Prague Spring had set in.

The Dubček Leadership's Broadened Base of Support

As had become manifest already in the months preceding January 1968, reformists of various backgrounds were in the majority among the party cadres. This majority, however, was not overwhelming. In view of the magnitude of the problems to be solved and of the delicate international situation of the Czechoslovak Communist movement, a broader basis of support for the new regime appeared necessary. To unite in favor of the reforms all the forces that once had fought Novotný's political immobility, a common positive program was indispensable. It was also important to convert to the cause of the reform the nonnegligible membership segment known as the centrists, or at least to ensure their tacit approval. Last but not least, there was the challenging opportunity to awaken the interest of the non-Communist public in the liberal policies of the Dubček team. The task before the new leadership, therefore, was to develop a policy line that would appeal to all three categories. It seemed that Dubček and his collaborators were fortunate in hitting upon the right course relatively early. The public at large had received the news about Novotný's demotion with a certain surprise, but not much excitement, although the former first secretary had been generally disliked in non-Communist circles and his name had been associated with a number of unpopular measures, such as the monetary reform of 1953. Initially, the changes in the CPCS leadership had been viewed as a more or less internal Communist affair. This detached attitude, however, did not persist for long.

On January 30, 1968, a group of 175 party members with active records dating from the prewar period, among them several prominent victims of Stalinist justice such as Marie Švermová and Josef Pavel, submitted a memorandum to the new first secretary calling upon him to create "a climate of mutual trust in which every communist will be able to freely express his views."[1] It was still freedom for the privileged only that the memorandum demanded; yet the action the new leadership took in response to this petition was of immediate interest to every citizen, regardless of party affiliation. Meeting on March 4, 1968, the party Presidium issued several regulations concerning press and other mass communication media. Two of these regulations proved to be of great consequence. The Presidium abolished the decree of August 1966, which had assigned to the Central Publication Administration (CPA) the role of ideological supervisor over periodicals, radio, and television. No substitute agency was created in its place. Instead, the Presidium reminded the once all-powerful censorship authority to "strictly respect the spirit and the letter of the law."[2] This was a major change, since in the terms of the valid press law the individual editorial boards had been given relatively great autonomy: the editors-in-chief were responsible for the material to be published or released. Before January 1968, the systematic, and actually illegal, interference of the Central Publication Administration (CPA) had restricted this autonomy. The application of the letter of the law by the party Presidium therefore meant the abolition of preventive censorship, a move unheard of in the Communist world since the early days of the Bolshevik revolution. The new freedom of the press was underscored by the exemption of the CPA from the jurisdiction of the Ministry of the Interior—that is, the removal of matters concerning the mass media from police controls.

The effect upon the public and political life of the suspension of censorship was penetrating. The party press, and soon all the press in the country, profoundly changed the content and form of its publications as it took advantage of the reform. Subjects that hitherto had been considered too delicate to address, or even taboo, were now discussed quite openly: Stalin's crimes, the misuse of justice at the political trials, internal party disputes, and details of the Communist take-over of 1948, among many others. As for the official party press organs, it could be claimed that they began to show independence and a critical attitude previously unknown, greater even than in the conditions of objective freedom before 1948. It was not only the coverage of political topics in the mass media that changed, however. More balanced reporting on all aspects of social life—economic, cultural, and scientific—sharply contrasted with the previously politically biased presentations.

The end of preventive censorship alerted both the party rank and file and the non-Communist public that the January events had not merely been due to individual and group rivalries in the CPCS, but that they actually ushered in a new policy course. The previous indifferent attitude of the unorganized majority gave way to an interested wait-and-see position. Thus a first step was made toward a general political mobilization. There is every reason to believe that the success of this move greatly alarmed the Soviet power center and was one of the principal reasons for the later intervention. Not only was the idea of free media unpalatable to the Soviets, the leaders of the CPSU perceived it as an unpardonable heresy that the Dubček team had solicited support outside the party framework and thereby indicated that it was prepared to share the established monopoly of power with the non-Communist majority of the population.

Another element in the strategy of the new party leadership in its efforts to secure the liberalization course from the danger of a reversal was the attempt gradually to eliminate conservative officials. The conservatives were not expelled, purged, or liquidated in any way known in the Stalinist era, but rather exposed to pressures from grass-roots organizations. These pressures were often very effective, and led to a number of resignations on the part of the opponents of the new line. Changes in the executive organs of the intermediate and lower party units—regional, district, and local—were usually carried out by specially convened conferences. The resignations appreciably weakened the conservative faction among the elected party functionaries, but the conservatives nevertheless maintained a sizable percentage among the workers of the party apparatus. Further organizational measures appeared necessary if this opposition was to be reduced and if the reforms planned by the Dubček group were to be implemented with sufficiently strong support. One rather subtle measure was built into a recommendation by a new Central Committee commission, the third in succession, that was charged with the investigation of the political trials and chaired by the Presidium member Jan Piller. Reporting to the Central Committee plenum, which was in session from March 28 to April 5, 1968, the Piller commission proposed that no person who had held a seat in the Central Committee or in the Control and Revision Commission without interruption since the Ninth Ordinary Party Congress in 1949 should be nominated or elected into these two party governing organs. The Piller report further urged the Central Committee to recall immediately from all party posts all individuals who "actively participated in fabricating the political trials, and in the reassessments of 1955–1962."[3] The consequent implementation of these two principles would have dealt a decisive blow to the conservative wing and might have secured the reform work of the Dubček leadership had the Central Committee had the chance to act upon the recommendation, and had external forces not interfered with the liberalization process.

In view of the contemplated reform of the entire party constitution, however, the defeat of the Stalinists at the top level might not have solved all the problems of the reformists now at the helm. Ironically, the democratization of the party structure that Dubček and his associates desired, especially the increase in the autonomy and the powers of the party base, contained the risk that the surviving bastions of Stalinism might be stabilized rather than removed. Nationwide party elections seemed to be the only way to make sure that the cleansing process would effectively reach the grass-roots units. Such elections could be best organized in the wake of an extraordinary party congress. The idea of convoking such a congress emerged in the early phase of the Prague Spring and soon took concrete shape. There seemed to be strong pressure from the lower-level party organizations to hold the congress as soon as possible. A passage in Dubček's speech at the Central Committee plenum on April 1 indicated that the leadership was aware of the pressure, but also of the necessity of carefully preparing the agenda before the congress could be scheduled. Officially, the Extraordinary (Fourteenth) Congress of the CPCS was called by the decision of the Central Committee of June 1, 1968. The various local, district, and regional conferences held in the late winter and spring were viewed as preliminaries to the congress, and the congress itself was to open on September 9.

The Action Program of 1968:
Blueprint for Democratization

Dubček and his associates were anxious to have the forthcoming meeting of the supreme party body endorse all the basic principles of liberalization or—as the party spokesmen and the media used to put it at that time— democratization. To this purpose it was essential that the policies be clearly formulated and thoroughly discussed at all levels far enough in advance of the congress. The leadership was confident that if its goals were fully known to the public, support would not fail to come from citizens in all walks of life. Later experience seemed to justify this expectation. The policies of the Dubček group were laid down in an important document approved by the plenary session of the Central Committee on April 5, 1968, titled "The Action Program of the

Communist Party of Czechoslovakia."⁴ Considering its extent and comprehensive nature, the Action Program had no precedent in the history of the CPCS or, for that matter, in the history of the entire world Communist movement. Its publication within a relatively short time after the January 1968 events was made possible by impressive groundwork accomplished during the last years of the Novotný regime by several groups of experts recruited mostly from the unorthodox young party élite.

Although the authors of the Action Program pursued their discussions and research prior to the Prague Spring, they did not know that they were helping to speed up the most dramatic crisis of the Communist system. Their objectives were the same as those of the more visible and articulate liberal opposition: new, more solid economic, political, and cultural foundations for a system that was increasingly failing to cope with the challenges of modern times. As Nikita Khrushchev had intuitively recognized in the 1950s, the non-Communist party intellectuals in Czechoslovakia in the 1960s concluded after a thorough analysis of the situation that a modern industrial society cannot operate on the purely coercive basis provided by the Stalinist type of communism. If Stalinism failed in the Soviet Union, they reasoned, it was even less suitable for Czechoslovakia, considering the incomparably higher level of economic and societal development in the latter. To overcome the difficulties of the system required, in their opinion, a radical departure from the policies advocated and practiced by the regime prior to January 1968, since these policies had been based on the discredited Stalinist principles.

On the other hand, the promoters of the reform who contributed to the formulation of the Action Program remained committed to the pattern of power distribution characteristic of a Communist party-state, with the monopoly of political initiative and decision making vested in the CPCS. They neither desired, nor considered as a realistic alternative, a change in this monopoly position of the party. This set fairly narrow limits to the range of solutions they could offer and created a number of dilemmas. Strictly speaking, their objective was a kind of a contradiction in terms: they wished to counteract the noxious impact of the totalitarian state upon the society while maintaining the totalitarian state intact. Implicitly, and sometimes explicitly, they shared the view of many Western social scientists that pluralism and participation were essential to the successful functioning of modern nations. But the task they had set for themselves consisted of bringing about the benefits of pluralism and ensuring wider participation within a framework that was the very negation of both principles.

The Action Program of the CPCS of April 1968 bore clear marks of all these dilemmas. Nevertheless, some of the solutions to the complicated political, economic, and cultural problems suggested by the document were original and highly interesting. They were the basic elements of what was later known as the Czechoslovak Model of Socialism, in the gallery of Communist polycentrism. Although sometimes labeled by the Czechoslovak Communist intellectuals themselves an attempt at "squaring the circle," the Czechoslovak model ranks in theoretical importance with other alternatives to the Soviet type of socio-economic system that have had better chances for application, for example, the Yugoslav and the Chinese models. It was as comprehensive as its counterparts, and sometimes even more so since it proposed solutions in all major areas of social life. It was indeed a blueprint for the restructuring of the whole society.

The Action Program contained all the principal elements of the Czechoslovak model, albeit in a rudimentary form. It focused on the individual goals that were to be achieved by the reform: the problems to be solved rather than the theoretical underpinnings of the reform or the technicalities of the solutions. The program was divided into four main parts. The most important issue was addressed in the first section, where the need for a "new system for the political management of society" was acknowledged. This was the most daring criticism of the prevailing order ever undertaken in a Communist country. It was in this area that the squaring of the circle was attempted. The solutions here proposed were the fruit of the work of a semi-official ad-hoc group of young theoreticians who had studied the problem under the leadership of Zdeněk Mlynář, during the last two years of Novotný leadership, and who identified themselves as the "Interdisciplinary Research Team to Study the Social and Human Context of the Scientific-Technical Revolution." Although the task of constructing a model of socialist democracy while preserving the one-party system was a superhuman one, the theoreticians exploited with great skill and imagination the extremely narrow room left to them. Of course, they could not work miracles. The weakness of the proposed new system of political management was not in the quality of theoretical analysis, but in the paucity of institutional mechanisms that were to guarantee the satisfactory performance of the system. Despite the commitment to classical principles of democracy, such as the legitimacy of alternative opinions and policy initiatives, no channels were identified in the Action Program through which this free market of ideas was to operate. The only concrete reference along those lines was to the recently restored freedom of the press. It seemed as if the ideologists of the Prague Spring had expected the various shades of opinion represented in the mass media to simulate the opposition in the new socialist democracy. If the media did not meet this expectation, it was not because of the unwillingness of the journalists. The latter were fully aware of their responsibilities, and were prone to overestimate rather than underestimate their own influence. The reason was a simple law of politics: the mere opportunity to express various opinions cannot be a substitute for organized interests capable of lending clout to these opinions. It is only in a pluralist order that organized interests can be properly articulated.

As genuine pluralism was out of the question, the only open avenue of change was that of the reform of the party itself. The Action Program, and even more the final report of the interdisciplinary research team published in June 1968, indicate that the proponents of the reform realized this necessity. They called not only for the democratization of the political system, but also for a revision of the party's power structure. In entering upon this path, however, they were confronted with the historical dilemma Lenin faced during the first years after the October Revolution. How much internal democracy can be afforded by a party that claims a monopoly of power over the society? Can it survive as an island of pluralism in the totalitarian sea of its own creation? Lenin tried to resolve this problem through the formula of democratic centralism: initiative from the top, comments and criticism from the lower levels, discontinuation of the discussion after a majority vote has been taken, and a strict ban on the formation of permanent groupings, proscribed as factions. We know that the recipe had not always worked under Lenin himself and that it actually paved the way for Stalinism, the most despotic personal power ever known.

The Czechoslovak reformers proposed another solution to this dilemma, although the principle of democratic centralism continued to be involved, even under Dubček, as the foundation of socialist democracy. Some important elements of this solution were included in a memorandum of the interdisciplinary research team of June 28, 1968. It was argued there, in the section on the "Humane Mission of the Party," that the minority "must be given the right to strive, before the eyes of the whole party, to become a majority." What is needed is not unanimity on all points and at any price, continued the memorandum, but the capacity to act in a given situation. The Action Program stated, in more general terms, "the right of every Communist to act according to his conscience, with initiative and criticism," and saw it not only as a right, but also as a duty of those holding different views on the matter in question "to oppose any party functionary."

Precisely how far the party was willing to go in this direction is difficult to say. An indication may be found in a draft of party statutes made public by *Rudé právo* on August 10, 1968.[5] The draft addresses the topic of democratic centralism in the very first paragraph. It specifies, among other things, that the principle of democratic centralism requires "the entire system of leading and controlling officials to be built from the base upwards, through elections, evaluation and supervision by the membership body." The implementation of this principle would have meant a radical change in the practice of delegating representatives to party congresses and conferences, filling the executive posts, and conducting daily party business—in brief, a departure from the practices used since the end of the Second World War or even since the bolshevization of 1929. Another sign of a changed image of the party as an association, produced by the reform movement, was the stress in the draft statutes upon the voluntary nature of party affiliation. The statutes provided for a voluntary loss of party membership or resignation. This was an unusual provision in the rules of a Communist party. The Communist movement on the whole had always rejected the notion of membership as a commitment revocable by individual decision. The orthodox party spokesmen derided such regulations as suitable for a dovecote, not for a socialist party, insisting that to be a Communist was a pledge for life that could be terminated only upon the member's failure, that is, by expulsion. The introduction in 1968 of the notion that party members were free to join and free to leave underscored the sovereignty of the grassroots units and the will of the reform leaders to make the CPCS more democratic. This modification of the statutes has never been carried into effect, any more than the principles of building the party "from the base upwards" have. Both proposals became casualties of the so-called normalization course imposed upon the CPCS after the Soviet-led military intervention. The efforts at the democratization of the party structure might even have been one of the elements in the decision of the Soviet power center to use force in Czechoslovakia; the deviations from the established practices of party governance were significant, and alarming enough in the eyes of the Kremlin to justify this decision.

The Democratization Experiment Threatened

Reading the Action Program of the CPCS and other major documents published during the Prague Spring, an observer could acquire a fairly accurate idea of the liberal leadership's objectives, its order of priorities, and the timetable it planned to follow. The leaders contemplated ambitious goals in areas pertaining to human and civil rights, economic management, and culture. Taken as a whole, the reforms represented a new model of the entire society. It was also easy to see that among the various reform goals the leaders put the main emphasis upon the restoration of the consitutional rights of citizens, full rehabilitation of the victims of political justice, and improvement of the methods of industrial management. The date set for the Fourteenth Party Congress, September 9, 1968, played an important role in the working calendar of the Dubček team. By the time the congress was to open, the liberal leaders hoped to have initiated the most urgent measures of their program. The supreme gathering of the party was then to provide the endorsement of the general line of democratization and to elect new executive bodies cleansed of conservative elements. This was to facilitate the implementation of the reforms that would still be pending at that point.

For the adversaries of the new course, too, the date of the congress was crucial. They realized that if the reform trend were not reversed by then, the chances of restoring the pre-January line would be less than ever. Dubček's opponents in the USSR and other Communist countries reasoned similarly. Unfortunately for the reform movement in Czechoslovakia, most Communist parties and governments in Central and Eastern Europe began, soon after the change in the CPCS leadership, to perceive the liberalization course as a threat. The East German regime was the first to sound the alarm. Its own deeply conservative, Stalinist orientation and the geographical proximity of Czechoslovakia gave it sufficient grounds for concern. Relaxation in Czechoslovakia, both internal and external, could nullify the effect of the formidable border barriers between the two Germanies and of the Berlin Wall. When in the late spring of 1968 the Czechoslovak border police began to remove the barbed wire fences along the Bavarian border, there seemed to be a real danger, since the border between Czechoslovakia and East Germany was not fortified, that Czechoslovakia might become a halfway house on a new mass escape route from the German Democratic Republic (GDR) to the West.

The position of the remaining two Communist neighbors of Czechoslovakia, Poland and Hungary, on the democratization policies of the Dubček regime was more balanced than that of the GDR. The attitude of the Hungarian Communists was one of reserved sympathy mixed with fear lest the Czechoslovak experiment get out of control and invite Soviet reaction. Such reaction, in the opinion of the Hungarian party leaders, would necessarily be a general stiffening of Soviet policies toward all satellites, and thus would threaten the recently introduced program of economic reforms in Hungary. The stand of Bulgaria, as the most loyal Soviet ally, was fairly predictable, and it was equally safe to assume that the Rumanian Communist party would abstain from any public assessment of the Czechoslovak reform program, and from any act of censure, ideological, diplomatic, or otherwise, against Czechoslovakia.

The Soviet leadership soon became uneasy about the developments in Czechoslovakia. The Soviet attitude was a disappointment to Dubček, who believed that he had received from Brezhnev himself tacit but unmistakable approval of the new course when the Soviet party boss had demonstrated his indifference to Novotný's fate at the height of the crisis, in December 1967. The Czechoslovak reformers read the CPSU's passive stand as a sign of acquiescence in the liberalization movement that Novotný's fall had released. It proved to be largely wishful thinking. On the whole, the team that had succeeded Khrushchev in the Kremlin was rather conservative, certainly more circumspect than the dynamic first secretary with whose name the idea of destalinization had been associated. In the spring of 1968, Brezhnev and his associates had been in control for more than three years. They did not seem to be inclined to take many chances at home or abroad: after all, one of the reasons they had replaced Khrushchev in 1964 was his penchant for taking too many risks.

Dislike of what the Brezhnev group perceived as political adventurism might not have been the only determinant of this group's mistrust of the Prague Spring. A more subtle reason, and one that is more significant to a historian, was the recurrent charge voiced by Soviet leaders and their media that the Czechoslovak party had renounced, or was just about to renounce, its guiding role in society. The charge may sound curious in the light of the fact that the power monopoly of the party was the only requisite of the pre-January regime that the reforms introduced by Dubček had left entirely intact. However, the Soviet spokesmen claimed that there was evidence to support their charge. The so-called Soviet White Book published after the August invasion summed up this evidence in two or three major points. It attributed special significance to the establishment and activities in the post-January period of two voluntary non-Communist organizations: the Club 231 and the Club of Politically Engaged Nonpartisans. The former was set up March 31, 1968, as an interest group of the victims of political justice. The figure 231 denoted the paragraph of the penal code according to which the defendants of the political trials, non-Communists as well as Communist party members, had been sentenced. The Club 231 did not pretend to be a political organization, let alone a political party, as the Soviet commentators claimed; one of its stated goals was to help create a political order in which the misuse of justice for political purposes would not be possible. It seems that the Soviet critics were not so much alarmed by what the Club 231 said or published about the political trials of the 1950s—after all, the Czechoslovak media, free from censorship, were often more outspoken on this subject than the members of the club—but rather by its potential role as an organizational platform for political opposition. For the same reason, they found objectionable the Club of Politically Engaged Nonpartisans, which was founded in June 1968. The political character of this second body was more pronounced than that of the Club 231, but "KAN," as it was called by the press (an abbreviation of the Czech name Klub angažovaných nestraníků) was still far from a political party; in fact it was little more than a dynamic discussion group composed of individuals of all shades of opinion. Of the two clubs, KAN, at least in theory, seemed more likely to challenge the leading role of the Communist party.

The Soviet observers' apprehension about the activities of the voluntary organizations outside the framework of the CPCS and the relaxed attitude of the Dubček leadership to these organizations was an indication of the different ways the Moscow power center and the Czechoslovak Communists interpreted the concept of the leading role. To the Soviets, the leading role of the party meant a monopoly of political initiative and tight control over all sectors of public life. The reformist leadership in the CPCS, however, felt that it should be something more subtle than "a monopolistic concentration of powers in the hands of party bodies." It believed, as it expressed in the Action Program, that "the party's goal is not to become a universal 'caretaker' of society, to bind all organizations and every step taken in life by its directives." In short, the party was "to lead, not to command."[6] The abolition of the "cadre ceiling" and of the famous "nomenclature" (a principle requiring party membership as the condition for assuming positions and entering occupations above a certain level of authority), which the Action Program called for, testified to the Dubček team's intention to translate the new image of the party role into everyday practice. It also might have reinforced the fears and suspicions of the Soviet decision makers.

It is difficult to tell with certainty whether the associations outside the CPCS system would have evolved into full-fledged political parties if the democratization trend in Czechoslovakia had been allowed to take a free course. The closest developments during the Prague Spring came to this point was the constitution, in July 1968, of an "Action Council of the Social Democratic Workers Party." The actual support of this body among the public cannot be estimated accurately, but the intention in this case was clear and explicit. Considered separately, this initiative seemed to substantiate the fears expressed by Dubček's critics in the neighboring Communist countries that the party was gradually losing its grip on the society. On the whole, however, such concerns about the situation in Czechoslovakia in the summer of 1968 were in many respects exaggerated. It is not easy to guess, of course, what turn events would eventually have taken if the Extraordinary Party Congress had been allowed to take place as originally scheduled. The endorsement of the post-January policies by the party's supreme organ and the elimination of the opponents of these policies could have had a stabilizing effect upon the party, which then could actually have asserted its leading role, possibly with the support or acquiescence of the public. On the other hand, it could have speeded up the rate of change and made it increasingly difficult for the leadership to cope with the situation. Uncertainty about the outcome of the congress might have been among the factors that ultimately prompted Soviet action.

The Dialogue of the Deaf

The situation in Czechoslovakia before the dramatic events of August 1968 was the topic of a number of bilateral and multilateral consultations among the ruling Communist parties of Europe. The first international meeting of this series was initiated by the leadership of the United

Socialist Party of East Germany. The events that stimulated this initiative were probably the resignation of Antonín Novotný from the office of president of the republic and the suspension of preventive censorship by the party Presidium on March 4; these must have convinced the East German observers in Prague of the serious nature of the ongoing change. The meeting was called for March 23, 1968, on relatively short notice, in the Saxon capital of Dresden. Although the real purpose of the talks was not officially spelled out—the communiqué spoke only of "consultations on urgent questions of political and economic development and cooperation"—commentators in both the East and the West as well as the Czechoslovak public knew very well what was to be discussed.[7] The choice of the conference site was ironic: it had been in Dresden, forty-seven years earlier, that the emissaries of the Komintern had successfully exerted pressure on the leaders of the Czechoslovak socialist left to make them join the Third International as the CPCS. The 1968 talks in Dresden, in which all the Communist parties of the Soviet bloc except Rumania took part, did not attain their objective. The confidence expressed in the final resolution that the "working class and all working people of Czechoslovakia will ensure, under the leadership of the CPCS, further development of socialism in their country"[8] only poorly papered over the growing differences of opinion on many crucial questions between the CPCS and most of its East European counterparts.

The Czechoslovak delegation in Dresden was no more impressed by the arguments of the representatives of the fraternal parties than these latter were convinced by the arguments of their Czechoslovak comrades. The democratization trend in Czechoslovakia continued on its course. The plenary session of the Central Committee held from March 27 to April 5, the longest meeting of its kind in the history of the party, made a number of important decisions, among them the adoption of the aforementioned Action Program. It reconstructed the party Presidium, to the further detriment of the conservative group, and proposed changes in the composition of the government that were made necessary by the election of Ludvík Svoboda to the office of president of the republic. These changes, too, signified the retreat of the conservative forces from influential positions both in the state and in the party. Amidst these signs of advancing liberalization, a delegation of the CPCS headed by Alexander Dubček traveled to Moscow on May 4 to hold talks with the Soviet leaders. This time, the official communiqué was more explicit than in Dresden: it stated that the consultations took place upon the invitation of the Central Committee of the CPSU and the Soviet government, and was to serve as "an exchange of views on the situation in both countries and on the activities of the CPSU and the CPCS."[9] It is unlikely that the apprehensions of the Soviet power holders about developments in Czechoslovakia were greatly lessened as a consequence of these talks.

Shortly after the return of the Czechoslovak party delegation from Moscow, a Soviet military mission arrived in Czechoslovakia to negotiate army exercises of the troops of the Warsaw Pact on Czechoslovak territory. The negotiations lasted six days. No one who was even superficially informed about the current situation could fail to see the political significance of the planned troop movements. As if inspired by the impact of this rather alarming news, *Rudé právo* carried an editorial on May 17 in which it called for "an independent Czechoslovak road to Socialism." The subsequent events in the party suggested that no brake had been applied to the liberalization process in response to Soviet criticism and apprehensions. The plenary session of the Central Committee held from May 25 to June 1 approved the full rehabilitation of the victims of Stalinist justice recommended by the Piller commission, and fixed the opening date of the Fourteenth (Extraordinary) Party Congress. Changes were effected in various party functions that gave the liberals a new opportunity to make inroads into the executive and party apparatus. The constitutional reform introducing the federative principle into the Czechoslovak political system was approved. The Dubček team was moving ahead according to its timetable.

On June 27, 1968, seventy leading personalities of intellectual and cultural life published a "Manifesto of 2000 Words" in which the inconsistencies of the liberalization process and the slow elimination of the dogmatic heritage were deplored.[10] This brief document received an extraordinary amount of attention in the Soviet and other East European Communist media and later played an important role in the justification of the August military intervention. In these media, the manifesto was equated with a "program for bourgeois-capitalist counterrevolution."[11] This charge, of course, cannot be taken seriously, but there was a passage in the manifesto that could have aroused specific fears in the Soviet Union and its allies about the direction of the whole democratization trend. The signatories regretted the unchanged monopoly power position of the Communist party in the state; in other words they rejected the party's leading role. In view of the fact that Czechoslovak authorities took no measures against the document's authors, save for mild criticism, and that the National Assembly formalized the earlier abolition of censorship by a law of June 26, the anxiety of the Communist neighbors of Czechoslovakia deepened. New initiatives were developed to contain the liberalization movement in Czechoslovakia.

In June, Soviet Politbureau member Alexei Kosygin stayed in the Czechoslovak health resort Karlovy Vary, allegedly to obtain a cure, but it was a public secret that he had met for informal talks with several prominent members of the CPCS. In July, it became known that the Communist parties of Bulgaria, East Germany, Hungary, Poland, and the Soviet Union had sent letters to the Central Committee of the Czechoslovak party in which they protested some specific measures taken by the Dubček leadership in the wake of democratization.[12] At that point the Czechoslovak public at large began to feel apprehensive about possible foreign interference. The risk of such intervention became salient when the Soviet troops that had participated in the June exercises of the Warsaw Pact armies in Czechoslovakia were not immediately withdrawn after the end of the maneuvers. It required a special diplomatic demarche in Moscow before these units were recalled from Czechoslovak territory.

A Settlement That Was None

The pressure on Czechoslovakia meanwhile increased. On July 11, an editorial of the Moscow *Pravda* compared the current Czechoslovak situation with that of Hungary in October 1956, on the eve of the national uprising and Soviet intervention.[13] The same day, five Communist parties of the Soviet bloc invited the Czechoslovak leaders to new consultations to be held in Warsaw on July 14 and 15. The Czechoslovak party declined the invitation and suggested instead bilateral talks with the individual party delegations to be held on Czechoslovak territory. The open letter of the five parties was answered by the CPCS Presidium on July 17.[14] The reply, calm and balanced, hardly carried any weight with those to whom it was addressed. Czechoslovakia's Warsaw Pact partners had already made up their minds, or had them made up by the Soviet Union, to put a stop to the Czechoslovak liberalization experiment. The conference in Poland took place without Czechoslovak representation, but this time the subject of the talks was quite openly indicated in the final communiqué: it was an exchange of opinions on the events in Czechoslovakia.[15] An open letter to the Central Committee of the CPCS, prepared at the Warsaw conference, went considerably farther than all the previous memoranda and recommendations of the fraternal parties. In quite unambiguous terms the letter stated that the internal affairs of one socialist country were legitimate objects of concern for all other socialist nations if they threatened the "achievements of Socialism" or the "interests of the international proletarian movement."[16] This was the essence of what later became known as the Brezhnev Doctrine. The letter also offered "all possible help to the working class of Czechoslovakia in its efforts to block the way to the reaction."

There could be little doubt after the Warsaw meeting that foreign intervention was a real possibility. The Dubček leadership did not seem to have many options for coping with such a contingency except for advancing the date of the Extraordinary Congress to demonstrate the will of the party's majority. Dubček and his colleagues may have hoped that an intervention, although technically feasible, would appear too costly to the Soviet Union in terms of international prestige, especially if the party congress established the extent of the support for democratization among the membership and the population. It was known in Prague that the Soviet leaders were very eager to bring about a new world conference of Communist and workers' parties, similar to the summits of 1957 and 1960, that would reconfirm their claim to the leadership of the international Communist movement and vindicate their position in the dispute with the People's Republic of China. The idea of the conference had made little progress toward realization during the second half of the 1960s. A consultative meeting held in Budapest in February and March 1968 failed to assemble the representatives of all key parties because of a continuing reluctance on the part of many Communists to be involved in the Sino-Soviet dispute. A forcible action against another Communist party or country was likely to worsen the international climate to the point of making a new conference impossible. Also, the signs were multiplying in the summer of 1968 that several Communist parties not under direct Soviet control were becoming concerned about a possible repetition in Czechoslovakia of the 1956 events in Hungary. This was especially true of the two largest West European parties, the Italian and the French.

Whereas the Italian Communists made no secret of their sympathies for the Czechoslovak liberalization experiment, the French party was more circumspect, but also more resourceful. The leadership of the Communist Party of France took concrete steps aimed at reconciling the

Soviet and Czechoslovak positions. Shortly after the Warsaw conference of the five Communist parties, the French Communist party's Politbureau approached the CPCS with a proposal for a European meeting of Communist parties to deal with the crisis. It was probable that if such a continent-wide conference of Communist parties could be convened, the atmosphere at it would be move favorable to the cause of the Czechoslovak reform movement than at gatherings where the CPCS was confronted with only the Soviet and other Soviet-obedient ruling European parties. However, the Czechoslovak leaders knew that precisely because of this circumstance the French initiative had little chance of being favorably received by the Soviet Union, the key partner in the controversy, and that Czechoslovak support of the proposal would only exacerbate the strained relations between Prague and Moscow. The party Presidium politely declined the French suggestion on July 22, hoping nevertheless that the obvious concern of the French and Italian comrades over Soviet-Czechoslovak relations would have a restraining effect upon the CPSU.[17]

In reply to the joint message of the five parties that had participated in the Warsaw conference of July 14 and 15, the Presidium pointed out that the meeting had been called in disregard of the clearly expressed opinion of the CPCS that no useful end could be served by such talks. It reminded the five parties that it had already recommended bilateral consultations with each interested party instead of large multinational conferences. The reply of the CPCS Presidium also contained a reference to the well-known and yet somewhat mysterious "Declaration of the Government of the USSR" of October 30, 1956, which had preceded the Soviet intervention in Hungary. The CPCS Presidium quoted a passage from this declaration that at the time of its first publication had been understood as a pledge by the USSR not to intervene in the internal affairs of Hungary, and expressed the somewhat wistful hope that the document was still valid in 1968. It also connected the declaration with a final communiqué of the first world conference of Communist and workers' parties in Moscow in November 1957, where the principle of "full equality of rights, full respect of territorial integrity, national independence and sovereignty" had been internationally endorsed.[18] Recalling these two documents and making a connection between them was a subtle move on the part of the Czechoslovak leadership, although the reference to the fall of 1956 might have evoked rather unpleasant associations in audiences familiar with recent European history.

It seemed for a short time that the views of the Czechoslovak party, as expressed in the reply to the five signatories of the open letter and endorsed by the Central Committee plenum on July 19, were receiving attention in the fraternal parties' headquarters. Shortly after the Central Committee plenum, it was announced that representatives of the CPCS would meet with the leaders of the Soviet party in the Slovak town Čierna nad Tisou, at the Soviet-Czechoslovak border, on July 29. The form of the meeting, a bilateral consultation, and the choice of the site, Czechoslovakia, seemed to correspond to the wishes expressed by the CPCS's governing bodies. On the other hand, certain news items appearing at that time in the press and on television did not exactly allay the fears of foreign interference. The Soviet troops, which had been withdrawn from Czechoslovak territory upon an urgent request of the the Czechoslovak government, were stationed in the immediate vicinity of Czechoslovakia. On July 23, the Soviet government made a formal proposal to the government in Prague that in view of "imminent danger from the West," permanent Soviet garrisons be set up along the Czechoslovak western frontier. Soviet military intervention thus remained a subject of speculation among political observers and commentators. The more optimistic of them, however, inferred that the military build-up was but a means of exerting pressure on the CPCS and that the Soviet side was as anxious to reach an acceptable compromise as its Czechoslovak counterpart. Public opinion therefore was turned to the border railway station of Čierna, where a special train carrying prominent members of the CPSU arrived on July 29, 1968. The Soviet delegation to the talks was impressive. Virtually the whole Politbureau came—a rare event in the history of the Soviet party, comparable only to the visit of Khrushchev and his associates to Warsaw at the height of the Polish October crisis of 1956. The Soviet turnout provoked some thought on the Czechoslovak side, which made an effort to match the rank of the Soviet guests by including in the CPCS delegation the president of the republic, Ludvík Svoboda. The talks lasted four days, until August 1, 1968. They were conducted in the carriages of the Soviet government train, an ingenious compromise by which both partners had their way: the meeting was held on Czechoslovak territory but on Soviet premises. In view of the length of the consultations, the joint final communiqué was surprisingly short. Moreover, it indicated no specific agreement, nor even an agreement in principle. It stated that "broad comradely exchange of opinions on problems interesting both parties . . .

had developed in an open and sincere climate of mutual under-standing."[19] This amounted to an admission, in diplomatic language, of failure to reach an understanding. The communiqué, however, an-nounced another impending multilateral consultation involving repre-sentatives of all five Communist parties, to open in the Slovak capital of Bratislava on August 3.

The Soviet delegation traveled to this meeting directly from Čierna, through Czechoslovak territory. It largely maintained its original compo-sition: only a few lesser personalities returned to the Soviet Union. The representations of the other four Communist parties were equal in rank to the Czechoslovak and Soviet delegations. Thus the Bratislava meeting became a seldom-seen parade of the highest statesmen of the world Communist leadership, a circumstance that only further emphasized the seriousness of the situation of the reformist cause. It has to be assumed that the talks in the Slovak capital city did not bring the sides any nearer than had the consultations at Čierna, considering that only one day was reserved for the entire agenda and no less than six large delegations were present. The closing communiqué was more eloquent but no more to the point. It stressed the agreement on "all problems of international politics," the willingness of the participants to "develop and strengthen their cooperation in economic matters," and their determination to fight "against imperialism and reaction, for European peace and security."[20] The topics that really mattered, namely, the internal problems of Czechoslovakia, were left out, obviously with the intention of concealing the lack of agreement.

The facts available at that time appeared inconclusive to many observers. It was possible to see the brief resolution of the Czechoslovak-Soviet meeting in Čierna and the verbose but empty communiqué of the Bratislava consultations either as a sign of resigned acceptance by the Soviets of the development in Czechoslovakia or as an ominous silence before a storm. The only extensive official comment was given by Alexander Dubček in his television speech on August 4. Dubček was optimistic. He described the results of Čierna as positive and affirmed that the consultations among the six Communist parties had been "equally successful and met our expectations."[21] Dubček also pointed out that the participants in the Bratislava meeting had approved only one document, the closing communiqué. This statement, which Dubček repeated once more during his TV address, was made presumably to dispel speculations about possible secret protocols. According to Dubček, the negotiations at Čierna had "acquired more room necessary for our socialist reform process." The only concrete restriction that Dubček mentioned as resulting from the Bratislava talks was the commitment, supposedly made by all parties, to discontinue public polemics; this agreement benefited Czechoslovakia more than its partners since it had long been the main target of attacks in the Soviet and East European media.

Chapter Eleven

History Returns as Farce

After the 1968 Soviet Military Intervention

It appeared to be business as usual after the Čierna and Bratislava meetings. Somewhat disquieting were the reports about new military exercises of the Warsaw Pact armies in East Germany, Poland, and Hungary, in areas very close to the Czechoslovak border. The Czechoslovak public was also aware that the question of permanent stationing of Soviet troops in Czechoslovakia, tabled by the Soviet government in July, still remained open. Nevertheless, some events during the first two weeks of August seemed to indicate that the leadership wished to stress the independence of the Czechoslovak party and national sovereignty. From August 9 to August 11, Yugoslav President Tito was an official guest in Prague. This was Tito's second visit to the Czechoslovak capital; the first was in 1946, during the period of conditioned pluralism. The enthusiastic reception Tito enjoyed this time was a tribute to the politician who had had the courage to resist Soviet claims to the tutelage of European Communist countries, and whose example the population wished to see emulated. There is little doubt that the message of the Czechoslovak welcome to Tito was duly monitored and understood in Moscow. The Soviets had to conclude that if the domestic forces in Czechoslovakia were given free rein, the reformist course, with all the grave risks the Soviet power center perceived in it, would continue unabated.

Another political event soon after Tito's trip to Prague was the visit to Czechoslovakia of the Rumanian Communist party boss, Nicolae Ceausescu, at the head of a large delegation, August 15–17, 1968. Rumania represented a rather conservative element among the Communist regimes of Central and Eastern Europe, more conservative in certain aspects than the Soviet Union. There was little affinity between the political line adopted by Dubček and that observed by his Rumanian counterpart. Nevertheless, for reasons of principle, the Rumanian Communist party took a stand favorable to the post-January leadership of the CPCS. As it rejected the right of any socialist country to impose its will on any other socialist nation, it also openly disagreed with the Soviet attempts to curb the liberalization movement in Czechoslovakia. From the very beginning of the Czechoslovak crisis, the Rumanian party abstained from the Soviet-sponsored initiatives aimed at reversing the prevailing course. Rumanian Communists did not participate in any of the conferences on Czechoslovakia called by the Soviet Union or its allies. As in the case of Yugoslavia, the popularity among Czechs and Slovaks of the Rumanian concern for independence and the sovereignty of smaller Communist states was reinforced by a tradition of friendship and alliance between Czechoslovakia and Rumania dating from the prewar period. Consequently, the three-day visit of the Rumanian party and government delegation in Prague turned out to be yet another demonstration of the Czechoslovak will to independence that was impossible for Moscow to ignore.

Considering that the Soviet leaders had from the beginning of the Czechoslovak liberalization process watched with apprehension the behavior of the unorganized Czechoslovak public, for fear that Dubček might eventually be swayed by the pressure of the non-Communist majority to surrender the leading role of the party, the goodwill occasioned by the Yugoslav and Rumanian state visits could not but cause alarm in the Kremlin. There were also other indications that the talks in July and August might not, after all, have put an end to the dispute between the CPCS and the five fraternal parties. It was difficult to understand, for example, why on August 12, barely a week after the Bratislava meeting, a large delegation from the United Socialist party of Germany, led by Walter Ulbricht, came to Karlovy Vary, again to discuss "the situation of the two countries and the policies of the two parties."[1] The public also speculated about an August 17 meeting between Dubček and the first secretary of the Hungarian Workers party, János Kádár, in Bratislava. Later it became known that on this occasion Kádár had warned his Czechoslovak colleague of an imminent military action planned by the Soviet Union against Czechoslovakia. At the time of the meeting, however, political observers and the public were limited to guesswork and speculation.

It was on the same day, August 17, 1968, that the Politbureau of the CPSU sent a letter to the Presidium of the CPSC urging "immediate implementation of the agreements reached in Čierna." The letter was followed by an editorial in the August 18 issue of the Moscow daily *Pravda* in which the Czechoslovak Communists were criticized for their unwillingness to carry out their obligations resulting from the talks of the six party delegations in Bratislava.[2] Apart from the fact that the editorial was a breach of the promise made in Bratislava that all polemics would be suspended, it was a curious case of media pre-empting an important move by the supreme party organ. It was equally difficult to see why the letter of the Soviet party's Politbureau, a copy of which was sent to the headquarters of all Communist parties and released by a telex message to all press agencies in Europe on August 17, reached the actual addressee, the Presidium of the CPCS, only on August 19. The contents of the letter were no less surprising than was the way in which it was made public. If it was true, as Dubček had affirmed in his TV address on August 4, that no document other than the final communiqué had been adopted in Bratislava, to what agreements and obligations did the CPSU Politbureau's letter and the *Pravda* editorial refer?*

Analysts of Soviet and East European politics then often wondered what actually had happened in Dresden, Čierna, and Bratislava during the three meetings and why the time allocated to the talks should not have been sufficient for the Soviets to state their position and to spell out

---

*Let us assume for a moment that Dubček was not telling the whole truth and that secret agreements had indeed been made in Čierna, as well as in Bratislava, pertaining to definite measures to be taken by the CPCS to ensure the leading role of this party and to preserve "the Socialist achievements." Such agreements might have been only oral, in which case the risk of a misinterpretation would have been great. This hypothesis seems to be quite plausible. A very strong argument in its support is the time element: it appears incredible that four days of intensive talks at Čierna would have produced no more than eighteen lines of ambiguous generalities. Yet, plausibility apart, another theory could be constructed that in the end might be more helpful in explaining the apparent mystery than supposed secret agreements. It is quite conceivable that no formal agreements, either written or oral, were reached in Čierna and in Bratislava apart from the official closing resolutions, but that there had been radical differences in the interpretation of these resolutions. A thoroughly different meaning might have been given to them by the Czechoslovak party leaders on the one hand and by their Soviet and East European comrades on the other. This theory has the advantage that in not postulating the existence of separate unpublished agreements it relieves us of the burden of explaining why the CPCS leadership failed to comply with them, even though it must have been fully aware of the consequences. The differences in meaning attributed by the spokesmen of each of the two parties to the various key terms of the Communist vocabulary can also account for the apparent paradox of protracted negotiations yielding such modest results.

their demands and expectations. The answer to their question, surprisingly enough, is that indeed the time was not sufficient. Four days, four
months, or four years are of little use when the partners do not speak the
same language, as was the case with the Czechoslovak CPCS and the
fraternal ruling parties. The only remedy would have been the Dubček
leadership's acceptance of the Soviet interpretation of the crucial notions
involved—that is, if the "leading role of the party" were understood as
tight power monopoly; if any public initiative not emanating directly
from the party organs and agencies were seen as "subversive activity"
and every idea not conforming to the Soviet version of Marxism-
Leninism as "bourgeois ideology"; and if all organizations and groups
outside the framework of the Communist-directed National Front were
viewed as antisocialist forces. If the CPCS leaders could have been
converted to these views, there would have been no problem in reaching
an agreement between Prague and Moscow. Moreover, there would have
been no democratization or liberalization, since Dubček's concept of
politics would have been identical with Novotný's.

Soviet Military Action and the
Extraordinary Party Congress

Eventually, the Soviet power center had no other choice but to resort to
force to eliminate what it had long perceived as a threat not only to Soviet
control of Central Europe, but also to the internal stability of all
Communist regimes, including the USSR itself. On the strength of the
available data, it is not possible to identify with full accuracy the actual
precipitant of the intervention—that is, the event or the move by the
Czechoslovak leadership that actually triggered the Soviet-led military
action. The decision to invade Czechoslovakia was taken at an extraordinary session of the Central Committee of the CPSU held on August 19,
1968,[3] two days after the letter of the CPSU's Politbureau urging the
implementation of the Čierna agreements had been despatched to
Prague, and the day on which it was received by the addressee. There
might be reasons to believe that the delay in delivering the letter was a
deliberate attempt to take action before the Czechoslovak side had a
chance to comply with the Soviet demands. However, other circumstances of the invasion appear to contradict this hypothesis. One of them
is a surprising lack of preparedness on the part of the Soviet sponsors in
the political, the most important, aspect of the operation. The occupa-

tion of Czechoslovakia started during the evening of August 20 and was completed by the following day. Troops of all Warsaw Pact countries, with the exception of Rumania, participated in this deployment. It was on the whole a smooth military maneuver, with very few, exclusively civilian, casualties because the Czechoslovak government had given the order to the armed forces and the police not to offer resistance. Politically, however, failures, complications, and difficulties followed each other in quick succession.

Observers familiar with Soviet propaganda methods and remembering the way in which the political aspect of the 1956 intervention in Hungary had been handled expected that the Soviet media would present to the world an alternative CPCS leadership, allegedly composed of truly Leninist officials upon whose request the selfless assistance of the fraternal parties and governments was given to the Czechoslovak working class in distress. In reality, although it was affirmed in the official communiqué of the Soviet press agency and by the Soviet delegate to the United Nations that the troops of the five powers had entered Czechoslovak territory "upon the demand of Czech and Slovak patriots and communists,"[4] no such patriots and Communists have ever been identified by name. The Soviets apprehended and deported to Moscow nearly all the prominent members of the CPCS Presidium, but they were patently unable to replace them. On the contrary, the decimated party Presidium, headed by President of the Republic Svoboda, and the Central Committee immediately undertook feverish activity. They issued a proclamation "to all people of the Czechoslovak Socialist Republic" in which the Soviet action was condemned not only as a contradiction of all principles of the relationship among socialist nations, but also as a negation of all basic norms of international law. An emergency meeting of the government and the National Assembly endorsed this position.[5] The Soviets faced a crisis whose diplomatic consequences were comparable to those created by the Hungarian uprising of 1956, but whose impact upon the international Communist movement far exceeded any previous experience.

According to a plan prepared earlier, the date of the Extraordinary Party Congress was advanced and the supreme party gathering occurred in the industrial Prague suburb of Vysočany on August 22. It was attended by 1,219 delegates previously elected by the regional party conferences and representing 1,687,565 members. Neither the emergency situation nor the possibility of Soviet retaliation seemed to discourage the participants. The congress launched an appeal to Communist and workers' parties of the world protesting the Soviet-sponsored intervention. Alexander Dubček, interned in Moscow, was enthusiastically re-elected first party secretary, and all other Presidium members sharing his fate were confirmed in their positions. Conservative functionaries lost further ground when the new Central Committee, composed of 144 members, and a new Central Supervisory Commission were constituted. A group of high party officials, known for their support of Novotný and therefore suspected of condoning the intervention, made a public declaration denying any part in the alleged invitation of Soviet troops to Czechoslovakia.[6]

Meanwhile, the diplomatic representatives of Czechoslovakia informed the governments and the international organizations by which they were accredited about the illegal character of Soviet intervention. The Czechoslovak minister of foreign affairs, Jiří Hájek, lodged a protest with the Security Council of the United Nations against the occupation. By far the most forceful reaction, however, came from the Czechoslovak public at large. It seemed as if the political mobilization of the unorganized populace, which the reformist leadership had pursued from the beginning of the new course, finally took effect under the shock of foreign interference. Unlike in Hungary in 1956, this mobilization assumed the form of unarmed mass demonstrations and passive resistance. Invading troops could not secure the cooperation of the population beyond what could be enforced by sheer threat. In sustaining the spirit of the resistance, the key role was played by mass communication media. These in a sense substituted themselves for the partly absent, partly paralyzed government. Those few days of mass protest in Czechoslovakia and the apparent indecision in the USSR gave birth to a unique phenomenon that is of great interest to political sociology: government by media. The efficiency of the communication networks—press, radio, and television—in this situation suggested the vital importance of these means in emergency conditions, and justified the concern that all totalitarian systems have always shown with maintaining the monopoly of information.

A Brief Truce

The massive resistance of the population, coordinated by mass media, compelled the Soviet power center to modify its original plans. In view of the absence of an alternative leadership and singularly poor preparation of the political side of the intervention, a compromise, at least temporary, became inevitable. On August 28, 1968, the Czechoslovak party and government officials who had been interned in the Soviet Union were allowed to return to Czechoslovakia and to resume their positions. The success of the resistance in retaining incumbents in key posts seemed complete. The offices of first party secretary, of prime minister, and of chairman of the National Assembly remained in the hands of Alexander Dubček, Oldrich Černík, and Josef Smrkovský, the most outspoken representatives of the democratization course. No significant changes occurred, either, in other important cabinet seats. Jiří Hájek retained the portfolio of foreign affairs and Josef Pavel kept that of interior. The plenary session of the Central Committee held on August 31 acknowledged the "changed situation created by the entry of the troops of the five countries of the Warsaw Treaty into our country"[7] and the contents of the negotiations in Moscow that had preceded the return of the reformist leaders. At the same time, however, it declared its commitment to the principles of the Extraordinary Party Congress and coopted eighty-seven members, mostly liberals, from the candidates and delegates to this congress.

The reformists also appeared to be advancing in the CPS. The Extraordinary Congress of the CPS (a sequel to the national meeting in Vysočany), which took place in Bratislava August 26–29, expressed full confidence in the CPCS leadership headed by Dubček. It also demanded that the constitutional reform included in the Action Program of April 1968 whereby Czechoslovakia was to be transformed into a federation of two republics, the Czech Socialist Republic and the Slovak Socialist Republic, be implemented by the next National Liberation Day, October 28.[8] By setting this date as the deadline, Slovak Communists demonstrated their respect for the political traditions of the First Czechoslovak Republic. At the constitutive meeting of the Central Committee of the Slovak party, on August 29, First Party Secretary Vasil Bil'ák, who was known for his conservative and pro-Soviet leanings, lost his position and was replaced by Gustav Husák. To a contemporary observer, considering Husák's past role as the most prominent Slovak victim of the dogmatic persecution in the 1950s and his active part in the democratization movement, this change appeared to be a victory for the reformists. Subsequent events were to show that Husák's comeback could not be interpreted in such simple terms.

Indeed, as the message of the returning leaders addressed to the "whole Czechoslovak people" on August 28 had already cautioned, the hard realities were not the composition of the party and state governing bodies but the presence of the military force in the country, which made all pretensions to Czechoslovak sovereignty and to the right of self-determination only conditional. Although the troops of the other four Warsaw Pact nations evacuated Czechosovak territory relatively soon after the reinstatement of Dubček and his associates, it could be anticipated that the units of the Red Army would not follow their example. Talks were initiated almost immediately to legalize the "temporary" presence of Soviet garrisons.[9] The details of this arrangement were worked out by a Czechoslovak government delegation led by Prime Minister Černík and the Soviet authorities in Moscow on October 14 and 15, 1968. They were laid down in the "Treaty on Temporary Location of Warsaw Pact Troops in Czechoslovak Territory," which was signed in Prague on October 16 by Alexei Kosygin.[10] Thus the Soviets implicitly admitted that a uniform policy line in the world Communist system could not be assured without coercion. This was the plain substance of the Brezhnev Doctrine: the socialist camp could survive only where Soviet troops could be deployed. Although this stand was not a very commendable one, it nevertheless signified a change for the worse in the international status of Czechoslovakia and reduced the hopes of its population that it would ever be able to determine its own destiny.

The developments within the CPCS following the first plenary session of the new Central Committee also indicated that Soviet pressure would not subside so soon. As early as September 3, Deputy Prime Minister Ota Šik, the main architect of the economic reform, was relieved of his position. Three days later, the Presidium of the National Front dismissed František Kriegel, one of the most active reformists, from the office of chairman. On September 9, Jiří Hájek lost his post as minister of foreign affairs. These three men had become intolerable to the occupying power because of specific actions they had undertaken during the August crisis. This was particularly true of Hájek, who had lodged an official protest against the Soviet intervention in the Security Council and the General Assembly of the United Nations. Kriegel made himself persona non grata in Moscow because of several proclamations he co-authored and signed in the name of the National Front, in which the invasion was condemned in vehement terms. Šik's unpardonable crime was to promote the idea of a socialist market economy, which the dogmatic Soviets considered tantamount to the restoration of capitalism, and of workers' participation in management, which the Soviets had viewed since its first application in Yugoslavia as an anarcho-syndicalist deviation of the worst kind.

Yet in the fall of 1968 it did not seem that the reform movement would be either stopped altogether or reversed soon. Not only did the relatively uninhibited way of reporting and commenting on political issues in the mass media continue long after the intervention; there were also certain parts of the Action Program whose implementation was not affected by the presence of the Soviet troops. The revision of the political trials of the 1950s and the rehabilitation of the victims were in this category. Another important area was that of the constitutional order, more precisely of the relations between the two nation-building ethnic groups, the Czechs and the Slovaks. The pertinent constitutional reform was endorsed by the National Assembly on October 27, 1968, and promulgated in a ceremony held at the Bratislava Castle on October 30.[11] The date of the ceremony was not an accidental choice. It coincided with the fiftieth anniversary of the Slovak declaration of national independence in Turčiansky Svätý Martin, the Slovak parallel to the proclamation of the Czechoslovak Republic in Prague on October 28, 1918. Thus the solemn enactment of the new constitutional law was symbolic in two ways: on the one hand, the CPCS leadership demonstrated its will to live up to the commitments of the Action Program; on the other hand, the party showed that it subscribed to the great pre-February traditions. In a way, the new constitutional order could be seen as a belated fulfillment of the aspirations of those who had signed the St. Martin Declaration of 1918.

The Action Program had originally contained a provision that general elections would precede the constitution of new legislative and executive bodies in the two parts of the federative state, the Czech Socialist Republic and the Slovak Socialist Republic. The Soviet political advisers, however, insisted that no election be held at that point; they feared (with good reason) that such elections might provide the population with an opportunity to show its real feelings towards Czechoslovakia's big brother. Thus the reform went into effect without a popular vote, on January 1, 1969, when the Czech National Council and the Slovak National Council were set up and elected the governments of each of the two republics. The structural change in the Czechoslovak polity also had a bearing upon the Communist party organization. It seemed in the fall of 1968 that after many years of ambiguity concerning the position of the

Slovak component within the national party—a kind of asymmetric centralism—the Communist movement was ready to adopt the federalist principle. On November 16, 1968, a new organ set up by the Central Committee, the Bureau for the Administration of Party Work in the Czech Provinces, met for the first time in Prague under the chairmanship of Václav Hájek, a member of the Central Supervisory Commission. Following an earlier decision of the Central Committee, the bureau's task was to prepare a constituent congress of the future Czech Communist party, an equal partner to the Communist Party of Slovakia.[12] The title of this new party must have caused some headaches in the CPCS headquarters. As the standard designation of the individual Communist parties had been based, since the times of the Komintern, on geographic rather than ethnic criteria—Communist Party of France, of Germany, of Czechoslovakia—the title of the party to be created should have read in Czech "Komunistická strana Česka" (in English, "Communist Party of Czechia"). This was unacceptable because the term Czechia had been used by Slovak right extremists during the Nazi occupation to refer to the German Protectorate of Bohemia and Moravia. Actually we do not know what terminology the CPCS leadership would have applied to the organization planned for the Czech provinces if the plan had not been eventually shelved.

The name, however, was not the thorniest problem in the efforts of the Dubček leadership to adapt the organizational structure of the party to the new conditions created by the constitutional reform. There could be no illusion about the nature of the intended change: it required a departure from the principle that for almost half a century had governed the Czechoslovak Communist movement and had engendered the absurd and unsatisfactory compromise of asymmetric centralism. The difficulties encountered by the Bureau for the Administration of Party Work in the Czech Provinces underscored the magnitude of the problem. The Soviet intervention had appreciably narrowed the scope of possible solutions. It was inconceivable that the power center in Moscow would tolerate any major deviation from what it claimed to be the Leninist form of socialist government. Thus while the federalization of Czechoslovakia was to enter history as the most significant, and possibly the only, lasting achievement of the short-lived Prague Spring, the adjustment of the party's organizational framework to this new type of polity appeared at least uncertain at the end of 1968.

Normalization

Meanwhile, the uneven struggle continued between the reformists, on the one hand, who were striving to preserve as much as possible of the democratization legacy, and the Soviets, on the other, who were bent upon destroying the work of the Prague Spring. It was increasingly evident that the unanimous opposition of the population, so impressively shown in August 1968, had only slowed down but not stopped the Soviet advance. Moscow had changed its tactics, but not its ultimate objectives. Nothing short of the restoration in the CPCS of a leadership unreservedly obedient to the Soviet power center could allay its fears. Soviet spokesmen and media coined a special term for this rolling-back process: normalization. The term truly reflected the Soviet idea of what was normal in the relations between the Soviet Union and its allies: a posture of unqualified subservience of the latter. The Soviets relentlessly worked toward this goal by all means available to them, political, ideological, diplomatic, and military.

To an outside observer, the luck in this silent but merciless battle might have appeared to be occasionally changing sides. Shortly after the talks between the top officials of the Czechoslovak and the Soviet Communist parties in Moscow in October 1968, Zdeněk Mlynář, a member of the party Presidium and secretary of the Central Committee, the principal initiator of the reform project concerning the political institutions of the country, resigned all his offices. He was succeeded by Lubomír Štrougal, who had a rather conservative reputation. On the other hand, the reformists still held a number of key positions at the start of the new year. With Alexander Dubček in the office of the first party secretary and Oldřich Černík and Josef Smrkovský in the Presidium, the champions of the liberalization were far from eliminated. On January 7, 1969, Josef Smrkovský was nominated to the prestigious function of chairman of the Chamber of the People, one of the houses of the federal Parliament established by the constitutional law of October 29, 1968. On the same occasion, the party Presidium decided that Smrkovský should retain his functions in the top organs of the CPCS, the Executive Committee of the Presidium and the Central Committee. One may infer that in explicitly stating no opposition to the cumulation of high state and party offices in the hands of Smrkovský the Presidium was responding to some unofficial objections on the part of the Soviet advisers.

The main elements of party policy under Soviet occupation were laid down in the resolution on the "Principal Tasks in the Immediate Future" that was adopted by the Central Committee plenum at its session held November 14–17, 1968. The resolution's headline indicated the pragmatic and short-term nature of the policy line. It was a compromise between the reformist and centrist approaches, made to avert the still worse alternative of a dogmatist comeback.[13] The dogmatists represented a very small faction in the CPCS, but the Dubček leadership feared that they might receive support from the Soviet side. As the Soviet strategy in the postinvasion period suggested, however, it seemed more likely that Moscow would look for collaborators among the centrists than among the right extremists. The actual Soviet option was a surprise: their man to replace Dubček was chosen from the very middle of the former anti-Novotný coalition.

While the reformist leaders endeavored to steer a safe course in the pre-invasion period without sacrificing too much of the ground they had gained, the spirit of resistance awakened in the population at large by the August intervention followed its own momentum. The goals of these two factions whose efforts were hardly ever coordinated, were often at odds now. Manifestations of hostility to the occupying power were frequent, even though more reserved behavior by the citizenry was necessary for the success of the Dubček policy, this time literally the art of the possible. The rebellious mood was partly encouraged by the media, which pretended to ignore the reality of the Soviet military presence. A very dramatic form of protest was chosen, in January 1969, by student Jan Palach, who burned himself publicly in Václavské Square in Prague. His funeral provided the public with yet another opportunity for a nonviolent but very impressive manifestation of defiance. Ironically, although these spontaneous outbursts testified to the loss of control by the Czechoslovak authorities over the population, it was the leadership of the Communist party that was in the end made responsible for their occurrence. For the occupying power, this was actually expedient; the incidents supplied a welcome lever for removing from the command posts of the CPCS all those whom the Soviets could not trust but who enjoyed too much popularity to be attacked directly.

A suitable occasion for this long-planned move offered itself in the early spring of 1969. The anti-Soviet demonstration that triggered Moscow's action was apparently of nonpolitical origin. The crowds in the center of Prague watching the telecast of the world championship hockey match between Czechoslovakia and the Soviet Union gave free rein to their enthusiasm on learning of the Czechoslovak victory, and the situation eventually got out of hand. There could be little doubt that along with the joy over the success of the national team the demonstrators also vented their feelings about the hated power represented by the defeated team. During riots on March 28 and 29, 1969, the premises of the official Soviet travel agency, Intourist, located in downtown Prague, were ransacked. Moscow found the destruction of Soviet property by the mob a sufficient pretext for radical action. The Soviets charged that the crowds in Prague had been incited by opportunistic party leaders and counterrevolutionary mass media. Under the threat of a new military intervention, which the Soviet leaders underscored by dispatching to Czechoslovakia a special delegation headed by the commander-in-chief of the armed forces of the Warsaw Pact, Marshal Yakubovsky, the CPSU insisted that energetic measures be taken to bring about the overdue normalization. The Kremlin was not willing to accept as satisfactory the resolution of the extraordinary session of the party Presidium of April 1, 1969, in which several members of the Central Committee, among them Josef Smrkovský, were reprimanded for "incorrect interpretation of the decisions of the November CC Plenum."[14] A thorough change at the helm of the party was demanded.

It was at the plenary session of the Central Committee on April 17 that the CPCS yielded to Soviet pressure. Alexander Dubček submitted his resignation as first party secretary and proposed Gustav Husák as his successor. At the same time, twelve Presidium members, including Smrkovský, were relieved of their functions. The situation was described as exceptional in the Central Committee discussions, and the need for a speedy consolidation was recognized. The party crisis was also the topic of an extraordinary session of the Central Committee of the CPS on April 18, and of the session of the Bureau for the Administration of Party Work in the Czech Provinces on April 21. Both organs approved the decisions of the Central Committee of the national party organization.[15] Normalization of conditions in Czechoslovakia, in the form in which the Soviets had imagined and desired it, took a giant step forward.

Although the name of the new first secretary of the CPCS was then still connected with memories of the struggle against the conservative Novotný regime prior to January 1968, and associated with those of the victims of Stalinist justice, everybody was aware of the fact that the change in the top executive party post had ushered in an entirely different era. Considering the circumstances in which Husák had been elected, it was evident that under his leadership the Soviets would be able to implement their normalization goals much faster. These goals consisted, above all, in replacing their opponents, avowed or potential, with more docile individuals. It was characteristic of the situation after the April 1969 plenum of the Central Committee that the very position that had become vacant through Husák's promotion to the office of first secretary of the CPCS was filled by Vasil Biľák, who was notorious for his dogmatic and pro-Soviet orientation. Dubček himself remained in the party Presidium after his resignation, but it was only a matter of time until he, too, would be eliminated. A similar fate awaited Josef Smrkovský, who, after his ouster from the party Presidium, lost his membership in the Central Committee on September 26, 1969, and his position as chairman of the Chamber of the People on October 15. Oldřich Černík resigned as prime minister of the federal government on January 18, 1970, was relieved of his Presidium membership two days later, and finally was expelled from the party on December 12 of the same year. Many other, less prominent personalities of the liberal leadership followed a similar path into disgrace.

Gustav Husák made an official trip to Moscow in the week following his election by the Central Committee. In the Soviet capital he met not only the first secretary of the CPSU, Leonid Brezhnev, but also his counterparts from Eastern Germany and Hungary, Walter Ulbricht and János Kádár. Their presence indicated that the April 1969 changes in the Czechoslovak party leadership were perceived as a matter of primary concern to all Communist neighbors of Czechoslovakia. No details about the Moscow talks were made public, but it can be assumed that the new CPCS executive boss was briefed by his three opposite numbers on the minimum requirements involved in the consolidation. Another point on the agenda was the planned third world conference of Communist and workers' parties. It is very likely that the Soviet hosts had little difficulty in enlisting Husák's support for the idea of a new Communist summit, but Czechoslovakia remained one of the major obstacles to the realization of the Soviet project. This was not because of any reluctance on the part of the team now in control, but rather because of the repercussions in the international Communist movement of the Soviet intervention, from which the world Communist system has not yet fully recovered.

The subsequent plenary sessions of the Central Committees of the CPS on May 4, and of the national party organization on May 28 and 29,

1969, took cognizance of, and approved, the results of the Moscow negotiations. The Slovak Central Committee also elected Štefan Sádovský to succeed Gustav Husák. In the Central Committee of the CPCS important personnel changes were carried out that further reduced the representation of the liberal element. Josef Špaček, who was known as one of Dubček's most loyal supporters lost his office as Central Committee secretary. Three outspoken and very popular leaders of the democratization era, Ota Šik, František Kriegel, and František Vodsloň, were expelled from the party. The party Presidium, in its session on May 31, 1969, declared Vasil Bil'ák and a number of other conservative members of the executive organs of the party "not guilty of any objectionable behavior during the August 1968 events."[16] This move was interesting for two reasons. The rehabilitation of the conservatives and dogmatists indicated the way the wind was blowing after the April 1969 plenum. On the other hand, the fact that such rehabilitation was considered necessary testified to the still strong feeling among the party rank and file in support of the aborted liberal experiment and against the foreign interference with which the names of the conservatives had been associated. A similar attestation of good patriotic behavior had been given to a group of ten party leaders by the Executive Committee of the Presidium in the session that had preceded the April 17 plenary meeting of the Central Committee.

From June 4 to June 17, 1969, a consultative meeting of Communist and workers' parties took place in Moscow at which the new CPCS leadership was duly represented. It was but a truncated convention of the world Communist movement, however. (Shortly before the Moscow talks, the Sino-Soviet conflict had assumed dramatic and dangerous forms in a military confrontation on the Ussuri River.) The events in Czechoslovakia in August 1968 and the Soviet-enforced change in the CPCS leadership of April 1969 had created a serious crisis of confidence. The two most important West European Communist parties, the French and the Italian, never ceased to deplore Soviet interference in the internal affairs of the Czechoslovak party. A few other key parties, such as the Yugoslav and Chinese parties, were not represented. Their position on what meanwhile had become the Czechoslovak question was clear. They repeatedly called for the evacuation of Czechoslovakia by Soviet troops and recognition of the right of the CPCS to determine its own policy course. Under these conditions, there was little hope that an impressive majority could be found to vindicate the Soviet cause in the

Sino-Soviet dispute. It did not help much that the spokesmen of the very party that was considered the victim of inadmissible foreign manipulation outdid themselves in their manifestations of loyalty to the USSR and in their unqualified support of the Soviet side in the conflict with the People's Republic of China. Husák's endorsement did not bring the Kremlin any nearer to its goal, which was the excommunication of the Communist Party of China from the international Communist movement and the reinstatement of the Soviet Union as the supreme infallible arbiter in matters of Communist theory and policy. As an exercise in obedience to the presumably infallible mother country of socialism, however, it may have been duly appreciated in the Kremlin, especially after the uncertainties and apprehensions about the intentions of the Czechoslovak ally it had experienced during the democratization era.

Rewriting History: The "Genuine" Fourteenth Party Congress

The gradual elimination of prominent reformist leaders, begun in September 1968, was but a prelude to a large-scale purge of all elements suspected of sympathizing with the Dubček course or otherwise considered unreliable by the occupying power. The purge, like several previous operations of this kind, officially took the form of an exchange of party cards. The principles of this restructuring of leading cadres were first openly discussed at the plenary session of the Central Committee held January 28–30, 1970. The report then submitted by the first secretary indicated that the CPCS was facing a shake-up in its membership base comparable only to the mass purge of 1949–51. It was clear, too, that nothing short of such a surgical intervention would satisfy the Soviet advisers. This impression was confirmed by the tone and content of the report of the planned action submitted by Jozef Lenárt to the Central Committee plenum of the Slovak party on February 5 and 6, 1970.

The review of membership began shortly afterward and lasted until the fall. At the Central Committee plenum of the CPCS in December 1970, the officials of the Control and Revision Commission announced that the exchange of party cards had been concluded, and provided a statistical summary of its results. According to these figures, 67,147 members had been expelled because of "violation of party statutes, opportunistic ideas and behavior, anti-Soviet attitudes" and other explicitly stated transgressions. The number of those whose membership was "simply not renewed" was much higher: 259,670. Some of the official grounds given for the nonrenewal were "lack of participation in party life" or failure to pay dues.[17] However, it can be assumed that some of those included in this larger group were lesser supporters of, or sympathizers with, the reformist cause. To strike their names from the membership registers instead of expelling them formally was a choice dictated by political expedience rather than by tact or humane consideration. The new leadership could not admit that Prague Spring had had such strong support among the rank and file.

The purge might have had one additional objective: to meet Soviet criticism of the mass nature of the party. It may have been an attempt to restore a more Leninist aspect to the party organization, to make it again a more elitist body. If so, the effort fell far short of the goal. Even after the elimination of more than three hundred thousand party cardholders, about 20 percent of the entire membership, the CPCS still remained one of the largest Communist parties in the world in relation to the country's population. This fact did not seem to disturb the leaders to any great extent; immediately after the December 1970 Central Committee plenum, the party launched a recruitment campaign geared especially to a particular class background and age group. Preference was to be given to applicants of worker or peasant origin who were about twenty-five years old. The campaign continued for a long time before yielding some of the expected results, but it eventually pushed the number of party effectives close to the 1.5 million mark once more.

There are good reasons to doubt whether even the main purpose of the exchange of party cards, the exclusion of the reformist element and the neutralization of possible opposition to the Soviet-sponsored course, was an unqualified success. To achieve this end, the purge, however extensive, was not drastic enough; the reformist and proreformist wing constituted more than the 20 percent expelled in 1970. It can also be argued that the very mass character of the CPCS, which the purge did not influence in any significant way, has contained a permanent threat of new shifts, unpredictable and undesirable from the viewpoint of the post-1969 leadership and its Moscow protectors. Among the 10 percent of the entire population organized in the party, practically all shades of opinion are likely to be represented. The stress placed by the power holders on the class criterion in new admissions could not overcome the effects of this heterogeneity.

Nevertheless, the team in control felt that the purge had been a step ahead on the path of normalization that was important enough to permit envisaging the convocation of a party congress. Husák, as well as the Soviet supervisors, had until then hesitated to take this step for fear of having to face a more representative and therefore more hostile audience at the congress. On the other hand, their options in this respect had been restricted for several reasons. The congress was already overdue unless the new masters of the CPCS were prepared to acknowledge the Extraordinary Congress of August 1968 as valid—an unthinkable alternative. The normalizing leadership not only had to avoid this at any price, it also perceived it as necessary to wipe the Vysočany congress out of the party annals, a move that in a sense amounted to rewriting history. Its objective could best be attained by substituting another convention of the supreme party body for the unwelcome event. At the start of 1971, the situation seemed to be favorable to this solution.

The decision to convene the congress was made at the plenary session of the Central Committee held on February 4, 1971. The congress was scheduled for the last week of May in that year, to coincide with the fiftieth anniversary of the Constitutive Congress of the CPCS, which had taken place in 1921. Obviously, the slated party gathering had to be upgraded in advance through historical symbols to obliterate more easily the memories of the emergency meeting during the dramatic days of Soviet intervention. Even more indicative of the new situation than this manipulation of symbols was another decision taken by the Central Committee on the same occasion: to discontinue the activity of the Bureau for the Administration of Party Work in the Czech Provinces. This spelled the end of prospects for a party reform matching the constitutional changes of October 1968. The federalization of the party structure was shelved and the CPCS returned to the previous practice of asymmetric centralism. This time, however, the discrepancy between the party and the state was much more salient: a federated polity was governed by a party that was 75 percent centralist. The only surviving legacy of the democratization era remained restricted to the governmental level. Dubček's opponents could now claim that the party had lost none of its totalitarian innocence in the upheavals of 1968.

Following long-established tradition (suspended only once, precisely during the August events of 1968), the congress of the CPS was held prior to the congress of the national party organization, in Bratislava May 13–15, 1971; 586 delegates representing about three hundred thousand members participated in its dealings. The total membership did not seem to be very much affected by the 1970 purge, certainly not in the same measure as the membership in the western provinces. Party First Secretary Jozef Lenárt, who had replaced Vasil Bil'ák in 1970, presented a "report on the development of the party and the society since the Thirteenth CPCS Congress (1966) and the main tasks of the party in the immediate future." This was the Slovak counterpart to the principal document to be circulated at the national congress in Prague two weeks later.[18] Like the latter, the Slovak party gathering was expected to give its sanction to all measures taken since the extraordinary congress in 1968, especially to changes in the leading positions of the party's governing organs. The new Central Committee elected in Bratislava reflected a net progress of normalization. From this point of view, it was indicative that Laco Novomeský, a prominent reformist and opponent of Novotný, was not re-elected. On the other hand, the fact that Gustav Husák did not figure among the CPS officials reflected his previous appointment to the supreme function in the national party body.

The national congress of the CPCS opened in Prague on May 25, 1971. Twelve hundred delegates participated in the deliberations. Membership at that time was estimated at about 1.2 million after the recent expulsions and nonrenewals of party cards. The congress reviewed party activities "in the critical period since the last congress." All speakers and all documents took good care that the public should understand the term last congress to mean the Thirteenth Ordinary Party Congress of May–June 1966; the extraordinary congress of August 1968 was thus reduced to a nonevent and buried in silence. The leadership was also anxious to turn the congress into a show of the further progress of normalization. If this notion implied the liquidation of the work of the Prague Spring, the meeting of the top party organ certainly lived up to expectations. It not only approved all ousters and demotions of liberals and the mass purge, as well as the mothballing of the project of a separate Czech Communist party, but also endorsed new statutes from which all the reforms contained in the July 1968 proposal had been expurgated, especially the principle of the control of the governing organs by the grass-roots units and the voluntary character of membership.[19] The version adopted at the congress signified the restoration of the status quo ante.

Party First Secretary Gustav Husák assumed the function of principal reporter. Addressing the congress, Husák stated that the Soviet military action against his predecessor Dubček had been "a fraternal act of assistance" for which the CPCS was "greatly indebted" to its Moscow counterpart. This interpretation reflected an adjustment to the official Soviet version of the August 1968 events; until then Husák had often referred to the intervention and to the subsequent occupation as "unfortunate" and "painful," albeit "inevitable" facts. A similar position on these issues was taken by the official evaluation of the Prague Spring period in a brochure widely circulated among the delegates and all party members titled "The Lessons of the Crisis-Like Developments of the Party and the Society since the Thirteenth Congress." The publication depicted the attempt at the democratization of the system undertaken after the fall of Novotný as a plot seeking to undermine the socialist order. It nevertheless put a part of the blame for the "crisis-like evolution" on the Novotný leadership, which "had refused to redress the injustices of the past."[20] This formulation seemed to show the hand of the first secretary, himself a former victim of such injustices; it also appeared to express the desire of the leadership not to let its policy line be understood as simply a continuation of that of the pre-1968 era.

The Central Committee elected at the Fourteenth Congress comprised 115 full members and 45 candidates. It was one of the largest top governing bodies ever appointed. The details of its composition, however, were not surprising. All important personnel shifts and changes had already been accomplished before the congress. Economic questions occupied a prominent place in the congress's agenda; they centered around the Fifth Five-Year Plan, which then had entered its initial phase. There were also political reasons for the special emphasis upon the economy. On the one hand, Gustav Husák and his associates were anxious to prove that the process of normalization, with all the upheavals it had brought about, had not led to an economic crisis, as many had anticipated. On the other hand, the advertised success in the management of the national economy by the postinvasion leadership was to supply an argument against the now neutralized but not yet wholly silenced reformist wing. As we know, specific economic policies had been an essential part of the reformist program. Economic survival without major difficulties since August 1968 was to prove that the shelving of the New Economic Model had been no great loss to the Czechoslovak party and people.

It is difficult to determine to what extent the team in control of the party was at that time sincerely convinced of the cogency of this argument or about the progress of normalization. For the purpose of window dressing, there seemed to be enough indicators to point to: the general election held in November 1971 brought in the usual 99 percent vote for the ballot of the National Front. The elections, not unlike the party congress, had been postponed for a long time because the power holders and their Soviet advisers had been concerned about the general mood of the population during the first years after the military intervention. The result of the November 1971 vote effectively reassured them that if popular support for the Soviet-imposed course might still have been questionable, the period of dangerous political mobilization was over and a general feeling of resignation prevailed.

The proofs, real or apparent, of advancing consolidation in the postinvasion era were addressed to two audiences: they were to convince the rank-and-file party membership and the population at large that the Prague Spring had been but a brief folly, an utterly unrealistic course, and at the same time to demonstrate to the Moscow power center that its trust in the Husák team had been wisely invested. To achieve the latter goal, the Husák leadership never missed any opportunity of showing unconditional obedience to the Soviet Union. World political events and the activities of the international Communist movement often provided such opportunities, but they also sometimes created delicate problems. Lending unqualified support to Soviet views and policies inevitably estranged other partners in the dispute who, as often as not, were Communist parties or nations, such as Yugoslavia or China. Even more delicate was the fact that in many of these disputes Czechoslovakia, or Soviet action in Czechoslovakia, was the central issue. On such occasions the CPCS spokesmen had the ungrateful task of asserting that far from being a victim of Soviet interference, Czechoslovakia had benefited by it. In most cases, their declarations could not prevent lively exchanges between the Soviet party and many of its counterparts on the subject of the events of August 1968. These tensions overshadowed practically all international contacts among Communists at that time.

Between Center and Dogmatic Right:
Husák Emulates Novotný's Example

Understanding the policies and tactics of the Husák group during the early 1970s requires acknowledging the constraints to which they were subject. In addition to the obvious limits imposed by the determination of the Moscow power center not to allow a repetition of any of the heresies that had led to the occupation of Czechoslovakia in August 1968, there were constraints stemming from some irreducible uncertainties. It was not quite clear whether the line implemented by Husák could entirely dissipate the apprehensions of the Soviet supervisors. The notion of normalization was a vague one; the CPSU officials never specified what exactly they meant by the "return to normalcy." This ambiguity actually was but a new version of the equivocation familiar from Soviet polemics against the Dubček team before the intervention concerning concepts such as the leading role of the party, preservation of socialist achievements, and proletarian internationalism. The Brezhnev Doctrine appeared to mean little more than the assertion by the USSR of the right to intervene in the internal affairs of other Communist states. It said nothing about the nature of events that might justify intervention, nor about the precise conditions in which it could be discontinued or avoided.

To add complexity to the situation, there was no agreement within the ruling segment of the Czechoslovak party on the most appropriate course of action. The new leadership, as it gradually emerged after the April 1969 plenum of the Central Committee, was a mix of centrists, dogmatists, and former supporters of the Prague Spring converted to the cause of normalization. Husák himself belonged to the last-named category despite a rather varied record of allegiances in the more remote past. One thing was certain: Husák belonged to those who had helped to topple the Novotný regime and thus open the door to Dubček. It was therefore difficult to expect an identity of opinion between him and the dogmatic wing merely because Soviet pressure had brought all these heterogeneous elements to power. It would have been equally unrealistic to expect that the Soviet intervention should not greatly stir the hopes of the dogmatists. However much wishful thinking there may have been in their perception of the situation, the dogmatists read the message of the August 1968 events as one of the return to the status quo ante, as the vindication not only of Novotný's policies but also of those that had preceded them—in short, as a rehabilitation of Stalinism. Husák's line, for all its relentless dismantling of the reform achievements, appeared too lenient to them.

The best-known representatives of this group were the Politbureau and Central Committee members Antonín Kapek and Vasil Bil'ák. They spoke for a relatively small faction, but the possibility that their ideas on some important aspects of the postinvasion policies might be closer to what the Soviets actually desired made them dangerous rivals to Husák. It is not easy to decide whether their chances of coming to power were real; after all, it was Husák and not Bil'ák whom the Soviets had accepted as Dubček's successor. Nevertheless, they could be seen struggling for more influence on several occasions after the April 1969 plenum, especially on the eve of the Fourteenth Congress. Some observers had expected that either the Fourteenth or the Fifteenth Congress would become a scene of open controversy, if not of a showdown, between Husák and the right extremists.[21] These anticipations did not materialize; on the contrary, it seemed that Husák's position became more solid, with time.

In the spring of 1975, the protracted illness of the president of the republic, Ludvík Svoboda, who had been re-elected in 1973, presented the leadership with the dilemma of his succession. It was a thorny problem, and the aspirations of the dogmatic faction may have played a significant role in its solution. The situation appeared to favor a formula auspicious for the extreme conservatives. If the tacitly accepted principle that the two most important offices in the nation, those of the first party secretary and of the president of the republic, should be evenly distributed between the two ethnic groups (the Czechs and the Slovaks) had then been applied, it would have followed that Husák, as a Slovak, either should not be considered Svoboda's successor or else should relinquish his top party post. This course of action appeared all the more logical since the cumulation of the two functions, practiced by Novotný before 1968, had been viewed with strong disapproval by many party factions. Husák himself had severely criticized Novotný on this account. Respecting the principle of the separation of the two key responsibilties, on the other hand, would have given the dogmatists the chance to make a bid for more power. The new president of the republic or the new first secretary would have to be a Czech, recruited possibly from the extreme right wing.

It was therefore a considerable surprise for the party rank and file as well as for the Czechoslovak public at large when on May 29, 1975, following the nomination by the CPCS Central Committee, Gustav Husák was elected president of the republic but retained the function of first party secretary. The new head of state thus replicated the political career of the man he had hated the most. Moreover, the election of Husák to this second highest office in the country could also be seen as an implicit rejection of a more general principle, established by the Action Program of the CPCS in April 1968, that had called for a consistent separation of party and governmental functions. It can be said that in emulating Novotný's example, Husák took one more step on the road to normalization; his new position in the power hierarchy negated an important point of the democratization program. It is also possible to infer, however, that this decision may have been dictated by the concern of the leadership majority about possibly undesirable reinforcement of the dogmatist group. The solution of the presidential crisis of 1975 thus indirectly confirmed the extent of the polarity of tendencies within the party's power structure.

The pressures from the conservatives may also have limited the range of options open to Husák in his dealings with the reformist opposition. The Soviet party endorsed the cumulation of both top functions in the hands of Husák; the reception he enjoyed during his subsequent visit to the USSR and the enthusiastic commentaries in the Soviet press clearly indicated approval.[22] However, it was necessary for the first secretary to avoid any action that could supply the right wing with arguments that he was too lenient toward the representatives of Dubček's course. Already in the period immediately following the Fourteenth Party Congress, signs of a toughening attitude towards liberal dissent had become visible. The general amnesty proclaimed on the occasion of the twenty-fifth anniversary of liberation was not extended to political offenders. A revised penal code was enacted in 1973 that introduced new notions of crime, such as "spreading untrue news about the Republic," a flexible definition applicable to practically any case of unorthodox opinion. A year later, a new method of neutralizing opponents previously applied in the Soviet Union was adopted: that of forcing dissenters into exile. The dissidents were given a choice between emigrating to the West with the permission of the authorities and standing trial for subversive activities. Not all spokesmen of the opposition agreed to leave the country. Many preferred to stay and face persecution rather than evacuate the field to the adversary. The new approach, while more subtle than the open terror of the 1950s, hardly signified any softening of the political course.

Repressive measures notwithstanding, reformist opposition was still fairly articulate. Letters of protest were sent in 1973 to the leading party and state officials by former liberal party functionaries and members such as Alexander Dubček, Jiří Hájek, Karel Kosík, and Ludvík Vaculík. Memoirs of the former Presidium member and chairman of the National Assembly Josef Smrkovský, who died in 1974, were published in that year by the Italian Communist review *Vie Nuove*. The protesters found the regime's actions to have violated the constitution and all international treaties on the protection of human rights. The support given by the Western Communist parties to these appeals complicated the relations of these parties with the CPCS. Prague officials saw it as a particularly unfriendly act when the Presidium of the Communist Party of Italy provided the exiled Communist writers from Czechoslovakia with the means to continue in Rome the publication of their once influential biweekly *Listy* under the editorship of Jiří Pelikán. In February 1974, French Communist intellectuals called a symposium about political, ideological, and moral consequences of the Soviet occupation of Czechoslovakia at the conference center at Bièvres, near Paris. Their initiative was acknowledged with indignation by the CPCS leaders, who countered by sponsoring an international colloquium in the Prague Institute of Marxism-Leninism in September of the same year on the "dangers of revisionism." On the whole, if normalization was to mean an improvement of the general political climate within Czechoslovakia and among the various components of the international Communist movement, it made little progress in the period between the two postinvasion party congresses.

The revision of the statutes endorsed by the Fourteenth Congress included the extension of the interval between the meetings of the supreme party body from four to five years. The first quinquennium came to its close in 1975. At its session on July 2 and 3, 1975, the Central Committee discussed the agenda of the impending Fifteenth Ordinary Party Congress. It was to be expected that economic questions would occupy an important place because the congress was to coincide with the beginnings of the Sixth Five-Year Plan. The plenum of the Central Committee, at its subsequent meeting held October 11, 1975, scheduled the Fifteenth Congress for April 1976.

The Fifteenth Party Congress

The congress of the national party organization was preceded, as usual, by a congress of the CPS held in Bratislava on March 25, 1976. An important detail of the Slovak party congress was the assertion by its first secretary, Jozef Lenárt, that party membership had reached a record level of 319,000 cardholders.[23] The statistics revealed an interesting aspect of the distribution of party membership between the two main ethnic groups: the record membership of March 1976 for the CPS amounted to less than a quarter of total membership in the CPCS even though Slovaks made up more than one-third of the Czechoslovak population at that time. It is difficult to determine the real causes of this disproportion. Differences in occupational pattern between Slovakia and the western provinces might have accounted for it three decades earlier, but by 1976 industrialization in Slovakia had made considerable progress. Moreover, both the CPS and the CPCS have always been keen on recruiting the rural proletariat as well, a fact that, incidentally, had led to appreciable electoral support for the Communists before the war. It could be that formal affiliation with the party has been less popular among the Slovaks than among the Czechs or, better yet, that party membership has not been perceived as a channel of social mobility in Slovakia as much as in the Czech provinces.

The Fifteenth Ordinary Congress of the CPCS opened in Prague on April 12, 1976. It assembled 1,215 voting delegates representing 1,382,860 members organized in 43,500 local sections. Since the previous congress, membership had increased about 15 percent, indicating that the mass character of the party was most likely to remain one of its salient aspects. The chairman of the Central Control and Auditing Commission, Miloš Jakeš, reported that of the roughly 350,000 individuals expelled from the party during the postinvasion purge, 64,926 or about 18.3 percent had appealed the expulsion. More than half of the appeals had been dealt with by lower level organs, but 23,669 cases had been heard by the Central Control and Revision Commission.[24] The figures suggested that the partisans of democratization had not accepted their elimination without protest. Only in a minority of instances, however, had the complainants' arguments been recognized as valid by the commission and their memberships reinstated.

According to the report, the trend of development of the membership structure had been on the whole satisfactory. The worker and the peasant elements were better represented than on any earlier occasion during the entire postwar period. Also, the age distribution among the party cardholders had improved. Among the 333,952 members admitted between the Fourteenth and the Fifteenth Congresses 50 percent were twenty-five years of age or younger and 90 percent were thirty-five; 60 percent were of working-class origin. The commission's report claimed that these improvements had resulted chiefly from a better-organized recruitment campaign and a more careful choice of new members.[25]

Husák's address to the congress stressed all these encouraging changes, for the team in control, and painted a generally satisfactory picture of the state and society. The only point causing the first secretary concern was the situation of the country's economy. Labor productivity, far from increasing, had instead diminished, and the shortage of skilled labor, typical of an advanced nation expanding its potential, persisted. Industrial output continued to lag behind the planned targets; agricultural production did not seem to fare much better; and investments also fell short of established goals. Very serious was the growing deficit in the balance of foreign trade, which was vital for a Czechoslovak economy dependent on exports for its supply of essential raw materials. A drastic rise in the price of Soviet oil, adjusting to the high price in the world markets, was one of the reasons for the deficit. Economic difficulties must have been particularly unwelcome to the Husák leadership at this juncture, as good performance in this area was one of the few avenues of legitimation left to the Soviet-sponsored regime.

Actually the Fifteenth Congress was supposed to be a milestone on the way to further normalization. This goal had been postulated since April 1969 but not yet attained, and some aspects of the congress testified to its elusive nature. The Yugoslav and the Rumanian delegations' spokesmen seized the opportunity to stress the need for every Communist party to take its decisions "independently and in harmony with the interests of their own societies."[26] The thrust of the message was not hard to see. The French and Italian delegations, on the other hand, were not allowed to present orally the message they had submitted in writing, again for obvious reasons. The coverage of the Czechoslovak party congress in the Italian Communist press, which was critical of the imposed restrictions, elicited an irritated response from the Czechoslovak hosts.[27] Thus the Fifteenth Congress, instead of marking a successful return to the state of affairs in the CPCS that had been dramatically upset by the Soviet intervention of 1968, showed that relations within the world Communist movement, which had been equally disturbed by the Soviet action, were no more back to normal in 1976, eight years after the event, than was the situation in Czechoslovakia itself.

The visibly slow normalization could hardly be compensated for by the predictably unanimous endorsement of the regime in the general elections of October 1976, in which the single ballot of the National Front polled 99 percent of the votes, a picture typical of all totalitarian elections. In Czechoslovakia, by that time, dissent had assumed other forms of expression than voting. As signs of the prevailing mood, the voices of the partisans of the reformist cause were far more important; on several occasions they criticized the regime's policies or protested against the discrimination they had to suffer. Thus the former Central Committee secretary Zdeněk Mlynář sent an open letter to the participants in the Communist summit held in East Berlin at the end of June 1976.[28] The host party did not allow the letter to be tabled or discussed; nevertheless, the head of the Italian delegation, Communist Party of Italy Secretary-General Enrico Berlinguer, in his speech criticized Soviet interference in Czechoslovakia. The Czechoslovak media, which otherwise extensively covered the summit, deleted this passage from the text. In the course of 1976, prominent reformists such as Jiří Hájek and František Kriegel gave various interviews in the Western press, radio, and television. In these interviews, they either corrected the official version of the 1968 events or supplied new, hitherto unpublished details, none of which pleased the group in control of the party.

The Unending Legitimation Crisis

As Czechoslovakia entered the tenth year since the Soviet-led military intervention, a new initiative was developed by the domestic opposition, both Communist and non-Communist, that proved the crisis of legitimacy was still acute. In the first days of 1977, a group of intellectuals, artists, economic experts, and former politicians, identifying themselves as citizens concerned with respect for human rights in Czechoslovakia, launched an appeal to the government and to world opinion. They called for an end to the persecution of liberal and reformist ideas and admonished the power holders to abide by the principles of the constitution as well as by those of universal law. The group took as its point of reference the final act of the European Conference on Peace and Security held in 1974 and 1975 in Helsinki, Finland, especially the part dealing with free circulation of persons and ideas. This part of the treaty, known in journalistic terminology as the "Third Helsinki Basket," had been endorsed, along with other stipulations of the final act, by Czechoslovakia in a ceremony attended by President of the Republic Gustav Husák on July 30, 1975. It was later ratified by the Czechoslovak National Assembly and enacted for internal implementation as a special Czechoslovak federal law. The manifesto of the dissident group of January

1977, which has been referred to as "Charter '77," blamed Czechoslovak authorities for violating the spirit and the letter of this law. Thus the Charter was, strictly speaking, an internal petition seeking redressment of injustices within the framework of valid Czechoslovak legislation.[29]

The government, however, understood the document as an "act of sedition instigated by domestic and foreign enemies of Socialism."[30] It might have been the scope of the protest that frightened the regime. Indeed, in terms of the number of signatories, initially about three hundred and soon reaching one thousand, it exceeded by far any similar initiative undertaken in the past. The proponents came literally from all walks of life, although the intellectual elite among them prevailed. It may also have been the fact that the Chartists included a large number of Communists, including some who had been expelled from the party and some in good standing, that alarmed the party leadership. Among them figured prominent names such as Jiří Hájek, Zdeněk Mlynář, Milan Huebl, and Lieutenant-General Vilém Sacher. Whatever the actual reason, the reaction of the authorities was forceful. The sponsors were harassed and persecuted, some of them were arrested and condemned for "distributing subversive literature," some were deported, some were made subject to police supervision and continuous investigation, and all were dismissed from their employment. It was during an interrogation that one of the Chartist leaders, philosophy professor Jan Patočka, suffered a brain hemorrhage and died. Persecution only exacerbated the resistance. By the end of 1977, the number of signatures under the Charter had multiplied fourfold.

Even taken as a purely internal matter, the Charter movement was significant enough. It suggested that the opposition to the Soviet-sponsored course had not yet been silenced. However, it soon overgrew national boundaries and began to influence Czechoslovakia's international relations, both on the diplomatic and on the party level. The Charter spokesmen, after petitioning the Czechoslovak authorities in vain, submitted the document to several foreign representatives in the country and to members of foreign delegations visiting Czechoslovakia. Many of the foreign diplomats, recognizing the legally unassailable form of the protest, responded positively and met with the Charter leaders for informal talks. This was viewed by the government as a breach of civic loyalty by the Chartists and as interference by the foreign officials. New searches, arrests, and interrogations followed, accompanied by a campaign in the media that reminded the public of the worst times of

Stalinism. Contrary to the intended purpose, the offensive against the Charter movement not only discredited the system in world opinion, but also strained the relations between the CPCS and its counterparts abroad.

The Communist Party of Italy condemned in very vigorous terms the treatment of the Charter proponents by the Czechoslovak authorities. As a gesture of solidarity, the press and publication department of the Italian Communist Party offered Milan Huebl a position in the party's publication network. The reactions of the rest of the West European Communist parties and of the Japanese Communist party were similar to that of their Italian comrades. The ruling parties in Central and Eastern Europe voiced their disapproval by default, as it were: they did not undertake any repressive action against those in their countries who voiced sympathy with the Chartists, for example, the Soviet physicist Sakharov and sixty other Soviet personalities, the Polish Workers' Defense Committee, a group of thirty Hungarian intellectuals and artists, and ninety-two Yugoslav signatories of a message of encouragement to the Czechoslovak dissidents.[31] According to reliable sources, the Czechoslovak party's inept handling of the Charter issue was also criticized by the top officials of other ruling parties at the meeting in Sofia in March 1977.[32]

In the same month, independently of the Charter manifesto, eleven former members of the Central Committee of the CPCS addressed an appeal to all European Communist parties to use their influence in Prague and make the Czechoslovak party live up to the commitment to free comradely discussion made by all participants in the East Berlin summit in 1976. Among the authors of the appeal were Jiří Hájek, František Kriegel, Zdeněk Mlynář, Josef Špaček, and František Vodsloň. Only the West European Communist parties officially acknowledged receipt of the plea, but the move of the Czechoslovak reformists drew considerable attention everywhere.[33]

The year 1977 also saw other controversies in the world Communist movement that did not concern Czechoslovakia directly, but nevertheless owed much of their heat to the unresolved issue of the legitimacy of Soviet intervention in Czechoslovak matters. One of these was a dispute over the concept of a specific policy line for the West European Communist parties, often labeled Eurocommunism. The merits and feasibility of a distinct West European road to socialism had long been discussed; the idea had been formulated in the late 1950s by the Italian Communist leader Palmiro Togliatti in connection with his polycentrist theory. However, the dispute between the partisans and the opponents of the concept flared up again with the publication in Paris in 1977 of a brochure by the secretary-general of the Communist Party of Spain, Santiago Carillo, under the title *Eurocommunism and the State.* The Czechoslovak party soon became involved in the controversy.

Czechoslovak involvement was due to the action of one of the most prominent representatives of the dogmatic wing in the CPCS, former First Secretary of the CPS Vasil Bil'ák. Bil'ák took the opportunity of the already mentioned meeting of the Communist party leaders in Sofia in March 1977 for a scathing attack on Carillo and other Communists who shared Carillo's views.[34] He repeated his invectives at the subsequent plenary session of the Central Committee of the CPCS in Prague in April. The argument gained in importance when Bil'ák summed up his position in the form of an article, published in the Soviet review *Voprosy Istorii.* According to Bil'ák, Eurocommunism was "a bourgeois device for the purpose of diverting attention from genuine Socialism." Bil'ák continued his broadside against Eurocommunism at a press conference given in Vienna while he was guest of the Austrian Communist party, and in the opening speech at the congress of the Union of Czechoslovak Journalists in Prague in June. The thrust of his attacks was directed against the Communist Party of Italy, which did not fail to refute his diatribes energetically.

The article in *Voprosy Istorii* contained an interesting passage in which Bil'ák asserted that "Eurocommunism had been invented as a substitute after the gimmick of so-called Socialism with a Human Face had failed."[35] Thus the Czechoslovak question was brought into the center of the Eurocommunism dispute. To be sure, a certain affinity between the two cannot be denied: the Czechoslovak democratization of 1968 and Eurocommunism of the late 1970s both constituted a challenge to the Soviet claim to supremacy over the world Communist movement. Whoever rejected the first also had to reject the second. Bil'ák took care that this connection, which may have not been evident to everybody, should become known. From then on, the regular exchanges between the CPCS spokesmen and the media of the West European Communist parties on the subject of Eurocommunism always touched upon the theme of the Prague Spring and of the Soviet intervention that had put a sudden end to it. The controversy showed how little the conflicting opinions among the various centers of world communism on the rights or wrongs of the Soviet action had been reconciled during the ten years since the fateful days of August 1968. At the start of the 1980s, everything seemed to indicate that no end was yet in sight to the legitimacy crisis, internal as well as international, that had been triggered by the application to Czechoslovakia of the Brezhnev Doctrine.

Chapter Twelve

Concluding Note

After having followed the Communist Party of Czechoslovakia through more than sixty years of its turbulent history, what conclusions can we make and what future developments can we anticipate? We have seen that communism in Czechoslovakia had drawn its initial élan mainly from the perception of itself as the legitimate heir to the great traditions of the workers' movement. This driving force was as powerful as the inspiration of the October Bolshevik Revolution. However, the failure of early attempts to lead the working class into revolutionary action showed the radical left that it had overestimated its influence. This experience made the leaders more receptive to the idea of the Czechoslovak Communist movement above all as an important link in a centrally controlled world revolutionary organization.

This new self-image opened the door to dominance by the power center in Moscow, which gradually triumphed over all groups and currents trying to assert autonomous policies that would be in greater harmony with Czechoslovak social conditions and political culture. Although the experience of political apprenticeship in a democratic polity to a certain extent marked all Communist leaders, including those most hostile to the bourgeois state and its constitutional game, service to a universal movement bent on changing the whole human condition appealed strongly enough to a sufficient number of them to permit the integration of Czechoslovak communism into a conspiratorial world system governed from Moscow. In 1929, the CPCS became what the Soviet politicians had always wanted it to be: a tool among other tools of an international revolutionary operation. This was the essence of the successful bolshevization that was accomplished by the Fifth Party Congress.

After bolshevization, the CPCS led the exalted but marginal and not very auspicious existence of a political sect, prey to an interminable series of violent crises and conflicts, until through the historical accidents of Munich and the Second World War it hit upon a new source of life. Since the dismemberment of Czechoslovakia, but especially since the involvement of the USSR in the war, it succeeded in identifying itself in the eyes of a large part of the population with the liberation struggle of the Czechs and the national aspirations of the Slovaks. These two concerns were easier to adopt than to reconcile within one political party, but because of the special conditions created by the division of Czechoslovak territory and by foreign occupation, the Communist cause was able to profit from both events.

The prestige the CPCS vicariously enjoyed as an unofficial representative of the most powerful war victor in the Central European area brought it to a new peak of popularity. The party became a mass movement, a status it has not shed since. Ironically, this happened under the very same leadership that two decades earlier had carried out the bolshevization program calling for a small elite party organization. In its new form, the party again played the role of a tool and a spearhead, no longer of a world revolutionary force but of a totalitarian superpower. The policy choices the CPCS made in this period no more represented the interests of those for whom it claimed to speak than did those made before the war. The seizure of control through the February coup of 1948 was a tactical move on the chessboard of international politics, calculated to aid the USSR in its conflict with the West, rather than a genuine revolution.

The policies of the party during the first twenty years of undisputed rule, too, were little more than adaptations of the Czechoslovak economy and politics to the needs of the Soviet Union. This dependence brought serious social dislocations and arrested the development of Czechoslovakia, already in progress, into an advanced industrial society. In the party itself, its most appalling impact was the terror of the 1950s, so strangely out of tune with all previous Czechoslovak experience. The mistakes of the personality-cult era, as the brutal repression of all dissent, initially outside and later within the Communist ranks, is now somewhat apologetically called by the party's spokesmen, caused a permanent trauma in the Czechoslovak Communist movement. As a consequence, the destalinization launched by the Soviet leaders in 1956 seemed a particularly risky course to the team in control of the Czechoslovak party: the admission of the inhumane acts committed during the early years after the seizure of power severly undermined the authority of the regime. Therefore, the new policy was only reluctantly followed in Czechoslovakia, otherwise an obedient ally of the Soviet Union, a circumstance that brought about the first discrepancy in the policy line between the two parties.

Although the leaderships tarnished by their participation in Stalinist crimes initially resisted the polycentric trend manifest in the Soviet bloc since the death of Stalin, this trend nevertheless provided the Czechoslovak Communist movement with a new, third chance to find a more solid basis in society than power delegated from Moscow. The search for such a basis actually seemed to be undertaken when the Novotný group, which had been at the helm since 1954, lost its position to the coalition of younger Czech nonconformists and Slovak nationalists in January 1968. Socialism with a Human Face had never been articulated as a program for Czechoslovak withdrawal from the Soviet orbit, but its orientation toward the great Czechoslovak liberal and radical heritage was unmistakable. Those probably were the danger signals to the power center in Moscow, which feared not the disintegration of a Communist party in a strategic spot, but the passage of an entire movement into an alien ideological universe. An intervention by naked force became inevitable to stop this transition.

The end of the democratization experiment marked the party's return, for the third time in its history, to the status of a remote-controlled subsidiary of the CPSU. However, some aspects of the present situation indicate that this may not be the most stable of all arrangements. The Czechoslovak crisis of 1968, in its impact upon the Communist party itself, was comparable to the bolshevization crisis of 1929. In its national consequences and its effect upon the world Communist movement, of course, it has been far more important. There were, besides, significant differences in the nature of the two events. Whereas bolshevization had been an intraparty coup, a palace revolution only morally supported by the Communist world center of the time, the establishment of the present regime, both in the party and in the state, required direct military action from outside. The rule imposed over the CPCS and the country in the period of normalization has not been entrusted to an ideologically motivated party faction (no *karlínský kluci* this time) but to a rather heterogeneous, cautious, and conservative segment of the party. This choice betrays the embarrassment of the foreign sponsor more than it reflects a real distribution of allegiances.

The present leadership, a peculiar mix of the victims of Stalinism and of its former advocates, is held together by a shared apprehension of change, and rules by Moscow's grace over a party which the events of 1968 split down the middle. It faces not only a hostile majority of the nonorganized population but also considerable opposition among the rank and file party membership, who question the legitimacy of the prevailing order. The problem is compounded by the size of the party, which since the end of World War II, through the February coup and the Prague Spring, has remained one of the strongest Communist parties in the world. It has to be assumed that the opposition was not eliminated in the 1970 purge. Even if all the three hundred thousand or so expelled members had been supporters of the liberal course, which is unlikely, a sizable number of dissenters would still have remained.

The progress of normalization, which has been very slow considering that even after ten years things have not returned to what the Soviet power center regards as normal, will to a large extent depend on how successful the Moscow-backed leaders will be in pre-emptively identifying and neutralizing the potential heads of the unreconstructed opposition. The various protest actions, the latest of which was the Charter 1977 movement, show that it has not yet been silenced. On the other hand, the regime can pin some hopes on the changing distribution of party membership by age: the statistics published during the Fifteenth Congress indicate that 90 percent were thirty-five years old or younger. Soon, too, many will not remember the events of the Stalinist period and those preceding the Dubček episode. These facts in themselves, however, give no guarantee that there will be more conformity to the Soviet-determined line.

By far the most serious handicap of the postintervention leadership has been its patent unwillingness or inability, or both, to suggest and implement alternative solutions to the problems that the 1968 democratization current had proposed to resolve. These problems have not even been acknowledged by Husák and his aides. Yet they have been there, looming large: the hopelessly outdated character of the political system in a relatively advanced modern nation; the inconsistency of the relationship established between the two ethnic groups, which is anchored in the constitution but not respected by the Communist party; and the unfinished business of the break with the deformations and crimes of the Stalinist past. As long as these issues are not confronted, instability is likely to continue. To be sure, the preference of the team in control for immobility has been nothing more than the Czechoslovak version of the same attitude displayed by the Soviet decision makers, whose interests Husák and his associates are expected to protect. Politics being always the art of the possible, there has been not much room for more imaginative moves on the part of the CPCS leaders, even if they had been able to conceive of such moves.

On the other hand, a return to the conditions prior to 1968 is hardly possible. That situation in itself was an anachronism; Novotný's CPCS constituted an island, artificially sheltered from currents that agitated all other leading parties of the Communist bloc. Since then, the world Communist movement has traveled a long way. Destalinization took its toll in the replacement of enthusiasm by more pragmatic attitudes. Also, the temper of the time is now different from that prevailing after the Second World War. Not even the devoted supporters of Soviet supremacy can believe that the ultimate battle between the two major types of modern sociopolitical order is imminent. The call for closing the ranks' and giving unqualified obedience to Moscow's leadership, which is supposed to justify the suppression of dissident thought, has thus a somewhat hollow ring.

However, the greatest obstacle to such a return is the change in the CPCS brought about by the 1968 experience. The relatively brief period of liberalization left a deeper imprint among Czechoslovak Communists than it would appear. The Prague Spring was more than just one dramatic event in the party's history. In its impact, it surpassed all attempts at independence ever undertaken. It was crucial that the basic elements of the Czechoslovak political culture were assimilated into the reform program: until then they had only challenged, contained, or occasionally influenced Communist actions—that is, they had been merely external factors in the process of shaping Communist policies. However difficult the implementation of this program might have been if the process had not been forcibly interrupted, it remains true that the proponents of Socialism with a Human Face became spokesmen of the national liberal and progressive legacy. Under their guidance the CPCS no longer seemed to be a spearhead of a remote-controlled international operation. Since then much effort has been expended to obliterate the memories of the Czechoslovak road to socialism, but the fact that a truly

Czechoslovak political platform was formulated for the Communist party cannot be changed. Although temporarily shelved, that program will continue to exist as an alternative in case there is a major shift in relations within the Communist world.

An interesting aspect of the CPCS has been the mass character it has retained for more than thirty years, in spite of countless purges and upheavals of all kinds. It may not be toally unrealistic, therefore, to expect that new reform currents resembling those before the Prague Spring could take shape among this large and heterogeneous body at some later time. Nevertheless, it is difficult to overlook an important lesson of the liberalization intermezzo and its sudden end: in the given constallation of world forces, no change originating from within the Czechoslovak Communist movement will be permanent unless it is completed by its international counterpart. Future events in Czechoslovakia may bring surprises, but they will not in themselves ensure any lasting transformations. At present, the political system is probably less stable than ever, since no significant problem has been seriously tackled by the current power holders, and the trust of the ruled, including a large segment of party membership, is at a very low point. Yet the answer to the question whether the CPCS will ever again play a more independent role that is in greater harmony with the interests and the needs of the nation has to be sought in the development of the Soviet core to which the CPCS, for the greater part of its existence, has only been peripheral.

Notes

Preface

1. Pavel Reimann, *Dějiny Komunistické strany Československa* (Prague, 1931). The author of the present volume had at his disposal the German version: *Geschichte der Kommunistischen Partei der Tschechoslovakei*, published by Carl Hoym Nachfolger in Berlin and Hamburg, 1931. Reimann wrote his second book on CPCS history in 1961, this time as head of an authors' collective, *Dějiny KSČ* [History of the CPCS] (Prague: Státní nakladatelství politické literatury, 1961). The later brochure *Dějiny KSC: Studijní příručka* [History of the CPCS: A Study Manual] (Bratislava: Vydavatelstvo politickej literatúry, 1965) cannot be viewed as a historical study; it is a political pamphlet, plainly and deliberately omitting all facts that could be embarrassing to the power holders of the time. It has been used mostly for indoctrination work ("party schooling").

Chapter 1: A Difficult Birth

1. Čestmír Amort, "Československé komunistické hnutí v Rusku," *Život strany*, no. 10 (1973), pp. 49–51.

2. Karel Pichlík, *Zahraniční odboj 1914–1918 bez legend* (Prague: Svoboda, 1968), pp. 324–342 (This presentation of the events concerning the Czechoslovak Legion in Russia after the October 1917 revolution, although written from the point of view of a CPCS member, is remarkably well balanced; especially striking is the unbiased portrayal of T. G. Masaryk). A detailed discussion of the conditions in which the evacuation of the Czechoslovak troops from the USSR was negotiated and carried out can be found in the First World War memoirs of the two main leaders of the Czechoslovak liberation campaign, T. G. Masaryk and Eduard Beneš. See T.G. Masaryk, *Světová revoluce* (Prague: Orbis-Čin, 1923; the English translation is *The Making of a State* [London: Allen and Unwin, 1927]); and Eduard Beneš, *Světová válka a naše revoluce* (Prague: Orbis-Čin, 1927), 2:173–314.

3. See T. G. Masaryk, *The Making of a State*, pp. 169–178.

4. There is a large body of literature about the adventures of the Czechoslovak Legion in Siberia. A good, objective account of the events that ultimately led to

the involvement of the troops in the Russian civil war can be found in George F. Kennan's *Soviet-American Relations*, vol. 2: *The Decision to Intervene* (Princeton, N.J.: Princeton University Press, 1958).

    5. Kennan, *Soviet-American Relations*, 2:471.

    6. This work by Masaryk appeared first in German as *Die philosophischen und soziologischen Grundlagen des Marxismus* in Vienna in 1899 (reprinted by Zeller Verlag, Osnabrueck, Germany, 1964). It was translated into English by Erazim V. Kohák as *Masaryk on Marx* (Lewisburg, Pa.: Bucknell University Press, 1972).

    7. M. A. Silin, *A Critique of Masarykism* (Moscow: Progress Publishers, 1975), p. 56.

    8. A book on this subject by Masaryk was published only after World War I, and that in unfinished form: *Rusko a Evropa* (Prague: Orbis, 1927), vols. 1 and 2. The English translation of the unfinished third volume, by Robert Bass, appeared in the United States as *The Spirit of Russia* (New York: Barnes and Noble, 1967). However, Masaryk was already lecturing extensively on Russia, as Professor of Sociology at the Prague University, at the turn of the century. Cf. Julius Dolanský, *Masaryk a Rusko předrevoluční* (Prague: Nakladatelství Československé akademie věd, 1959).

    9. Milan Machovec, *T. G. Masaryk* (Prague, Melantrich, 1968). The German translation of this volume was published by the Verlag Styria in Graz, Austria, in 1969, under the title *Thomas G. Masaryk*. The charge that the ideological heritage of the First Republic founded by Masaryk had "poisoned" the CPCS was contained in the so-called White Book circulated in all world languages after the military intervention of August 1968. See Group of Soviet Journalists, *On Events in Czechoslovakia: Facts, Documents, Press Reports and Eye-Witness Accounts* (Moscow, 1968). The same charge was developed in great detail in Silin, *Critique of Masarykism*, especially in Chapter 6, "Revival and Failure of Masarykism," pp. 239–299.

    10. Rudolf Medek, *Plukovník Josef Jiří Švec* [Colonel Josef Jiří Švec], is a drama about a legion officer who commits suicide to shake his troops out of lethargy and to stop further progress of their conversion to Bolshevik ideas. The problem of the defection of the legionnaires to the Soviet side has also been mentioned by Eduard Beneš, in his *Světová válka a naše revoluce* and has been dealt with more recently by Communist scholars; see Karel Pichlík, Vlastimil Vávra, and Jaroslav Křížek, *Červenobílá a rudá: vojáci ve válce a revoluci 1914–1918* (Prague: Svoboda, 1967), p. 271.

    11. Reimann, *Dějiny Komunistické*, p. 74.

    12. Ibid., p. 36.

    13. James A. Davies, "Towards a Theory of Revolution," *American Sociological Review* 23, February 1958.

    14. Reimann, *Dějiny Komunistické*, p. 56.

    15. Joseph Stalin, *On the National and the Colonial Question* (Moscow: Foreign Languages Publishing House, 1936); the Russian original appeared in 1909.

    16. Heinrich Kuhn, *Zeittafel zur Geschichte der Kommunistischen Partei der*

Tschechoslowakei [Chronology of the History of the CPCS] (Munich: Fides-Verlagsgesellschaft, 1973), pp. 29–30; also Miroslav Buchvaldek et al., *Dějiny Československa v datech* [History of Czechoslovakia in Dates] (Prague: Svoboda, 1968), p. 290.

17. Buchvaldek et al., *Dějiny Československa*, p. 296; also Reimann, *Dějiny Komunistické*, pp. 87–89.

18. Reimann, *Dějiny Komunistické*, p. 79.

19. Oscar Jászi, *Revolution and Counter-Revolution in Hungary* (London: King and Son, 1924), pp. 88, 92.

20. Eva S. Balogh, "Nationality Problems of the Hungarian Soviet Republic," in *Hungary in Revolution 1918–19*, ed. Ivan Volgyes (Lincoln, Nebraska: University of Nebraska Press, 1971), p. 117.

21. Ibid., p. 120.

22. Ibid., p. 115.

23. The title of the information pamphlet published by the left wing of the Social Democratic party was *Zásady a cíle marxistické levice Československé sociálně demokratické strany dělnické* [The Principles and the Goals of the Marxist Left of the Czechoslovak Social Democratic Workers Party] (Prague, 1920).

24. Wolf Oschliess, "Die Kommunistische Partei der Tschechoslowakei in der Ersten Tschechoslowakischen Republik (1918–1938)," *Berichte des Bundesinstituts fuer Ostwissenschaftliche und Internationale Studien*, no. 61 (1974), p. 17.

25. Reimann, *Dějiny Komunistické*, p. 127.

26. Ibid., pp. 149–151.

27. Ibid., p. 148; also Buchvaldek et al., *Dějiny Československa*, p. 302.

28. Reimann, *Dějiny Komunistické*, p. 124.

29. *Zásady a cíle*, p. 7.

30. Reimann, *Dějiny Komunistické*, pp. 93–94.

31. Oschliess, "Kommunistiscshe Partei," pp. 16–17.

32. Reimann, *Dějiny Komunistické*, p. 97.

33. Ibid., pp. 149–151.

34. *Protokol XIII. řádného kongresu Československé sociálně demokratické strany dělnické*, Prague: Delnické nakladatelství Ant. Němec, 1920.

35. Reimann, *Dějiny Komunistické*, pp. 112–114.

36. Ibid.; all of Chapter 8 (pp. 110–119) is devoted to the claim that the situation in Czechoslovakia in December 1920 was a revolutionary one, but that the "leaders of the Marxist left . . . lagged behind the proletarian mass movement" (p. 110).

37. Zdeněk Kárník, "Založení KSČ a Kominterna," *Revue dějin socialismu*, no. 2 (1962), pp. 163–202.

38. Karel Gorovský, "O založení KSČ—Drážďanská konference v dubnu 1921," *Revue dějin socialismu*, no. 3 (1968), pp. 415–451.

39. Kárník, "Založení KSČ," p. 192.

40. Václav Šplíchal, "K historii závěrečného procesu vytváření KSČ a jejího přijetí do Komunistické Internacionály," *Příspěvky k dějinám KSČ*, no. 6 (1966), pp. 858−877.

41. J. Galandauer, "Slučovací sjezd KSČ," *Nová mysl*, no. 10 (1971), p. 1489.

Chapter 2: The Road to Bolshevization

1. Reimann, *Dějiny Komunistické*, p. 171.

2. Ibid., p. 174.

3. Ibid., pp. 185−186.

4. The strength and the influence of the Communist-controlled unions in Czechoslovakia at that time are presented in Vladimír Dubský, *KSČ a odborové hnutí v Československu na počátku dvacátých let* [The CPCS and the Trade Union Movement in Czechoslovakia in the Early 1920s] (Prague: Státní nakladatelství politické literatury, 1966).

5. Reimann, *Dějiny Komunistické*, pp. 184−185.

6. *Ústava Československé republiky* [The Constitution of the Czechoslovak Republic], Preamble (Prague: Státní nakladatelství politické literatury, 1920).

7. *Protokol prvního řádného sjezdu Komunistické strany Československa, 2. − 5. února 1923* (Prague, 1923).

8. Reimann, *Dějiny Komunistické*, pp. 193−194.

9. Kuhn, *Zeittafel*, p. 39.

10. Ibid., p. 40.

11. Reimann, *Dějiny Komunistické* p. 195.

12. Ibid., pp. 189−190.

13. "About the Tactics of the Komintern," Supplement 6 to *Protocol of the Fourth Congress of the Komintern* (Moscow, 1924), pp. 1014−1018.

14. Reimann, *Dějiny Komunistické*, p. 188.

15. Grigori J. Zinoviev, "On the Bolshevization of Communist Parties," *Communist International*, no. 1 (1925).

16. Reimann, *Dějiny Komunistické*, pp. 201−205.

17. *Protocol of the Fifth World Congress of the Communist International* (Moscow, 1925).

18. Reimann, *Dějiny Komunistické*, p. 224.

19. Ibid., p. 207.

20. *Protokol druhého řádného sjezdu Komunistické strany Československa* (Prague, 1924).

21. Reimann, *Dějiny Komunistické*, pp. 216−217.

22. *Protokol druhého.*

23. *Rudé právo*, February 11, 1925.

24. Reimann, *Dějiny Komunistické*, p. 229.

25. *Za bolševickou orientaci KSČ* [For a Bolshevist Orientation of the CPCS] (Prague: Svoboda, 1954), p. 31.

26. Ústřední výbor Svazu komunistické mládeže, *Leninismus nebo . . . ?* (Prague, 1925).

27. *Protokol třetího řádného sjezdu Komunistické strany Československa* (Prague, 1925).

28. *Rudé právo*, September 30, 1925.

29. R. V. Burks, *The Dynamics of Communism in Eastern Europe* (Princeton, N.J.: Princeton University Press, 1961), pp. 187–195.

30. S. M. Lipset and Stein Rokkan, *Party Systems and Voter Alignments* (New York: Free Press, 1967), pp. 1–64.

31. K. W. Deutsch, *Nationalism and Social Communication* (Cambridge, Mass.: M.I.T. Press, 1962), pp. 125–153.

32. Reimann, *Dějiny Komunistické*, p. 251.

33. J. Pollak, *Boj o Komunistickou Internacionálu* [Struggle for the Communist International] (Prague, 1927).

34. *Protokol čtvrtého řádného sjezdu Komunistické strany Československa* (Prague, 1927).

35. Ibid.

36. *Rudé právo*, October 31, 1927.

37. *Rudé právo*, June 18, 1928.

38. Reimann, *Dějiny Komunistické*, pp. 310–312.

39. Jarmila Menclová, "Po Rudém dni. K předhistorii V. sjezdu KSČ," *Příspěvky k dějinám KSČ*, 1961, pp. 674–691.

40. Reimann, *Dějiny Komunistické*, p. 318.

41. Stern's defense was described by Pavel Reimann in *Dějiny Komunistické*, p. 315.

42. Ibid. pp. 315–316.

43. *Protocol of the Sixth World Congress of the Communist International* (Moscow, 1928).

44. Ibid.

45. *Open Letter of the Executive Committee of the Communist International to the Members of the CPCS* (Moscow, 1928).

46. *ČETEKA* (Czechoslovak Press Agency) Press Release, June 25, 1928.

47. *Protokol pátého řádného sjezdu Komunistické strany Československa* (Prague, 1929).

48. Jos. Guttmann, *Wer sind und was wollen die Liquidatoren: Eine informative und polemische Broschuere* (Berlin and Hamburg: Carl Heym Nachfolger, 1929), p. 31.

49. Ibid., pp. 96–100.

50. Viliam Plevza, *KSČ a revolučné hnutie na Slovensku 1929–1938* (Bratislava: Vydavatelstvo Slovenskej akadémie vied, 1965), p. 52.

51. Buchvaldek et al., *Dějiny Československa*, p. 466.

Chapter 3: From Bolshevization to Munich

1. David E. Apter, *The Politics of Modernization* (Chicago: University of Chicago Press, 1965), pp. 12–16.

2. Reimann, *Dějiny Komunistické*, p. 286.

3. Plevza, *KSČ a revolučné*, pp. 55–57.

4. Ibid., p. 85.

5. *Protokol šestého řádného sjezdu Komunistické strany Československa* (Prague, 1931).

6. Zdeněk Hradilák, "Josef Guttman—konflikt rozumu a svědomí," *Revue dějin socialismu*, no. 5 (1968), pp. 645–680.

7. *Rudé právo*, December 31, 1933.

8. *Tvorba*, no. 23 (1935).

9. The speech by Georgi Dimitrov at the Seventh World Congress of the Communist International in Moscow, in Hermann Weber, *Die Kommunistische Internationale* (Hanover: J. H. W. Dietz Nachfolger, 1966), pp. 294–299.

10. Buchvaldek et al., *Dějiny Československa*, p. 466.

11. Ibid.

12. Klement Gottwald, *Desel let* (Prague: Svoboda, 1949), p. 11.

13. *Rudé právo*, May 26, 1935.

14. Gottwald, *Deset let*, p. 27.

15. *Protokol sedmého řádného sjezdu Komunistické strany Československa* (Prague, 1936).

16. Ibid.

17. Ibid.

18. Ibid.

19. *Rudé právo*, November 6, 1936.

20. Gottwald, *Deset let*, p. 19.

21. See *Příruční slovník k dějinám KSČ* [Dictionary of the History of the CPCS], vol. 1, entry "Mezinárodní brigáda ve Španělsku"; see also *Bojovali jsme ve Španělsku: Čs. dobrovolníci mezinárodních brigád ve Španelsku 1936–1939* (Prague, 1956).

22. Weber, *Kommunistische Internationale*, pp. 302–304.

23. See *Příruční slovník*, vol. 1, entry "Mezinárodní brigáda."

24. Editorial by Henri Kerillis in *L'Epoque* (Paris), September 28, 1938.

25. Eduard Beneš, *Mnichovské dny* [The Days of Munich] (Prague: Svoboda 1968), pp. 310–312.

26. Speech by the Soviet Commissar of Foreign Affairs, Maxim M. Litvinov, at the General Assembly of the League of Nations in Geneva, September 21, 1938; see also *Rudé právo*, September 22, 1938, and Beneš, *Mnichovské dny*, pp. 313–317.

27. Gottwald, *Deset let*, p. 168.

Chapter 4: From Munich to Liberation

1. Buchvaldek et al., *Dějiny Československa*, p. 339.

2. Ibid., pp. 339–340.

3. Resolution of the First Illegal Central Committee of the CPCS, December 15, 1940, published in the clandestine edition of *Rudé právo* circulated in Bohemia and Moravia in January 1941; reprinted in Eduard Beneš, *Paměti: Od Mnichova k nové válce a novému vítězství* (Prague: Orbis, 1948), pp. 214–217.

4. Beneš, *Paměti*, p. 212.

5. See *Příruční slovník*, vol. 1, entry "Illegální ÚV KSČ."

6. The cooperation between the clandestine Communist organization in Slovakia and the non-Communist components of the anti-Tiso resistance, especially the story of the Christmas agreement of 1943, is presented in Jozef Jablonický, *Z illegality do povstania: Kapitoly z občianskeho odboja* (Bratislava: Stání nakladatelství politické literatury, 1969).

7. Beneš, *Paměti*, pp. 366–398.

8. Wolfgang Venohr, *Aufstand fuer die Tschechoslowakei* (Hamburg: Christian Wegner Verlag, 1969), pp. 93–112.

9. Venohr, *Aufstand*, pp. 125–137.

10. Ibid., pp. 306–307.

11. Resolution of the Communist Party of the Transcarpathian Ukraine, endorsed by the Ruthenian National Council in Užgorod, November 26, 1944. See also Buchvaldek et al., *Dějiny Československa*, p. 355.

Chapter 5: From Liberation to the Coup d'Etat

1. Jaroslav Stránský, minister of education in the coalition National Front government, made this statement in his lecture on the politics that had led to the 1948 coup d'état, given in the Eduard Beneš Institute in London in July 1950.

2. In the border regions, for a time after the war, a situation prevailed that was comparable to that at the American frontier during pioneer times: all power was in the hands of local organs and central authority was almost nonexistent. Unlike the American situation, however, this one did not promote the spirit of democratic self-government, but served the interests of the best-organized force, the Communist party.

3. Gottwald, *Deset let*, pp. 350–353.

4. *Pražská květnová revoluce* [Prague May Uprising], publication of the Czech National Council, Prague, 1946, p. 70.

5. George S. Patton, *The War as I Saw It* (Boston, Mass.: Houghton Mifflin, 1947), p. 327.

6. Omar Bradley, *A Soldier's Story* (New York: H. Holt Company, 1951), p. 549.

7. Hubert Ripka, *Czechoslovakia Enslaved* (London: Victor Gollancz Ltd., 1950), pp. 36, 37.

8. *Pravda* (Bratislava), August 13, 1945.

9. Gottwald, *Deset let*, p. 447.

10. *Protokol osmého řádného sjezdu Komunistické strany Československa* (Prague, 1946).

11. *Rudé právo*, September 27, 1946.

12. Radio Prague, Domestic Service, July 4, 1947.

13. Josef Belda et al., "K otázce účasti Československa na Marshallově plánu" [On the Question of Czechoslovakia's Participation in the Marshall Plan], *Revue dějin socialismu*, 1968, pp. 81–100.

14. *Radio Moscow*, September 28, 1947.

15. Eugenio Reale, *Avec Jacques Duclos, au banc des accusés à la réunion constitutive du Kominform à Szklarska Poreba* (Paris: Plon, 1958), pp. 43–45.

16. Ibid., pp. 98–106; Slánský's report is reproduced verbatim.

17. *Právo lidu*, November 17, 1947.

18. Ripka, *Czechoslovakia Enslaved*, pp. 109–118.

19. Ibid., p. 196.

20. Otto Friedman, *The Break-Up of Czech Democracy* (London: Victor Gollancz Ltd., 1950), pp. 88–91.

21. Ibid., pp. 94–95.

22. *Rudé právo*, February 23, 1948.

23. Friedman, *Break-Up*, p. 78.

24. Ibid., pp. 110–118; for a more detailed presentation of the events that led to Jan Masaryk's death, see Claire Sterling, *The Masaryk Case* (London: 1968). From the point of view of Communist reformists, the story is told in an editorial by Jiří Hochman in *Rudé právo* dated April 16, 1948.

25. It is interesting to note that in referring to the seizure of power in February 1948, Communist spokesmen have never used the term revolution. On solemn occasions, they sometimes recall "Victorious February"; in everyday contexts we are likely to hear them speak of "the February events."

Chapter 6: From Victorious February to the Death of Stalin

1. Buchvaldek et al., *Dějiny Československa*, p. 468.

2. *Pravda* (Bratislava), September 28, 1948.

3. Reimann, *Dějiny Komunistické*, especially the chapter entitled "The CPCS and the Nationalities Problem."

4. *Protokol devátého řádného sjezdu Komunistické strany Československa* (Prague, 1949).

5. *Rudé právo*, February 25, 1949.

6. Jiří Pelikán, *The Czechoslovak Political Trials, 1950–1954* (Stanford, Ca.: Stanford University Press, 1971), pp. 64–66.

7. Ibid., pp. 74–75.

8. Ibid., pp. 72–75.

9. Ibid., p. 103.

10. Ibid., p. 104.

11. Radio Prague, February 26, 1950.

12. Jiří Pelikán, *Czechoslovak Political Trials*, pp. 88–89.

13. Ibid., pp. 90–93.

14. Ibid., p. 106.

15. *Rudé právo*, November 29, 1951.

16. Pelikán, *Czechoslovak Political Trials*, p. 113; for a detailed official account of this trial, see Ministry of Justice of the Czechoslovak Republic, *Proces s vedením protistátního spikleneckého centra v čele s Rudolfem Slánským* [The Trial of the Anti-State Conspiratorial Center Led by Rudolf Slánský] (Prague, 1953).

17. *Rudé právo*, January 9, 1953.

Chapter 7: From Stalin's Death to the Hungarian Uprising

1. Pelikán, *Czechoslovak Political Trials*, p. 122.

2. Ibid., pp. 123–124.

3. Ibid., p. 122.

4. Ibid., p. 123.

5. Ibid.

6. Ibid., p. 126.

7. Ibid.

8. Ibid., p. 127.

9. Radio Prague, August 1, 1953.

10. *Protokol desátého řádného sjezdu Komunistické strany Československa* (Prague, 1954).

11. Pelikán, *Czechoslovak Political Trials*, pp. 198–200.

12. Ibid., p. 201.

13. Ibid., p. 117.

14. *New York Times*, February 26, 1956.

15. *Rudé právo*, June 12, 1956.

16. *Literární noviny*, April 28 and 29, 1956.

17. See Novotný's comments in Pelikán, *Czechoslovak Political Trials*, pp. 216–217, 230; see also pp. 227–228 for views on Slánský expressed by Central Committee members B. Laštovička and V. Škoda.

18. Pelikán, *Czechoslovak Political Trials*, p. 194.

19. *Rudé právo*, December 7, 1956.

Chapter 8: From the Hungarian Uprising to the Crisis of the 1960s

1. *Pravda* (Moscow), November 2, 1957.

2. H. Gordon Skilling, "People's Democracy and the Socialist Revolution: A Case Study in Communist Scholarship," *Soviet Studies* 12, no. 3, pp. 241–262.

3. Skilling, *Czechoslovakia's Interrupted Revolution* (Princeton, N.J.: Princeton University Press, 1976), p. 46.

4. *Protokol jedenáctého řádného sjezdu Komunistické strany Československa* (Prague, 1958).

5. Jiří Hendrych's report on the Twenty-Second Congress of the CPSU, submitted to the Politbureau of the CPCS on November 14, 1961; see the pertinent passage in Pelikán, *Czechoslovak Political Trials*, p. 216.

6. See Skilling, *Czechoslovakia's Interrupted Revolution*, p. 400. According to this source, the report of the Piller Commission criticized Barák for "highly illegal" proceedings but did not discuss whether, and to what extent, the charges that had led to Barák's arrest and imprisonment in 1962 had been justified.

7. Pelikán, *Czechoslovak Political Trials*, pp. 218–219.

8. Zdeněk Eliáš and Jaromír Netík, "Czechoslovakia," in *Communism in Europe: Continuity, Change and the Sino-Soviet Dispute*, ed. William E. Griffith (Cambridge, Mass.: M.I.T. Press, 1966), 2:241.

Chapter 9: Belated De-Stalinization

1. Pelikán, *Czechoslovak Political Trials*, p. 220.

2. *XII. sjezd Komunistické strany Československa* (Prague, 1963).

3. Pelikán, *Czechoslovak Political Trials*, pp. 235–237.

4. Ibid., pp. 41–242.

5. Ibid., p. 242.

6. Karel Kosík, *Dialektika konkrétního* (Prague: Czechoslovak Academy of Sciences, 1965).

7. Machovec, *Masaryk*.

8. Ivan Sviták, *Lidský smysl kultury* (Prague: Československý spisovatel, 1968).

9. Radoslav Selucký, *Někomu chléb, někomu růže* (Prague: Mladá fronta, 1966); see also Radoslav Selucký and Milada Selucká, *Člověk a hospodářství* (Prague, 1967).

10. Selucký, *Západ je Západ* (Prague, 1967).

11. Radovan Richta et al., *Civilisace na rozcestí: Společenské a lidské souvislosti vědeckotechnické revoluce* (Prague, 1966). The English translation of this volume was published under the title *Civilization at the Crossroads* (White Plains, N.J.: International Arts and Sciences Press, 1969), and commented on by Daniel Bell in *The Coming of Post-Industrial Society* (New York: Basic Books, 1973), pp. 105–112.

12. Miroslav Kusý, "Strana a riadenie našej spoľočnosti," *Predvoj*, February 24, 1964.

13. Július Strinka, "Dve koncepcie socialistickej dialektiky" [Two Concepts of Socialist Dialectics], *Otázky marxistickej filozofie* 18, no. 1; see also idem, "Apologetický dogmatizmus a revolučná dialektika" [Apologetic Dogmatism and Revolutionary Dialectics], *Filozofia*, no. 1, 1966.

14. Michal Lakatoš, *Občan, právo, demokracie* (Prague: Svobodné slovo, 1966; this is the Czech version. The book was originally written in Slovak).

15. Bruno Štainer, "Tvrdá slova" [Harsh Words], *Svět motorů*, no. 22, 1966.

16. Strinka, "Apologetický dogmatizmus a revolučná dialektika"; Strinka's article in *Filozofia* became widely known thanks to the earlier publication of a somewhat condensed version in the popular review of the Union of Writers, *Kultúrny život* (Bratislava), November 6, 1965.

17. *XIII. sjezd Komunistické strany Československa* (Prague, 1966).

18. Ibid.

19. *Literární noviny*, June 28. 1967.

20. Dušan Hamšík, *Writers Against Rulers* (London, 1971), pp. 74–93.

21. *Frankfurter Allgemeine Zeitung*, August 11, 1967.

22. *Rudé právo*, September 2, 1967.

Chapter 10: Spring Without Summer

1. Kuhn, *Zeittafel*, pp. 107–108.

2. *Rok šedesátý osmý v usneseních a dokumentech ÚV KSČ* (Prague: Svoboda, 1969), p. 33.

3. Pelikán, *Czechoslovak Political Trials*, p. 298.

4. *Akční program Komunistické strany Československa* (Prague, 1968); the English translation appeared in London under the title *The Action Programme of the Czechoslovak Communist Party* (London: The Bertrand Russell Peace Foundation Ltd., 1968). The present discussion and the occasional quotes are based on the English text.

5. The final draft of the new party statutes was distributed as a special supplement to the August 10, 1968, edition of *Rudé právo*. Its English translation was published in Jirí Pelikán (ed.), *The Secret Vysočany Congress: Proceedings and Documents of the Extraordinary Fourteenth Congress of the Communist Party of Czechoslovakia, 22 August 1968* (London: Penguin Press, 1971), pp. 128–185.

6. *Action Programme*, p. 7.

7. Comment by Miloš Weiner, Radio Prague, March 23, 1968.

8. *Rok šedesátý osmý*, p. 44.

9. *Rudé právo*, May 6, 1968.

10. The manifesto was originally published in *Literární listy*, June 27, 1968. Its English translation can be found in Robin A. Remington, *Winter in Prague: Docu-*

ments on Czechoslovak Communism in Crisis (Cambridge, Mass.: M.I.T. Press, 1969), pp. 196–202.

11. See "Dopis pěti komunistických a dělnických stran ústřednímu výboru KSČ" [Letter from Five Communist and Workers' Parties to the Central Committee of the CPCS], *Rok šedesátý osmý*, p. 238; for the English version, see Remington, *Winter in Prague*, p. 227.

12. Skilling, *Czechoslovakia's Interrupted Revolution*, p. 288.

13. I. Alexandrov, "Attack on the Socialist Foundations of Czechoslovakia," *Pravda* (Moscow), July 11, 1968; the English translation of this editorial was published in *Current Digest of the Soviet Press* 20, no. 25, pp. 3–7.

14. *Rok šedesátý osmý*, pp. 243–250; for the English text see Remington, *Winter in Prague*, pp. 234–243.

15. PAP (Polish Press Agency) release of July 15, 1968.

16. *Rok šedesátý osmý*, pp. 239–240; Remington, *Winter in Prague*, p. 229.

17. *Rok šedesátý osmý*, p. 259.

18. Ibid., p. 249; also Remington, *Winter in Prague*, p. 243.

19. *Rok šedesátý osmý*, pp. 262–263; see also Remington, *Winter in Prague*, pp. 254–255.

20. *Rok šedesátý osmý*, pp. 263–267; see also Remington, *Winter in Prague*, pp. 256–261.

21. Czechoslovak Television, August 4, 1968.

Chapter 11: History Returns as Farce

1. *Rok šedesátý osmý*, p. 291.

2. The text of this letter was published by the Czechoslovak media on the first anniversary of the Soviet-led invasion; see Radio Prague, August 21, 1969. For the English version, see BBC International Program (London), August 22, 1969. The *Pravda* editorial was written by I. Alexandrov and entitled "Insolent Attacks by Reactionaries," *Pravda* (Moscow), August 18, 1968. The English translation of the editorial appeared in *Current Digest of the Soviet Press* 20, no. 33.

3. At least this is the date on which most observers and commentators seem to agree. The question has been addressed in great detail in Skilling, *Czechoslovakia's Interrupted Revolution*, the chapter entitled "Military Intervention."

4. The text of the alleged appeal for help was published, without signatures, in *Pravda* (Moscow), August 22, 1968; the English version can be found in Remington, *Winter in Prague*, pp. 295–299.

5. *Rok šedesátý osmý*, pp. 297–298.

6. Ibid., p. 304.

7. Ibid., p. 299.

8. Pelikán, *Secret Vysočany Congress*, pp. 254–255.

9. *Rok šedesátý osmý*, p. 302.

10. *Pravda* (Moscow), October 19, 1968.

11. *Rok šedesátý osmý*, pp. 329−330.

12. Ibid., pp. 336−337.

13. Ibid., pp. 372−392.

14. *Rudé právo*, April 3, 1969.

15. *Rudé právo*, April 19, 1969; *Pravda* (Bratislava), April 22, 1969.

16. *Rudé právo*, June 2, 1969.

17. Ibid., December 15, 1970.

18. *XIV. sjezd Komunistické strany Československa* (Prague, 1971). This document also exists in English as *14th Congress of the Communist Party of Czechoslovakia* (Prague: Orbis, 1971). This is an official English edition of a party congress report, a rather rare publication that may have been prompted by the need to defend the Soviet-sponsored policies of normalization among the English-speaking components of the international Communist movement. The English version is abridged and focuses mainly on speeches and reports by top party officials and distinguished guests.

19. *Rudé právo*, May 31, 1971.

20. *Poučení z krizového vývoje ve straně a společnosti po XIII. sjezdu Komunistické strany Československa* (Prague, 1971). This document was published in several languages; the English title is *The Lessons of the Crisis Development in the Party and Society Since the Thirteenth Congress of the CPCS.*

21. Among the right extremists, the observers claimed to identify party Presidium members Alois Indra and Vasil Bil'ák. The expected showdown had not taken place when these lines were written.

22. *Pravda* (Moscow), March 5, 1975.

23. *Pravda* (Bratislava), March 26, 1976.

24. *XV. sjezd Komunistické strany Československa* (Prague, 1976).

25. Ibid.

26. Ibid.

27. *Sunday Times* (London), April 11, 1976.

28. *Frankfurter Allgemeine Zeitung*, June 27, 1976.

29. *Frankfurter Allgemeine Zeitung*, January 7, 1977.

30. *Rudé právo*, February 12, 1977.

31. Reuter from Prague, March 13, 1977.

32. Deutsche Presse Agentur in its Paris dispatch of January 19, 1977; Agence France Presse, March 1, 1977; United Press International from Warsaw, March 14, 1977.

33. *Le Monde* (Paris), March 19, 1977.

34. Reuter from Prague, March 17, 1977.

35. *Voprosy Istorii* (Moscow), no. 5, May 1977.

Review of Bibliography

More details on the prehistory of the Communist Party of Czechoslovakia and the origins of the Czechoslovak workers' and socialist movement can be found in the writings of both Communist and non-Communist authors published before and after the Second World War. Most of these writings are in Czech or in Slovak; nevertheless, some basic sources will be accessible to readers knowing German. The following are of particular interest:

Aktionsprogramm der Kommunistischen Partei der Tschechoslowakei [Action Program of the Communist Party of Czechoslovakia]. Reichenberg: "Vorwaerts" Verlag, 1921.

Authors' Collective under the Leadership of Pavel Reimann. *Dějiny KSČ* [The History of the CPCS]. Prague: Státní nakladatelství politické literatury, 1961.

Dubský, Vladimír, and Kárník, Zdeněk. "Otázka masovosti strany v boji za vytvoření KSČ" [The Problem of the Mass Character of the Party in the Struggle for the Constitution of the CPCS]. *Příspěvky k dějinám KSČ*, 1961, pp. 180–207.

Gajan, Koloman. *Příspěvek ke vzniku KSČ, od prosincové stávky do slučovacího sjezdu* [Contribution to the History of the Origin of the CPCS, from the December Strike till the Merger Congress]. Prague: Státní nakladatelství politické literatury, 1954.

Gorovský, Karel. "O založení KSČ: Drážďanská konference v dubnu 1921" [On the Constitution of the CPCS: The Dresden Conference in April 1921]. *Revue dějin socialismu*, 1968, pp. 415–451.

Husar, Jozef. *Zjazd v Lubochni 1921* [The Lubochňa Congress of 1921]. Bratislava: Epocha, 1969.

Kuhn, Heinrich. *Der Kommunismus in der Tschechoslowakei* [Communism in Czechoslovakia]. Cologne: Wissenschaft und Politik, 1965.

———. *Von der Massenpartei zur Staatspartei* [From a Mass Party to the State Party]. Vol. 1. Cologne: Bundesinstitut fuer wissenschaftliche und internationale Studien, 1977.

Oschliess, Wolfgang. "Die Kommunistische Partei der Tschechoslowakei in der Ersten Tschechoslowakischen Republik" [The CPCS in the First Republic].

Berichte des Bundesinstituts fuer Ostwissenschaftliche und Internationale Studien,
no. 61, 1974.

Protokol XIII. řádného sjezdu Československé sociálně-demokratické strany dělnické [Minutes of the Thirteenth Ordinary Congress of the Czechoslovak Social Democratic Workers Party/the Center-Right]. Prague: Lidový dům, 1920.

Protokoll der Verhandlungen des Gruendungsparteitages der ersten Frauenreichskonferenz Der KSC, 12.–15. Maerz 1921 [Minutes of the Constitutive Congress and of the First National Women's Conference of the CPCS, March 12–15, 1921]. Reichenberg: Runge Verlag, 1921.

Reimann, Pavel. *Geschichte der Kommunistischen Partei der Tschechoslowakei* [History of the Communist Party of Czechoslovakia]. Berlin: Verlag Carl Hoym Nachfolger, 1931.

Veselý, Jindřich. *Entstehung und Gruendung der Kommunistischen Partei der Tschechoslowakei* [The Origin and the Constitution of the Communist Party of Czechoslovakia]. Berlin: Duncker & Humboldt, 1955.

Založení KSČ 1917–1921 [The Foundation of the CPCS, 1917–1921]. Prague: Ústav dějin KSČ, Státní nakladatelství politické literatury, 1954.

Zásady a cíle marxistické levice Československé sociálně demokratické strany dělnické [The Principles and the Goals of the Marxian Left of the Czechoslovak Social Democratic Workers Party]. Prague: Executive Committee, Czechoslovak Social Democratic Party (Left), 1920.

The crises of the formative years, especially the events that led to the bolshevization of the party at the fifth congress of the CPCS, are described in the following sources:

Čihák, Miloš. *Dějiny ČSR a KSČ v letech 1918–1923* [The History of the Czechoslovak Republic and of the CPCS in the years 1918–1923]. Prague: Vysoká škola politická, 1967.

Gorovský, Karel. "Bohumír Šmeral." *Revue dějin socialismu,* no. 4 (1969), pp. 893–922 and no. 1 (1970), pp. 112–39.

———. *Der heutige Stand der KSČ: Diktatur der Apparatchiki oder Demokratie?* (The Present Stand of the CPCS: Dictatorship by Apparatchiks or Democracy?]. Prague: Verlag der marxistischen Opposition, 1928.

Klír, Miroslav. *Studijní materiály k dějinám KSČ v letech 1921–1924.* Prague: Státní nakladatelství politické literatury, 1959.

———. "Úloha Bohumíra Šmerala při vypracování strategicko-taktické orientace KSČ [The Role of Bohumír Šmeral in Working Out the Strategic and Tactical Orientation of the CPCS]. *Příspěvky k dějinám KSČ,* 1964, pp. 651–84.

Koudelková, Jarmila. "Rudý den 1928" [The Red Day, 1928]. *Příspěvky k dějinám KSČ,* 1969, pp. 389–412.

Menclová, Jarmila. "Po rudém dni. K předhistorii V. sjezdu KSČ" [After the Red

Day: A Contribution to the Prehistory of the Fifth Congress of the CPCS]. *Příspěvky k dějinám* KSČ, 1961, pp. 674–91.

Plevza, Viliam. *KSČ a revoluční hnutie na Slovensku 1929–1938* [The CPCS and the Revolutionary Movement in Slovakia 1929–1938]. Bratislava: Vydavatelstvo Slovenskej akadémie vied, 1965.

Štern, Viktor. "Eine wichtige nationale Konferenz der Kommunistischen Partei der Tschechoslowakei" [An Important National Conference of the CPCS]. *Internationale Pressekorrespondenz*, June 28, 1928, pp. 644–45.

Vebr, Lubomír. *Mostecká stávka* [The Most Strike of 1928]. Prague: Státní nakladatelství politické literatury, 1955.

More extensive presentations of the party's history after the bolshevization of 1929, of its role in the Spanish Civil War and in the creation of the International Brigade, as well as of the gradual change in its position on Czechoslovakia and on the peril from National Socialist Germany, can be found in the following material:

Bareš, Gustav. *Proti Mnichovu: KSČ v čele lidové obrany* [Against Munich: The CPCS in the Lead of People's Defense]. Prague: Státní nakladatelství politické literatury, 1958.

Beneš, Eduard. *Mnichovské dny* [Munich Days]. Prague: Svoboda, 1968.

César, Jaroslav. *Komunistická strana Československa v boji proti fašismu: Sborník k 50. výročí založení KSČ* [The CPCS in the Struggle Against Fascism: An Almanach on the Occasion of the 50th Anniversary of the Foundation of the CPCS]. Prague, 1971.

The complex history of the Czechoslovak Communist movement, which was broken up into various local and ethnic groups after the dismemberment of Czechoslovakia during the years of exile and clandestinity, particularly the history of the Communist Party of Slovakia, is presented in these studies:

Beneš, Eduard. *Paměti: Od Mnichova k nové válce a novému vítězslví* [Memoirs]. Prague: Orbis, 1948.

———. *Šest let exilu a druhé světové války* [Six Years of Exile and World War II]. Prague: Orbis, 1948.

Feierabend, Ladislav. *Ve vládě v exilu* [In the Exile Government]. Vols. 1–3. New York: Universum Press, 1964–1965.

Fierlinger, Zdeněk. *Ve službách ČSR* [In the Service of Czechoslovakia]. Vols. 1 and 2. Prague: Orbis, 1947.

Friš, Eduard. "Moskevský pobyt Karla Šmidkeho v auguste 1944" [The Stay of Karol Smidke in Moscow in August 1944.] *Příspěvky k dějinám KSČ*, 1964, pp. 439–44.

Graca, Bohuslav. *Komunistická strana Slovenska v príprave slovenského národného povstania* [The Communist Party of Slovakia in the Preparations for the Slovak National Uprising]. Bratislava: Nakladatel'stvo politickej literatúry, 1969.

Husák, Gustav. *Svedectvo o slovenskom národnom povstaní* [Testimony about the Slovak National Uprising]. Bratislava: Nakladateľstvo politickej literatúry, 1964.

Jablonický, Jozef. *Z illegality do povstania: Kapitoly z občianskeho odboja* [From the Clandestinity to the Uprising: Chapters from the Nonworker Resistance]. Bratislava: Nakladateľstvo politickej literatúry, 1969.

Křen, Jan. *Do emigrace* [Into Exile]; Vol. 1: *Západní zahraniční odboj 1938/39* [The Liberation Action in the West]; Vol. 2: *V emigraci: Západní zahraniční odboj 1939/40* [In Exile. The Liberation Action in the West]. Prague: Československa akademie věd, 1963.

KSČ proti nacismu: KSČ v dokumentech nacistických bezpečnostních a zpravodajských orgánů [The CPCS Against Nazism: The CPCS in the Documents of the Nazi Security and Intelligence Organs]. Prague: Ústav dějin KSČ, 1971.

Laštovička, Bohuslav. *V Londýně za války* [In London During the War]. Prague: Svoboda, 1964.

Venohr, Wolfgang. *Aufstand fuer die Tschechoslowakei: Der slowakische Freiheitskampf 1944* [Uprising for Czechoslovakia: The Slovak Liberation Struggle of 1944]. Hamburg: Wegner Verlag, 1969.

Readers interested in learning more about the party's activities and policies during the three years of restricted pluralism, 1945–1948, can turn to the following literature:

Belda, Josef. "Some Problems Regarding the Czechoslovak Road to Socialism." *History of Socialism*, vol. 1968, Prague: Lístav dějin KSČ, pp. 113–154.

Kotrlý, Josef (ed.). *Pražské povstání* [The Prague Uprising 1945]. Washington, D.C.: Rada Svobodného Československa, 1965.

Kozák, Jan. *K některým otázkám strategie a taktiky KSČ v období přerůstání národní revoluce v revoluci socialistickou* [On Some Problems of the CPCS Strategy and Tactics in the Period of the Transformation of the National Revolution into a Socialist Revolution]. Prague: *Rudé právo* Publications, 1956.

Opat, Jaroslav. *O novou demokracii* [For a New Democracy]. Prague: Academia, 1966.

Reiman, Michal. "O významu hesla 'Za většinu národa!' " [About the Meaning of the Slogan 'For the Majority of Popular Vote!']. *Příspěvky k dějinám KSČ*, 1964, pp. 400–14.

Ripka, Hubert. *Czechoslovakia Enslaved*. London: Victor Gollancz, 1950.

Šťovíček, Ivan. "Zápis o zasedání ČNR ve dnech 4.–9. května 1945" [Minutes of the Session of the Czech National Council, May 4–9, 1945]. *Historie a vojenství*, no. 4 (1967), pp. 919–1019.

The first years of absolute Communist rule in Czechoslovakia, which were overshadowed by the Great Terror, have been the subject of many analyses published in the West. Moreover, the brief span of relative press freedom and freedom of scientific inquiry around the Prague Spring made possible the publication of a few more objective studies by domestic authors. These titles include the following:

Gerard-London, Arthur. *The Confession.* New York: William Morrow & Company, 1970.

Korbel, Pavel. *Purges in the Communist Party of Czechoslovakia.* New York: National Committee for a Free Europe, 1952.

Loebl, Eugen. *Sentenced and Tried.* London: Elek Books, 1969.

Nedvěd, Jaroslav. *Cesta ke sloučení sociální demokracie s KSČ* [The Road to the Merger of the Czechoslovak Social Democracy with the CPCS]. Prague: Academia, 1968.

Pelikán, Jiří. *The Czechoslovak Political Trials, 1950–1954.* Stanford, Ca.: Stanford University Press, 1971.

Proces s vedením protistátního spikleneckého centra v čele s Rudolfem Slánským [The Trial of the Anti-State Conspiratorial Center Led by Rudolf Slánský]. Prague: Ministry of Justice, 1953.

Slánská, Rudolfa. *Report on my Husband.* London: Hutchinson, 1969.

Relatively little material is available on the party's history since the deaths of Stalin and Gottwald in 1953 and the beginning of the reform movement of the 1960s. Here the reader will have to depend chiefly on the comments of Western observers of the Czechoslovak scene and on publications by Czechs and Slovaks living in the West. The following sources based on party data and records could be of use:

Kabrhel, Jaroslav. *Boj KSČ o socialistickou vesnici* [The Struggle of the CPCS for Socialist Agriculture]. Prague: Ministry of Agriculture, Research Department, 1971.

Lhotka, J. (et al.) *K problémům politiky KSČ v letech 1953–1955* [On the Problems of the CPCS Policies in the Years 1953–1955]. Prague: Ústav dějin KSČ, 1967.

Usnesení a dokumenty ÚV KSČ od IX. sjezdu do celostátní konference 1960 [Resolutions and Documents of the Central Committee of the CPCS from the Ninth Congress till the National Party Conference of 1960]. Prague: Svoboda, 1960.

The economic, political, and moral crisis of the 1960s has been commented on more extensively than the party's history in the period before the Twelfth Congress. Readers able to read Czech or Slovak can have recourse to original sources that explain or evaluate this crisis. The following are recommended:

Další rozvoj socialismu a úkoly společenských věd [Further Development of Socialism and the Tasks of Social Sciences]. Prague Státní nakladatelství politické literatury, 1963.

Hamšík, Dušan. *Writers Against Rulers*. New York: Random House, 1971.

Komarnickij, Miroslav (ed.). *Soubor článků a statí k úkolům strany po XIII. sjezdu KSČ* [Collection of Articles and Theses on the Tasks of the Party After the Thirteenth Congress]. Prague: Svoboda, 1968.

Lakatoš, Michal. *Občan, právo, demokracie* [Citizen, Law, Democracy]. Prague: Svobodne slovo, 1966.

Mlynář, Zdeněk. *Stát a člověk* [State and Man]. Prague: Svobodne slovo, 1964.

Roell, F., and Rosenberger, G. (eds.). *ČSSR 1962−1968: Dokumentation und Kritik* [Czechoslovakia 1962−1968: Documents and Critique]. Munich: B. Kyncl Verlag, 1968.

Šik, Ota. *Plan and Market Under Socialism*. White Plains, N.Y.: International Arts and Sciences Press, 1967.

IV. Sjezd Svazu československých spisovatelů, Praha 27.−29. června 1967 [Minutes of the Fourth Congress of the Union of Czechoslovak Writers in Prague, June 27−29, 1967]. Prague: Československý spisovatel, 1968.

Skilling, Harold Gordon. *Czechoslovakia's Interrupted Revolution*. Princeton, N.J.: Princeton University Press, 1976.

More can be learned about the key role of the intellectual élite in the development that led to the liberalization of the regime at the end of the 1960s from several well researched and documented studies published in the West. The following four merit special attention:

Golan, Galia. *The Czechoslovak Reform Movement: Communism in Crisis*. Cambridge: At the University Press, 1971.

―――. *Reform Rule in Czechoslovakia: The Dubček Era 1968−1969*. Cambridge: At the University Press, 1973.

Kusin, Vladimir V. *The Intellectual Origins of the Prague Spring*. Cambridge: At the University Press, 1971.

―――. *Political Groupings in the Czechoslovak Reform Movement*. New York: Columbia University Press, 1972.

The prelude to the Prague Spring, the whole history of the democratization experiment, and the essence of the reform projects of 1968 are topics of a large number of studies, most of them sympathetic to the reform movement. At the beginning of the 1970s, pro-Soviet presentations of the 1968 events began to appear both in Czechoslovakia and in the Soviet Union. Among the specific studies of the Dubcek interlude, I would like to list the following:

Action Program of the Communist Party of Czechoslovakia. London: Bertrand Russell Peace Foundation, 1968.

Dahm, Helmut. *Demokratischer Sozialismus* [Democratic Socialism]. Analysen Series. Opladen, Germany: Leske Verlag, 1971.

Dubček, Alexander. *K otázkam obrodzovacieho procesu v KSČ* [On the Problems of the Regenerative Process in the CPCS]. Bratislava: Vydavateľstvo politickej literatúry, 1968.

Gruber, L., and Rambousek, O. *Zpráva dokumentační komise K 231* [Report of the Documentation Commission of the Club 231]. Toronto, Ontario: Nakladatelství 68, 1973.

Oschliess, Wolfgang. *Demokratisierungsprozess und Herrschaftstechnik in Partei und Gewerkschaften der Tschechoslowakei* [The Process of Democratization and the Technique of Rule in the Party and in the Unions of the Czechoslovak Republic]. Trittan i. Holst., Germany: Juergen Scherbath Verlag, 1970.

Pielkalkiewicz, Jaroslaw A. *Public Opinion Polling in Czechoslovakia 1968−69*. New York: Praeger, 1972.

Rebro, Karol. *The Road to Federation*. Bratislava: Epocha, 1970.

Rok šedesátý osmý v usneseních a dokumentech ÚV KSČ [The Year 1968 in the Documents and Resolutions of the Central Committee of the CPCS]. Prague: Svoboda, 1969.

Sviták, Ivan. *The Czechoslovak Experiment 1968−1969*. New York: Columbia University Press, 1971.

Zeman, Zbyněk A. *Prague Spring: A Report on Czechoslovakia*. New York: Hill & Wang, 1969.

The Soviet military intervention of August 1968, its peculiarly weak political preparation, the reactions of the party leadership and membership, and of the entire nation as well as the world, have received considerable coverage in scholarly and popular Western literature. Of these titles I can recommend the following:

Littel, Robert (ed.). *The Czech Black Book*. Prepared by the Institute of History of the Czechoslovak Academy of Sciences. New York: Praeger, 1969.

Pelikán, Jiří. *The Secret Vysočany Congress: Proceedings and Documents of the Fourteenth Congress of the Communist Party of Czechoslovakia, 22 August 1968*. London: Allen Lane, The Penguin Press, 1971.

Remington, Robin. *Winter in Prague: Documents on Czechoslovak Communism in Crisis*. Cambridge, Mass.: M.I.T. Press, 1969.

Solomon, Michael. *Prague Notebook: The Strangled Revolution*. Boston: M.I.T. Press, 1971.

Among the rich material in original languages, the most informative may be those listed below:

Dokumenty o okupácii ČSSR [Documents about the Occupation of Czechoslovakia]. Bratislava: Ústredný výbor KSS, 1968.

Dopis předsednictva ÚV KSČ všem základním organisacím strany z 31. srpna 1968 [The Letter of the Central Committee of the CPCS to All Party Organizations, Dated August 31, 1968]. Prague: *Rudé právo*, 1968.

Zpráva o současné politické situaci Československé socialistické republiky a podmínkách činnosti KSČ (srpen 1968) [Report about the Present Political Situation of the Czechoslovak Socialist Republic and the Conditions of Work of the CPCS]. Prague: *Rudé právo*, October 1968.

Normalization, which began with the appointment of Gustav Husák as first party secretary in April 1969, has been closely watched by observers in both East and West. However, sources directly addressing the issue of the return to normalcy are understandably pro-Soviet or of Soviet origin. The following could be of use:

Bil'ák, Vasil. *Pravda zůstala pravdou: Projevy a články, říjen 1967—prosinec 1970* [Truth Remained True: Speeches and Articles from October 1967 till December 1970]. Prague: Svoboda, 1971.

On Events in Czechosovakia: Facts, Documents, Press Reports and Eyewitness Accounts. Moscow: Group of Soviet Journalists, 1968.

Hájek, Jiří (not Jiří S. Hájek, Minister of Foreign Affairs in 1968). *Demokratisierung oder Demontage?* [Democratization or Liquidation?]. Munich: Damnitz Verlag, 1969.

Husák, Gustav. *Projevy a stati* [Talks and Theses]. Prague: *Rudé Právo*, 1970.

Lessons of the Crisis Development in the Party and Society Since the Thirteenth Congress of the Communist Party of Czechoslovakia. Approved by the Plenary Session of the Central Committee of the CPCS in December 1970. Prague: *Rudé právo*, December 1970.

All regular congresses of the CPCS and their transactions are described in detail in the corresponding protocols, which are published separately for each congress, including the Merger Congress of 1921. These publications constitute a regular series that since the end of the 1940s has been given a uniform aspect and format. The editorial board is responsible to the Central Committee. Beginning with the Twelfth Congress, these publications carry a somewhat simplified title: *XII.* (XIII., etc.) *sjezd Komunistické strany Československa* [The Twelfth (Thirteenth, etc.) Congress of the Communist Party of Czechoslovakia].

Simple data and facts about the party or its important individual leaders and officials can be obtained from the *Manual Reference Book on the History of the CPCS* (Příruční slovník k dějinám KSČ) published in 1964 by the Státní nakladatelství politické literatury in Prague. Apart from its inevitable obsolescence, this two-volume documentary source has the disadvantage of being strongly biased by the party line prevailing in the mid-1960s; names of prominent members who were then nonpersons are simply omitted. The volume *Dějiny Československa v datech* [History of Czechoslovakia in Dates] by Miloslav Buchvaldek et al. (Prague: Svoboda, 1968) can compensate for some of the shortcomings of the *Manual Reference Book*, since it was published in 1968—four years later and under political conditions much more favorable to objective historiography.

Index

DATE D